An Introduction to Physical Science
for Christian Schools®

the PHYSICAL WORLD

An Introduction to Physical Science
for Christian Schools®

Donovan Hadaway
David Hurd
John E. Jenkins
George Mulfinger Jr.

Bob Jones University Press
Greenville, South Carolina 29614

NOTE:
The fact that materials produced by other publishers may be referred to in this volume does not constitute an endorsement of the content or theological position of materials produced by such publishers. Any references and ancillary materials are listed as an aid to the student or the teacher and in an attempt to maintain the accepted academic standards of the publishing industry.

The Physical World: An Introduction to Physical Science for Christian Schools®
formerly *Basic Science for Christian Schools®*
Authors
Donovan Hadaway
David Hurd, Ph.D.
John E. Jenkins, M.S.
George Mulfinger Jr., M.S.

Consultants
Verne Biddle, Ph.D.
George Matzko, Ph.D.

Design and Typesetting
Preface, Inc.
Schaumburg, Illinois

for Christian Schools is a registered trademark of Bob Jones University Press.

Produced in cooperation with the Bob Jones University Division of Natural Science of the College of Arts and Science, the School of Religion, and Bob Jones Academy.

ISBN 1-59166-641-4

15   14   13   12   11   10   9   8   7   6   5   4   3   2   1

Contents

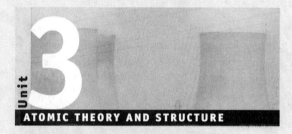

Unit 4

CHEMICAL APPLICATIONS

Unit 5

PHYSICS IN ACTION

Unit 6

WAVE AND PARTICLE MOTION

Introduction

Do you know how television pictures are transmitted or why an atomic bomb can release enough energy to destroy an entire city? If you have questions like these about the world around you, then you are a curious person.

The Physical World: An Introduction to Physical Science for Christian Schools was written for you, the curious student. We have filled this textbook with answers to puzzling questions about why things happen and how things work. But this text should do more than simply answer your questions. It is intended to stimulate new questions that will cause you to expand your knowledge.

You will be introduced to realms that you have never before explored. This book will take you "inside" an atom; let you "see" what happens in solids, liquids, and gases; help you to discover the forces that make things move or keep things from moving; and show you forms of matter and energy that scientists are just beginning to understand.

The Physical World was also written for you because you are a Christian student. Christians have a very special reason for being curious about the world around them: the physical universe reveals the power and majesty of our God. We can see the Creator clearly in His creation. Patterns in nature, from the ordered movement of planets through space to the intricate movement of minute particles in matter, attest to His power. The entire universe, from atoms to galaxies, is governed and maintained by the infinite power of our God.

We have even deeper reasons for studying the physical universe. Not only did God create the universe for us, but He sent His Son to reconcile us to Himself when we rebelled in sin. Paul tells us in Colossians 1:12-17,

> Giving thanks unto the Father, which hath made us meet to be partakers of the inheritance of the saints in light: Who hath delivered us from the power of darkness, and hath translated us into the kingdom of his dear Son: In whom we have redemption through his blood, even the forgiveness of sins: Who is the image of the invisible God, the firstborn of every creature: For by him were all things created, that are in heaven, and that are in earth, visible and invisible, whether they be thrones, or dominions, or principalities, or powers: all things were created by him, and for him: And he is before all things, and by him all things consist.

Here Paul reveals to us a very special truth: God used His Son, our Savior, to frame the worlds (Heb. 1:2). In this course you will study the world that Christ created. As a Christian student you will have an opportunity to see Christ in His creation.

Paul continued his description of Christ to the church at Colosse by saying, "And he is the head of the body, the church: who is the beginning, the firstborn from the dead; that in all things he might have the preeminence" (Col. 1:18).

May your studies this year help you to honor Christ and to keep Him first in your life.

Format for *The Physical World*

The Physical World is divided into six units with a single theme: matter, the "stuff" of the universe. The units are divided into chapters, and each chapter is divided into at least two sections. At the end of these sections, there are questions that will help you review the material that you have just read.

Each chapter has several features that will help you study. Illustrations, captions, special notes, and tables will help you understand the material. Many important scientific terms are printed in **boldface**, each in the portion of text where it is defined. These terms are gathered after the text of each chapter in a list titled "Scientifically Speaking." Use this list as a tool for reviewing important concepts in the chapter. "Chapter Review Questions" will focus on key ideas in the chapter, most of which will show up at test time. Also at the end of each chapter appears "What Did You Learn?" You will not find answers for these questions in the text! They are designed to stimulate class discussion and to help you think of ways to apply what you have learned.

Some important terms appear in *italic* type. Many of these were boldfaced in earlier discussion and are important for you to note again. Other times, italic print is used to point out significant ideas, contrasts, or conditions. (If you cannot remember what a term means, look it up in the glossary at the back of the text.) You will also find pronunciation guides in parentheses if the word is difficult to pronounce. The pronunciation key on page xi will tell you how to read them.

In addition to the normal text, you will find various "Facets of the Physical World." These highlighted sections of information or application add dimension to the topics you are studying. Be sure to read them; they are an important part of the text. The facets cover a wide range of topics from the historical to the present day, from normal day-to-day occurrences to bizarre disasters. Some of

the facets are biographies of scientists who served God. These men have been selected as examples of the balance that God expects in a Christian's life.

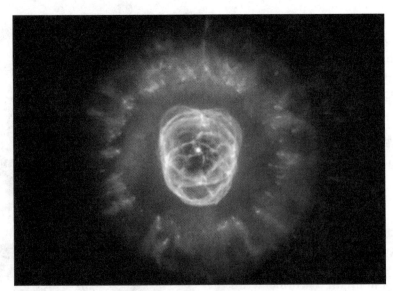

Study Skills

As you have learned during your years in school, study methods vary depending on the assignment and the course. Study methods that work for one class may not be as helpful for another class. Here are some study tips that will help you throughout the school year.

Maintain a positive attitude—there will be times when things get tough. You may not understand something, or you may earn a bad grade. Proverbs 24:16 says, "For a just man falleth seven times, and riseth up again." Stay consistent with your work and eventually it will pay off.

Ask your teacher questions! He is there to help you understand the material and more than likely can provide all the answers you will need to finish this course successfully. When you read, keep in mind possible questions so that you can ask them in class the next day.

Read assignments ahead of time or follow the reading schedule your teacher has given you.

Prepare for tests by listening well in class and taking good notes. Your best study time is your class time. When you study at home for tests, prepare a little bit each night so that you will not have to do everything the night before the test.

If you have trouble concentrating, the best thing to do is to find a quiet place to study and remove those things that are distracting you. When reading or doing homework, schedule some breaks ahead of time and set goals for yourself to complete certain sections in the book. You may want to have a pen or pencil nearby and some paper to write down important concepts, but don't waste time by trying to rewrite paragraphs. Whatever study methods you use, try to get advice from your teacher on what works best. Studying is very similar to practicing a musical instrument—you get better at it as time goes by.

Pronunciation Key

The pronunciation key used in this text is designed to give the reader a self-evident, acceptable pronunciation for the word as he reads it from the page. For more accurate pronunciations, the reader should consult a good dictionary. This pronunciation key will help the student who has difficulty interpreting the diacritical marks used in most dictionaries.

Stress

Syllables with primary stress appear in LARGE CAPITAL letters. One-syllable words and syllables with secondary stress appear in SMALL CAPITAL letters. Unstressed syllables appear in lowercase letters. For example, the pronunciation of *kilogram* appears as (KILL uh GRAM).

Symbol	Example
c	voice = voyce
g	get = get
j	gentle = JEN tul
th	thin = thin
th	then = then
zh	vision = VIZH un

Vowel Sounds

Symbol	Example
a	cat = KAT
a-e	cape = KAPE
ay	paint = PAYNT
e	jet = JET
eh	special = SPEH shul
ee	fiend = FEEND
i	swim = SWIM
ih	pity = PIH tee
eye	ivory = EYE vuh ree
i-e	might = MITE
y	pint = PYNT
	mighty = MY tee
ye	Levi = LEE vye
ah	cot = KAHT
ar	car = KAR
aw	all = AWL
o	potion = PO shun
oa	don't = DOANT
o-e	groan = GRONE
oh	own = OHN
u	some = SUM
uh	abet = uh BET
oo	tune = TOON
oo	push = P*OO*SH
ou	loud = LOUD
oy	toil = TOYL

A Philosophy of Science

Science and the Christian

1A A Framework for Science

1B An Outlook on Science

1C Science in the Bible

Man has an unquenchable thirst to know and understand the world around him. From the moment a baby is born, he opens his eyes and ears and begins to ponder the colorful, noisy world. Later, he begins to taste and touch things his parents bring to him. Eventually, he will grow dissatisfied and crawl to find things on his own. One day he will communicate his findings to others, perhaps in a church nursery or later on in a classroom.

The first activities related to science are found in the Word of God, when the Lord told Adam and Eve to "be fruitful, and multiply, and replenish the earth, and subdue it" (Gen. 1:28).

Chapter

1

Fig. 1-1 As we grow older, we satisfy our desire to know and understand the world around us in different ways.

In order to subdue and use something, you must have some basic understanding of it. Over the course of history, science has helped man subdue many things that in many minds were just fantasy, such as air travel. Science has brought us medical advances, the telephone, air conditioning, automobiles, computers—the list goes on and on. But none of these wonderful pieces of technology appeared by accident. What do all the activities that we call science have in common?

A Framework for Science

Every scientist uses his or her senses to record information about the physical universe. A scientist might be looking at the microscopic structure of an insect's wings, recording the sounds of a great gray whale, or examining the information and photographs sent back by a deep space probe, but in each case the scientist is using the senses to collect pieces of information called **data** (DAY tuh). Any collection of data through the senses (taste, touch, smell, sight, and hearing) is an **observation.** Scientists must carefully plan and control their observations. They also record them in minute detail so that other scientists can study the events that led up to a particular observation and confirm the results by duplicating it.

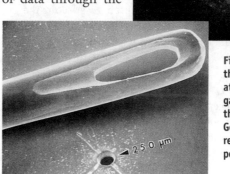

Fig. 1-2 Scientists can observe things that are as small as an atom or as far away as another galaxy, but they can observe only the physical universe. Part of God's creation—the spiritual realm—lies beyond scientists' power to observe.

A Definition for Science

There are many definitions of science. Some emphasize a method, some a body of knowledge, and others experimentation. Observation plays a key role in all these definitions. In this book **science** is defined as man's observation of the physical world. We can make accurate predictions of natural phenomena through the systematic use of observations in our physical universe. The process includes methods used, instruments used, and the use of the scientific method. The methods or the instruments by themselves are not science; they are simply the tools of the people who accomplish

FACETS of the physical world

Making a Choice

On December 2, 1942, the world's first nuclear reactor powered up, and with it came the promise of bountiful, safe, clean energy. Four and a half minutes later the world had its first nuclear waste.

There are two categories of nuclear waste, high-level and low-level. High-level wastes include used reactor fuel and materials from the development of atomic weapons. As the name implies, high-level waste is highly radioactive and will stay that way for thousands of years. Low-level wastes include contaminated gloves and clothing, building materials, and medical isotopes. These materials are less radioactive because they either have a smaller concentration of radioactive material or will remain radioactive for a shorter time. With either kind of waste, storage is a problem. This problem, like many others, requires not only a solid understanding of scientific principles but also appropriate value judgments.

Each state is responsibile for dealing with its own low-level nuclear waste, and the states have formed regional compacts to dispose of it properly. Since low-level waste is significantly less hazardous, extreme safety precautions are not required. But what about the high-level waste? It is very hazardous and remains so for long periods, so extreme care must be exercised in deciding how to dispose of it. The federal government has taken the responsibility of disposing of the high-level wastes.

Since high-level wastes persist for thousands of years, the disposal method must likewise secure the wastes for thousands of years; government regulations say 10,000 years. Come storm, fire, earthquake, sabotage, radiation damage, or natural aging, the waste must not be released into the environment. The question authorities want answered is "Scientifically, what is the best way to dispose of this waste?"

Scientists have examined the following disposal alternatives and found advantages and disadvantages to each.

"Shoot it into space."
The advantage of this idea is that when sent toward the sun or deep space, the waste will be gone forever. The disadvantage is that rockets occasionally fail (explode or otherwise malfunction) on liftoff. Radioactive waste rockets would likewise occasionally fail. The spilled radioactive contents of such a rocket could pollute the atmosphere.

the activities we call science. Science cannot exist without purposeful observations and interpretations.

Pure and Applied Science

Within the realm of science fall numerous specialties ranging from astrophysics to zoology. Some of these sciences attempt to discover new data just to satisfy our basic curiosity about the physical universe. These sciences are called **pure science.** Often, however, scientific activities are directed toward solving a particular problem. These activities are called **applied science.** For example, a pure

"Dilute it in the vast ocean."
The advantage of this proposal is that once the waste is uniformly dissolved in the ocean, the radiation at any one point would be very small. Disadvantages include that until it is uniformly dissolved, danger would certainly exist. Also, international treaties currently prohibit such ocean dumping.

"Store it on Antarctica."
The advantage is that it would be stored far from people and other living organisms. One disadvantage comes from the fact that this nuclear waste not only is "hot" from a radioactive point of view but also

produces heat. It might melt part of the icepack, and the liquid water might flow to the sea or evaporate into the atmosphere, carrying radioactive waste with it.

"Bury it under the sea."
In this plan the waste would be loaded into streamlined containers and dropped overboard. Sinking rapidly, the containers would reach high speeds and imbed themselves several meters deep in the mud of carefully selected seafloor sites. The advantage is that the selected sites would be remote and seismically stable. A disadvantage is that it would take only one canister that accidentally ruptured on impact to pollute a great volume of water. This solution also might violate international treaties about ocean dumping.

"Change it to a different substance."
It is possible to change one material to another, but the technology to do this on a large scale does not exist at the present time. An additional storage or disposal plan would be needed because the changed waste would still be radioactive, though not as much.

"Store it underground."
The advantage of this idea is the protection offered by hundreds of meters of rock. Disadvantages include that ground water could eventually dissolve the waste and bring it back to the surface and that earthquakes might open faults and thereby expose the waste.

Even after all the scientific studies, the question still remains: "Scientifically, what is the best way to dispose of this waste?" The scientists involved generally favor one or two of the options above. A few favor a third option. Why the disagreement? Why is there not a clear scientific answer? Why did science not answer this question? The answer to these questions is that the final answer requires a value judgment. To identify "best" requires value judgment and cannot be answered by science alone.

Does this mean that there is no best way to dispose of high-level nuclear waste? No, it simply means that the decision is not strictly a scientific decision, since it draws on human values.

scientist might study how matter conducts electricity at very cold temperatures, while an applied scientist might examine how such cold matter could be used in electrical devices.

Technology and Science

Technology is the practical use of knowledge gained through pure and applied science. Science and technology are a research and development team: one discovers the information needed to solve a problem, and the other works out the everyday methods of applying the solutions. When the pure scientist Charles Townes developed the laser, for example, other scientists used his discovery in new methods of surgery, in checkout scanners, and in CD players.

It is this important union between scientific information and its application that increasingly affects us. As we learn to apply scientific knowledge to more areas of our lives, we will be able to make informed decisions with respect to difficult choices. For example, does technology always "benefit" humans? We soon will have the technology to put men on Mars—but is it wise to risk lives and money on this endeavor? Many people would enthusiastically say, "Yes!" but there are also those who would reply with an equally resounding "No!" We already wrestle with issues about genetic engineering (including manipulating a baby's physical and mental characteristics before it is born), food processing (as the world's population increases, might we turn to processed seaweed for our staple diet?), and the energy needs of our country, to name just a few.

Fig. 1-3 Can you find anything in this photo that is not a product of applied science?

Fig. 1-4 Imperfect beings often make imperfect observations.

6

A Basis for Choosing

The accuracy of scientific principles is dependent upon the accuracy of the observations. Some questions cannot be answered by scientific observations, so science has its limitations. Whether he wants to admit it or not, man has limitations as well. We are mortal and imperfect beings. Our eyes have not seen the entire universe, and our minds are only so powerful. Science is limited because our senses, though powerful, cannot answer all the questions of the universe. Our senses can fool us as well. When we look at the horizon, we see a flat earth at first glance. But with mathematics, astronomy, and some careful thought, we realize that the earth is actually round. In our present-day society, many people have a "seeing is believing" philosophy and believe that philosophy to be a good measure of scientific accuracy. But many scientific facts that have been established today were scoffed at in the past because people could not see that facts could exist outside the realm of normal, everyday experience.

On the other hand, scientists often make the same mistake when they declare something as true and irrefutable that has not been adequately examined. Or they try to address issues that no amount of observation could ever solve. In these cases, scientists try to use science as a giver of truth. Science cannot be a giver of truth. At best it is a tool that we use to help us understand natural phenomena. The government collects crime statistics every year and tries to use scientific principles to combat any rise in crime. Science has helped police identify criminals through DNA and fingerprint testing. Police everywhere use state-of-the-art bullet-proof vests. But can science solve the greatest of all challenges—what causes people to commit crimes in the first place? Although poverty, discrimination, childhood abuse, and neglect may contribute to a person's leap into a life of crime, the ultimate decision lies within a person's heart and the wicked thoughts and actions he decides to act upon. James 4:1 says, "From whence come wars and fightings among you? come they not hence, even of your lusts that war in your members?" Although the Bible is clear on this issue, many scientists still believe that there is a scientific, physical reason behind criminal behavior. While these scientists may mean well, they are allowing people to avoid responsibility for their crimes. Other sins, such as homosexuality and drunkenness, are now described as being inherited, something ingrained from the moment of conception. Science practiced in the absence of biblical values yields choices based upon the opinions and observations of man—not those of God.

Fig. 1-5 DNA science can help solve crimes, but it will never be able to solve sin problems in the heart.

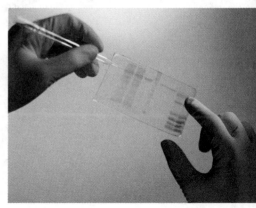

Fig. 1-6 Citizens must make wise decisions to balance the preservation of the beauty of God's creation with the need for additional energy resources.

Deciding whether something is right or wrong, good or bad, valuable or worthless is called a **value judgment.** Scientific observations cannot be used to make value judgments. Whether or not a painting is beautiful is based solely on the values and opinions of the observers, not upon recorded data. The same goes with a television program or musical recording. Technology offers applications, and science offers information, but neither can offer a basis for determining the worth of a choice.

Television, radio, and computers are pieces of technology that can be used for good or for tremendous evil. Christians must make the right decisions when using these tools to ensure that they are used for God's glory. Choices must be based on a system of values. To make correct choices, you must have correct values.

Since science cannot determine value, where can you find correct values? Many people trust their own or other people's ability to determine value. Relying on human abilities is called **humanism,** for humanity is the center of the belief. Science plays an important role in humanism. When asked to make value judgments, humanists often reply with the "anything goes" philosophy. That means any entertainment or lifestyle choice is acceptable. To the humanist, watching television and listening to the radio are value-free activities—you do whatever you feel like doing. Abortion (to the humanist) is also a value-free activity—whatever the woman and her doctor decide is truth—making what the Bible says about the value of human life totally irrelevant. Christians look to Christ and the Word of God as their authoritative source of values. For the born-again believer, the Bible is the framework of truth with which to test the advantages and disadvantages of technology usage.

You will be faced with many technological choices in your lifetime. As a citizen you may face choices between preserving wilderness areas and developing them to provide energy resources. You may be asked to decide questions about genetic engineering. You may even be offered the option of choosing characteristics you would like to have implanted in your unborn child. How will you decide these complex issues? You cannot look to science for answers; it can only provide you with options. You can look either to God or to man. Whom will you choose?

SECTION REVIEW QUESTIONS 1A

1. Give a definition of science.
2. Describe data and give an example of how a scientist might collect it.
3. Is a geologist who helps a mining company locate mineral deposits a pure scientist or an applied scientist?

An Outlook on Science

Two Basic Outlooks

Scientists interpret data in the light of their outlooks. They may misinterpret data if they do not have a correct perception of the whole. Some scientists interpret data to support their view that the physical universe somehow structured itself out of self-existing matter and that its parts continue to organize themselves into more complex structures as time progresses. This outlook is called **evolution.**

It should be noted here that the word "evolution" can have different meanings. Sometimes it is used to refer to general and simple change over time. For example, the changes we see taking place within specific species is often referred to as evolution or adaptation. This is not a problem for a Christian. Think about the many different kinds of cats there are! What about a changing (or evolving) river system? Is this inconsistent with the Bible? Certainly not!

The evolution that Christians should have a problem with is sometimes referred to as modern evolutionary theory or the **mutation-selection theory.** In this definition of evolution, the origins of life are left to chance and time. In classical evolution, people

Fig. 1-7 Decay, degeneration, and general disordering are natural processes in a world cursed by sin.

somehow "evolved" from more primitive life forms that developed random genetic mistakes (mutations) in the DNA. The mutation-selection theory deals specifically with the origin of living things but not with the origins of the earth, sun, moon, and stars. Evolutionists have a very difficult time harmonizing biological sciences with physical sciences. They say not only that the seas, mountains, and rivers evolved by chance but also that all two million types of species on the earth are a result of genetic "mistakes."

Scripture tells us that God spoke the universe into existence by the miraculous acts described in Genesis 1 and 2. Those that hold the belief in a created universe are called Creationists.

An evolutionary view of the physical universe assumes that modern-day observers would see continued evolving, or improving, of our world. However, rather than improvement and increased organization, we observe decay, degeneration, and general disordering processes in nature. Well-established scientific principles indicate that nature is running down, not building itself into more ordered and complex forms.

The Creationists' view of the physical universe, or **Creationism,** is founded on the written record of the Creator. Scientific observations of a world that is running down do not conflict with the biblical record of a world under God's curse.

A Comparison of Evolution and Creationism

With respect to the beginning of our universe (origins), evolution and Creationism are complete opposites. The evolutionary outlook holds that chance and natural processes can explain the origin of the physical universe, while the Creationist view recognizes that supernatural (miraculous) acts were needed. Genesis 1 and 2 detail the supernatural acts of God in creating our physical universe and all that is in it. Concerning Creation, Psalm 33:9 states, "For he [God] spake, and it was done; he commanded, and it stood fast." The universe and all living things were created to bring honor and glory to God. From that perspective, any endeavor that is scientific or otherwise will be looked at from a biblical standpoint—a biblical worldview.

These two outlooks are so directly opposed to each other that it seems impossible that a person could hold to both at the same time. Yet some Christians try to believe evolution. Their attempt to join these two conflicting outlooks is called **theistic** (thee ISS tik) **evolution.** (*Theistic* means "pertaining to belief in a god.") It is based on the belief that God used evolutionary processes to create the universe.

1-8 Viewpoints of Origins

	Evolution	Creation	Theistic Evolution
Action	Natural processes/chance	Supernatural act	Supernatural direction
Time	Billions of years	Six days	Billions of years
End Result	Evolving	Finished: change taking place but degenerating	Evolving under direction

Theistic evolution might appear to be a way of satisfying the demands of both sides, enabling a person to hold onto Christian beliefs with one hand and evolutionary ideas with the other. However, those who hold firmly to the Bible know that it allows no room for evolution; and those who hold firmly to evolutionary theories allow no room for God. Therefore, the person who attempts to "harmonize" the two does not have the blessing of either side.

Evolutionary Bias

Everyone has some form of **bias** in thinking. You believe what you want to believe based on your mental inclinations and leanings. Your bias on any subject will depend largely on what you have been taught about it. Bias is not necessarily bad. The right kind of bias often indicates knowledge or experience in a given subject. An electrician will be biased in favor of using copper wire, rather than tin or nickel wire, in motors. Electricians have learned that copper has the best combination of important qualities, such as good conductivity and low cost. If you play on a sports team, you think your team is the best and will encourage others to believe the same, although you may not have a lot of evidence to support your claim. A person cannot be completely unbiased about something unless he or she has either no knowledge of it or no interest in it.

There is another form of bias that is not desirable. If a person closes his mind on a subject before learning enough about it to form a sensible opinion, that person harms himself and others. The Bible says, "He that answereth a matter before he heareth it, it is folly and shame unto him" (Prov. 18:13). It is best to examine a subject thoroughly, and if the evidence supports a position that runs counter to your particular bias, you

Fig. 1-9 This shoe print was found in rock that evolutionists claim was formed over 500 million years ago—long before man supposedly "appeared." Evolutionists often reject evidence like this because of their bias.

would do well to discard your bias in favor of a better position. Evolutionists are constantly finding evidence that runs counter to their claims, yet they discard the evidence because their bias for evolution is too strong. This type of bias is more precisely called *prejudice.*

A Bias for Order

The bias of a Creationist is based on his belief in design or purpose in nature. An evolutionist must rely on accidental events to explain

the ultimate origin and evolution of everything observed. The Creationist seeks to uncover God's design in nature. He believes that God is actively controlling and purposefully directing His creation. When studying an object or an event in nature, the Christian man or woman of science will try, in the words of a famous German astronomer, "to think God's thoughts after Him."

Many avenues of scientific research point to God. The Christian researcher readily recognizes that the human body is "fearfully and wonderfully made" (Ps. 139:14). The Christian sees each part of the human body as a marvelously engineered device, expertly designed for its assigned function(s).

Fig. 1-10 People exhibit bias in almost every area of life—even when deciding which products to buy.

There is scientific evidence to support Creation, but science cannot prove it. If you recall, science is observation. The question of origins lies outside the realm of scientific observation because no one but God witnessed it. Therefore, one must compare the evidence for Creation and evolution and make a judgment based on faith—the evidence of things not seen. But is faith in the creative works of God a blind faith? Each new day brings with it new evidences for a belief in an all-wise Creator. The Scripture has many fulfilled prophecies and accurate descriptions of the physical world. If the Bible is accurate in the areas of prophecy and history, we can then accept by faith that it is accurate when it describes the Creation of the universe in Genesis 1 and 2. Evolution has no such comparison to offer—it is indeed a blind faith. Belief in God's

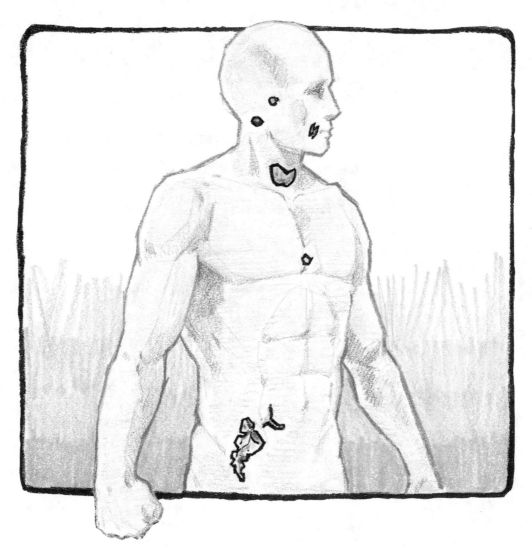

creative works will establish us in our salvation as well, because we know that the God who has the power to create us has the power to save us for eternity.

We also see clear evidence of design when we look at the earth and its near surroundings. The earth is just the right distance from the sun. The sun provides a steady supply of exactly the right kinds of energy for living things on the earth. Our atmosphere contains the best possible mixture of oxygen and other gases. The earth's magnetic field protects us from cosmic rays. The ozone layer in the stratosphere (upper layer of the earth's atmosphere) protects us from ultraviolet rays. The earth's rotational speed provides ideal periods of day and night. All these things speak of God's creative design.

Fig. 1-11 These organs were once thought to be useless "leftovers" from the evolutionary process. Modern medical science has discovered the purpose for many of these "vestigial" organs.

Sometimes God's design is not apparent to us. Some of our observations seem unexplainable. With further study, however, many of these begin to make sense. Even if we are not capable of understanding a certain fact of nature, every such fact exists and operates in accordance with some part of God's overall plan.

SECTION REVIEW QUESTIONS 1B

1. Give the term used to describe the modern theory of evolution.
2. Why must any theory of origins be accepted by faith?
3. Give two evidences that support the Bible as the true, inerrant Word of God.

Science in the Bible

Although the Bible is not meant to be a textbook of science, it contains much valuable information that relates to science. In fact, Scripture answers questions that science cannot test directly—such as, where did the universe come from? What will eventually happen to it? Scripture tells us that the universe came into being by the miraculous acts of an omnipotent Creator. This event, called Creation, occurred at a definite time in the not-too-remote past. Scripture also states that the present universe will be dissolved and a new heaven and a new earth will be established (Isa. 34:4; II Pet. 3:10; Rev. 21:1).

Remember that the definition of science includes purposeful observations and prediction. Since scientists cannot now observe either past events or future events, science can only speculate about how the universe began and how it will end. The Bible can speak with authority on these subjects because it is God's Word and He sees all eternity; science cannot speak about what it cannot observe.

Science is concerned mainly with physical observations; the Bible, with spiritual observations. Yet sometimes the two overlap. When they do, science does not contradict the Bible. In fact, science has made observations that confirm the Bible's accurate descriptions of the physical universe. Some portions of Scriptures show an understanding of natural processes that science has now been able to observe. When those portions were written, however, there was no way to make the observations necessary to test those ideas about nature. By confirming the truth of these statements, scientific observations evidence the divine inspiration of Scripture. For

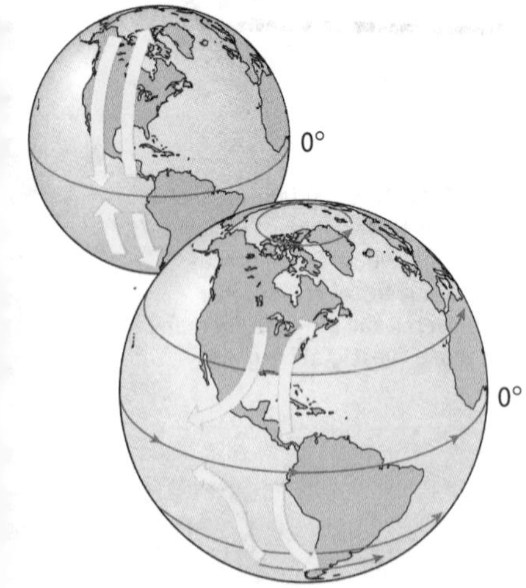

0°

0°

Fig. 1-12 Solomon described the circular motion of wind currents in the Bible.

1 Science and the Christian

example, Ecclesiastes 1:6 declares that the winds move in cycles: "The wind goeth toward the south, and turneth about unto the north; it whirleth about continually, and the wind returneth again according to his circuits." King Solomon wrote this statement approximately three thousand years ago when no special equipment was available for observing wind currents aloft.

Jeremiah wrote, "The host of heaven cannot be numbered" (Jer. 33:22). Scripture compares the number of stars to the number of grains of sand on the seashore (Gen. 22:17). In contrast, many of the ancients thought there were only about a thousand stars, those that could be seen with the naked eye. Not until A.D. 1609, when Galileo (GAL uh LAY oh) turned his first telescope skyward, did humans appreciate the truth of these verses. The stars are innumerable to us; there are so many stars in the Milky Way galaxy that many are hidden by others and cannot be seen to be counted. God not only sees all the stars and knows their total number, but He knows each one by name: "He telleth the number of the stars; he calleth them all by their names" (Ps. 147:4). Modern astronomers have estimated that there are at least ten sextillion stars in our universe! Written out this number looks like this:

Fig. 1-13 Galileo Galilei

$$10,000,000,000,000,000,000,000$$

Other astronomers estimate that the number is as high as one hundred octillion:

$$100,000,000,000,000,000,000,000,000,000,000$$

Fig. 1-14 As God allows mankind to develop his ability to see deeper into space, the truth of Scripture is again borne out: "the host of heaven cannot be numbered."

Of course, these estimates are mere guesses. The true number remains, as the Bible says it will, beyond the scope of our counting.

To the ancients, nature must have seemed disorderly and mysterious. Planets wandered through the sky; comets and eclipses appeared suddenly and without warning, inspiring terror and predictions of doom. Such events would have seemed random, as if they had occurred by chance. But God's Word revealed even then that there are "ordinances of heaven" (Job 38:33): the celestial bodies move according to patterns. Not until perhaps thirty centuries later did Copernicus (ko PUR nih kus), Kepler, and Newton establish that these motions follow a predictable pattern.

Science and the Christian

Some students are naturally attracted to science. They enjoy investigating nature or tinkering with machines. They may have a natural aptitude in mathematics. They pursue extra projects and reading just to satisfy their curiosity about the world around them.

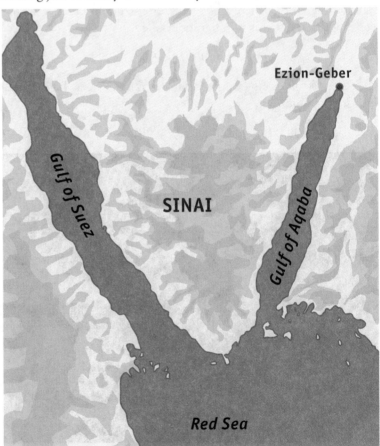

Fig. 1-15 When Nelson Glueck discovered the location of Solomon's mines, many critics of the Bible's accuracy were silenced. The mines were located in an ideal location for trade—just at the tip of the Gulf of Aqaba in the city of Ezion-Geber.

Many of these students will train for careers in science. They will become the nurses, doctors, dentists, research scientists, engineers, and technologists of the future. Yet you may not be one of those students. You may be thinking about a career as a businessman, homemaker, teacher, or pastor. Will this science course be of any lasting benefit to you?

As you explore the physical universe and study the principles that govern its operations, you will learn to appreciate the complexity and order of God's creation. The psalmist held God's creation in such awe that he wrote, "When I consider thy heavens, the work of thy fingers, the moon and the stars, which thou hast ordained; what is man, that thou art mindful of him? and the son of man, that thou visitest him?" (Ps. 8:3-4) The psalmist's observations of the creation helped him understand his smallness as compared to God's greatness.

Science has played an important role in supporting the inerrancy of the Bible. Once liberal scholars and archaeologists scoffed at the passage in Deuteronomy 8:7-9: "For the Lord thy God bringeth thee into a good land, . . . out of whose hills thou mayest dig brass." Brass is an alloy of copper, and the skeptics questioned the existence of copper deposits anywhere in Palestine.

Conservative scholars had long believed that Solomon mined and traded copper to the Persian kings in exchange for gold and spices. To confirm this, Dr. Nelson Glueck began the task of locating the lost mines. His team first uncovered the ancient city of Ezion-geber, the actual port from which eastbound copper had been shipped. Aerial surveys soon revealed water holes that had been used in ore smelting. Finally the abandoned mines were unearthed. In 1957 the unworked copper veins were put back into production and proved to be a profitable business. A literal reading of the Scripture had borne fruit.

The study of science can also help you develop your thinking skills. The activities of science require careful thought. You must make detailed observations, develop a clear understanding of what you observe, and evaluate how it fits with what you already know. This skill—*critical thinking*—will help you in every area of your life, whether in examining news reports for the true story of an event or in applying Scripture in your daily life.

Science is also a vital topic in our world. Almost every day some aspect of science is the subject of debate, investigation, or legislation. The ability to speak intelligently on subjects such as atomic energy or genetic engineering might gain for you the respect of people who would not otherwise give credit to your views. Such knowledge will also be a tool to help you detect error and false reasoning and make wise decisions in today's technology-oriented society.

Finally, by studying science you can satisfy some of your curiosity about the world around you. You will develop a better understanding of what things are made of, how they work, and the laws that govern their relationships and reactions to one another. As you satisfy your curiosity about matters of science, you may decide you want to pursue them further. If the Lord calls you into a science-related field of work, you will want to be well prepared by your early, foundational studies in science.

SECTION REVIEW QUESTIONS 1C

1. How does Ecclesiastes 1:6 support the viewpoint that the Bible is scientifically accurate?
2. Give an example of how supposedly "current" scientific theory contradicted the Bible.

CHAPTER REVIEW

SCIENTIFICALLY SPEAKING

data
observation
science
pure science
applied science
technology
value judgment

humanism
evolution
mutation-selection
  theory
Creationism
theistic evolution
bias

CHAPTER REVIEW QUESTIONS

1. What is information collected by observation called?
2. Give an example of a controversial use of technology.
3. How do pure science and applied science differ?
4. Identify some of the limitations of science.
5. How do theistic evolutionists differ from Creationists in respect to the amount of time required for Creation?

FACET REVIEW QUESTIONS

1. What are the two categories of nuclear waste, and how are they generated?
2. List seven options for disposing of high-level nuclear waste.

WHAT DID YOU LEARN?

1. Can you name some ways that newspapers, magazines, and television shows display evolutionary bias?
2. Describe the different uses of the term "evolution."
3. How does your point of view bias your judgment about handling a harmless garden spider?
4. List some of the orderly processes that you observe in creation that point to a designer of the universe.
5. If you were called to be a preacher or a Bible teacher, how would the study of science help your future ministry?

The Scientific Method

Chapter

2

At a birthday party Randall vigorously shakes two cans of soft drink and places them in the icy tub of drinks. Someone unsuspectingly picks up one of the booby-trapped cans—and foaming soda pop sprays everywhere. Randall picks up the second booby-trapped can, taps it on the bottom with his finger, and calmly opens it. Surprisingly, it does not spray like the other one did.

Why did the second can not spray? Randall smugly claims that tapping the bottom of the can cancels the effect of all the shaking. Someone else claims that the second can was deeper in the ice and that the additional cooling is the answer. Another friend suggests that the extra time that elapsed before the second can was opened is the reason.

While you may not realize it, you have taken the first steps in a scientific investigation. You have observed, and you have recognized a problem or question. But the investigation is incomplete. You have not completed the process of inquiry and problem solving unless you have logically considered the details of the data collection, carefully analyzed the data, and drawn logical conclusions. Scientists call this process the **scientific method.**

A Pattern of Thought

The experimental method is a pattern of thought that results in a certain approach to problem solving. It is a very effective approach to finding the solution to a problem. You have probably used the experimental method without even knowing it. Yet it is the consistent use of this approach by scientists that makes science the discipline of discovery.

TABLE

2–1	The Steps of the Experimental Method
1.	State the problem.
2.	Form a hypothesis.
3.	Do a controlled experiment.
4.	Analyze the data.
5.	Make a conclusion.
6.	Verify the conclusion.

State the Problem

Before you can solve a problem, you need to know exactly what the problem is. A clearly stated **problem** helps to focus your attention on how to solve it. In the soft drink example, you could begin by considering information relevant to the situation. You remember that both cans were shaken equally, recall their locations in the pile of iced drinks, and realize that the two cans were not opened at the same time. In this example, the problem could be stated, "What canceled the effect of shaking one of the cans of soft drink?"

Form a Hypothesis

Next, from your information you choose a possible solution from the variety of explanations. At this point you have no proof that this possible solution is any better than the others, but you suspect that it is the best one. This possible solution is your **hypothesis** (or educated guess); and it should be clearly stated as a sentence, not as a question. One possible hypothesis in the soft drink example could be, "Cooling an unopened can of soft drink cancels the effect of vigorously shaking it." Can you think of other good hypotheses for this example?

Do a Controlled Experiment

Your next goal in solving the problem scientifically is to prove that your hypothesis is right or wrong. Proof in science usually comes by performing a controlled experiment. A **controlled experiment** attempts to look at just one factor (or variable) that could help answer the original problem. In the example hypothesis, cooling (or temperature change) is the key factor. Thus, the controlled experiment to test the hypothesis would compare the spraying from cooled and uncooled shaken soft drink cans.

Imagine how you could perform this experiment. First, you would need to get cans of a soft drink. Might different brands or even different shipments of the same brand give different results? Perhaps. Thus you need to get cans which are as nearly identical as possible. Next, they both need to be shaken equally (same time, same amount of vigor, etc.). Then you need to chill one can more than the other while keeping all other conditions the same. Why should all the other conditions remain the same? Is it possible that something other than chilling might affect the foaming? Unless you are certain that the only difference between the cans is the temperature, you cannot be certain that some other factor will not affect the results. Finally, you need to open each can at the same time and in the same manner and observe the results.

In controlled experiments, the factor that is deliberately changed or altered is called the **variable.** The group(s) in which the variable is altered is called the **experimental group(s).** The example experiment had only one experimental group—the chilled soda can. We could have designed an experiment with many treatment groups, each one being chilled to a different temperature. The group in which the variable is not changed is called the **control group** (hence the term "controlled experiment"). Treatment groups are compared with the control group to determine if the altered variable had any effect in that treatment. The unchilled soda can is the control group in the example.

Scientists keep records of what they do in their experiments and what happens. They record their observations, measurements, and results in a variety of ways, including pen and paper, computer files, photographs, and audio recordings, to name a few. The information contained in these records is called *data.*

Gathering data is a crucial part of the experimental method. Good researchers learn to record observations immediately. They will not trust memory, even for a short period of time. They double-check each observation to ensure that their data are accurate. Good researchers record details carefully so that their experiments and observations can be repeated or compared with similar observations. In most research, if an observation cannot be duplicated, it should not be accepted.

Some data are **qualitative** (KWAHL uh TAY tiv) **data.** They do not involve the use of numbers or measurements; rather, they describe an event or condition. Some examples of such data are descriptions of the color of a liquid before, during, and after a chemical reaction; the physical characteristics of a certain biological species; and the quality of a certain sound.

Measurable or numerical data are **quantitative** (KWAHN tuh TAY tiv) **data.** Doctors order tests that count blood cells and measure chemicals in the blood. Nurses take blood pressure and temperature readings. Scientists in the laboratory use complex instruments to detect light, measure volumes and masses, and calculate exact times. Scientists generally prefer quantitative data because they are less affected by the observer's bias.

In the soft drink experiment the data collected would include exact timing of the shaking and chilling periods, temperature

Fig. 2-2 Audubon's sketches of American wildlife are classic examples of the collection of qualitative data. He recorded the colors and feathers of hundreds of birds, using watercolor paintings to record his data.

Developing Data

Participating in science fairs enables many students to learn more about the steps of the scientific method.

When Mr. Behn assigned science projects, Julia decided that she wanted to experiment with photography. After talking with her teacher and with her father's friend Mr. Wilt, Julia decided to test the effect of temperature on the development of color prints. Mr. Wilt was a professional photographer, and he told Julia that he would help her in any way he could. She studied his photography manuals until she understood the developing process. Then she bought the necessary chemicals and asked the photographer to help her print some photos on color paper.

For each print, Julia carefully adjusted the temperature of the developing solution and timed the period needed for processing. She timed the process at five different temperatures and then repeated the experiment to ensure the accuracy of her results. She carefully recorded all her data in a notebook.

The next day Julia showed the data to Mr. Behn.

"What do my results mean?"

"Well, Julia, it's hard to find a relationship when you simply list your data. You were trying to show the effect of temperature on the development time, right? I think the best way to show that type of relationship is to graph your results."

"How do I do that?"

This is how Mr. Behn set up Julia's graph:

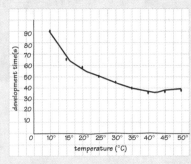

Then Julia plotted her data.

"Now what does your graph show?"

"The graph shows me that increasing the temperature speeds up the developing process. The bottom of the graph begins to level out. That probably means that after the solution reaches a certain temperature, heating it anymore doesn't help."

"I think you've done an excellent science project, Julia!"

"Thanks, Mr. Behn!"

readings, and of course the subsequent foaming. Timing and temperature are clearly quantitative data. Data related to the amount of spray could be either quantitative or qualitative. Since quantitative measurements are preferred, a method to measure the spray should be devised. For example, the volume of the spilled soda or the height of the spray could be measured and recorded as data.

Analyze the Data

After the scientist has collected data, the next step is to decide what the collected information means. Organizing scientific data involves **classifying** the data (separating data into groups) and then **analyzing** those groups. When analyzing, the scientist looks for relationships in the data. Did the data suggest a trend? Did they indicate a steady condition? Did they reveal a cause-and-effect relationship in which one factor caused a change in another?

In the soft drink experiment, the analysis would consist merely of comparing the control and treatment groups. If you had several treatment groups or performed the experiment several times, it would be best to perform more analysis. Calculating averages for each group or organizing the data in the form of a chart would then be appropriate.

Charting or graphing groups of data is often the best way to analyze them. Charts and graphs both make the relationships in the data visible and help the scientist to answer the question or problem statement. Today's researcher often depends on the computer when organizing and analyzing data.

Make a Conclusion

After a scientist organizes the data from the experiment, he or she sifts through the numbers, measurements, and descriptions for an answer to the problem being investigated. Sometimes this involves the use of the analyzed data and personal judgments to draw a **conclusion** (answer) that seems best.

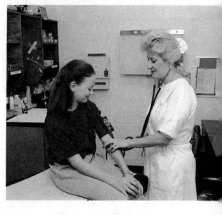

Fig. 2-3 Those in the medical profession rely greatly on quantitative data.

Fig. 2-4 Scientists look for the most workable answer to a problem.

PROBLEM

PROPOSED SOLUTIONS

It may come as a surprise to you that the conclusions of science are not discovered but are chosen from an array of alternatives. This makes the scientist's ability to make correct choices very important. A scientist is looking for the most workable answer to the problem. The hypothesis may prove to be correct, or the hypothesis may have to be changed to make it better fit the data. In some cases, the hypothesis is rejected altogether.

Good conclusions should
1. relate to the hypothesis.
2. account for the data.
3. predict new data.
4. stay as simple as possible.

The scientist's conclusion should have certain characteristics. It should relate back to the original hypothesis. It must agree with the data gathered from the experiment. The chosen conclusion should also predict what would happen in similar circumstances, and it may direct the scientist to applications or further research. Finally, a good conclusion should be kept as simple as possible. Not all problems will have simple answers.

The selection of an answer by scientists is influenced by their bias. Therefore not even careful scientific conclusions are considered absolute or final. Any answer is subject to possible challenges and may eventually be rejected.

Verify the Conclusion

The data from a single experiment are rarely enough to isolate the correct answer. People make mistakes, data seem to vary, and answers are not always clear the first time. You may have a good idea of what the answer should be after one experiment, but in order for the answer to be valid, you should **verify** the conclusion. Verifying means repeating the experiment at least once and perhaps many times.

An answer may be verified by methods other than repeating the entire experiment. One way is to perform a different experiment that should lead to similar results. Another method is to make a prediction based on the solution and to test whether the prediction is accurate. Even verification, however, does not make a hypothesis absolute fact; it simply makes it more likely to be true.

Fig. 2-5 Verifying the results of an experiment can uncover a large problem.

QUICK!!! VERIFY THIS EXPERIMENT WITH A CAT!

Sometimes a researcher's work does not "check out." The equipment may have malfunctioned during the experiment, or the scientist may have made an error in judgment when choosing the answer. However, the scientist who later disproves his or her own conclusions still makes progress. If the scientist is convinced that the equipment caused the problem, then he should modify or replace the equipment and perform the experiment again. Sometimes a scientist must completely rethink and restructure the research. It may take several times, but with perseverance, a scientist should eventually produce verifiable results.

Variations

Whether they are searching for specific applications or new information, most scientists use some form of the scientific method. Lists of the steps of an experimental method may mislead you into thinking that there is a single unchanging path to an answer. There is no single, simple list of the exact steps that all scientists follow. Some scientists use five steps, others six, and still others seven. How can this be? The explanation lies in the fact that different problems are best studied in different manners. The steps presented in this chapter are a broad outline of the procedures used in most scientific problem solving.

Consider an experiment examining the effect of a new medicine on human beings. Since all people, even identical twins, are different, it would be impossible to perform perfectly controlled experiments. Does this mean that data obtained from such experiments are invalid? No, it simply means that the method used has to account for the additional variability.

Consider the science of astronomy. Is it possible to experiment with a star? Of course not. Does this mean that most of astronomy is not science? No. To astronomers, science is mostly observation and mathematical models rather than experimentation. Their conclusions are often predictions that can be verified by even more observations.

Intelligent guesswork teamed with the experimental method helped Charles Goodyear develop a way to make rubber products practical. In the early 1800s, companies making India-rubber caps, shoes, coats, and wagon covers sprang up at a phenomenal rate. However, within two years after rubber was introduced into the American marketplace, the India-rubber boom was over. The heat of summer reduced the rubber products to molten masses that gave off such an offensive odor that they had to be buried.

Goodyear had just sold his interest in a hardware store so that he could devote his life to a career of invention. He decided to take on the challenge of making rubber useful. He felt that he could solve the problem with this "gum elastic" (rubber) in just a few months but later wrote that he was "blessed" with ignorance of the obstacles he would meet. Several winters and summers would pass before he could successfully test his products with observations.

His road to discovery was not an easy one. He tried mixing witch hazel, black ink, and even cream cheese into the rubber to make it stable, but his efforts failed dismally. His lack of training in chemistry handicapped him. Nevertheless, his persistent use of trial and error, tested by observations, kept him on the road to discovery. It was not until he treated crude rubber with sulfur and subjected it to heat that he found success. This process, now called vulcanization, resulted in a stable compound that had both strength and elasticity (ih LAS TIS uh tee). Soon factories were producing Goodyear's rubber all across Europe and America. Goodyear's careful observations and use of the scientific method finally paid off.

Science sometimes involves intelligent guesswork, intuition, and prediction, but it subjects them all to the rigorous test of observation. All proposed solutions must be tested and retested by carefully controlled experimentations. The strength of the experimental method lies in its ability to test its solutions. Guesswork, intuition, or prediction alone cannot do this, but combined with the experimental method they can play an important role in discovery.

Fig. 2-6 Astronomers use observation and mathematical models more than they perform experiments.

Observing the Lord

The value of observation is not limited to the field of science. Observations are significant in the Scriptures as well. Beginning in Genesis with the mark of Cain and the first rainbow, God called on man to observe many things. One of the most important calls was to observe His Son.

"Behold the Lamb of God, which taketh away the sin of the world" (John 1:29).

John the Baptist first called men to look upon Jesus Christ. The Lord was about to begin His public ministry when John asked men to observe Him—to use their physical senses to perceive the precious Gift of God. Later, when John sent two of his disciples to ask Jesus if He were indeed the Promised One, "Jesus answered and said unto them, Go and shew John again those things which ye do hear and see" (Matt. 11:4). They were to testify to others the things they had observed of Christ.

"Behold the man!" (John 19:5)

This time it was Pontius Pilate who called men to behold the Lamb of God. The Savior was on His way to the cross, which would thrust Him high above the stark hill of Calvary, into view for all the ages to come. When the jeering crowd at the foot of the cross saw Him hanging there, they demanded, mocking, "Let Christ the King of Israel descend now from the cross, that we may see and believe" (Mark 15:32).

He did not come down from the cross. But the mockers heard for themselves His last words and His last breath, and saw for themselves the darkness, and felt the earthquake that declared this to be the death of the Son of God.

His disciples, too, saw Him there. They "stood afar off, beholding these things" (Luke 23:49). Then, because they were trusting in their physical vision alone, they went their way in grief and not in hope.

Procession to Calvary by Giovanni Antonio Bazzi, called Il Sodoma. From the Bob Jones University Collection.

1. What is a hypothesis?
2. What type of data is not recorded in measurable units?
3. Which step of the experimental method often involves making charts and graphs?

"Behold my hands and my feet, that it is I myself: handle me, and see; for a spirit hath not flesh and bones, as ye see me have" (Luke 24:39).

The risen Savior spoke to calm His troubled disciples. Already He had given them proof of His resurrection: the angel at the empty tomb had told the two women that He lived again; then Mary Magdalene had seen Him and had spoken with Him in the garden. But the apostles would not believe these reports; "their words seemed to them as idle tales" (Luke 24:11).

That same day, the Lord had appeared to two of His followers as they traveled to Emmaus. He kept them from knowing who He was; they told Him all that had happened, and of their disappointment and sadness. The Lord responded, "O fools, and slow of heart to believe all that the prophets have spoken" (Luke 24:25). To these who had believed neither His promise nor the witness of others, He explained the Scriptures that testified of Him. Only then did He open their eyes so that they could see and know Him, and return to Jerusalem to testify, "The Lord is risen indeed" (Luke 24:34).

Now He stood before them as He had promised and as Scripture had prophesied—and they were afraid. He invited them to observe for themselves His resurrected body, to see and to touch, and to "be not faithless, but believing" (John 20:27). Christ was truly the Lord; He lived again as He had promised.

"Ye men of Galilee, why stand ye gazing up into heaven? this same Jesus, which is taken up from you into heaven, shall so come in like manner as ye have seen him go into heaven" (Acts 1:11).

The disciples stood staring at the sky as the heavenly messengers spoke to them. A moment before, the Lord had been with them, talking with them and instructing them as He had so many times before. Then, as they watched, "he was taken up; and a cloud received him out of their sight" (Acts 1:9). He had left them again—not alone or hopeless, but with the promise of the Holy Spirit, and of power, and of His coming to earth again as they had seen Him go. He had also left with them a mission—to bear witness of Him throughout the earth.

They did go to the ends of the earth—preaching, teaching, and writing, to share with the lost world what they had observed of the Savior. "That which was from the beginning, which we have heard, which we have seen with our eyes, which we have looked upon, and our hands have handled, of the Word of life; . . . That which we have seen and heard declare we unto you, that ye also may have fellowship with us: and truly our fellowship is with the Father, and with his Son Jesus Christ" (I John 1:1, 3).

People on earth will behold the Lord again when He returns as He promised. For those who have heard and believed the witness of Christ, seeing Him will bring great joy and reunion with their Redeemer. For those, however, who have not believed the report, seeing Him will not bring joy, but judgment.

"Behold, He cometh with clouds; and every eye shall see him, and they also which pierced him: and all kindreds of the earth shall wail because of him. Even so, Amen" (Rev. 1:7).

Theories and Laws

A research project may have a variety of outcomes. It may provide only a specific answer to the original problem. It often raises more questions than it answers. It could lead to a broader conclusion, such as a theory or a law.

A **theory** is a partially verified idea that ties together a number of different observations. Theories should not be confused with hypotheses. A theory is an idea that has been tested by many experiments or observations. A hypothesis is an "educated guess" that guides scientists as they plan their experiments and observations. A hypothesis is unconfirmed. A theory has been verified to some extent.

Scientific **laws** are chosen to describe consistent patterns of phenomena in nature. When scientists observe a sequence of events that occurs nearly the same way every time, they can frame a scientific law. Some scientific laws are expressed by mathematical relationships. Coulomb's Law is a mathematical equation that lets us calculate the strength of the force between electrical charges. This is an example of a quantitative physical law. Other physical laws are qualitative; they describe relationships that are not expressed in numbers. For instance, the law of electrical charges says that like charges repel and opposite charges attract. It does not state how strongly they attract or repel.

[handwritten margin note: or numerical / measurable or / event or condition]

Some laws describe relationships very accurately. Others are only approximate. Some laws work well under ordinary conditions but break down under unusual ones. Scientific laws, like scientific theories, are chosen rather than discovered. How well they work depends on how well they are chosen. Can nature "violate" a scientific law? Yes it can, if the law is not well chosen or not well stated. If a "violation" of the law is observed, the law should be written so that it more accurately describes what actually happens. We also believe the "laws of nature" can be changed or modified if God so chooses—we call such events *miracles.* Even unbelievers sometimes admit that there are some events that qualify as miraculous. Numerous miracles are mentioned in the Bible, so we marvel at them. But God is all-powerful, and it should not surprise us that He can do anything He wants to. "Is anything too hard for the Lord?" (Gen. 18:14)

Communication

Communication is an important part of science. Not only are conclusions shared with others in the field of science, but the experiments and reasoning leading to the conclusions are submitted for all to examine. It takes courage to expose your research to scrutiny.

Fig. 2-7 One purpose of publishing articles in scientific journals is the opportunity to benefit from having peers examine a scientist's work.

However, the benefit from having peers examine your work and check your reasoning and observations is worthwhile.

How do scientists communicate? Forms of communication in the scientific community include publishing research in journal articles, presenting work at professional meetings, and discussing findings at informal gatherings. The benefits from such scientific communications can be great. But the benefits are far greater when scientists can communicate their theories plainly to people who may not be scientists or specialists. A good scientist realizes that just having a lot of knowledge or wearing a white lab coat does not give a person all of the answers. Pride sometimes leads scientists to word their theories in such vague terms that even other scientists have a difficult time understanding them. Or some scientists will accept a theory as fact even though they have not given it much thought or scrutiny. The lesson here is that scientists, like everybody else, are capable of mistakes, bias, and even lies. You should not believe everything you read or hear unless you have first checked to see what the Bible says about it. Since the Bible is always accurate, we can use it to judge the accuracy of any scientist's observations or theories. There are three possible categories.

- It may contradict the Bible and be wrong (evolution).

- It may agree with the Bible and be accurate (the winds in Eccl. 1:6).

- It may not be discussed in the Bible and may or may not be accurate (extraterrestrial life).

Hand Over the Data!

Theories play a double role in research. While showing patterns in data, they also introduce new lines of research. The famous research of Lord Rayleigh at Cambridge University's Cavendish Laboratory illustrates these roles. In 1882 Rayleigh noticed that the liquid nitrogen he had condensed from the air differed slightly from the nitrogen he had produced from other sources. First he guessed that nitrogen might have several different chemical forms.

When he could not support that idea, he attributed the difference to impurities. Some other gas or gases must have condensed with the nitrogen. With the help of William Ramsay, Rayleigh soon isolated the impurity. The newly detected gas was very stable and highly unreactive. They named it argon, from the Greek word for "lazy."

Their work caught the eye of a French scientist, Lecoq de Boisbaudran. He projected a theory from the data. Argon must belong to a family of unreactive gases that were present in very small quantities in the air. Ramsay took this new theory as a challenge and began to experiment. He eventually located four more gases that fit Lecoq's theory: helium (from the Greek word for "sun"), krypton (Greek for "hidden"), neon (Greek for "new"), and xenon (Greek for "stranger"). This family of elements is now known as the noble gases. Boisbaudran devised his theory using much of the data that Lord Rayleigh supplied, thus demonstrating the importance of communication in scientific research.

Fig. 2-8 Lord Rayleigh

SECTION REVIEW QUESTIONS 2B

1. Which has more evidence to support it, a hypothesis or a theory?

2. Explain the difference between a theory and a law.

3. List three ways that scientists typically communicate with each other about their research.

Limitations of Science

Some people have exaggerated ideas of what science is and what it can do. Although science does occupy an important role in modern life, it cannot solve all our problems. Science is only a means of gathering information, and that information poses questions: Is the information correct? How should it be used? To properly answer these questions, we must understand the limitations of the experimental method.

Limitations in Collecting Data

A scientist collects information by observing physical phenomena. Only information that a scientist can gather through the senses, either with or without the aid of instruments, can be scientific data. Information can be collected only from the physical universe. Some phenomena are too small, occur too quickly, or happen too far away to be observed with unaided senses. Much of our scientific information has come through instruments that allow us to "extend" our senses so that we can collect data about events not readily observable. When a scientist investigates the impact of a bullet, the event occurs too quickly to be seen. Using stroboscopes and high-speed photography, one can "slow down" the event to an observable rate. The origin of the universe is an example that cannot be redone, and no human observer was present to collect information when it was created. In a similar way, science cannot deal with the spiritual realm, because it can use only the physical senses to collect data.

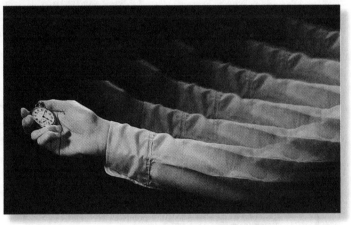

Fig. 2-9 Stroboscopic photography can "slow down" events that occur too briefly for us to observe.

If something cannot be observed, then it cannot be subjected to the experimental method. One must be especially careful not to make statements using *all* or *none,* called **universal statements.** A statement such as "there is no life on other planets" or "all animals have been discovered" seems very foolish in light of the limitations we have. Since it is impossible for our eyes to see everywhere, calling such statements science is simply wrong. It is not wrong to have an opinion or viewpoint based on the present evidence, but only God knows the absolute truth about the universe.

We also must recognize that the terms scientists use are man-made terms. The concept of gravity is one of the most basic concepts of science. But what is gravity? Can you touch it or handle it? It is the same way with energy. Energy is the ability to do work, not a substance that can be stored in a test tube. We do not know all the mysteries of gravity or energy—but we really do not need to know everything about these concepts in order to use them. Our present theories of these concepts are workable and usable. Scientific theories are not necessarily meant to explain but rather to describe phenomena.

Limitations in Using Information

Scientists use information to develop laws and theories that describe the way things work. With this information they have found cures for diseases, reached into the heavens, and uncovered the inner workings of matter. But there are things that science cannot do.

Science cannot establish truth. Scientific conclusions are always subject to change as new information is collected. There is only one Truth. Christ said, "I am the way, the truth, and the life: no man cometh unto the Father, but by me" (John 14:6). This truth does not change. With God there "is no variableness, neither shadow of turning" (James 1:17). His Word reveals to us His truth.

Scientists are subject to all the limitations of human nature. They can miscalculate, misunderstand, and misapply information. Therefore, science is limited by the persons who practice it. History records many scientific blunders that happened because of misinterpreted natural phenomena. Scientists used to think that

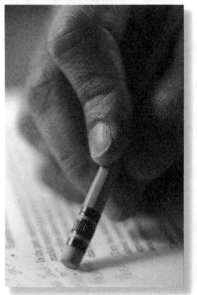

Fig. 2-10 All human activity—including scientific research—is subject to error.

mice came from old rags stored in dark places. Today such a theory sounds like madness since scientists have clearly established that life comes only from life, not old dirty rags. This is just one illustration of the fact that all human activity is subject to error.

Remember, scientific information is changeable. If you were to compare the "facts" held by science fifty years ago with what science holds today, you would be surprised at the number of "proven facts" that have changed. For example, biologists do painstaking research when they search for an animal that is possibly extinct. They interview villagers, look for bones, and literally search worldwide for any trace of life. When they have exhausted every possible effort, they will declare extinction. Imagine their suprise (and frustration) when several creatures that they believed to be extinct are found years later, alive and well, in a remote area they had missed. That is part of the beauty of science. New information, new things, and new hypotheses are constantly being generated. On the other hand, people who put their faith in science are bound to be disappointed.

Scientific information cannot form the basis of **value judgments.** We make these decisions based on the rightness or wrongness of a particular choice. Consider the following "scientific" view of a bank robbery. Every Friday, the First National Bank receives a one-million-dollar cash shipment to cover the cashing of payroll checks. The security system at the bank is outdated, and no cameras cover the delivery entrance. Security is lax; there is only one guard. The data show that you could rob this bank. Should you rob it? We also make value judgments when we decide the worth of a material or action, such as the beauty of a dress or the worth of a painting.

There is no scientific way to collect information on the morality of robbing a bank. Science cannot tell right from wrong. It can tell you only if something might work. Through scientific investigations we have obtained atomic energy but not guidelines for its use. If a thief programs a computer to choose which banks could be robbed, the computer will produce the information without

The Limitations of Science

1. Science must deal with observable, physical phenomena.
2. Science cannot establish truth.
3. Science is limited by the persons who practice it.
4. Science cannot prove a universal statement.
5. Science cannot make value judgments.

any judgment. The moral judgment was made by the programmer. Science can provide only information, not the guidelines for making moral judgments.

Science, by its very nature, can never answer all our questions. Scientific inquiry is limited, and the work of scientific research is never finished. We will never know everything about the physical universe. It has been estimated that for each question science is able to answer, ten new questions are raised. This is precisely what God has ordained. If we could understand everything God did, we would be thinking on His level. But we know that His thoughts are infinitely higher than our thoughts. "God thundereth marvellously with His voice; great things doeth he, which we cannot comprehend" (Job 37:5).

SECTION REVIEW QUESTIONS 2C

1. List three limitations of science.
2. Can the statement "This is a beautiful dress" be proved using science? Why or why not?

CHAPTER REVIEW

SCIENTIFICALLY SPEAKING

scientific method	classifying
problem	analyzing
hypothesis	conclusion
controlled experiment	verify
variable	theory
experimental group	laws
control group	universal statements
qualitative data	value judgments
quantitative data	

measurable or numerical

event or condition

CHAPTER REVIEW QUESTIONS

1. How does stating the problem assist a scientific investigation?
2. What is the key element that makes an experiment a controlled experiment?
3. In an experiment, what is the factor which differs from one treatment group to the next?
4. What type of data can be recorded with numbers or measurements?
5. Why do you think scientists prefer quantitative data?

6. Which is the more firmly established concept, a theory or a law? Why?

7. Why is the conclusion to a scientific investigation rarely the end of the inquiry?

WHAT DID YOU LEARN?

1. Why should a scientist verify data before making a conclusion?

2. Why might different scientists follow different experimental methods?

3. A scientist communicates his research to other scientists who then find some possible mistakes in his work. What should he do next?

4. In what ways is science a better problem solver than guessing?

5. Susan wonders if food drops into her stomach because of gravity or if the muscles in her esophagus push it downwards. She believes it is gravity. How can she test her hypothesis?

A Description
of Matter

The Measurement of Matter

3A Metric Units

3B Mass and Volume

3C Density

3D Reporting Measurements

What is matter? Every object in the physical universe is made up of matter. The air you breathe, the food you eat, the clothes you wear, and a multitude of other things that you encounter every day illustrate the numberless forms that matter takes. No one could describe all the different forms of matter that God has created. Faced with this infinite variety, scientists have chosen to describe matter by the properties it has. All physical objects have two characteristics in common. All objects have a certain quantity of matter (mass), and all occupy space (volume). Therefore, **matter** is described by its measurable properties of mass and volume.

Why do scientists choose measurable properties to define matter? Scientific information is useless unless it can be communicated. Such information can be communicated in either numerical measurements (quantitative data) or word descriptions (qualitative data). Why have scientists chosen numerical data?

Suppose you observe a ball swinging at the end of a string. The name of this apparatus is a pendulum. Observations of the setup could include many things: How long is the string? How big is the ball? How much time does one swing take? How high does the ball swing? If you reported that a light ball on the end of a short string took a surprisingly long time for one swing and rose quite high, would this word description be worth anything to a scientist? How long is "long"? What is "quite high"? What seems "light" to one observer might be "heavy" to someone else.

What if you reported that the length of the string was 25, the ball had a mass of 30, the time of one swing was 1, and the height of the swing was 5? Would these numbers be any better than the first data? Numbers alone are not very useful. Is the length of the string 25 inches, 25 feet, or 25 meters? No one could tell from this information! Numbers must go with units to have meaning. **Units** are descriptive notes that accompany numbers. For the observations of the pendulum to be useful, all of the data should be recorded in numbers with corresponding units. A correct form for the data from the observation would be, "A 30-gram ball on the end of a 25-centimeter string took 1 second to make a complete swing and rose to a height of 5 centimeters." This data might also be abbreviated in a table of "known" values like:

Mass of ball	= 30 g
Length of string	= 25 cm
Time for complete swing	= 1 s
Height of swing	= 5 cm

The most precise information is communicated with *numerical* (or quantitative) data. Lord Kelvin knew how important precise measurements are in science. He said, "When you can measure what you are speaking about, and express it in numbers, you know something about it; but when you cannot express it in numbers, . . . it may be the beginning of knowledge, but you have scarcely, in your thoughts, advanced to the stage of science."

When Is an Ell Not an Ell?

How would you react if you went to the store this evening, bought a "2-liter" bottle of cola, took it home, and discovered that it was only three-fourths as large as the "2-liter" bottle you bought yesterday in a nearby town? If we did not have a common system of units that were the same size everywhere, you would encounter situations like this every day. You would never know how much of anything you were actually buying.

That was the state of affairs in England until the thirteenth century. The people constantly battled fraud and confusion because they had not agreed on any consistent units for their country. Because each baron was free to establish his own units for his domain, trade was almost impossible. It is no wonder that when the English barons demanded basic political rights in the Magna Carta, they also forced King John to establish standard units of measure. One clause of the charter says,

"Throughout the kingdom there shall be standard measures of wine, ale, and corn; namely two ells within the selvedges [edges]. Weights are to be standardized similarly."

Even though men in the Middle Ages did not have a "technologically advanced" society like ours, they knew how important consistent

units were. Today SI *(Système International)* is a system of measurements that is consistent worldwide, eliminating many problems of trade, aiding the scientific community, and generally simplifying communication.

The Word of God also condemns the use of divers weights and divers measures (Prov. 20:10).

It is a sin to tell someone that he is buying a certain amount of goods when in reality he is receiving less. Since people generally do not carry around balances and meter sticks to check the truthfulness of vendors, a certain amount of trust goes into all business transactions.

Metric Units

Man has used many different systems of units. In Bible times length was measured in cubits and spans. (The giant Goliath was 6 cubits and 1 span tall.) Since then ells, fathoms, leagues, miles, yards, feet, and inches have been used to designate lengths. While the names of some of these units are fascinating, using them can be frustrating. Why are these units difficult to use?

First, they are based on *changeable* standards. The inch was originally defined as the length of three barley seeds placed end to end. In ancient times inches varied with the quality of the barley crop. King Henry I of England established the yard as a unit of measurement. He defined it as the distance from the tip of his nose to the end of his outstretched hand. Unfortunately, when he died a new standard had to be found. Barley seeds and arms are not the best standards for units of scientific measure, but they did become the basis of the English system of measurement.

Second, there are too many different units. In the English system alone, length is measured in miles, furlongs, rods, yards, spans, feet, hands, and inches. This list does not include units of nautical length or surveyors' lengths. There are literally hundreds of different units in the English system. You can imagine what confusion they can create!

Finally, the *conversion* from one unit to another can be very difficult. Try this English system conversion quiz.

Cubit = 44.45 cm	Gen. 6:15; John 21:8
Finger = 1.85 cm	Jer. 52:21
Handbreadth = 7.40 cm	Exod. 25:25
Span = 21.21 cm	Exod. 28:16
Talent = 34 kg	I Kings 16:24; Rev. 16:21
Shekel = 11.4 g	II Sam. 14:26
Litra (Roman Pound) = 0.373 kg	John 12:3; 19:39
Bath = 22.71 L	I Kings 7:26
Homer = 227.1 L	Lev. 27:16; Ezek. 45:14
Omer = 2.3 L	Exod. 16:16

1. How many feet tall is a horse that measures 15 hands in height?

2. What is the weight in ounces of a pickup truck weighing one ton?

3. How many pints of gasoline are there in a full 18-gallon tank?

Give up yet? To answer these questions you would need to know how to relate one English unit to another. There are 3 hands in a foot, 16 ounces in a pound, and 2000 pounds in a ton. A liquid gallon contains 8 pints. Converting one English unit into another is not easy. (See Appendix A for help.) In the metric system, however, conversion from one unit into another is simple.

The International System

The measurement of mass, distance, and volume in the **metric system** is based on a unit of length called the **meter** (m). This unit of measure is not based on the changing human anatomy. It was based on a more permanent standard. The meter was originally defined as one ten-millionth of the distance from the North Pole

Fig. 3-1 The standard kilogram is kept by the International Bureau of Weights and Measures. It is stored under three vacuum domes to ensure that it remains accurate.

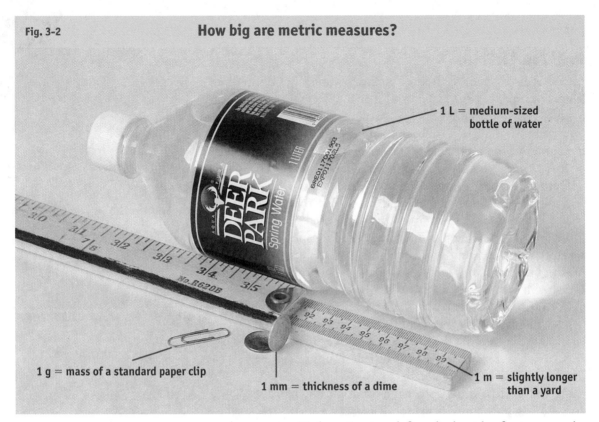

Fig. 3-2 How big are metric measures?

1 L = medium-sized bottle of water

1 g = mass of a standard paper clip

1 mm = thickness of a dime

1 m = slightly longer than a yard

to the equator. Today scientists define the length of a meter as the length traveled by light in a vacuum during 1/299,792,458 of a second. This allows scientists to have an extremely precise standard for the meter.

The metric system is a *decimal* system. Since all the units are related to each other by multiples of ten, you can make smaller or larger units simply by moving the decimal place. From the basic unit of length, a *unit of volume* called the **liter** (L) was derived. A liter is the volume of a cube with sides one-tenth of a meter (0.1 meter, called a decimeter) long. This unit of volume was then used to produce the basic unit of mass. The mass of one liter of pure water at 40°C is one **kilogram** (kg), or 1000 grams.

Scientists can easily check the accuracy of these units in the laboratory. To confirm the weight of a pound, the volume of a quart, or the length of a foot, however,

SI Basic Units		
Unit	**Quantity**	**Symbol**
Meter	length	m
Kilogram	mass	kg
Second	time	s
Ampere (AM peer)	electrical current	A
Kelvin	temperature	K
Mole	amount of substance	mol
Candela (kan DEL uh)	light intensity	cd

3 The Measurement of Matter

would require a trip to the National Institute of Standards and Technology near Washington, D.C. Over the decades, the metric system has been systematized into what is now known as **SI**, or *Système International.* SI units include a basic unit of time (the second), a unit of temperature (the Kelvin), and a unit of electrical current (the ampere). This unified system simplifies and standardizes all scientific work.

Metric Prefixes

Many times the basic SI units are too small or too large to use for a specific measurement. The meter is too small to measure the distance between cities and much too large to measure the thickness of aluminum foil. The volume of a hypodermic syringe is too small to be measured in liters. Likewise, it would be difficult to express a dosage of medicine in kilograms. A prefix system was developed to allow us to modify the basic unit into units that can apply to other situations. The prefix tells how many starting units are to be used. For example, the prefix *kilo-* means "1000"; therefore, a kilometer (km) is 1000 meters, and a meter is $\frac{1}{1000}$ of a kilometer.

TABLE 3-3 **Metric System Prefixes**

Abbreviation	Prefix	Pronunciation	Meaning	Decimal Relationship
M	mega-	MEG uh	1,000,000 times the basic unit	1,000,000X
k	kilo-	KIL oh	1000 times the basic unit	1,000X
h	hecto-	HEK to	100 times the basic unit	100X
da	deka-	DEK uh	10 times the basic unit	10X
	(no prefix)		the basic unit	1X
d	deci-	DESS uh	1/10 of the basic unit	0.1X
c	centi-	SEN tuh	1/100 of the basic unit	0.01X
m	milli-	MIL uh	1/1000 of the basic unit	0.001X
μ	micro-	MY kroh	1/1,000,000 of the basic unit	0.000001X

Milli- means $\frac{1}{1000}$. A milliliter (mL) is $\frac{1}{1000}$ of a liter—in other words, it takes 1000 mL to make 1 L. Adding one of the standard prefixes changes the starting unit by a multiple of ten.

We can adapt the basic metric units for almost any measurement. Distances between cities are measured in kilometers. The thickness of aluminum foil is measured in millimeters. Hypodermic syringes are calibrated (KAL uh BRATE id) in milliliters, and the dosages of many medications are calculated in milligrams.

Metrication

Can you imagine a world in which airline pilots and air traffic controllers spoke different languages? Fortunately for pilots and their passengers, the worldwide language of aviation is English. Companies such as Microsoft and General Motors do business on almost every continent, yet they use English as their official business language so that they spend less time translating and more time building their product.

The worldwide language of measurement is the metric system. Political leaders have long recognized the need for an easy-to-use system. In fact, in 1790 Thomas Jefferson first proposed a *decimal-based* system for the United States. To this day, however, the United States has not fully adopted the metric system.

Proponents of the metric system want a true change from the old English system to SI units. That would mean that pounds, feet, and miles would go out of everyday use and into the history books. This proposed process is called *metrication*.

It is said that the metric system was first developed by a Frenchman named Gabriel Mouton in the late 17th century. However, it was not until 1795, over a hundred years later, that France officially adopted the metric system as the official system of measurement. As time passed, the meter as well as the kilogram became standardized. In 1875, the Treaty of the Metre was signed by several nations, and it led to the establishment of the General Conference on Weights and Measures (CGPM). At that time, the standard meter was a platinum bar. The other countries that signed the treaty received prototypes of that bar so that most of the Western world now had a standard meter that would be recognized for shipping, trade, and travel around the globe. Since then, the definition of a meter has changed several times, but its length has never changed. It has merely been defined with greater precision (see inset).

In 1960, the CGPM gave the offi-

Definitions of the Meter

Year	Definition
1793	1/10,000,000 of the distance from the North Pole to the equator.
1795	Provisional meter bar constructed in brass.
1799	Definitive prototype meter bars constructed in platinum.
1889	International prototype meter bar in platinum-iridium, cross section X.
1906	1,000,000/0.64384696 wavelengths in air of the red line of the cadmium spectrum.
1960	1,650,763.73 wavelengths in vacuum of the radiation corresponding to the transition between levels 2p10 and 5d5 of the krypton 86 atom.
1983	Length traveled by light in vacuum during 1/299,792,458 of a second.

3 The Measurement of Matter

TABLE
3-4

Metric Measures of Length

Unit	Abbreviation	Size Compared to Meter
megameter	Mm	1,000,000 times as large
kilometer	km	1000 times as large
hectometer	hm	100 times as large
dekameter	dkm	10 times as large
meter	m	the basic unit

These products are labeled in both ounces and liters.

cial symbol SI to the metric base units, and several nations rapidly put metrication efforts into place if they had not already done so. By 2000, all but three countries of the world had officially adopted SI units for all government and business activity. The three countries were Myanmar (Burma), Liberia, and the United States.

Why has metrication had such a hard time in the United States? It is definitely not for lack of trying. The National Bureau of Standards in Washington, D.C., issued a report to Congress in 1971 entitled "A Metric America: A Decision Whose Time Has Come." Politicians took

notice, and Congress passed and President Ford signed the Metric Conversion Act of 1975. The act established the United States Metric Board to coordinate the increased use of metrics in public and private life. However, no deadlines were set for compliance, and the law had minimal effect on Americans' attitudes towards the "new" system. In 1988, Congress passed a law that required all federal agencies to use the metric system by 1992. Soon after that, the Food and Drug Administration (FDA) required the use of inch-pound and metric units on all consumer products. Today almost every product in the grocery store is labeled in both ounces and liters.

Metrication in the United States is far from complete, especially in the construction industry.

But most agree that eventually a "metric nation" will result, though no one speculates about when. The United States may be forced to convert because other countries are becoming increasingly irritated with the old system. In fact, the European Union is requiring that all products sold in Europe from the United States be labeled in SI units only and set a 2009 deadline for compliance. The more people start to "think metric" the sooner we will be measuring our mass in kilograms and asking questions like "how many more kilometers to Grandma's house?"

The National Institute of Standards and Technology (formerly the National Bureau of Standards) is a leading proponent of metric usage in the United States.

Unit Conversions

Unit analysis is a way to convert between units. It is a mathematical tool for expressing the way we think about these conversions. If someone asks you how many dozen eggs is 6 eggs, you might stop and think and then answer that 6 eggs is $\frac{1}{2}$ dozen. How did you perform the conversion from single-egg units into dozen units? The conversion was based on two facts: there are 12 eggs in 1 dozen, and 6 is one-half of twelve.

If you summarized your thoughts in a mathematical equation, they could be stated this way:

$$12 \text{ eggs} = 1 \text{ dozen}$$

$$\text{Therefore, } \frac{1 \text{ dozen}}{12 \text{ eggs}} = 1$$

because a number divided by itself or its equivalent is always equal to one.

$$6 \text{ eggs} \times \frac{1 \text{ dozen}}{12 \text{ eggs}} = \frac{6}{12} \text{ dozen or } \frac{1}{2} \text{ dozen}$$

Remember that multiplying by 1 does not change the value of the measurement. It changes only the units.

You may not have realized that you used all these steps as you thought, but this type of analysis is the key to the conversion of units.

Three groups of students were given the assignment of measuring a table in their classroom. Each group was supplied with a different measuring device. One device was calibrated in meters, another in centimeters, and the third in millimeters. The teacher recorded the results on the blackboard:

Group A	Group B	Group C
2000 millimeters	200 centimeters	2 meters

Fig. 3-5 Thinking through the cancelling of units

Do their measurements agree? We can check the results by converting all of the measurements into the same unit. The first meas-

1. Multiply a number equal to 1   2. Cancel the units   3. Multiply and divide

3 The Measurement of Matter

urement, 2000 millimeters (mm), can be converted into meter (m) units by applying the fact that there are 1000 millimeters in a meter. (See Table 3-3.) If 1000 millimeters are the same as one meter, then 2000 millimeters must be equal to 2 meters. The following equation summarizes this process:

$$2000 \text{ mm} \times \frac{1 \text{ m}}{1000 \text{ mm}} = 2 \text{ m}$$

Because $\frac{\text{mm}}{\text{mm}} = 1$, the millimeter units cancel, and the answer is expressed in meters. We have simply multiplied the number and the unit by the relationship between the two units. This relationship is stated as a ratio that is equal to 1. A meter and 1000 millimeters are exactly the same length. If you divide a length by itself the answer is 1! Multiplying by 1 does not change the size of the measurement. It changes only the units of the measurement. The same process can be used to convert other metric units.

Check the measurements made by the second group. Are 200 centimeters the same as 2 meters? We can solve for the answer by using this relationship: 1 meter = 100 centimeters.

$$200 \text{ cm} \times \frac{1 \text{ m}}{100 \text{ cm}} = 2 \text{ m}$$

EXAMPLE PROBLEM

Practicing unit analysis

How many milliliters are there in a 2-liter bottle of soft drink?

RELATIONSHIP: 1000 milliliters = 1 liter

UNIT ANALYSIS: $\frac{2 \text{ L} \times 1000 \text{ mL}}{1 \text{ L}}$

ANSWER: 2000 milliliters

Which contains more mass, a 350-gram box of breakfast cereal or a 3.5-kilogram box of breakfast cereal?

RELATIONSHIP: 1000 grams = 1 kilogram

UNIT ANALYSIS: $\frac{350 \text{ g} \times 1 \text{ kg}}{1000 \text{ g}} = 0.35 \text{ kg}$

ANSWER: The 3.5-kilogram box contains much more mass!

The unit that you are converting into is always on the top of one fraction. Can we use this method to confirm that 2 meters are the same as 2000 millimeters? What is the relationship between the two units? 1 meter = 1000 millimeters. How would we set up the unit analysis? We start with meters and convert into millimeters:

$$2 \text{ m} \times \frac{1000 \text{ mm}}{1 \text{ m}} = 2000 \text{ mm}$$

Why did we use the relationship 1000 millimeters = 1 meter? Why did we place the millimeters on the top of that relationship?

In checking our work, we have confirmed that the groups made identical measurements. They simply expressed them in different units. You will often need to convert several different units into the same units for comparison. Be sure to learn the metric prefixes so that you can convert units easily. The real benefit of unit analysis is being able to see which units cancel. This is particularly helpful when dealing with more than one unit at a time, such as length and time.

SECTION REVIEW QUESTIONS 3A

1. What is the unit of volume in the metric system?
2. The systemized metric system is known as _____.
3. How many millimeters are in a kilometer? Use unit analysis and show your work.

Section

Mass and Volume

In making a snowball, you pack a certain amount of snow into a sphere. As it is packed, the snow decreases in size, but does it lose matter? Is size a dependable measure of the amount of matter in an object? What about the astronauts as they travel through space? In the ready room of the launch pad, an astronaut weighs 160 pounds. Far out in space, the astronaut is "weightless." Is part of the astronaut lost as he travels into space? Could weight be a dependable measurement of the amount of matter in an object?

The Measurement of Matter

Mass is defined as the quantity of matter in an object. Mass does not change when an object is compressed. It will not change with the pull of gravity. An object that has a mass of 4 kilograms on earth will have that same mass in space. Mass is a constant. It does not change unless matter is added or removed.

The mass of an object can be determined on a **balance.** Balances are measuring devices that compare the amount of matter in an object to a known amount of matter. The simplest type of balance is the double-pan balance. The object to be measured is placed on

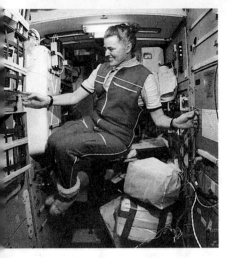
Fig. 3-6 This astronaut's weight is zero, but her mass is the same whether she is in space or on the earth.

3 The Measurement of Matter

one pan, causing the balance to shift to that side. Separate masses with known values are placed on the other pan until the center scale shows that the pans are balanced. Since each pan now holds an equal amount of mass, the sum of the known masses equals the mass of the object being measured.

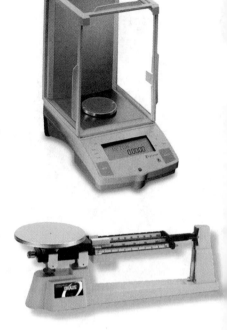

Multiple-beam balances are very practical devices for determining the mass of an object. They are simpler to use because they require no separate known masses. These balances usually have two to four specially marked beams. The marks are called calibrations or calibrated beams. The calibrations might stand for hundreds of grams, tens of grams, grams, and tenths of grams. The object to be measured is placed on the pan, and the riders (known masses that slide on the beams) are moved until the scale balances. Measurements can be made to the nearest centigram. When more accurate measurements are needed, analytical balances are used. These precision instruments give readings to the nearest $\frac{1}{10}$ of a milligram (0.0001 gram). Recall that if you convert from milligrams to the base unit (g), you move the decimal 3 places to the left (1 mg = 0.001 g).

The Conservation of Mass

Matter undergoes many changes. It can be crushed, powdered, or subjected to chemical reactions. It can be frozen, melted, or boiled. Yet it cannot be destroyed. When an object is crushed or powdered, it retains its original mass. When objects undergo chemical reactions, the products of those reactions will have the same mass as the original objects. Water does not gain or lose mass as it is

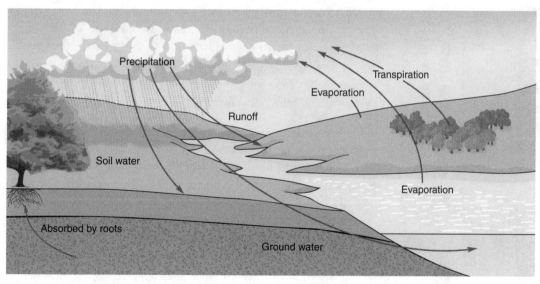

Fig. 3-7 The water cycle is a natural process that illustrates the conservation of mass.

Fig. 3-8 Antoine Lavoisier

frozen or boiled. In all physical and chemical changes, matter is neither created nor destroyed. It is conserved.

In the eighteenth century the French chemist Antoine Lavoisier (lah VWAH zyay) stated this important principle:

We must lay it down as an incontestable axiom [rule], that in all operations of art and nature, nothing is created; an equal quantity of matter exists before and after the experiment.

Scientists call this principle the **law of mass conservation,** and it states that *in all chemical and physical changes, matter is neither created nor destroyed.* It describes one way that God sustains the physical universe. Water evaporates from the oceans, falls as rain, and returns to the oceans in streams and rivers. Trees feed on the nutrients in the soil, grow, die, and decompose to fertilize other plants. In all chemical and physical changes, matter is conserved. The matter that God created is continually recycled. He sustains His creation without creating new matter.

A Comparison of Mass and Weight

Weight is the measure of the force of gravity on an object. We measure this force in SI units called **newtons** (N). One newton equals 0.225 lb. This textbook weighs about 10 newtons (2.25 lb.—where lb. is the abbreviation for pounds). The average ninth grader weighs 500 newtons (112 lb.). Since gravitational forces vary, the weight of an object can change as conditions change. An astronaut who weighs 710 newtons (160 lb.) on earth seems "weightless" in space. Yet his mass has not changed; he has moved to a location where the gravitational pull is less. On the moon's surface the astronaut weighs only one-sixth of his weight on earth. Since the moon has less mass than the earth, the gravitational pull of the moon is one-sixth that of the earth. Your weight changes when you ride in an airplane. At an altitude of 8000 meters, the average ninth grader weighs 13.5 newtons less than he does at sea level!

The words *mass* and *weight* are often confused. Weight is not a measure of matter. It is the measure of the attraction of one object (such as the earth) for another (such as you). We *weigh* objects on **spring scales.** The more the object weighs, the more the spring in the scale stretches.

Let's use the example of an elevator ride to help us see the difference between mass and weight. Jill gets on an elevator armed with a 2.2-pound ball of clay resting in the pan of a spring scale. While the elevator is at rest, the weight remains steady at 2.2 pounds. Jill notes (as do the other curious occupants) that as the

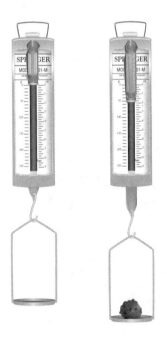

Fig. 3-9 An object in the pan of a spring scale stretches the spring, moving a weight indicator down the scale.

elevator begins to ascend, the weight of the ball increases, as shown by the indicator moving down the scale. But once the elevator achieves a steady rate of speed, the weight readjusts to 2.2 pounds. But then when the elevator slows as it reaches the top floor, the weight of the ball actually decreases! The reverse of this process holds true as Jill descends in the elevator.

So the weight, or measure of the force of gravity on the ball of clay, changed with the motion of the elevator. But did the ball's mass change as well?

Jill enters the elevator a second time, still carrying the same ball of clay. But this time she has placed it on a double-pan balance, which she places on the floor of the car so that other passengers won't accidentally bump it. The two pans are evenly balanced. On one side is the clay ball (its mass, measured in kilograms rather than in pounds, equals one kg), and on the other side she has placed masses equivalent to one kg. As the elevator ascends and descends this time, the balances do not move one way or the other!

So the mass, or quantity of matter in the ball of clay, did not change with the motion of the elevator even though the weight of the ball did change.

Volume

All matter takes up space. To occupy space, matter must have three dimensions: length, width, and height. The space described by these dimensions is called **volume.** We find out the volume of rectangular solids using a simple mathematical formula:

> **Formula for the volume of a rectangular solid**
> $$v = lwh$$
>
> or volume = length × width × height

The unit of volume is the liter (L) for measuring large volumes and the cubic centimeter (cm^3) for smaller volumes. (The cubic centimeter has exactly the same volume as the milliliter.) Volume calculations are essential to finding out just how much space an object takes up. It could be as simple as finding out the volume of a soft drink can or as serious as calculating the amount of fuel an airliner can hold. Consider this example of a typical problem involving volume.

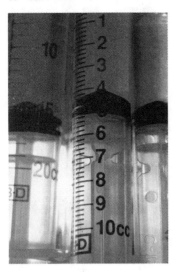

Fig. 3-10 One cubic centimeter (cc) is equal to 1 milliliter (mL); cc = cm^3 = mL.

EXAMPLE PROBLEM

How to calculate volume

What is the volume of a rectangular solid 6 cm long, 3 cm wide, and 2 cm high?

KNOWN: length (l) = 6 cm
width (w) = 3 cm
height (h) = 2 cm

UNKNOWN: volume (v)

FORMULA TO USE: v = length × width × height, or v = lwh

SUBSTITUTION: v = 6 cm × 3 cm × 2 cm

SOLUTION: v = 36 cm^3

The unit of volume here is the cubic centimeter (cm^3), which is sometimes abbreviated "cc." It is the *same* volume as a milliliter.

As long as an object has a standard geometric shape (such as a cube, cylinder, or sphere), we can calculate its volume by simple arithmetic. These mathematical formulas were worked out by ancient Greek mathematicians. Familiarize yourself with the common shapes and their volume formulas. (See Table 3-12.)

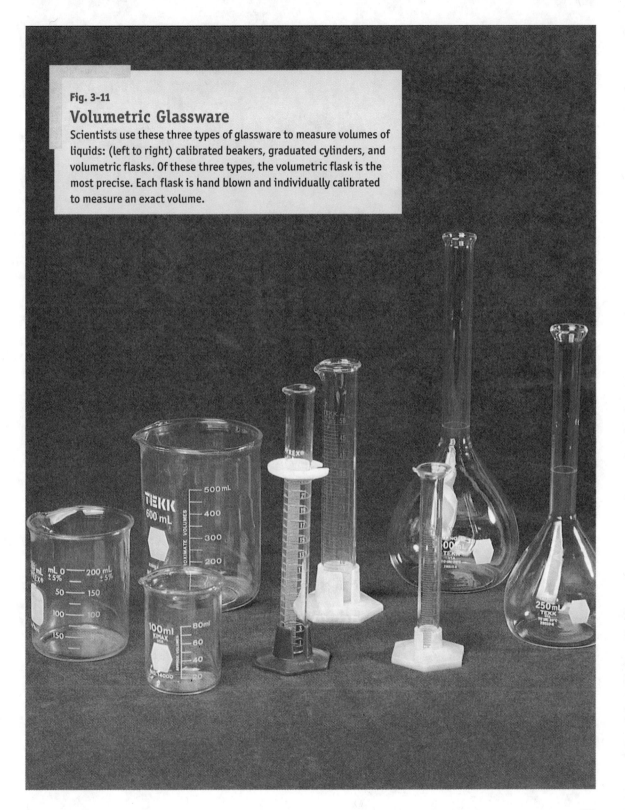

Fig. 3-11

Volumetric Glassware

Scientists use these three types of glassware to measure volumes of liquids: (left to right) calibrated beakers, graduated cylinders, and volumetric flasks. Of these three types, the volumetric flask is the most precise. Each flask is hand blown and individually calibrated to measure an exact volume.

3-12 Calculating Volumes

Shape	Relationship	Formula
cube	side • side • side = volume	$v = s^3$
solid rectangle	length • width • height = volume	$v = lwh$
sphere	$(4\pi$ • radius • radius • radius$) \div 3 =$ volume	$v = \dfrac{4\pi r^3}{3}$
cylinder	π • radius • radius • height = volume	$v = \pi r^2 h$
cone	$(\pi$ • radius • radius • height$) \div 3 =$ volume	$v = \dfrac{\pi r^2 h}{3}$

Fig. 3-13 In a graduated cylinder, the volume is measured at the lowest point of the meniscus.

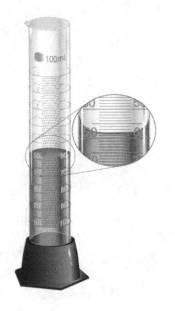

When scientists measure the volume of large solids or large amounts of fluids (liquid or gas), they use liters. A chamber that is 100 cm on each side will have a volume of 1,000,000 cm³, or 1,000 liters.

For even larger volumes, scientists use cubic meters. A cubic meter has a volume of 1000 liters. An empty room that measures 5 m × 6 m × 4 m contains 120 m³ of air.

Measuring Volume

You can easily find the volume of a *regular solid* by measuring it with a ruler or meter stick and using arithmetic. But how can you measure liquids and irregular solids? Scientists use many types of specialized glassware to measure liquids. Some types measure volumes as small as $\frac{1}{100}$ of a milliliter or even smaller! One one-hundredth of a milliliter is 0.01 mL.

Graduated cylinders are used to measure liquids in most laboratories. The volume of the liquid is indicated by precise markings on the side of the cylinder. Study Figure 3-13. You will notice that the surface of the liquid in the cylinder is not flat. This curve is a **meniscus** (muh NIS kus). When using a graduated cylinder, be sure to read the markings at the *lowest* point of the meniscus if the liquid is water or behaves like water.

The volume of *irregularly shaped solids* can be measured by the **water displacement method.** A graduated cylinder is filled with enough water to cover the object being measured. A reading is taken at the bottom of the meniscus. The object is then carefully placed in the water and the water level is read, again using the bottom of the curve. The volume of the object is the *difference* between the first reading and the second reading. If the first reading was 33 mL and the second reading was 78 mL, the volume of the object can be calculated: 78 mL – 33 mL, or 45 mL.

Imagine trying to calculate the volume of an object such as a stone without using this simple method. The process would require an extremely complex mathematical formula, and even then the answer would be only approximate.

Overflow cans are used to measure irregular objects too large to fit into graduated cylinders. The overflow can is filled until the water begins to flow out the spout. An empty beaker is placed below the spout, and the object is carefully placed in the overflow can. The water that runs out is measured in a graduated cylinder. This volume is the same as the volume of the object.

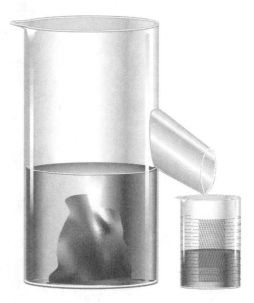

SECTION REVIEW QUESTIONS 3B

1. State the law of mass conservation and provide an example of it from nature.

2. What is the unit of weight in the SI system?

3. What is the curved surface of a liquid in a graduated cylinder called? How does this curve affect the accuracy of scientific measurements?

Density

Which has more mass, a kilogram of paper or a kilogram of lead? Think about it for a moment. Even though both items have the same mass (1 kg) you would need a larger volume of paper than of lead to equal a kilogram. Why do you need less lead than paper to equal a kilogram? It is because of lead's greater density compared to that of paper. The term density relates mass and volume. **Density** is the amount of mass in each unit of volume. We calculate the density by dividing the mass of an object by its volume.

Formula for density

$$d = \frac{m}{v}$$

or density = mass/volume

Density is measured in units such as kilograms per liter (kg/L) or grams per milliliter (g/mL) for liquids and grams per cubic centimeter (g/cm^3) for most solids. The density of lead is 11 g/cm^3. The density of most paper is less than one-tenth of that. Lead is not the most dense naturally occurring substance on earth. That substance is osmium (22.48 g/cm^3). A brick-sized chunk of osmium would weigh more than half as much as an average ninth grader! You can find the density of any material by dividing its mass by its volume.

EXAMPLE PROBLEM

How to calculate density

If a chunk of lead displaced 36.0 cm^3 (mL) of water and had a mass of 407 grams, what would its density be?

KNOWN: volume (v) = 36.0 cm^3
mass (m) = 407 g

UNKNOWN: density (d)

FORMULA TO USE: $d = \frac{m}{v}$

SUBSTITUTION: $d = \frac{407 \text{ g}}{36.0 \text{ cm}^3}$

SOLUTION: $v = 11.3 \text{ g/cm}^3$

Note the way the units are handled. Grams divided by cubic centimeters gives grams per cubic centimeters in the answer.

TABLE
3-14

Densities of Some Elements and Common Substances
(in g/cm^3)

osmium	22.48	opal	2.2
iridium	22.42	rock salt	2.18
platinum	21.45	bone	1.85
gold	19.3	magnesium	1.74
uranium	18.7	brick	1.7
mercury	13.6	sugar	1.59
lead	11.3	gelatin	1.27
copper	8.92	hard rubber	1.19
iron	7.86	seawater	1.03
diamond	3.26	pure water	1.00
cement (set)	2.8	ice	0.92
aluminum	2.7	butter	0.86
glass	2.6	ethyl alcohol	0.79
chalk	2.4	seasoned oak	0.75
clay	2.2	cardboard	0.69

A university science department was once asked to determine the composition of the ancient Roman coins in a special collection. The museum caretaker who sent them specified that the coins could not be tested chemically or defaced in any way. He assured the science department that the coins were mostly copper or gold or some mixture of the two metals. Fortunately, copper and gold have widely different densities. Each coin was weighed and its volume determined by the water displacement method. The mass of each coin was then divided by its volume. For instance, one coin had a volume of 1.2 cm^3 and a mass of 10.5 grams. Its density was therefore 8.7 g/cm^3.

The densities of the ten coins tested ranged from 7 to 10 g/cm^3. Since copper has a density of 8.92 g/cm^3 and gold is more than twice as dense (19.3 g/cm^3), the scientists concluded that all the coins were predominantly copper. The composition of the coins varied, but if they had contained very much gold, their densities would have been much higher.

The density of a material also gives a clue to its strength. This is important for engineers and building designers, who must determine what materials will work best during construction. Iron is denser and stronger than concrete, so it is often used to reinforce poured concrete. Metals, such as iron, are usually more dense than other solids, but not all metals are particularly strong. Even though lead is a metal and is denser than concrete, it is unsuitable for buildings because it is too soft and has a low melting point. You could melt lead on your stovetop!

Physicians use *bone density tests* to determine if a patient has weak bones. This condition is called *osteoporosis* and is usually caused by the loss of calcium from the bones as the body ages. In

FACETS of the physical world

Just a second . . .

The fundamental unit of time in both the Metric System and the English System is the **second** (abbreviated *s*). The first attempts to accurately measure seconds were made with mechanical clocks. A second was measured by the clicks of a pendulum-powered gear. Pendulum clocks were eventually replaced by a more efficient system. These new clocks used a wound spring and flywheel for power, but the second was still measured by the clicks of the clock's gear.

Science demanded a more accurate timing device. Advanced research required a highly accurate device that could be based on a natural phenomenon that any laboratory could reproduce. Scientists discovered that a quartz crystal would vibrate when voltage was applied to it. This phenomenon is called the piezoelectric (pee AY zo uh LEK trik) effect. Using that effect, scientists developed a timing device that measured the second by the vibrations of the quartz crystal—approximately 30,000 of them. This new clock was accurate to within one second per year. But even this level of accuracy was not sufficient for some of the demands of science.

Further research led to the development of the atomic clock. This highly accurate clock uses the vibrations of a cesium–133 atom to measure a second. Today we can define one second as 9,192,631,770 vibrations of a cesium atom.

cases of advanced osteoporosis, the slightest fall or stress on bones can cause them to break or bend. Bone density, as you can see, is crucial to maintaining good health and posture.

Some objects in deep space have such a high density that it is difficult to imagine. *Black holes* and *neutron stars* have been identified in space with the aid of extremely powerful telescopes. A black hole is a collapsed star that is so dense that one the size of a baseball would have the same mass as the earth. That would make its density almost 10^{15} g/cm³! A black hole has an enormous gravitational pull—so powerful that even light cannot escape it.

SECTION REVIEW QUESTIONS 3C

1. Given that this book has a mass of 1200 g and a volume of 1400 cm³, what is its density?

2. Which of the following is the most dense: ice, fresh water, or seawater?

3. Describe osteoporosis and how it is diagnosed.

$0.8571 \frac{g}{cm^3}$

$d = \frac{g}{v}$

Reporting Measurements

Three students were told to find the volume of a small cube. The first used a meter stick calibrated in centimeters. He found that each side of the cube was between 3 and 4 cm long. Since the smallest division on the meter stick was the centimeter, he estimated the length to be 3.4 cm and calculated that the volume was 39.3 cm³. The second student used a ruler marked in millimeters and measured the length to be 33.0 mm. She converted this measurement to 3.30 cm and found the volume to be 35.94 cm³. The third student measured the cube with a precise measuring device called a *caliper* (KAL uh pur) and found that a side was 32.70 mm or 3.270 cm long. She calculated that the volume was 34.966 cm³. Who was correct?

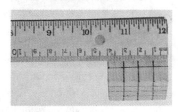

Fig. 3-15 A caliper (top) is a more precise instrument than a meter stick.

Student	One	Two	Three
Measuring device	meter stick	ruler	caliper
Calibration	centimeters	millimeters	1/100 mm
Length	3.4 cm	33.0 mm	32.70 mm
Volume	39.3 cm³	35.94 cm³	34.966 cm³

Each student's measurement was limited by his or her judgment and the precision of the instrument. Yet each student made the best measurement possible within these limitations. Scientists have long recognized that all measurements are limited by the instruments used to make them. They also recognize that many

How Far Is Around the World?

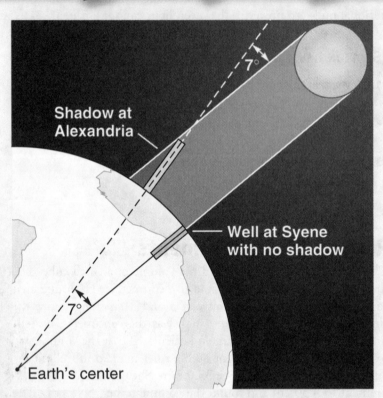

Shadow at Alexandria

Well at Syene with no shadow

7°

7°

Earth's center

Measuring a planet with a meter stick sounds like a long, hard job—especially if the planet is Jupiter! Yet an encyclopedia will list for you the circumference of each planet in our solar system and give you the same information about the sun.

How do scientists measure things they cannot reach or handle, even with the help of instruments? Some amounts are not measured in the usual sense. They are calculated. Centuries ago scientists and mathematicians discovered that they could find new information by using mathematical formulas with information they already had.

Eratosthenes (ehr uh TAHS thuh NEEZ), a Greek astronomer who lived more than two thousand years ago, was the first to accurately calculate the size of the earth. He knew that at noon on the first day of summer, the sun's rays cast no shadows and reached the bottom of a deep well in Syene, Egypt. This information told him that the sun was directly overhead. At the same time in Alexandria, a city 800 km to the

north, the sun did cast shadows. He could tell by measuring these shadows that the sun was about 7 degrees "lower" in the sky at Alexandria.

Eratosthenes already knew that the earth was round (360 degrees) and that all the sun's rays striking the earth were parallel. Using geometry, he figured out that an angle at the earth's center formed

by imaginary lines from the two cities would also be 7 degrees or approximately 1/50 of the circle of the earth. Therefore, he could multiply by fifty the distance between Syene and Alexandria and find the distance around the earth.

Erathosthenes' method worked so well that his result came within 1 percent of the correct circumference: 50 × 800 km, or 40,000 km.

measurements must be estimated. Often a scientist records measurements with a range of possible errors. If a geologist determines the mass of a rock by using a balance that is accurate to within one centigram, the mass of the rock could be reported as 45.45 ± 0.01 g.

When other scientists examine this work, they see that the measurement has specific limitations. Using a more precise balance, the geologist might be able to state the mass to the nearest milligram (0.001 g). Every measurement made, even with the most precise balance, will be limited to some degree.

Significant Digits

Suppose you use a ruler to measure the width of a piece of notebook paper. Also suppose that the smallest divisions on the ruler are millimeters. You carefully position the ruler across the paper and find that the paper is between 215 and 216 mm wide. What should you report as the paper's width? Reporting 215 mm would not be correct since you can see that the paper extends a little bit beyond the 215 mm mark. Likewise, 216 mm would be incorrect since the paper falls short of that mark. Should you split the difference and report 215.5 mm? Suppose the paper ends a little closer to the 216 mm mark? Should you report 215.7 mm? 215.75 mm? 215.75984 mm?

Scientists have developed a system to tell each other how accurate their measurements are. They use the concept of **significant digits.** In any measurement, all the digits that are known to be certain (the ones marked on the measurement tool) are used, plus one that is estimated. A measurement of 215.7 mm, for example, has four significant digits. The 2, 1, and 5 are certain and the 7 is an estimate. In this case, any 4-digit number between 215.0 and 216.0 could have been reported and would still be correct.

Does reporting more significant digits (215.76 mm) make a measurement more precise? If the measurement were made with a ruler calibrated only to mm, then you would be in error. You can estimate only one significant figure—in this example the tenths place (one place after the decimal). However, if you used a measuring tool calibrated to the nearest tenth of a mm, then you would be allowed to estimate the hundredths place and be more precise. A measurement of 215.76 mm means that the actual measurement fell somewhere between 215.7 mm and 215.8 mm, that you estimated the hundredths place (2 places after the decimal), and that your equipment is calibrated to the nearest tenth mm.

Fig. 3-16 This digital weight scale is calibrated to the nearest tenth of a pound.

Accuracy vs. Precision

Precise instruments can produce measurements with many significant figures. Precision and accuracy are not the same. *Accuracy* has to do with how close a measurement is to the true value. *Precision* has to do with the degree of agreement between replicate measurements of the same quantity.

We often assume that because our measurements are very precise they are also very accurate, but that is not necessarily the case. For example, suppose that you were to carry out the density determinations on the Roman coins that were mentioned in the main text, and the manufacturer did not draw the lines on the graduated cylinder at the proper intervals. The improperly calibrated glassware may give you the same answer time after time, but not the right answer. Yes, you have good precision . . . but poor accuracy.

On the other hand, you may have a well-made cylinder, but every time you repeat the experiment you sight the meniscus at a different angle. The average of your measurements may give you the true value, but your precision will be poor. Thus, significant digits tell us more about the precision of a measurement than about its accuracy.

What if a measurement falls exactly on one of the calibration lines? Suppose in the example above that your ruler gave a reading of exactly 215 mm. Since you can estimate the tenths place, you should report the measurement as 215.0 mm. Tacking a zero on to the end of the number does not make the measured paper any wider, but it does tell how sure you are of your measurement.

Calculations involving numbers with significant digits (usually measurements) follow certain rules. One such rule is that there can be no more significant digits in an answer than appears in the *least* accurate measurement that enters into the computation. How would you calculate the area of a room? The length of the room is measured very accurately to four significant digits: 5.824 m. The width is measured with less accuracy to three digits: 4.20 m. Substituting these numbers into the area formula, a = lw, gives the equation

$$a = (5.824 \text{ m})(4.20 \text{ m}) = 24.4608 \text{ m}^2$$

or expressed to three significant digits,
$$24.5 \text{ m}^2$$

Only three figures should be given in the answer, the same as the less accurate of the two original measurements. The last digits should not be used.

Scientific Notation

Science often involves numbers that are very large or very small. Astronomers have calculated the mass of the earth to be 5,980,000,000,000,000,000,000,000 kg. Atomic physicists have determined that the mass of a hydrogen atom is 0.00000000000000000000000000167 kg! Such large and small numbers are difficult to write and even more difficult to use in a mathematical operation such as multiplication or division.

These numbers can be much more conveniently expressed in **scientific notation.** Large or small numbers can be converted into the product of a power of 10 and a number between 1 and 10. This is done by first moving the decimal place to make the number fall between 1 and 10. Then count each space that the decimal was moved, and make that number the exponent for the power of ten. Consider the following illustrations:

3 The Measurement of Matter

Expressing scientific notation

Convert 5,600,000,000.0 into scientific notation.

THE NUMBER BETWEEN 1 AND 10 IS 5.6.

THE DECIMAL PLACE WAS MOVED 9 PLACES TO THE LEFT.

THEREFORE, THE SCIENTIFIC NOTATION IS 5.6×10^9.

If the number is very small, the decimal place will be moved to the right. The exponent on the power of ten will be negative. Consider this example:

Convert 0.000000045 into scientific notation.

THE NUMBER BETWEEN 1 AND 10 IS 4.5.

THE DECIMAL PLACE WAS MOVED 8 PLACES TO THE RIGHT.

THEREFORE, THE SCIENTIFIC NOTATION IS 4.5×10^{-8}.

SECTION REVIEW QUESTIONS 3D

1. Convert 150,000,000 km (the average distance between the earth and the sun) into scientific notation.

2. Dan reported that last week he put 10.2 L of gasoline in the family car. Ruth said she put in 11 L, and Robert claimed he put in 4.12 L as well. Using significant figures, calculate the total volume of gasoline put into the car last week.

SCIENTIFICALLY SPEAKING

matter

units

metric system

meter (m)

liter (L)

kilogram (kg)

SI

unit analysis

mass

balance

law of mass conservation

weight

newtons (N)

spring scales

volume

meniscus

water displacement method

density

second

significant digits

scientific notation

CHAPTER REVIEW QUESTIONS

1. Metric units are related to each other by multiples of what number?

2. Convert 35 cL to mL. Note that 1 step down makes the number ten times bigger.

3. Is *hectometer* a unit of volume, length, or mass?

4. Convert 25 km to mm.

5. Convert your answer for number four into scientific notation.

6. What tool should an astronaut take along to determine the mass of an object on the moon?

7. Describe the difference between a scale and a balance.

8. What volume of potting soil can a cylindrical flowerpot that is 13.0 cm tall and 12.0 cm in diameter hold? Show your work and express the answer in scientific notation using significant figures.

9. An object made of an unidentified material has a mass of 1400 g and a volume of 530 mL. Calculate the density of the object and use Table 3-14 on page 59 to identify it.

10. David measures a liquid using a graduated cylinder calibrated in milliliters. The bottom of the liquid's meniscus appears to line up exactly with the 31 mL line. What should David report as the volume of the liquid?

11. Copper atoms have an average diameter of 0.0000000256 cm. Convert this average into scientific notation.

FACET REVIEW QUESTIONS

1. The _____ clock is the most accurate timekeeping system in the world.

2. What does the Bible have to say about fair weights and measures?

3. Who was Eratosthenes, and what is he known for?

4. What is the "Metric Conversion Act"?

WHAT DID YOU LEARN?

1. Using Table 3-4 on page 47, choose the best unit(s) of length for measuring your height. Defend your choice(s).

2. Why is the moon's gravitational pull less than the earth's?

3. How could you increase the density of a dry sponge without adding any mass (such as water) to it?

4. What would you estimate the density of a human body to be? (Hint: What is the human body primarily composed of? Do you float or sink in water?)

5. Most notebook paper is 11 inches by 8.5 inches. Why is it unlikely that a paper manufacturer would ever state that his product was 11.0000 by 8.5000 inches?

6. Most people would agree that the metric system is easier to learn and use than the English system. Yet the United States still overwhelmingly favors the English units in most industries. Explain some reasons that this is true and what must happen for the United States to "go metric."

7. Why is it especially important for Christians to be accurate and precise when working in science?

The Properties of Matter

Chapter

4

We know that something is matter if it has mass and occupies space. That would include all of the materials that surround you. Various metals, plastics, fibers, foods, woods, and other solids, liquids, and gases—you probably will not be able to list them all. Even you are made of matter. The trillions of cells that make up your body are all made of matter. So the question is this . . . is there anything not made of matter?

The answer is yes. Light, radio waves, and television signals are not made of matter, yet they exist. Heat can be measured and felt, yet it has no volume or mass. God tells us that He is not a physical being made of matter but rather a spiritual being who must be worshiped in a spiritual way (John 4:23-24). Angels are spiritual beings as well. Some scientists falsely believe that if we cannot taste, touch, or handle something through our physical senses, then it does not exist. They do not take into account the fact that our brains are only so powerful and we have only so many senses. God has commanded us to learn as much as we can about matter through the physical senses that He has given to us (Gen. 1:28). Therefore, we describe the earth and living things on the earth according to their physical properties.

We can identify many kinds of matter by their physical properties. A **physical property** is one that can be observed and measured without a change in the kind of matter being studied. Some physical properties of matter are color, density, shape, electrical conductivity, hardness, and texture. These physical properties help determine the uses of materials. A diamond-tipped drill can pierce through bedrock, but if the diamonds were replaced with quartz crystals, the drill would grind to a halt.

Why do the diamonds work better than the quartz? They share several of the same physical properties. Both are transparent minerals. Both can be cut into beautiful faceted shapes. Yet the industrial diamonds used in drill bits are four hundred times harder than quartz. This physical property—hardness—makes diamonds ideal for drilling through layers of rock.

Matter can also be identified by its chemical properties. A **chemical property** describes how matter will react and change in the presence of other kinds of matter. The tendency of iron to rust is a chemical property, as is the resistance of chrome to rust. We

Fig. 4-1 The tendency for iron to rust is a chemical property.

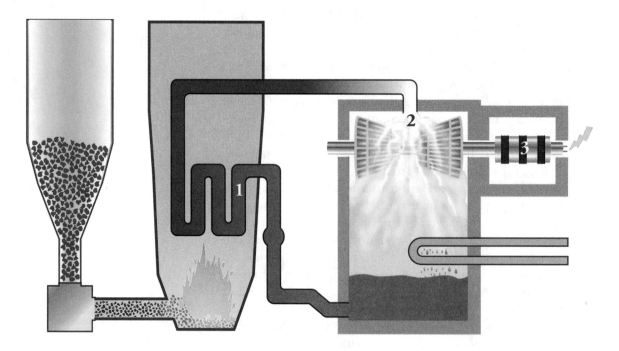

Fig. 4-2 Most electrical generating plants use a chemical change to produce electricity. In a coal-powered plant, burning coal heats water to make steam. (1) The steam travels through pressurized pipes until it reaches the turbines. (2) There the steam turns the turbines much like wind turns the blades of a windmill. The spinning turbine turns the generator to produce electricity. (3) The steam condenses in a cooling chamber and goes through the system again.

will study the chemical properties of matter in more detail in a later chapter.

When we observe the world around us, we see that matter is continuously changing. Some of the changes we observe are in the shape or state of the material. A change that does not alter the identity of the material is called a physical change.

Most kinds of matter on earth occur in the solid, the liquid, or the gaseous state. Matter can change its state and remain the same kind of matter. Water freezes, but it is still water. Alcohol may evaporate, but it is still alcohol. Matter may also change its physical form and still remain the same kind of matter. Sugar can be dissolved in water, but it is still sugar. Wood can be ground into sawdust, but it is still wood.

Many physical changes are harnessed for practical purposes. For example, much of our electrical energy is produced by huge steam turbines. These are powered by a physical change. Water is heated by coal, oil, or nuclear fuel to produce steam under high pressure. This steam turns the turbines, which turn the generators. As another example, many of our tools are made by die

Fig. 4-3 Sugar in any form is still sugar.

casting, a process that relies on physical changes. Metals are heated until they become liquid and then are poured into a mold. As the metal cools, another physical change occurs: the metal returns to the solid state. When the mold is broken away, the solid metal tool remains.

A change that alters the identity of the material is a **chemical change.** When a chemical change occurs, new kinds of matter are formed. Water can be chemically split into hydrogen and oxygen. Sugar will decompose when heated, and wood will burn. Each of these changes produces new substances. We will study chemical changes in Chapter 9. In this chapter you will explore the models that scientists have developed to describe physical properties and physical changes. These models will help you to understand and predict the behavior of matter.

The Particle Model of Matter

About four hundred years before Christ, Greek philosophers began a great debate about the nature of matter. Several philosophers proposed that all matter was continuous. They argued that any material could be subdivided an infinite number of times and still be the same kind of matter. If a water droplet were subdivided again and again, it would always be water. Other philosophers were convinced that matter could not be infinitely subdivided. They felt that if a material were broken into smaller and smaller pieces, it would eventually reach a point where it could not be subdivided any further and remain the same kind of matter. If a water droplet were subdivided again and again, at some point the smallest particle of water would be found. If this particle were subdivided further, it would no longer be water. This is referred to as the **particle model.**

This debate lasted for more than two thousand years, until scientists collected enough evidence to support one model over the other. Eventually the particle model was accepted, but only in recent times have scientists realized how small and complex particles of matter are, or how many particles a visible piece of matter contains. The diameters of these particles are measured in hundred-millionths of a centimeter (10^{-8} cm), called **angstroms** (ANG strumz). When referring to angstroms we use the symbol Å. If you could lay one million particles of water side by side, they would match the thickness of a piece of construction paper! The **nanometer** (10^{-9} m) is also a measurement for small particles and is the accepted SI unit being used by many scientists today.

Units of Particle Measurement

1 angstrom (Å) = 10^{-8} cm or 10^{-10} m

1 nanometer (nm) = 10^{-9} m

10 Å = 1 nm

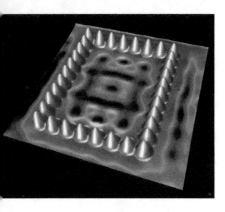

Fig. 4-4 An STM image of iron atoms on a copper surface

Particles can also be called **atoms.** Scientists generally describe all matter in terms of atoms now because we are familiar with their structure. Atoms are the smallest particles of matter. Two or more atoms can be joined together to form a *molecule.* We will discuss atoms in more detail in Chapters 5 and 6.

Can we observe anything so small? A technique known as scanning tunneling microscopy (STM) allows scientists to see atoms on the surface of some materials. In some cases they can even push the atoms around to spell words. Yet even before the development of STM, enough indirect evidence had been gathered to convince scientists that these particles did exist.

Evidence for the Particle Model

A good model should faithfully describe what we observe about matter. If the particle model is correct, then it should be able to describe everyday observations.

Why does a sweetened drink taste sweet? The answer must lie in the sugar particles. If you crush a lump of sugar into many small pieces and then grind those pieces into a fine powder with a mortar and pestle, you can still observe sugar. But when you dissolve that powder in a glass of tea, the sugar disappears. It has become subdivided until it cannot be seen with even the most powerful microscopes. We can observe that every part of the drink tastes sweet. Therefore, sugar must exist as tiny particles that can spread equally throughout the solution. These particles are so small that they cannot be seen, but each of them must have all the properties of sugar if every part of the drink tastes sweet.

Is your favorite instant drink mix made up of particles? We can observe some color changes to find out. When a packet of instant cherry drink mix dissolves in a pitcher of water, it makes a bright red solution. What would happen if that same packet were poured into a bathtub of water? Or a swimming pool? In each case the color of the resulting solution would be considerably lighter, but a faint color would still be present. For any color to appear in such a weak solution, the drink mix must consist of a very large number of particles.

Scientists have used observations such as these to reach the conclusion that all matter is made of particles. But there is more to the particle model of matter than merely particles. Other evidence that scientists have collected indicates that the particles that make up matter are in *constant motion.* Consider the following evidence.

Solid potassium permanganate occurs as purple crystals. If you place a crystal of potassium permanganate in a glass of water and stir, the water will turn purple. The particles of the chemical have been distributed throughout the solution. But what happens when

Using Models

What really takes place when something freezes, boils, or condenses? Scientists have long sought to describe what actually occurs in a physical change. They are not satisfied with simply labeling what they observe; they want to understand how it is happening.

When scientists cannot directly observe what is taking place, they rely on their instruments to extend their observing ability. Only recently have instruments been available that allow scientists to "see" what actually occurs during a physical or chemical change. Most of the clues, both direct and indirect, about the changes that matter undergoes have been pieced together by scientists into working representations, or models, of what might be happening.

To be good scientific models, these representations must have certain characteristics:
1. They should help us organize ideas.
2. They should faithfully describe what is observed.
3. They should help us visualize things that happen at a level that is too small, too large, or too complex for us to observe.
4. They should help us predict what will happen under certain circumstances.

One of the most famous scientific models is the Copernican model of planetary motion. Since the solar system is too large and too complex

The heliocentric theory of planetary motion has been modified since the time of Copernicus, but over the years this model has been extremely useful in helping scientists understand space.

to be observed all at once, Copernicus had to piece together many observations about the motion of the planets to make a model. He based his model on the heliocentric (HEE lee oh SEN trik) theory since his observations indicated that the sun (*helio-*) was the center (*-centric*) of the solar system. In his model the planets followed certain orbits around the sun. His model worked. It described the motion of the planets and allowed scientists to predict the approximate time when a planet should appear in the sky. Although the model has been modified, we still use it to plan space flights and planetary probes.

You may have heard about or seen scientific models without realizing that they were models. In recent years you have probably heard of El Niño? El Niño is a model of how warming in the Pacific Ocean affects climate worldwide. Tornadoes in a bottle, wave machines, artificial lightning, and wind tunnels are all models too. Can you think of how these models meet the characteristics of a good model listed above?

No model is absolutely perfect, and often we must choose among several different ones. Sometimes we will reject one model in favor of a better one. Can you think of some problems with the models mentioned above? The best model is the one that describes the most observations and makes the most accurate predictions—simply, the one that "works" the best. Yet even the best model will change as more information is collected.

Fig. 4-5 The constant motion of particles accounts for the diffusion of potassium permanganate in water.

you carefully drop a crystal into the water without stirring it? Patient observation will show that the crystal gradually breaks apart and slowly spreads throughout the liquid. How can we account for this mixing without stirring?

Scientists believe that the particles that make up water are in constant motion. These moving particles spread the purple potassium permanganate particles through the solution. The process of mixing by particle motion is **diffusion.** Diffusion can occur in all the states of matter, but it happens by far the most rapidly in gases. This leads us to believe that the particles of a gas move much more rapidly than the particles in a solid or a liquid. You have probably noticed that a few drops of perfume spilled from a bottle on one side of a room can soon be smelled on the far side of the room. As the perfume evaporates, the particles of the perfume change from the liquid state to the gaseous state. These particles are quickly scattered by the rapidly moving particles of the air until perfume particles have diffused to all parts of the room.

The motion of particles in matter was first observed in 1827. Robert Brown, an English botanist, was examining with a microscope tiny plant spores floating on water. Much to his amazement, he saw the spores jostle back and forth as if they were being struck repeatedly from different sides. Yet nothing was touching them except the water in which they were floating. He realized that the particles of water must be causing the motion of the spores. Since there was no pattern to this movement, he proposed that all the particles of a liquid are in constant random motion. Today, we call this movement of suspended matter in liquids and gases, **Brownian movement** in honor of its discoverer.

These are only a few of the many evidences that have led scientists to conclude that all matter is made up of tiny particles in constant motion.

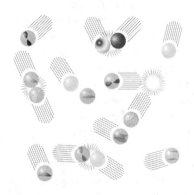

Fig. 4-6 Brownian movement

4 The Properties of Matter

1. Identify each of the following as a physical change or a chemical change.

   a. Gasoline and air burn in your car's engine.

   b. The defroster melts the frost on the windshield.

   c. Metal in the car's body begins to rust.

2. What units of length are often used when describing the particles of matter?

4B

Section

Solid, Liquid, and Gas

Normally, matter on earth can be found in one of three *states:* solid, liquid, or gas. Because many materials can exist in more than one physical state, scientists often refer to these as the **phases** of matter. In what phases have you observed water? Water occurs in nature as ice (solid), liquid, and vapor or steam (gas). Some kinds of matter are commonly observed in only one of their phases. Oxygen occurs most often as a gas, yet liquid oxygen is used to power rockets. How can one material occur in different physical states?

Our model of matter is based on the idea of constantly moving, extremely tiny particles. Scientists believe that the physical state of a material is determined by the positions and the energy of its particles.

Fig. 4-7 Old Faithful is a geyser that erupts steam from superheated water deep in the earth's crust.

Solids

Remember that we learned that the particles that make up matter are in constant motion—even the particles that make up this book! Although the particles are in motion, this book is considered a solid. Solids have two distinguishing characteristics. All **solids** have definite shape and definite volume. Your pencil, desk, chair, and even the room you are in are made of materials considered to be solid. Solid particles are in motion but have the least amount of movement of all phases of matter. The less the atoms are moving, the closer they are together. That would explain why solids are usually denser than liquids or gas. Since the atoms cannot be packed much closer together, solids are said to have low **compressibility.**

Fig. 4-8 Can you tell the difference between the crystalline and amorphous solids?

Solids occur in two basic forms, crystalline (KRIH stuh lin) and amorphous (uh MOR fus). In a **crystalline solid** the individual vibrating particles are held in a fixed, repeating pattern. In an **amorphous solid** the particles are held in a random placement with no apparent pattern. But both of these are still solid: both have definite shape and volume, yet they have very different physical appearances. Sometimes melting a crystalline solid into its liquid form and then cooling it quickly will produce an amorphous state. It will be amorphous because the particles have not had time to arrange themselves into a pattern. Cooling the substance slowly gives time for the atoms to arrange themselves into an orderly pattern. One of the most common amorphous solids you are familiar with is glass. Manufacturers melt certain types of sand, shape it, and then let it cool. Obsidian (from volcanoes) is also an amorphous solid.

Characteristics of a Solid

1. Definite volume
2. Definite shape
3. Low compressibility

Particles are packed closely together and vibrate in a fixed position.

Crystalline: Atoms are in a fixed, repeating structure.

Amorphous: Atom arrangement is random.

Liquids

Two distinguishing features can also characterize liquids. **Liquids** have definite volume but no definite shape. Liquids will take the shape of the container or region they are in. If placed in a rectangular fish tank, the liquid will be rectangular. Water in a lake "molds" around the shape of the bottom of the lake. The particles of a liquid are not completely independent, but their limited motion allows the liquid to assume the shape of the container.

The "flowing" of the particles in a liquid that allow it to take the shape of its container can vary a great deal from one liquid to another. The ease with

Characteristics of a Liquid

1. Definite volume
2. No definite shape
3. Low compressibility

Particle movement is random (Brownian movement), but particles are still fairly close together.

The rate of flow for a liquid is called the *viscosity*.

4 The Properties of Matter

Fig. 4-9 Some liquids are "thicker" or more viscous than others.

which a liquid will flow is called **viscosity**. A liquid with a high viscosity does not flow very easily (or quickly). Take, for example, the syrup you put on your pancakes. Compared to water, syrup has a higher viscosity.

Oils (liquid lubricants) used in motors have different viscosities, depending on the size and use of the motor. A 10W oil is "thinner," or has a lower viscosity, than a 20W oil. Oftentimes, motors use multi-viscosity oil, where the viscosity changes depending on the temperature. Since particles making up matter tend to slow down as the temperature drops, oil will get thicker in cold weather. In order for a car engine to be properly lubricated, drivers want lower viscosity oil when the engine is cold and higher viscosity when the engine is hot.

Gases

A **gas** has neither a definite shape nor a set volume. Unlike a solid or a liquid, a gas can be compressed into a small container and will expand to distribute itself evenly throughout a large container. In either case, the gas assumes both the volume and the shape of its

Fig. 4-10 Motor oil is clearly labeled to indicate viscosity.

Characteristics of a Gas

1. Indefinite volume
2. Indefinite shape
3. High compressibility

Particles are far apart and move at high speeds. Highest energy level of the three phases.

container. In the gaseous state, particles are relatively far apart and move at very high speeds. A typical particle in the gaseous state moves 490 meters per second, or 1.5 times the speed of sound! If a gas molecule could travel straight ahead without any collisions, it could cover the distance across the United States in less than three hours! But particles in the gaseous state can experience millions of collisions per second, and thus cannot travel in a straight line for very long distances. The particles are free to travel in all directions while their movement is limited only by the volume and the shape of their container.

Particles of a gas enclosed in a container collide not only with one another but also with the walls of the container. Imagine how the particles of the gas bombard the walls of the container—

Fig. 4-12 The balloon shrinks after it is placed in liquid nitrogen. Notice that as the air inside warms up, it returns to normal size, "growing" after being removed from the nitrogen.

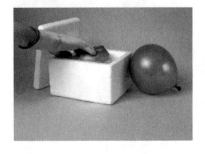

Comparison of Three Physical States of Matter

Solid	Liquid	Gas
at room temperature:	at room temperature:	at room temperature:
iron, sugar, salt, diamond, sand, gold	water, alcohol, mercury, gasoline, benzene, ether	oxygen, hydrogen, carbon dioxide, helium, ammonia

ice	water	steam
273 K (0°C) or below	274 K (1°C) to 372 K (99°C)	373 K (100°C) or above
Definite volume	Definite volume	Indefinite volume
Low compressibility	Low compressibility	High compressibility
Definite shape	Indefinite shape (assumes shape of container)	Indefinite shape (assumes both shape and volume of container)
Attractive forces overcome weak disruptive forces to hold vibrating particles in fixed positions.	Attractive forces and disruptive forces are balanced, allowing particles to move randomly (Brownian movement).	Attractive forces are completely overcome by very strong disruptive forces, causing particles to have rapid, random movement.

billions of them hit each square centimeter every second! The impact of a single particle would never be noticed, but the impact of billions of those particles can exert a great pressure. This is known as **gas pressure.** Heating a gas causes its particles to gain kinetic energy. The faster gas particles push harder on their surroundings. If the gas is contained, pressure rises. If uncontained, the gas expands. Cooling a gas has the opposite effects.

SECTION REVIEW QUESTIONS 4B

1. What phase of matter has the least amount of movement among its particles?
2. Which states of matter have an indefinite shape?

Solid, Liquid, and Gas

Unusual States of Matter

We have studied the states of matter in order of increasing energy. The particles in the solid state vibrate. The particles in the liquid state have limited random motion. The particles in the gaseous state have independent random motion. In two other states of matter, extreme temperatures (very high or very low) affect not only the movement of particles but the interior design of the particles as well. These two unusual states of matter are **plasma** and **Bose-Einstein condensate**. Particles in the plasma state travel at fantastic speeds, and therefore they are normally formed at high temperatures. Like gas particles, they collide many times each second. But unlike gas particles, plasma particles collide with such force that the very nature of the particle changes. Part of each particle is knocked away, and it receives an electrical charge.

Think of the energy that must be present on the surface of the sun, where temperatures exceed 6000°C. Plasma exists on the surface of the sun and stars; in fact, trace amounts of plasma have been found throughout outer space and in the magnetic belts (the Van Allen belts) that surround our planet. Right here on earth we can find plasma as close as the nearest fluorescent light! The gas present within these light bulbs is so energized that its properties no longer resemble those of a solid, liquid, or gas. In addition, auroras, lightning, and welding arcs are plasmas. Neon tubes and the halogen lights that illuminate our streets also contain plasma. Because the plasma state in nature is brief and generally rare, scientists know very little about it.

The Bose-Einstein condensate is a recent discovery, and it is explained best by *the quantum mechanical theory*. This theory goes beyond the particle model of matter to describe particles as waves and uses mathematical equations instead of particles to describe matter. The Bose-Einstein condensate forms only at temperatures near absolute zero (0 K or −273°C). As the temperature of the substance is lowered, the individual particles vibrate less and less, and their properties become more wavelike. Eventually, all of the

The Bose–Einstein condensate forms when particles of matter are super-cooled.

particles become so cold that they lose their "identities" and become one particle—the Bose-Einstein condensate. Of course, this phase of matter can be produced only in a laboratory, and many of its properties are still being determined.

Examples of plasma formation

The Phase Changes in Matter

If you drop several ice cubes into a hot frying pan, the spitting, popping cubes will dance about the pan as they melt into a liquid and then sizzle into steam. The matter changed physical states but remained the same kind of matter. This is called a phase change. Ice, liquid water, and steam are all composed of water particles. If the particles themselves were not altered, what changed as the ice melted into liquid and the liquid boiled into steam?

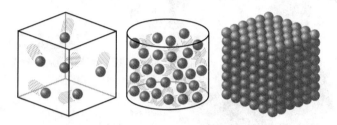

Fig. 4-13 The particles of a gas (left) have more energy than those of a liquid (middle). The solid particles (right) have the least amount of energy. Notice that as the energy and temperature increase, the amount of particle motion increases.

As phase changes occur, something happens to the position and movement of the particles. Just as a liquid normally becomes less viscous as the temperature goes up, the energy of the particles also increases. The energy of the particles is directly related to their temperature. In other words, as the temperature *increases,* the energy and motion of the particles goes up. As temperature *decreases* the energy and motion of the particles also goes down. Therefore, adding or removing energy by raising or lowering the temperature of a material can cause phase changes. In general, a liquid will have more energy than the same substance has in its solid state. A gas of the same substance has more energy than the liquid. As particles increase their motion, they also tend to move farther apart, explaining why a gas can expand its volume.

This model helps us to visualize the phase changes that we observe every day. If a solid is heated enough, it will melt. If a liquid is heated enough, it will boil. If a liquid is cooled enough, it will freeze. Each phase change occurs because the change in temperature alters the energy of the particles of that material.

Adding Energy in a Phase Change

Melting occurs when a solid changes to a liquid. The temperature at which this transformation occurs is the **melting point.** The melting point of ice is 0°C—but different substances have different melting points.

Fig. 4-14 Lead has a very low melting point.

Some solids have extremely low melting points. The addition of a very small amount of heat will allow the particles to flow over each other. Mercury can exist as a solid at temperatures below -39°C but will melt if the temperature is raised even one degree higher than that. That is why mercury is a liquid at room temperature. Cocoa butter melts at 34°C, only 3°C lower than average body temperature. Some metals and minerals will melt only at extremely high temperatures; copper, for example, melts at 1083°C. The melting point of a material is determined by the strength of the attractive forces between its particles.

Another phase change associated with adding energy involves changing a liquid to a gas. In the liquid state, particles constantly interact with one another. They roll, slide, and collide with one another. Because the movement in a liquid is random, not all the particles move at the same speed. Some might have a series of collisions that increase their speeds, while others might have head-on collisions that bring them to a "halt," only to be set in motion again by random collisions. Most of the particles are moving at a moderate speed, but a few are moving very quickly or very slowly. When one of the very fast particles reaches the surface of a liquid, it sometimes has enough energy to escape from the liquid.

This process is known as **evaporation.** The energy for evaporation comes from the uneven distribution of speeds in a liquid. Heat provided by warmer surroundings or by sunlight striking the surface of the liquid is able to increase the percentage of particles moving at higher speeds. Those possessing a speed high enough to escape from the surface of the liquid leave behind the slower or "colder" particles. This is why evaporation is sometimes referred to as a "cooling process" even though energy must be added to get evaporation to occur.

God designed our bodies to use the process of evaporation for cooling. When you perspire, your sweat glands produce a liquid on the surface of your skin. The particles in that liquid absorb the heat

Fig. 4-15 A pressure cooker can raise the boiling point of water by increasing the pressure.

energy of your body. When this occurs, heat energy is removed and your body cools.

If enough heat energy is added to a liquid, the particles inside the liquid gain enough energy to change to a gas. Inside the liquid the gas forms bubbles that rise to the surface in the action we call **boiling.** The temperature at which this action occurs is the **boiling point** of the liquid. The boiling point of water is 100°C.

The pressure on the surface of a liquid can affect the boiling point of that liquid. If this pressure is increased, then the boiling point will be higher. As the pressure increases, more energy will be needed to overcome that pressure. If, on the other hand, we reduce the pressure, less energy will be needed to change the liquid to a gas. In fact, if you put water in a vacuum chamber and reduce the pressure enough, you can boil water at room temperature! That is why some foods need to be cooked longer at higher altitudes, where the air pressure is less. Since the air pressure "pushing down" on the surface of the liquid is less, the boiling point is lower and the food must be cooked longer.

Fig. 4-16 Cooking directions are dependent on elevation.

Removing Energy in a Phase Change

Phase changes also occur when energy is removed from particles by lowering the temperature. **Condensation** is the phase change from gas to liquid. The temperature at which this occurs is called the **condensation point.**

Dew is a good example of condensation in action. In the cool of the evening, water vapor particles lose energy because of the drop in temperature. As the temperature drops, the particles move more and more slowly until they cannot exist as a gas any more. The

SUBLIMATION —The Phase Change that Skips a Step

By adding more heat energy, solids can be melted to form liquids, and liquids can be boiled to form gases. Is it possible for solids to change directly into gases without going through a liquid phase? **Sublimation** is the direct change of a solid to a gas. Not all matter can do this, but here is an example of a material that does.

Dry ice (frozen carbon dioxide, CO_2) is a very common substance that sublimates. Normally, carbon dioxide exists as a gas. But when supercooled it becomes solid enough to be sold in blocks to those who find it useful. For example, ice cream vendors use dry ice to keep their ice cream frozen. Not only does the dry ice keep the ice cream frozen, but it does not melt and make a mess of things. As particles of dry ice gain energy from their surroundings, they go directly from the solid state to the gas.

Most people know that paint must be mixed well before it is used. Making paint involves a great deal of mixing to make sure the colors and other additives are blended in just the right way. Paint manufacturers often produce specialized oil-based coatings that are very heat sensi-

tive. Mixing the paint too vigorously during production can ruin it. Dry ice is often added to paint while it is being mixed to help keep it cool. Trying to cool the paint with water would not work because oil and water do not mix. Keeping the large batch of paint refrigerated is impractical. Dry ice can be emptied directly into the paint while it is mixed and more can be added if needed. No cleanup is necessary because the carbon dioxide gas harmlessly bubbles into the air.

Sublimation can work in the opposite direction too—a gas can change to a solid without the intervening liquid state. Frost and snow are perhaps the most common examples of this change. In these two examples, water vapor changes directly to ice crystals. This phase change can be dangerous for aircraft flying in cold weather at high altitudes. Ice could

collect on the wings, causing the plane to lose lift and crash. Several crashes have been attributed to icing on the wings, and airlines have spent millions of dollars trying to come up with solutions. One of the most promising is installing special heaters on the wings to discourage ice formation.

Meteorologists have been experimenting for years with *cloud-seeding*, using airplanes to drop dry ice and other sublimating chemicals into clouds. This is usually done to encourage rainfall or to reduce dense fog over airports. There have also been attempts to use cloud-seeding to discourage dangerous hail formation in severe thunderstorms. Although its effectiveness has been questioned, cloud-seeding has had limited success. It seems unlikely, however, that it will ever eliminate the world's droughts.

slower-moving particles then condense on fallen leaves, blades of grass, cars, bicycles, spider webs, and other objects on or near the ground.

The other phase change associated with the removal of heat energy is **freezing.** Freezing is the phase change from liquid to solid. The temperature at which this occurs is the **freezing point.** The freezing point of a liquid is generally the same as the melting point. For example, ice melts at temperatures above 0°C, but water will freeze if the temperature drops below 0°C. The term "freezing" should not always be associated with what we consider "cold" temperatures. Molten iron freezes if the temperature is below 1500°C!

Measuring Energy in a Phase Change

We have stated that the energy of a particle is directly related to its **temperature.** For that reason, the temperature of a material acts as a "molecular speedometer." We measure the average **kinetic energy** (the energy of motion) of particles with *thermometers.* These tell us the range of temperatures in which a certain material will exist as a solid, a liquid, or a gas. For example, water is a gas above 100°C, a liquid between 0°C and 100°C, and a solid below 0°C.

The thermometer scale commonly used by many scientists is the Celsius scale. In 1742 Anders Celsius invented a temperature scale with one hundred degrees between the boiling point and the freezing point of water. Therefore, the Celsius scale is a type of centigrade scale (*centi-* $= \frac{1}{100}$). His scale has been very useful, but it has led to a popular misconception about temperature. Many people think that there is no kinetic energy below 0°C. This is not true—some materials have enough energy to exist as gases far below 0° on the Celsius scale. Oxygen is one of these materials. What would happen to life on earth if the atmosphere condensed from the gaseous phase to the liquid phase at 0°C?

To combat this misconception about temperature, Lord Kelvin developed a new temperature scale. He based it on temperature units the same "size" as the degrees Celsius used, but his scale had an important difference. On his scale, he defined 0 K as absolute zero. **Absolute zero** is the point at which there is the least possible kinetic energy. Absolute zero has been calculated to be approximately −273°C. At this temperature, almost all particle movement ceases, no matter what the substance. Kelvin used this calculation to define zero on his scale. The diagram to the right shows the relationship between the *Celsius* and *Kelvin* scales.

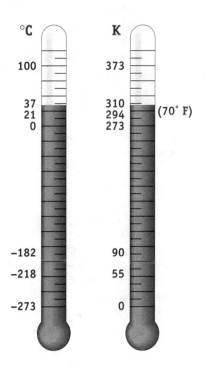

Fig. 4-17 Small droplets of water have formed on this spider web. These droplets are known as dew.

LORD KELVIN IRISH PHYSICIST (1824-1907)

Lord Kelvin (William Thomson) is probably best known for the scale of temperature that bears his name. He was also the mastermind behind the building of the first transatlantic telegraph cable and the first scientist to adopt the term "energy" to describe the most important of all quantities dealt with in physics. Kelvin was equally learned in both the theoretical and the practical branches of science. He contributed much to our knowledge of thermodynamics and pure mathematics. He also patented seventy inventions!

This giant of science was born in Belfast, Ireland, in 1824. He was the fourth of the seven children of James Thomson, a Scottish mathematics professor. The Thomson children were brought up in the Established (Presbyterian) Church of Scotland. The preaching they heard was fundamental and practical.

William responded favorably to the gospel message and was saved at an early age. During his years at Cambridge University, he was a brilliant scholar and maintained a good Christian testimony before his professors and fellow students. Upon graduation he was awarded, among other academic honors, a special citation "in consideration of his great mind and exemplary conduct."

After receiving his bachelor of arts degree in 1845, young Thomson chose to broaden his horizons by working for a year at the Regnault Laboratories in Paris, France. He earned his Master of Arts degree, also from Cambridge University, in 1848. At the age of twenty-two, Thomson accepted an appointment as professor of natural philosophy at the University of Glasgow, a post he filled until his retirement fifty-three years later.

Thomson and four of his contemporaries are generally credited with formulating the second law of thermodynamics. Thomson's definitive paper on the subject appeared in 1852. Although many people have never heard of this law, its meaning is extremely important to all of us. It indicates that the entire universe is degenerating (running down). The universe, therefore, cannot be eternal (infinitely old), or it would have run down completely long ago. Thus, by the mid-1800s, scientists had established the fact that there must have been a definite time of Creation. Skeptics could still deny that there was ever a moment of Creation, but they would now do so in opposition to the clear findings of science. Therefore, today the debate plays out not in whether there was a moment of Creation, but whether that moment was clearly a design by God or mere chance.

The second law of thermodynamics also clearly contradicts any theory of evolution that has ever been proposed. If, indeed, degeneration is the trend of nature, we could hardly expect increasing order and complexity to arise from less organized forms of matter. It was no secret that William Thomson strongly opposed the evolutionary teachings of Charles Darwin.

Moreover, the Irish physicist stoutly rejected the idea that life on the earth could have arisen spontaneously. "Mathematics and dynamics fail us," he wrote, "when we contemplate the earth, fitted for life but lifeless, and try to imagine the commencement of life upon it. This certainly did not take place by any action of chemistry, or electricity, or crystalline grouping of molecules under the influence of force, or by any possible kind of fortuitous concourse [lucky combination] of atoms. We must pause, face to face with the mystery and miracle of the Creation of living creatures." We can readily see the sharp contrast between Thomson's clear insight, derived from the biblical account of Creation, and modern philosophy, which regards life as a mere product of chance.

In 1856 Thomson was elected a director of the Atlantic Telegraph Company, the purpose of which was to install a transatlantic telegraph cable from Ireland to North America. By this time the use of Samuel Morse's telegraph had spread through much of the world. Wires were humming with messages on both the North American and

After experiencing several discouraging failures, the crews finally completed the cable on August 5, 1858. It connected Valencia Bay, Ireland, to Heart's Content, Newfoundland, Canada. Wild celebrations erupted on both sides of the Atlantic Ocean as Queen Victoria and President Buchanan exchanged congratulatory messages. Many newspaper headlines hailed the completed cable as the feat of the century.

For this and other accomplishments, Thomson was knighted. In 1892, he was again honored by the Queen of England, who conferred on him the official title Baron Kelvin of Largs. Although he had been born a commoner, William Thomson was now considered a nobleman and became known as Lord Kelvin. Kelvin's total list of distinctions grew to an imposing length and included honorary doctorates from twenty-one universities throughout Europe and America.

Kelvin's was an unusually full life. He derived a wonderful sense of fulfillment from his life's work, counting the privilege of scientific investigation one of the Creator's greatest gifts to mankind. He lived to the age of eighty-three, enjoying the blessings of good health and a keen mind until a month or two before his death. Lord Kelvin is buried in Westminster Abbey in London, where he has been honored with a magnificent Gothic stained glass window bearing this inscription: *In memory of Baron Kelvin of Largs, Engineer, Natural Philosopher, B: 1824 D: 1907.*

European continents. Short lengths of submarine cables, such as the cable connecting England with the Netherlands, had been successfully laid. But the feat of spanning the four thousand kilometers between the British Isles and America still posed many problems. The ocean was known to be almost five kilometers deep in places, and no ship in existence could carry the tremendous amount of cable needed to cross the Atlantic.

The Atlantic Telegraph Company decided to use two ships, the British battleship *Agamemnon* and the United States frigate *Niagara*. When the company's electrician fell ill and was unable to accompany the expedition, Thomson volunteered his services and supervised the operations from aboard the *Agamemnon*.

Rules for using the Kelvin scale

1. The word *kelvins* is lower-case but the symbol (K) is capitalized.

2. Say "73 kelvins" *not* "73 degrees Kelvin."

3. Conversion with the Celsius scale:

   Celsius to kelvins
      °C + 273 = kelvins

   kelvins to Celsius
      kelvins − 273 = °C

You can convert temperatures in Celsius degrees to kelvins by adding 273. Likewise, you can convert temperatures in kelvins to Celsius degrees by subtracting 273. One final detail—notice that the temperature unit on the Kelvin scale is the **kelvin,** not the degree. It is incorrect to report a temperature in degrees Kelvin.

SECTION REVIEW QUESTIONS 4C

1. List five phase changes.

2. What is the temperature at which a substance has the least possible energy and movement?

3. What is the difference between the Celsius scale and the Kelvin scale of temperature?

CHAPTER REVIEW

SCIENTIFICALLY SPEAKING

physical property
chemical property
chemical change
particle model
angstroms (Å)
nanometer (nm)
atoms
diffusion
Brownian movement
phases
solids
compressibility
crystalline solid
amorphous solid
liquid
viscosity
gas

gas pressure
plasma
Bose-Einstein
  condensate
melting
melting point
evaporation
boiling
boiling point
condensation
condensation point
freezing
freezing point
sublimation
temperature
kinetic energy
absolute zero
kelvin (K)

CHAPTER REVIEW QUESTIONS

1. Identify each of the following as a chemical or physical change.

   a. rusting iron

   b. burning paper

   c. dissolving sugar

2. What is the main idea of the particle model?

3. As the temperature of a material increases, what happens to its energy level and to the movement of the particles?

4. Which of the three usual phases of matter has the highest density?

5. Which phase of matter is most compressible?

6. Which state(s) of matter will most likely fill a container completely?

7. How are particles in crystalline form different from amorphous solids?

8. Name the process that occurs when a particle in a liquid gains enough energy to escape from the liquid.

9. Convert 1600 K to degrees Celsius.

FACET REVIEW QUESTIONS

1. What model is Copernicus famous for?

2. Of the two unusual states of matter, which one has the greater kinetic energy?

3. Explain the second law of thermodynamics and how Kelvin used it to combat evolution.

4. Describe the process of sublimation and give an example.

WHAT DID YOU LEARN?

1. In colonial days, a blacksmith would beat metals into usable items such as horseshoes, wheel rims, and household utensils. Why was it important for him to understand the physical properties of the metals he was working with?

2. Man's first "flying machine" was the hot air balloon. Explain how a hot air balloon works. Why does a helium balloon rise even though the gas is not "hot"?

3. Why is the cooking time for some foods dependent upon elevation?

4. What is the difference between evaporation and boiling?

5. Sometimes ice forms on the wings of planes as they fly at high altitudes. The added weight of the ice could cause the plane to plummet to the ground. Why does this ice form? What phase change is occurring? From your knowledge of phase changes, what would be the best way to prevent ice buildup on airplane wings?

The Classification of Matter

Chapter

5

Can you imagine how many different kinds of matter there are in the universe? If scientists could not classify this incredible jumble of items, there would be no way to study them successfully. Part of the physical scientist's job is to find ways to sort all the kinds of matter into different categories.

We have long probed for the basic pieces in God's design of the physical universe. At first we thought the puzzle was not complex, just as you would if you examined a puzzle from a distance. The individual outline or identity of each piece would not be clear. The early Greek philosophers thought that all matter was made from one element and that the different kinds of materials were simply different forms of that element. Some believed that this element was water, which by evaporating or condensing could produce all the other elements. Some identified this element as air. They believed that the atmosphere condensed into water, solidified into earth, and rarefied into fire. Other philosophers declared that fire was the central piece of the puzzle.

After many debates, the Greek philosophers settled on a theory of four elements. About 440 years before Christ, a Greek philosopher named Empedocles (em PED uh KLEEZ) proposed that all matter was made from particles of earth, air, fire, and water. This theory held sway over science for centuries.

Then people began to realize that God's creation was far more complex than had been imagined. In 1661 Robert Boyle published a book called *The Sceptical Chymist.* It was a very appropriate title indeed, for Boyle had just cause to be skeptical about the ancient definition of elements. In his book Boyle defined an element as any substance that could not be broken down into simpler substances by ordinary chemical means. He opened the door to the chemical exploration of matter. Scientists began to analyze substances to find their simplest parts—the pieces called elements.

In Boyle's day only a few of the elements we recognize today were known. Early civilizations knew of carbon, sulfur, antimony, and several metals, including zinc, gold, silver, copper, iron, tin, mercury, and lead. By the beginning of the eighteenth century, only about thirty substances had been classified as elements. Since then, many more elements have been discovered as science techniques improved.

To study matter in better detail, scientists have developed a system for classifying matter according to its makeup. They study what materials are composed of by the process of analysis. **Analysis** is the study of materials by breaking them down. In using analysis, scientists determine the kinds of matter or substances in a material. This process has allowed scientists to classify all the materials in the universe into three classes— elements, compounds, and mixtures.

Fig. 5-1 Scientists use flame spectroscopy to analyze elements by the color given off while the sample burns.

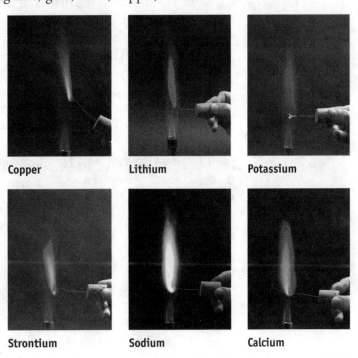

Copper

Lithium

Potassium

Strontium

Sodium

Calcium

Introduction

Atoms and Elements

The physical universe is like a complex puzzle made from a countless number of small individual particles. We describe these "particles" of matter as **atoms.** One of the most challenging parts of science is to determine what types of atoms make up a substance. Over the years, scientists have noticed that some substances can be broken down into several other substances. Water, for example, can be broken down into hydrogen and oxygen. But hydrogen cannot be broken down further. Neither can oxygen. An **element** is any substance that cannot be broken down into simpler substances by ordinary chemical means. Elements are composed of only one type of atom. Oxygen and hydrogen are both elements. Gold is an element too. There is no "recipe" to make gold. Gold is made out of gold atoms and nothing else. Scientists have identified over 115 indivisible elements on the earth, and the number will probably rise over time.

Fig. 5-2 Scanning Tunneling Microscopy (STM) uses technology to capture this image of iodine atoms on a platinum metal surface. The color was added by a computer. Notice the spaces between each of the atoms.

Scientists represent elements by **symbols**—a "shorthand" notation consisting of one or two letters derived from the element's name. For many common elements, the symbol is simply the first letter of its name: oxygen = O, nitrogen = N, hydrogen = H. For others it is the first letter of the name plus one other letter from the name: silicon = Si, magnesium = Mg, platinum = Pt. The first letter is always capitalized, and the second letter is always lowercase. The symbols of some elements come from their Latin names. Ag represents silver for *argentum,* sodium is Na for *natrium,* and iron is Fe for *ferrum.* Elements have been grouped according to their symbols, atomic structure, and properties on the periodic table. We will study the periodic table in more detail in Chapter 7.

Some Common Elements and Their Symbols

Aluminum	Al	Copper	Cu	Mercury	Hg	Silicon	Si
Argon	Ar	Fluorine	F	Neon	Ne	Silver	Ag
Arsenic	As	Gold	Au	Nickel	Ni	Sodium	Na
Barium	Ba	Helium	He	Nitrogen	N	Sulfur	S
Bromine	Br	Hydrogen	H	Oxygen	O	Tin	Sn
Calcium	Ca	Iodine	I	Phosphorus	P	Uranium	U
Carbon	C	Iron	Fe	Platinum	Pt	Zinc	Zn
Chlorine	Cl	Lead	Pb	Potassium	K		
Chromium	Cr	Magnesium	Mg	Radium	Ra		

A complete list of elements and symbols is found in Appendix B.

Nearly all elements are solids at room temperature. Mercury and bromine are liquids. Eleven are gases—hydrogen, helium, nitrogen, oxygen, fluorine, neon, chlorine, argon, krypton, xenon, and radon. When two atoms of the same element join together, we call the resulting particle a **diatomic** (DY uh TAHM ik) **molecule** (two-atom molecule). Both oxygen and nitrogen form diatomic gas molecules in the air you breathe. In nature, oxygen and nitrogen are usually found in the diatomic formation (O_2, N_2).

Some elements are very similar to each other, and others are as different as night and day. The behavior of elements is controlled by their chemical properties. Some elements are very *reactive.* Others are very

Fig. 5-3 Several elements have been manufactured in laboratories such as the famous Lawrence Berkeley National Laboratory at Berkeley, California. Scientists there discovered such elements as neptunium, berkelium, californium, einsteinium, mendelevium, nobelium, and lawrencium.

stable. Each element will combine with only a select few other elements that have the necessary chemical properties. Iron will react with oxygen in the air to form rust. Silver tarnishes because it reacts with sulfur in the air. Gold neither rusts nor tarnishes. The chemical properties of gold make it one of the most stable and least reactive metals. It is also important to keep in mind that some of the elements are very rare or exist in a laboratory setting only.

Whether silver comes from Mexico, Colorado, Australia, or any other location, it will be exactly the same element. No matter where the element comes from, atoms of the same element are similar to one another and different from atoms of any other element.

Fig. 5-4 *Plumber* comes from the Latin word *plumbum,* which is the Latin word for *lead.* Although plumbers no longer use lead pipes, knowing this may help you remember the symbol for lead—Pb.

SECTION REVIEW QUESTIONS 5A

1. List the four substances which the Greek philosopher Empedocles claimed all matter was composed of.

2. What was Robert Boyle's definition of *element?*

3. What element does the symbol Hg represent?

4. Define *atom.*

The Molecular World

Water is made out of atoms just like gold is, but water is made up of a *combination* of different types of atoms. Therefore, water is classified not as an element, but as a **compound.** Compounds are substances in which two or more different types of elements are chemically bonded together. The oxygen and hydrogen atoms that make up water are held together in units called **molecules.** A molecule is a group of atoms held together by strong attractive forces and is the smallest particle that can exist in a compound. Sugar is another example of a compound, but its molecules are

---

FACETS of the physical world

Elements in the Bible

Seven of over 115 known elements are mentioned in the Old Testament. Several of those are used to illustrate spiritual truths, and a few give significant evidence for the reliability of the Old Testament.

Copper—The words *bronze* and *brass* appear many times in the Bible. They are often used figuratively to represent strength or hardness (Job 40:18) and judgment (Lev. 26:19). Today, brass means an alloy of copper and zinc, but Bible

scholars believe that the brass mentioned in the Bible is simply copper, or sometimes bronze, an alloy of copper and tin. Deuteronomy 8:7-9 makes an important reference to copper, stating that God's chosen people could mine it from the hills of the Promised Land. For a long time, no one could find any copper deposits in Israel, and many liberal scholars tried to use these verses to deny the inspiration of the Bible. However, Dr. Nelson Glueck of the Hebrew Union College believed that the Bible was right and began to search the region for copper mines. He found not only the copper mines he was looking for but also copper smelters and refineries used in the time of Solomon!

Gold—Part of Job 23:10 says, "When he hath tried me, I shall come forth as gold." Gold is a remarkable element. Because it is

so beautiful and so easily worked and because it does not easily tarnish or corrode, gold has been a symbol of value and riches since the beginning of history. The Scriptures often use gold to represent the believer, who has a precious soul that should be beautiful and remain unaffected by the world.

Iron—The statue in King Nebuchadnezzar's dream had "legs of iron, his feet part of iron and part of clay" (Dan. 2:33). The iron part is generally thought to represent power and dictatorship. (See also Job 40:18.) Joshua 17:16-18 mentions the Canaanites' chariots of iron, which exemplifies the high level of technology achieved by some ancient societies.

Lead—Jeremiah 6:29 illustrates the character of lead when it says, "The lead is consumed of the fire." Most people would agree that lead is

atoms of elements gold

molecules of elements diatomic oxygen

molecules of compounds water

Fig. 5-5 We really do not know what atoms look like, so we use colored circles as models to represent them.

not an attractive metal. Because it absorbs impurities easily, its silvery surface becomes dull gray quickly when it is exposed to air. It also lacks strength and therefore has only limited uses in building. Scripture often uses lead to symbolize the corruptible and temporal.

Silver—Silver is mentioned often in the Bible. It has been used as currency since Old Testament times. Abraham paid 400 shekels (about 6 kg) of silver for the cave of Machpelah and the land around

it (Gen. 23:16-17). This metal was also used to make trumpets, platters, and bowls. In Solomon's time it was used to make tables and candlesticks for the temple.

In Proverbs 25:4-5 silver illustrates a principle of government: "Take away the dross from the silver, and there shall come forth a vessel for the finer. Take away the wicked from before the king, and his throne shall be established in righteousness." The dross is the layer of impurities that rises to the top of molten metal. The metal is pure when the dross is removed; in the same way, a government will be strong and righteous if wicked men are removed from it. Does this principle still apply today?

Sulfur—Known in Scripture as "brimstone" (Gen. 19:24), sulfur is a symbol of God's judgment. He used it to destroy the cities of

Sodom and Gomorrah, and He will use it for judgment in the future. Brimstone is mentioned no fewer than six times in the book of the Revelation (Rev. 9:17, 18; 14:10; 19:20; 20:10; 21:8).

Tin—The element tin is mentioned several times in Scripture (Num. 31:22; Isa. 1:25; Ezek. 22:18, 20; 27:12). During Bible times the Phoenicians mined it in the British Isles; some suggest that the name "Britain" comes from the Phoenician *barat-anac,* "land of tin." As we saw above, tin was often alloyed with copper to make bronze.

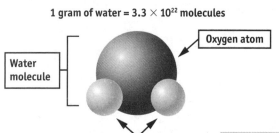

1 gram of water = 3.3×10^{22} molecules

Oxygen atom

Water molecule

Hydrogen atoms

much larger than water. One molecule of sugar contains 12 carbon atoms, 22 hydrogen atoms, and 11 oxygen atoms. Some protein molecules are composed of thousands of atoms. It is important to remember that even though molecules are too small to be seen individually, they still have all the characteristics of the compound.

Element or Compound?	
Silver	Element
Oxygen	Element
Hydrogen peroxide	Compound of hydrogen and oxygen atoms
Iron	Element
Sugar	Compound of carbon, hydrogen, and oxygen
Gold	Element
Sulfuric acid	Compound of hydrogen, sulfur, and oxygen
Sulfur	Element

Molecular Formulas and Symbols

A **molecular formula** gives the number of atoms for each element in a molecule. The molecular formula for water is H_2O. The subscript 2 tells us that there are *two* hydrogen atoms. Even though there is no subscript on the oxygen, it is implied that there is only *one* oxygen atom. So there are two atoms of hydrogen bonded to one atom of oxygen, giving a total of three atoms per water molecule. The molecular formula for baking soda is $NaHCO_3$. How many atoms total are there in the baking soda molecule? The answer is six—one sodium, one hydrogen, one carbon, and three oxygen. The diatomic oxygen molecule would be O_2, and a single oxygen atom is just O. The molecular formula is an easy way to tell what elements are in a molecule and how many atoms of each element are present. You can see the molecular formula for other common compounds in Figure 5-6.

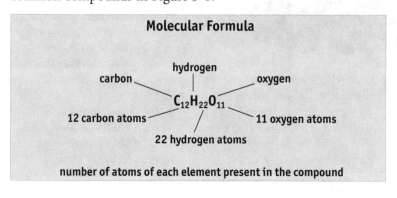

Molecular Formula

carbon — hydrogen — oxygen

$C_{12}H_{22}O_{11}$

12 carbon atoms — 11 oxygen atoms

22 hydrogen atoms

number of atoms of each element present in the compound

Fig. 5-6 Some Common Compounds

Name	Formula	Molecular model	Uses
Ammonia	NH_3		fertilizer, explosives, textiles, insecticides, cleaners, detergents
Baking soda (sodium bicarbonate)	$NaHCO_3$		beverages, fire extinguishers, baked goods, antacids
Carbon dioxide	CO_2		dry ice, fire extinguishers, air guns
Chalk (calcium carbonate)	$CaCO_3$		antacids, paint, ceramics, polishes, cosmetics
Natural gas (methane)	CH_4	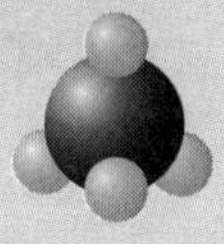	fuel
Sand (silicon dioxide)	SiO_2		glass, ceramics, filters, abrasives
Sodium fluoride	NaF		insecticide, drinking water, toothpaste, disinfectant
Sulfuric acid	H_2SO_4		steel cleaning, batteries, fertilizer production, explosives, dyes
Table salt	$NaCl$		seasoning, preservatives
Water	H_2O		universal solvent, essential for life processes

Once elements combine to form a compound, they lose their individual properties. In general, the properties of a compound are very different from those of the individual elements that formed it. In some cases, we benefit greatly by the change. Salt, for instance, is a very common compound that we use to season our food. A chemical union of sodium and chlorine produces salt. Sodium is a silvery metal that reacts violently with water. Chlorine is a greenish gas that is extremely poisonous. Individually these elements are dangerous, but in chemical combination they form a substance that is essential for our bodies.

SECTION REVIEW QUESTIONS 5B

1. Distinguish between atoms and molecules.
2. What atoms and how many of each kind compose the smallest unit (or molecule) of water?
3. How many atoms does the chemical formula Na_2SO_4 represent?
4. Explain why salt is such an interesting compound, taking into account the properties of sodium and chlorine.

5C

Section

Mixtures

Elements and compounds are each made up of a single kind of matter. A pure element consists of identical atoms. Any particular compound consists of similar molecules. Because both elements and compounds are the same throughout, they are both classified as **pure substances.** Yet most substances in the physical universe cannot be classified simply as elements or compounds. The overwhelming majority of substances are **mixtures.**

The Nature of Mixtures

Mixtures have three basic characteristics. *First,* all mixtures consist of two or more pure substances. Sugar water is a common example of a mixture. It consists of two compounds, sugar and water. *Second,* the parts of a mixture keep their own properties. Carbon, hydrogen, and oxygen lose their properties when the atoms chemically bond to form sugar. But sugar is still sugar, and water is still water in a sugar-water mixture. The sugar and water molecules do not bond or react; they just mix together. The two compounds are only physically associated and can be separated by ordinary physical means. If you boil away the water, the sugar will remain.

Some Common Mixtures

Brass

Chocolate

Concrete

Gasoline

14-karat gold

Ink

Milk

Orange juice

Seawater

Stainless steel

Fig. 5-7 Mixing iron filings with potassium dichromate crystals; we can illustrate that this is a heterogeneous mixture by using a magnet to easily separate the iron filings from the orange crystals.

TABLE
5-8
A Comparison of the Three Classes of Matter

	Elements	Compounds	Mixtures
Examples	lead, gold, carbon, zinc, neon, oxygen, copper, calcium	water, sugar, salt, ammonia, carbon dioxide	air, paint, rock, brass, concrete
Representation	symbols Example: C = carbon	represented by formulas using symbols and subscripts Example: CO_2 = carbon dioxide	represented by percent composition Example: 10% salt solution
Number	115 known	more than 16 million	unlimited number
Molecular models	Monotomic Diatomic	Molecular compound	Mixture of compounds and/or elements
Relationships among atoms	all atoms are identical	atoms of two or more elements joined chemically	two or more substances combined physically
Composition	definite composition	definite composition	indefinite composition
Properties	properties of all samples similar	components lose their individual properties; properties of compounds unlike those of components	parts keep their properties and identity
Chemical analysis	cannot be broken down into simpler substance through ordinary chemical means	can be separated into components only by chemical means	can be separated into parts by physical or chemical means

However, you cannot boil the carbon out of sugar ($C_{12}H_{22}O_{11}$). *Third,* the parts of a mixture may be associated in any proportion. The first grain of sugar added to the water makes it a sugar-water mixture. It remains a sugar-water mixture no matter how much sugar you add.

Elements use symbols, and compounds use formulas, but mixtures are most commonly described by percentage composition. Percentage composition is a way of comparing the amount of one substance with another. A salt solution that is made up of 10 g of salt dissolved in 90 g of water would be labeled a 10% salt solution by mass. An alcohol solution that is made up of 10 mL alcohol dissolved in 90 mL of water would be labeled a 10% alcohol solution by volume.

Some common mixtures are air (nitrogen, oxygen, argon, carbon dioxide, and very small amounts of other gases); milk (water, lactose, butterfat, proteins, etc.); seawater (water, sodium chloride, and small amounts of dissolved minerals); stainless steel (iron, carbon, and chromium); and 14-karat gold (gold and copper).

The Categories of Mixtures

Mixtures are divided into two categories—homogeneous (HO muh JEE nee us) and heterogeneous (HET ur oh JEE nee us). If a mixture is so well mixed that it appears the same throughout, it is called a **homogeneous mixture.** Air is a prime example of a homogeneous mixture, as are stainless steel and 14-karat gold. In fact, any alloy (a mixture of two or more metals) is a homogeneous mixture.

Another name for a homogeneous mixture is a **solution.** You might think that all solutions must contain water, but alloys are solid-solid solutions, just as salt water is a solid-liquid (salt-water) solution. Solutions are a very important part of the mixtures in the physical universe. We will study more about solutions in Chapter 10. If a mixture has different appearances in its different parts, it is called a **heterogeneous mixture.** One example of this is granite. If you closely examine a piece of granite, you can see the black grains of mica, white grains of quartz, and pink or brown grains of feldspar.

Colloids

Colloids are heterogeneous mixtures in which the particles of one substance are partially dispersed in another substance. The difference between a colloid and a true solution is that colloid particles

Fig. 5-9 Some examples of colloids

are larger and give the mixture a totally different appearance. The method of determining whether a mixture is a solution or a colloid is by passing light through it, and observing what is called the **Tyndall effect.** When a beam of light is passed through a solution (for example, salt water), the light will not disperse in the liquid and will be invisible. Pass a beam of light through a colloid (fog), however, and the beam of light will be visible as it strikes the large dispersed particles. Air inside most homes contains particles that can be seen in a sunbeam. These particles are dirt, dust, or mold that the lungs usually filter out during breathing. A **suspension** is a mixture in which the particles will eventually settle out, as with a mud and water mixture. Suspensions must be constantly stirred in order to maintain the dispersion. However, the substances that make up a colloid do not settle out.

Fig. 5-10 The Tyndall effect

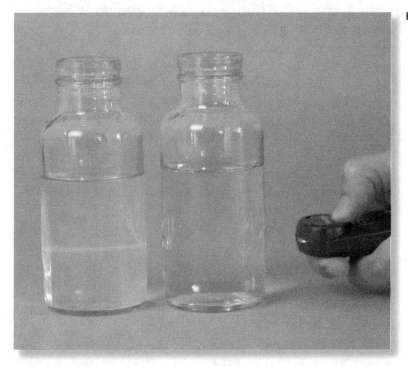

SECTION REVIEW QUESTIONS 5C

1. What is the minimum number of pure substances needed to make a mixture?

2. Is milk a heterogeneous or homogeneous mixture?

CHAPTER REVIEW

SCIENTIFICALLY SPEAKING

analysis

atoms

element

symbols

diatomic molecule

compound

molecules

molecular formula

pure substances

mixtures

homogeneous mixture

solution

heterogeneous mixture

colloids

Tyndall effect

suspension

CHAPTER REVIEW QUESTIONS

1. Give at least five elements that have been known since ancient times.

2. Compare *stable* elements with *reactive*.

3. What element is represented by the symbol K? H? Ni?

4. Which is more complex, an atom or a molecule? Why?

5. How is a diatomic molecule different from other two-atom molecules?

6. How many atoms are represented by the chemical formula $MgSO_4$? How many elements?

7. How does a compound differ from a mixture?

8. If a sugar-water mixture is 10% sugar by mass, what substance composes the rest of the mixture and what is the percentage of that substance by mass?

9. How is a homogeneous mixture different from a heterogeneous mixture?

10. Explain how the Tyndall effect helps us to analyze mixtures.

FACET REVIEW QUESTIONS

1. What seven elements are mentioned in the Old Testament?

2. Brass is a mixture of what two elements?

WHAT DID YOU LEARN?

1. Even in this age of technology, why is it still possible that there could be naturally occurring elements that have not yet been discovered?

2. Fish, like land animals, require diatomic oxygen (O_2) but take it from water rather than air. Do you think the water and oxygen combination in which fish live is a compound or a mixture? Why?

3. A scientist received a sample to analyze. It appeared to be made entirely of small, white crystals. When he heated the sample, he observed that the solid changed into a green gas and brownish liquid. Was the sample an element, a compound, or a mixture? Explain your choice.

Atomic Theory and Structure

Models of Atoms

6A The Development of the Atomic Model: A Historical Perspective

6B Nuclear Chemistry

Think back to one of your birthdays. Did you ever receive a mysterious package that you were told not to open before your party? It probably sparked your curiosity and made waiting very difficult. Since you could not open the package, maybe you tried to collect some indirect evidence about its contents. First, you noted the size of the box. Then you lifted it to find out how heavy it was. Finally, you shook it and listened for any telltale rattles. As a result of your investigations, you probably developed a mental image of your present.

Scientists are often faced with similar mysteries. Sometimes a scientist cannot directly observe the situation being studied. Just as you did with your gift, a scientist collects indirect evidence and uses it to form a conceptual or mathematical model. Your teacher will sometimes use examples and illustrations to explain difficult concepts. A scientific model serves the same purpose by making the complex seem simple.

As we saw in Chapter 4, scientists frequently use scientific models to represent the things they study. Like the birthday present, some items or processes cannot be directly observed. The scientist is forced to deduce what they are really like inside. Using bits and pieces of indirect evidence, he checks constructed models to see how each fits the observed data. After careful study, he selects a model that best describes the data, and other models are discarded. If the thing being investigated is too complicated to analyze completely, the scientist might use a simplified model to make the task more manageable. Kits assembling model cars or trains are available in varying levels of difficulty, usually related to the amount of detail present. In a similar manner, scientific models having varying degrees of detail may be utilized, depending on the degree of accuracy or detail that is desired. Calculations based on such a model may not be exact, but they are useful. If scientists did not use models, they could not make any calculations at all!

When scientists "shook" the mysterious package called matter, they discovered that it was made up of many smaller mysteries. It was just like a gift that is opened only to reveal even more wrapped packages inside. These smaller mysteries were atoms, the fundamental units of matter. Scientists have developed atomic models that describe the observed behavior of the atom. Even now our model of the atom is changing. Increasing evidence shows the atom may be far more complicated than we ever imagined, and made up of a variety of subatomic particles with names like leptons and quarks.

Different models of the atom are used for different applications. We will use *conceptual models* here because we want to represent the concept of the atom in physical terms that we can visualize so we can study how the atom appears to function. A nuclear physicist, however, might develop a *mathematical model* to study the amount of energy in the various parts of the atom. Although both models are useful for different purposes, neither model is exact. Remember, *models are simply useful tools,* their worth being determined by how well they predict the way atoms behave. When you see these models illustrated in a text or some other source, always remember that the colors, the sizes of the parts, and the shapes are *representations* chosen to help us understand or visualize the mysterious package called the atom.

Fig. 6-1 Like model trains, scientific models help us to simplify an otherwise complex concept.

The Development of the Atomic Model: A Historical Perspective

The first ideas about atoms can be traced to the ancient Greek philosophers. The concept of atoms was originated by Leucippus and developed by his student Democritus over four hundred years before the birth of Christ. Democritus coined the word *atom,* meaning "indivisible." He stated that these atoms are the only things that exist, that they have always existed, and that they will always continue to exist.

The Greek philosophers believed that reasoning, not experimentation, was the way to gain knowledge. Therefore, Democritus did not try to collect evidence to test his ideas. Today we realize that many of his ideas were wrong. For example, we know from Scripture that atoms have not always existed. God created them at

Fig. 6-2 In Democritus's model, matter was held together by means of little hooks covering the particles.

FACETS of the physical world

ROBERT BOYLE—IRISH CHEMIST (1627-91)

Robert Boyle, one of the most outstanding Christians in the field of science, was born in Munster, Ireland, in 1627. His father, the Earl of Cork, was reputed to be the wealthiest man in Great Britain. A devout Christian, the Earl attributed his great prosperity to the goodness and providence of God. Undoubtedly, his godly influence played an important role in shaping the thoughts of the young lad who was to become the leading chemist of the seventeenth century.

Although we usually associate the name Boyle with Boyle's law (Chapter 15), he made many more contributions than that to the field of chemistry. Many scientific histo-

rians have called him the Father of chemistry. It was Boyle who guided the great transition from alchemy to

true chemistry. Alchemy was the attempt by medieval "chemists" to change various metals into gold, find substances that could prolong life, and practice other mystical arts. Alchemists were those who practiced alchemy.

Before Boyle's time, men spoke of vague and mystic things making up matter. After his work had made its impact on the scientific world, men spoke in terms of elements and compounds. It took a man of courage to defy the traditions of the alchemists, and Boyle's spiritual makeup afforded him that courage in generous measure.

Robert Boyle studied the Scriptures in their original

a definite point in time (John 1:3). We also know from observations that some things that exist are not made of atoms. Light waves, for example, are not made up of atoms. Not all of Democritus's ideas were exactly right, but he was the first to develop the idea that matter was made of many very tiny particles.

It was not until the beginning of the eighteenth century that the first model of an atom was proposed by an English schoolteacher named John Dalton. He was the first to blend theory and experimentation in order to develop a workable atomic model.

Dalton and the Atomic Theory

Dalton used his knowledge of the way chemicals react to guide the development of his atomic model. One of the most important experimental evidences to influence his thinking was the **law of definite proportions.** Chemists had wondered for some time why every compound had a definite composition by mass. For example, they noticed that when 18 grams of water was decomposed, it

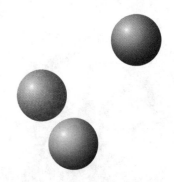

Fig. 6-3 Dalton pictured atoms as hard spheres.

languages and became familiar with the important theological writings of his day. Converted in his early teens, Boyle dedicated his scientific endeavors to attest to God's Creation and control of the universe. Boyle wrote on a variety of scientific and religious subjects, and became a powerful force for reproving evil and combating heresy. His influence continued long after his death. In his will he designated funds for the "Boyle lectures," a series of sermons to be delivered each year. These lectures were to demonstrate that Christianity is intellectually defensible and far more reasonable than the philosophies that oppose it.

Boyle was strictly orthodox in his Christian beliefs. He did his utmost in word and deed to defend the great doctrines of Scripture. He had no patience with preachers who spiritualized or allegorized important portions of the Bible rather than accepting them at face value.

Boyle read the Bible each morning throughout his life in spite of illness, eye trouble, and other difficult circumstances. As a result of his faithfulness and his clear-cut testimony, he was repeatedly offered the highest positions in the Anglican Church. Each time he refused; he believed that his testimony as a layman was a strong, effective ministry of the Christian faith.

During his later years Boyle became intensely interested in worldwide evangelism. A man of considerable means, he supported missionary endeavors in Ireland, Scotland, Wales, India, and North America. In addition, he commis-

sioned translations of the four Gospels and the book of Acts into Turkish, Arabic, and Malayan.

Boyle's greatest burden was for his fellow Irishmen. In spite of great opposition from the Irish clergy, Boyle financed a new Irish translation of the entire Bible, giving the Irish people access to the Word of God. Thousands of these Bibles were distributed throughout the British Isles at Boyle's expense.

When Boyle died in 1691, both the scientific community and the community of believers felt the loss keenly. He had made substantial contributions in both chemistry and physics, and he had steadfastly upheld the faith. Robert Boyle was an outstanding Christian researcher who used his science to exalt the name of the Lord.

Fig. 6-4 John Dalton

always yielded 2 grams of hydrogen and 16 grams of oxygen. If 9 grams of water were decomposed, the results would be 1 gram of hydrogen and 8 grams of oxygen. The ratio of hydrogen to oxygen was always 1:8 by mass. Dalton saw that *each compound is always made of the same elements combined in the same unique proportion by mass.*

To Dalton the atom was indivisible, a solid core surrounded by an envelope of heat. The heat envelopes helped to explain the varying sizes of atoms: the larger the heat envelope, the larger the atom. He believed that every element was composed of atoms and that each element had its own unique kind of atom. All matter, he asserted, must be made from combinations of these atoms. His ideas about the relationships among atoms, elements, and compounds were surprisingly accurate, but his "core-envelope" model of the atom was later disproved. Shortly after Dalton proposed his model, heat was shown to be energy, not matter. Nevertheless, Dalton had laid the foundation for modern atomic theory and had shown the correct relationship between atoms and elements.

J. J. Thomson and the Electron

A significant discovery by J. J. Thomson in 1897 dealt the death-blow to Dalton's "core-envelope" theory. Dalton had based his model on the belief that atoms were indivisible; J. J. Thomson discovered some astounding new evidence that led him to conclude that atoms consisted of charged particles. Scientists of that time knew that energized metals gave off streams of negatively charged energy. Was this stream a group of waves or a mass of tiny particles? Thomson proved that the metals were giving off *negatively charged particles* called **electrons.** This introduced a revolutionary new concept: could the atom be made up of even smaller particles?

Thomson knew that negative charges should repel each other. He reasoned that since atoms contained small negatively charged electrons, they must also contain positive charges that would hold the negative charges together. Therefore, Thomson pictured the atom as a mass of positively charged material containing the negatively charged electrons embedded in it like plums in a plum pudding. We frequently call Thomson's model the *plum-pudding model* for that reason.

If atoms were not electrically neutral, you would get a shock every time you touched anything. His model accounted for the fact that this does not happen. The positive charge on the material

Fig. 6-5 The Thomson model had negatively charged electrons embedded in a positive "pudding."

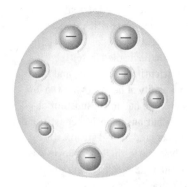

6 Models of Atoms

("pudding") balanced the negative charge on the electrons ("plums"). The electrons were held in place by the attractive forces between these opposite charges. He did not seek to change the idea that atoms were the fundamental "units" of matter; rather he gave us a better picture of how atoms are constructed. For his day, Thomson's model was quite remarkable.

It appears that electrons are the same no matter what the element. Electrons do not seem to vary in mass or charge. Early experiments indicated that the masses of all of the electrons in an atom formed a miniscule amount of the total mass of the atom, so there was still the question of what composed the rest of the matter in an atom. Scientists also did not know the reason for the vast chemical variety observed in nature. These questions would be answered in the first decades of the new century.

Rutherford and the Nucleus

In 1903 Philipp Lenard, a German physicist, succeeded in passing beams of electrons through sheets of metal. This came as a complete surprise to many people. Scientists realized that if rays of electrons could pass through the atoms of a metal, there must be empty space within the atoms and between them.

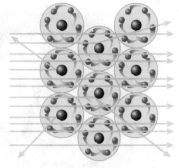

Fig. 6-7 Thomson's model couldn't explain how particles could pass right through a solid material.

Then in 1908 Ernest Rutherford penetrated a thin sheet of gold foil with positively charged particles, known as *alpha particles,* which were over 7000 times as massive as electrons. This was analogous to switching from BBs to cannonballs! Rutherford's experiment showed that the empty spaces inside of matter must be very large.

Figure 6-8 shows the experimental setup Rutherford used in this classic experiment. When the positively charged particles were shot at the gold foil, most of them went straight through it as if nothing were in the way, though some particles were deflected. The most astonishing thing was that some of them were bounced almost straight backwards! Rutherford exclaimed, "It was the most incredible event that ever happened in my life. It was . . . as if you had fired a 15-inch shell at a piece of tissue paper and it came back and hit you!"

Rutherford concluded, first of all, *that there must be a great amount of empty space in the atom.* Unless this was true, the relatively massive alpha particles would be unable to pass through the

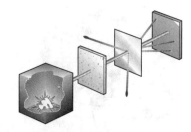

Fig. 6-8 In Rutherford's experimental setup, a radioactive source emitted a stream of alpha particles through a small hole toward a thin sheet of gold. Many particles passed right through, but a few bounced back.

Fig. 6-9 Rutherford's model of the atom

Fig. 6-10 Ernest Rutherford

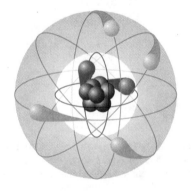

Fig. 6-11 The Bohr model was the first to have electrons travel in specific energy levels.

metal foil without colliding with something and being deflected. Second, *there must also be a very dense, very tiny, positively charged region in each atom* that was able to deflect some of the alpha particle "cannonballs."

By 1920 Rutherford had devised an atomic model to account for these facts. He calculated that the positive charge and practically all of the atom's mass were concentrated in a tiny region of space, which he called the **nucleus** (NOO klee us) (plural "nuclei" [NOO klee eye]). Furthermore, the nucleus contained *tiny, positively charged particles* called **protons,** which he also discovered. The electrons were thought to whirl around the nucleus at high speeds that kept them from being drawn into the positive nucleus.

At this point, Rutherford's model was still incomplete, since it had been determined that the mass of the nucleus was greater than the total mass of all the protons contained therein. Thus, the nucleus must contain something besides protons. It was not until 1932 that James Chadwick discovered **neutrons**—*particles that have no electric charge and have approximately the same mass as protons.* These particles reside in the nucleus along with the protons and account for the additional mass that was found to be in the nucleus.

Fantastic though it may seem, the diameter of an atom's nucleus is only $\frac{1}{100,000}$ as large as the diameter of the entire atom! If an atomic nucleus were as large as a period on this page, the atom would have a diameter equal to one-half of the length of a soccer field. With this comparison in mind, you can easily see why atomic representations are not drawn to scale!

Rutherford's modified atomic model gave us a working picture of the nucleus, but it did not explain the motion or location of the electrons. How far away from the nucleus were they? How were they arranged? These questions were to be answered by the Danish physicist Niels Bohr (1885-1962).

Bohr and Energy Levels

Any respectable fireworks display must have brilliant colors along with its sparks, smoke, and noise. How are these colors produced? In fireworks the color-producing compounds are added to an explosive mixture. The energy from the explosion of this mixture heats the atoms of the color-producing compounds. As these atoms cool, they release energy in the form of visible light. Each element releases light of a characteristic wavelength or color. Sodium compounds, for example, create yellow flames; strontium compounds burn red; barium compounds burn green. Changing the compound that produces the color alters the hue of the fireworks.

Niels Bohr (BOR) knew that certain atoms gave off specific colors of light when heated. When he passed these *emissions* through a prism, he was able to identify the specific wavelengths of light given off by each atom. Bohr suspected that these emissions were caused by the electrons in the atoms.

He theorized that when the atoms were heated, the electrons in them acquired enough energy to enable them to "jump" farther from the nucleus (they reached an excited state); they then returned very quickly to their original, lower-energy positions (ground states) when the atoms cooled. As the electrons returned to their original states, they gave off the excess energy as light energy, the magnitude of which depended on how far a given electron jumped away from the nucleus.

Different elements were known to give off different colors when they were heated; thus, the distances that the electrons jumped must vary from element to element. This meant that each element must have its own unique electron structure! Further, the fact that the same colors of light were always obtained for the same element indicated that *there were specific, "normal" energies that characterized the electrons in an atom, not random or arbitrary ones.*

Since light color, wavelength, and energy are all related (see Chapter 20), Bohr could mathematically calculate the distance between the electrons and the nucleus. He then developed a model of the atom that accounted for this color phenomenon. In his model, electrons occupied specific **energy levels,** or orbits. They could jump to higher energy levels if they were given enough energy and would return to their original levels when they cooled. Since his model looks like a miniature 3-D solar system, we often call Bohr's model of the atom the **planetary model.** The most important feature of his model is the concept that *electrons exist in specific energy levels.*

More sophisticated models of the atom have been developed since Bohr's time—models which more accurately portray the observed behavior of the atom. For example, the **quantum** (KWAHN tum) **model** represents the electron energy levels as general regions in space where electrons *most probably exist.*

Fig. 6-12 Niels Bohr

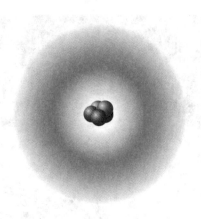

Fig. 6-13 In the quantum model, it is not possible to specify the exact position of an electron. Rather, there is a "cloud" of possible positions as if the electron were spread out all around the atom.

Picture an electric fan and an old-fashioned clock sitting side by side. The clock represents the Bohr model of the atom. The minute and hour hands of the clock move so slowly that we cannot see their movement. We can say with confidence exactly where they are at any given point in time. So it is with the position of the electrons in the Bohr model: they have specific, known locations ("orbits") in the atom.

The moving fan blades, however, representing the quantum model, are a different story. They move at such a high speed that we cannot see exactly where they are at a given time. We can see only a general region, a blur of blades or "cloud," where the blades are most likely to be located. Similarly, due to the nature of the electron, we cannot actually assign specific tracks ("orbits") to electrons or pinpoint their exact locations in an atom. We can only designate areas in which they will most likely be found. These *regions of most probable location for the electrons* are called **orbitals.** Chemists have even devised 3-D geometrically shaped "clouds" to represent these orbitals. It is often helpful to describe the appearance of the electrons in the quantum model as a cloud because neither has clearly defined boundaries. Which model we use depends largely on how accurate we wish to be and whether a simple model will suffice for the concept being discussed.

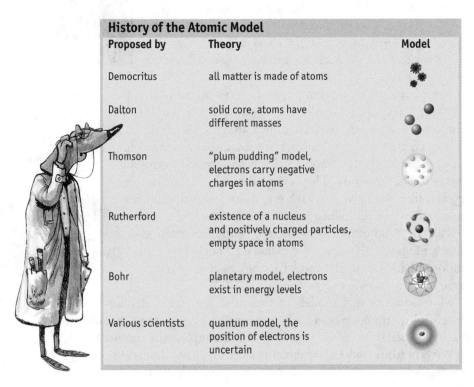

History of the Atomic Model		
Proposed by	**Theory**	**Model**
Democritus	all matter is made of atoms	
Dalton	solid core, atoms have different masses	
Thomson	"plum pudding" model, electrons carry negative charges in atoms	
Rutherford	existence of a nucleus and positively charged particles, empty space in atoms	
Bohr	planetary model, electrons exist in energy levels	
Various scientists	quantum model, the position of electrons is uncertain	

6 Models of Atoms

The Atom: Our Everyday Miracle

Modern science has aimed its most potent experimental weapons at the atom, trying to solve its mysteries. Over the years a progression of atomic models has led to our present description. On the surface all this knowledge seems very impressive. Dalton's ingenious ideas, Rutherford's exciting experiments, and Bohr's detailed calculations might tempt us to look back in pride and say, "We have it all figured out." Do we really? Stop and take a new look at the atom.

Even though it is extremely small, the atom is wondrously complex. It is so intricate that we have not been able to understand it fully. Its parts work together harmoniously like the pieces of a precision watch. Unlike even the finest watches, however, the atom does not wear out. The parts of most atoms function flawlessly for years, centuries, and millennia.

If we analyze our present theories, we will find that they explain only some situations. They leave several vital questions unanswered. For instance, has it occurred to you that as far as we know, a nucleus is an impossibility? The laws of electricity say that it is

impossible for many positive charges to "stick" together. According to these laws the protons should repel each other and fly apart with a tremendous release of energy. What holds the nucleus together? No one knows for sure. It seems that the nucleus is governed by rules that we do not yet fully comprehend. We may not know how these rules work, but we do know their source. In Colossians 1:16-17, the apostle Paul gives full credit to Jesus Christ for this marvelous act of Creation and preservation: "For by him were all things created, that are in heaven, and that are in earth, visible and invisible, . . . And he is before all things, and by him all things consist [hold together]."

Another entity that baffles physicists is the neutron. By itself, it is an unstable particle. It bursts into smaller particles in about seventeen minutes. But when combined with protons in the nucleus, it is stable!

Finally, think about the complex movements of the electron. Its speed and distance from the nucleus are just right to keep it from being pulled into the positively charged nucleus. It can jump to higher energy levels or drop back down and yet never upset the balance of forces. The atom is truly a complex wonder. God's hand is constantly working on every atom. Through studying the atom, we can see how marvelous and detailed God's creation is. The atom—our everyday miracle!

1. What is the main criterion by which scientists judge the usefulness of a model?

2. Who is given credit for proposing that matter is composed of atoms?

3. With which model do we associate the word "orbitals"?

4. What significant information about the atom was obtained by the work of Rutherford?

Nuclear Chemistry

The discoveries of the various subatomic particles have led us to a clearer, more accurate understanding of the structure of atoms. Our atomic model started off as an indivisible core surrounded by an envelope of heat; J. J. Thomson modified it with the addition of electrons; Rutherford and Chadwick gave it a nucleus filled with protons and neutrons; Bohr circled it with electrons in energy levels. Modern atomic physicists have changed our structural model even further. Now the electrons of the various energy levels are better described by orbitals that indicate their probable locations. In this section we will examine the particles within the nucleus in greater detail.

Atomic Mass

The two major types of particles in the nucleus of an atom are the proton and the neutron. A proton carries one unit of positive charge (+1) and is 1,836 times more massive than a single electron. A neutron is 1,839 times heavier than an electron, but it has no electrical charge. The masses of the proton and neutron are approximately equal; the difference is less than $\frac{1}{10}$ of 1 percent. The actual mass of either of these particles is approximately 1.6×10^{-27} kilograms, or 0.0000000000000000000000000016 kilograms! An electron is so much lighter than the particles in the nucleus that its contribution to the mass of the atom is considered negligible.

How is the mass of an atom calculated? Some assumptions can be made to make things simpler. First, since the masses of the protons and neutrons are close to being equal, they can be treated as if they *are* equal. Second, the masses of the electrons can be disregarded because they are so small. Therefore, to find the **atomic mass** we simply *add the masses of all the particles in the nucleus,* that is, the protons and the neutrons.

If scientists used kilograms (or even grams) to measure the masses of atoms, the numbers would be extremely small and difficult to work with. So scientists have chosen a special unit, called the **atomic mass unit,** or the amu. An amu is defined as *one-twelfth of the mass of a carbon atom that has 6 protons and 6 neutrons in its nucleus.* Thus, the amu is roughly equal to the mass of 1 proton or 1 neutron. To find the approximate mass of any atom, simply total the number of particles in the nucleus. For example, a typical sulfur atom has 16 protons and 16 neutrons. Its approximate mass would be 32 amus.

Atomic Number

Since each element is composed of a specific kind of atom, there must be something that makes the atoms of each element unique. But what is it? Each type of atom has a distinctive number of protons in its nucleus. For example, every gold atom has 79 protons in its nucleus. Likewise, all atoms with 79 protons in their nuclei are gold atoms. If a proton were removed from a gold atom, it would no longer be gold. One proton fewer would change the atom to platinum, because all atoms with 78 protons are platinum atoms. All the atoms of a given element must have the same number of protons.

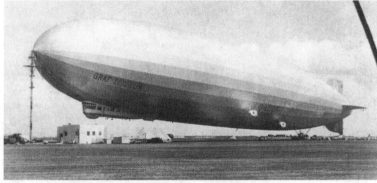

Fig. 6-14 Lithium, with an atomic number of 3, is a soft, silvery metal that reacts violently with water. Hydrogen, with an atomic number of 1, is a colorless, odorless, tasteless gas that reacts easily with oxygen. This lightweight gas was used to fill dirigibles. An atom of lithium has only 2 protons more than an atom of hydrogen, but what a difference those two protons make!

The number of protons in the nucleus determines the kind of atom; this number is known as the **atomic number.** The atomic number also tells us the number of electrons surrounding the nucleus. Since protons have a positive charge and electrons have a negative charge, the typical atom is electrically neutral, with a charge of 0. For example, the atomic number of carbon is 6, so the number of protons in the nucleus of each carbon atom is 6 and the number of electrons is 6. It might help for you to think of the atomic number as an element's "ID number" since scientists use it to identify elements; each element has a unique number to identify it. Hydrogen has an atomic number of 1; oxygen has an atomic number of 8; sulfur has an atomic number of 16. Thus, *any* atom with atomic number 1 is hydrogen; *any* atom with atomic number 8 is oxygen; and *any* atom with atomic number 16 is sulfur.

Mass Number

The sum of the protons and neutrons in the nucleus is called the **mass number.** Because the definition of atomic mass has been simplified in this chapter, the *mass number* and the *atomic mass* will have the same numerical value. However, the mass number does not have units since it is simply a number of nuclear particles. Except for the simplest hydrogen atom, all atoms have both protons and neutrons in their nuclei. Simple hydrogen has only a single proton in its nucleus. Most oxygen atoms have 8 neutrons in addition to the 8 protons in their nuclei, giving them a mass number of 16. A carbon atom with 6 protons and 6 neutrons would have a mass number of 12. What is the mass number of a helium atom that has 2 protons and 2 neutrons?

A typical sulfur atom has a mass number of 32 and an atomic number of 16. The mass number tells you that there are 32 total particles in its nucleus. The atomic number tells you that 16 of those particles are protons. You can find the number of neutrons by a simple subtraction operation:

$$\text{mass number} - \text{atomic number} = \text{number of neutrons}$$
$$32 - 16 = 16 \text{ neutrons}$$

Some sulfur atoms have a mass number of 33. Since they are sulfur atoms, their atomic number must still be 16. Therefore, the difference between these atoms and the more common sulfur atoms is in the number of neutrons that each possesses. The less common type of sulfur has 17 neutrons.

$$33 \text{ neutrons and protons} - 16 \text{ protons} = 17 \text{ neutrons}$$

Atoms of the same element that have different numbers of neutrons in their nuclei are called **isotopes** (EYE suh TOAPS). Most elements, as they occur naturally, are composed of several isotopic forms of their atoms. Isotopes of the same element have the same atomic numbers but different mass numbers because they have different numbers of neutrons.

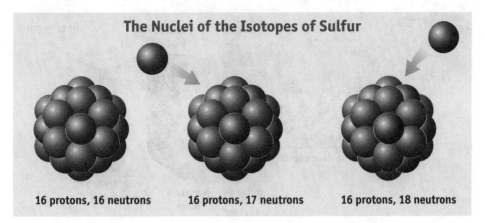

The Nuclei of the Isotopes of Sulfur

16 protons, 16 neutrons   16 protons, 17 neutrons   16 protons, 18 neutrons

An isotope is indicated by a special notation called the **isotopic notation,** which shows both the atomic number and the mass number of the element. The mass number is placed to the upper left of the element's symbol, and the atomic number is placed to the lower left. Usually, the symbol for an isotope is represented as follows, where "X" is the symbol for the element:

$$_{\text{atomic number}}^{\text{mass number}}\text{X}$$

Thus, the isotopes of sulfur would be written $_{16}^{32}\text{S}$ and $_{16}^{33}\text{S}$.

A third naturally occurring isotope of sulfur exists and has the notation $_{16}^{34}\text{S}$. How many neutrons are in an atom of this isotope?

Nuclear Radiation

Not all nuclei of all atoms are stable. Some require a specific stimulus, at which time they will break apart into smaller, more stable nuclei. Others become more stable naturally by simply emitting rays of high-energy radiation or small particles. *The study of reactions involving atomic nuclei* is known as **nuclear chemistry.**

The study of nuclear chemistry began with the accidental discovery of radioactivity. In 1896 Henri Becquerel (beh KREL) found that uranium compounds caused photographic film to become "exposed" when the two were placed near each other, even though the film was wrapped in paper to protect it from light. It was as if the film had been exposed to highly penetrating X rays. He had observed **radioactivity**—*the emission of high-energy rays and particles (protons and neutrons) from a nucleus.* Most elements are not radioactive—they will not release protons or neutrons under ordinary circumstances. However, elements with an atomic number over 84 are radioactive and exhibit some fascinating properties.

Becquerel's exciting discovery posed many questions about radiation. What is it? What causes it? Is it dangerous? How can it be used?

Fig. 6-15 The isotopes of sulfur have different numbers of neutrons.

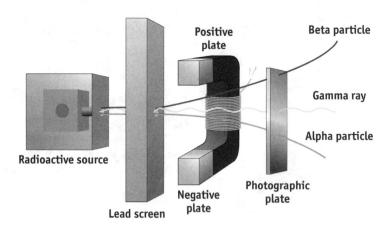

Fig. 6-16 Experiment for analyzing the charge on radioactive particles

Positive plate

Beta particle

Gamma ray

Alpha particle

Radioactive source

Photographic plate

Negative plate

Lead screen

TABLE 6-17	Three Types of Radiation				
Name	Symbol	Identity	Charge	Mass	Penetration
alpha	$^4_2 He$	helium nucleus	+2	4 amu	low
beta	$^0_{-1} e$	electron	-1	1/1,836 amu	medium
gamma	$^0_0 \gamma$	electromagnetic radiation	0	0	high

A detailed analysis of radiation was needed. In a later experiment, researchers used as their source of radiation an amount of uranium compound housed within a lead container that had a small opening. The lead container blocked all radiation except that which escaped through the opening, thereby producing a narrow beam of radiation that was passed through an electric field and aimed at a photographic plate. The field separated the one beam into three beams, which showed up as spots on the photographic plate.

One beam was deflected only slightly by the electric field, its path curving toward the negative plate. The slight deflection indicated that the beam was composed of fairly massive particles, and the attraction toward the negative plate indicated that the beam was composed of positively charged particles. These particles, called **alpha particles**, were later found to be composed of two protons and two neutrons—the same composition as helium nuclei.

The particles in the second, or beta (BAY tuh), beam were greatly deflected but in the direction opposite to the alpha particles—toward the positive plate. Since the beam was easily bent, the **beta particles** must have had very little mass; and because they were deflected in the opposite direction, they must have had a negative charge. These beta particles were later found to be *free electrons.*

The third beam was not affected at all by the electric field, indicating that it had no electrical charge. Nor were these **gamma rays** found to be particles; they were *electromagnetic waves* like radio waves, visible light, and X rays but with much more energy.

Once the beam of radiation produced by the radioactive uranium compound had been studied, scientists turned their attention to the changes in the nucleus that were causing this radiation.

Nuclear Decay

When nuclear changes occur, the nuclei end up with extra energy. They release this extra energy as gamma rays. However, because of their extremely high energy, gamma rays can penetrate deeply into matter; about a meter of concrete or two inches of lead is required to stop gamma rays! Also, because of their high energy, they can cause significant changes in materials, especially living tissue.

Fig. 6-18 How an alpha particle is emitted

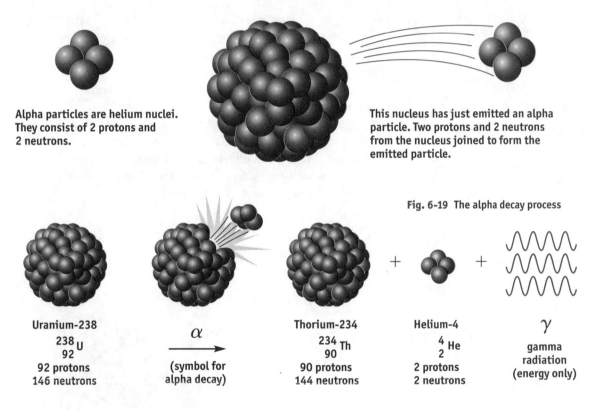

Alpha particles are helium nuclei. They consist of 2 protons and 2 neutrons.

This nucleus has just emitted an alpha particle. Two protons and 2 neutrons from the nucleus joined to form the emitted particle.

Fig. 6-19 The alpha decay process

Uranium-238
$^{238}_{92}$U
92 protons
146 neutrons

α
(symbol for alpha decay)

Thorium-234
$^{234}_{90}$Th
90 protons
144 neutrons

Helium-4
$^{4}_{2}$He
2 protons
2 neutrons

γ
gamma radiation
(energy only)

When nuclei emit alpha particles, they lose 2 protons and 2 neutrons. This **alpha decay** *decreases the atom's mass by 4 amu and the atomic number by 2, thereby transforming it to the element two atomic numbers before it in the periodic table.*

Nuclide symbols are very useful for writing nuclear reactions in a short form. For example, one type of atom that readily undergoes alpha decay is uranium-238 ($^{238}_{92}U$). Since the alpha particle, sometimes symbolized by the Greek letter alpha (α), is really a helium nucleus, we may also write it as $^{4}_{2}He$. The complete reaction includes the original atom and all the products.

Like any equation, nuclear equations *must* be balanced, both according to atomic number and atomic mass. That is, the totals of all the *mass numbers (sum of protons and neutrons in nucleus)* on both sides of the arrow must be equal, and the totals of all the *atomic numbers (number of protons in nucleus)* must also be equal. For the above example, the mass number of uranium-238 (238) must equal the sum of the mass numbers of the products (234 + 4), and the atomic number of uranium-238 (92) must equal the sum of the atomic numbers of the products (90 + 2).

Once the alpha particle has been emitted, it quickly attracts electrons from the first thing it hits and becomes an ordinary helium atom. Such a massive, highly charged particle has very low penetrating power and can be stopped by a sheet of newspaper.

Some unstable nuclei release electrons in a nuclear change known as **beta decay.** Since electrons do not normally exist in the nucleus, you may wonder where these electrons come from. Each beta particle (or electron) is formed when 1 neutron disintegrates into 1 proton and 1 electron. The electron leaves as beta radiation, but the proton remains in the nucleus, increasing the atomic number by one. The overall effect is *the emission of an electron from the nucleus and the transformation of the atom into a different element with the next higher atomic number.*

The product of the uranium-238 alpha decay is thorium-234. (Recall that 234 is the mass number and represents the number of

Fig. 6-20 How a beta particle is emitted

Beta particles are negative electrons.

This nucleus has just emitted a beta particle. A neutron has broken down into a proton and an electron.

6 Models of Atoms

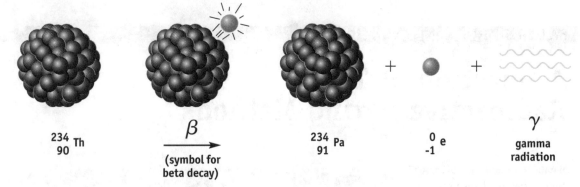

$$^{234}_{90}Th \xrightarrow{\beta} {}^{234}_{91}Pa + {}^{0}_{-1}e + \gamma$$

234 Th
90

β
(symbol for
beta decay)

234 Pa
91

0 e
-1

γ
gamma
radiation

Fig. 6-21 The process of beta decay

protons and neutrons in the nucleus.) Thorium (Th) has a very unstable nucleus and will quickly emit a beta particle (increasing the number of protons, and hence the atomic number, by 1) to produce protactinium (Pa). As in alpha decay, the sums of all the atomic masses and atomic numbers before and after the reaction must be equal. Since the atomic number of the product nucleus increases when a beta particle is emitted, the symbol for the beta particle must have a −1 subscript (atomic number) in order for the sums to come out right. Further, since an electron has virtually no mass, its mass number (superscript) is zero. Thus, the beta particle is symbolized $_{-1}^{0}e$ or by the Greek letter beta (β).

For the example given above, note that the mass number on the left of the arrow, 234, is equal to the sum of the mass numbers on the right (234 + 0), and that the atomic number on the left, 90, is equal to the sum of the atomic numbers on the right [91 + (−1)].

A *free electron* (that is, a beta particle) is subject to capture by any atom that it passes, making this form of radiation also easily stopped. It does travel farther than an alpha particle, but it takes only a piece of wood or aluminum to stop the electrons of beta radiation.

Fig. 6-22 Each of the three types of radiation has a different penetrating power. Can you identify them?

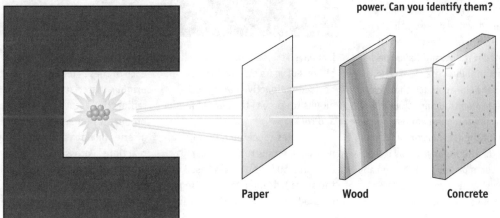

Paper   Wood   Concrete

A Question of Time: Radioactive Dating Methods

Numbers enjoy a special status in our culture. They have an almost magical way of authenticating the statements they embellish. A published report containing figures as well as facts will have better success and command greater respect from its readers than one without figures. The problem is that sometimes people use questionable statistics to bolster their ideas and pass them off as fact to unsuspecting people.

Have you ever read in the paper a headline such as "50-Million-Year-Old Bat Fossil Confirms Theory"? How do researchers arrive at the such a large figure, and how certain are they of its accuracy? If you study the biblical account of Creation, Scripture seems to indicate an earth that is between eight thousand and fifteen thousand years old, which would also imply that living things have been here for the same amount of time. Why such a discrepancy?

Even devoted evolutionists admit that the theory of evolution is doomed if it does not have one very important ally on its side: time. They take the approach that given enough time (roughly 3.5 billion years) anything can happen, including evolution. Evolutionists use dates of billions of years as if they were common knowledge—and anyone who challenges these dates is being "unscientific." So evolution-

ists have asserted that the earth is billions of years old and have also devised **radioactive dating** techniques to "prove" the ages of fossils and rocks.

Estimates concerning the ages of rocks and fossils run into the millions and billions of years based on the so-called "long-term" dating methods: uranium-lead, potassium-

argon, and rubidium-strontium. In each of these methods, an unstable original material is changing by radioactive decay to a stable end product. Uranium decays to lead in a series of alpha and beta decay reactions. Potassium decays to argon in a single step, and rubidium decays directly to strontium. It takes a certain amount of time for this decay process to occur. When a scientist measures the amount of argon in a rock sample, he can calculate the approximate age of rock assuming that when the rock was "formed" it contained only potassium. That would be similar to measuring the amount of gasoline in the gas tank of a car after a trip and then estimating how much time had elapsed since the beginning of the trip.

These "long-term" dating methods are not deceptive in themselves, but the scientist who uses them must make some basic *assumptions* that he has no way of verifying. For example, the scientist using the potassium-argon dating method has no way of knowing how much argon was originally present in the sample. Assuming there was no argon present when the rock was formed is foolish, since it has been proved that rocks of known age and formation (volcanic rocks) have been found with an abundance of argon.[1] The problem with these dating methods is that a key ingredient of the scientific method—*observation*—is missing.

Another assumption is that the radioactive decay rate is constant. Scientists use the principle of *half-life* to describe how long it takes for an isotope to decay. A 1.0-gram sample of iodine-131 will be present at 0.50 gram after only 8.0 days. So the half-life of iodine-131 is 8 days. Many radioactive isotopes have half-lives that have never been directly observed but rather *extrapolated* (graphing a projected trend). Uranium-238 is a good example because it is said to have a half-life of 4.51 billion years!

Obviously, scientists had to extrapolate that figure assuming that uranium has decayed at a constant rate since the origin of the universe. But we really do not know whether the rate of isotope decay is constant or not.

As you can see, these dating methods rely on some questionable assumptions. The main problem, however, with these "long-term" dating methods is in the interpretation of the results. Evolutionists say that these dating methods prove that the earth's rock layers are old, and therefore evolution occurred. But all that these methods ever really show is the amount of end product present within a rock, and that result can be interpreted many different ways. In fact, there are many Creationists who say some dating methods are accurate, and they have various theories to reconcile old-earth estimates and the Creation week described in Genesis 1. But on the whole, Christians who believe in a literal, six-day Creation are skeptical of old-earth estimates. The general mistrust that believers have for dating methods is understandable, considering that evolutionary theory was considered "scientific fact" long before radioactive dating techniques were developed.

Carbon-14 dating is a *short-term* dating method that is often used to determine the ages of fossils and manuscripts. Cosmic rays from the sun produce a heavy isotope of carbon with two extra neutrons—carbon-14. It decays at a constant rate and has a half-life of 5730 years. Carbon-14 properties are identical to those of carbon-12; and all living things, plants or animals, always contain a certain amount of carbon-14. When an organism dies, no more carbon-14 is taken in by the dead organism, and the isotope gradually decays to nitrogen. By measuring the amount of carbon-14 left, scientists can determine the approximate time of the organism's death. Most scientists would agree that carbon-14 dating gives accurate calculations for *living* things since they have an abundance of carbon molecules. The carbon-14 method starts to lose accuracy for organisms over 3000 years old, partially because scientists have determined (using tree rings) that C-14 levels in the atmosphere fluctuated significantly prior to 1000 B.C. As with the other dating methods, C-14 data is useful only if the limitations are recognized.

[1]Andrew A. Snelling, "The Cause of Anomalous Potassium-Argon 'Ages' for Recent Andesite Flows at Mt. Ngauruhoe, New Zealand, and the Implications for Potassium-Argon 'Dating'" (paper presented at the Fourth International Conference on Creationism, Pittsburgh, Pa., August 1998).

Nuclear Bombardment Reactions

A **nuclear bombardment reaction** *occurs when a nucleus is struck with atomic particles or other nuclei.* Scientists use nuclear bombardment reactions to release tremendous energy and particles. If controlled properly, they can even be used to produce new and different elements with different atomic numbers.

How does this type of reaction differ from nuclear decay reactions? For one thing, this procedure can release millions of times more energy and particles than alpha or beta decay. Also, alpha and beta decay occur spontaneously over a long period of time and without human intervention. Nuclear bombardment reactions occur only in specialized nuclear reactors or particle accelerators where the amount and rate of particle release can be tightly controlled. Bombarding radioactive nuclei is a very sensitive and complex process, but the results are staggering.

In the 1930s scientists found that they could make a nucleus unstable by striking it with a neutron. The unstable nucleus soon broke up to form two smaller nuclei and several neutrons. Nuclear **fission** (FISH un) *occurs when a nucleus is split into smaller, more stable nuclei, thereby releasing energy.* These emitted neutrons could, in turn, go on to hit other nuclei and cause them to split, and so on, ultimately releasing immense amounts of heat and light energy. This process is called a **chain reaction.**

Where does all the energy come from? When scientists measured the masses of the two new nuclei and the neutrons produced in the split, they found that the sum was less than the mass of the original atom! Somewhere, some mass had been lost forever. What had happened to this matter? Albert Einstein showed that mass could be changed to energy and developed the equation $E = mc^2$ to answer this question. In this equation:

E = energy
m = mass
c = the speed of light

Einstein's **theory of relativity** ($E = mc^2$) tells us, among other things, that a loss of energy equals a loss of mass. Whenever energy is released, a proportional amount of mass must be lost. How does this equation explain how such a small amount of mass yields fantastic amounts of energy?

The speed of light is 300,000,000 meters per second. When this already large number is squared and multiplied by even a tiny amount of mass, the resulting quantity of energy is *extremely* large. If you could completely convert 1 gram of matter (about the

Fig. 6-23 Nuclear fission splits a large nucleus into two smaller nuclei and releases energy.

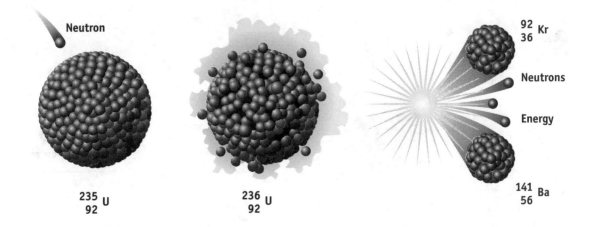

Neutron

$^{235}_{92}\text{U}$

$^{236}_{92}\text{U}$

$^{92}_{36}\text{Kr}$

Neutrons

Energy

$^{141}_{56}\text{Ba}$

mass of a paper clip) into energy, you would have enough energy to send 400 rockets into space, each of them with a mass of 4000 kilograms!

The process of fission was first used in the two atomic bombs that ended World War II. Now nuclear power plants harness that same type of energy to heat water to steam, which runs electrical generators. Approximately 20 percent of America's electricity is supplied by fission processes.

Nuclear **fusion** is *the process that joins small nuclei into larger ones.* Fusion produces even more energy than fission. The sun and stars derive their energy from a series of fusion reactions wherein hydrogen nuclei combine to ultimately form helium nuclei plus several other subatomic particles. Larger stars can even fuse other elements.

Fusion has rightly been called "the energy of the future," and it has many compelling selling points. First, it requires no hard-to-find fuels; the oceans contain all the hydrogen atoms that we would ever need. Second, while fossil fuels produce harmful pollutants and fission produces radioactive waste, fusion would produce only low-level radioactive products, which could be easily handled. Third, the fusion process produces an extremely large amount of energy from what is "invested" without depleting nonrenewable natural resources.

However, several major obstacles must be overcome before fusion can be controlled and used. In fact, controlled nuclear fusion has been called *the greatest technological challenge in the history of mankind.* The reason is that, in order for this reaction to occur, the hydrogen nuclei must be under conditions similar to those in stars, where the temperatures and pressures are incredibly high.

Fig. 6-24 In the fission of uranium-235, a neutron is fired at a uranium nucleus. This causes the nucleus to become unstable. It splits into two smaller nuclei, emits several neutrons, and gives off a large quantity of energy. What would happen if these neutrons hit other uranium nuclei in the surrounding area?

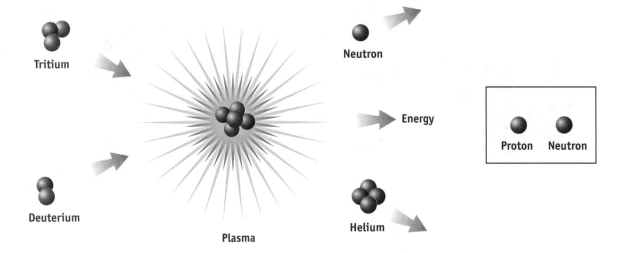

Tritium

Deuterium

Plasma

Neutron

Energy

Helium

Proton   Neutron

Fig. 6-25 In a deuterium-tritium fusion, a tritium nucleus and a deuterium nucleus fuse in the extreme heat of a plasma to form a neutron, helium, and energy.

One fusion reaction that has received a fair amount of study because it requires the lowest temperature—that involving fusion of two isotopes of hydrogen, *tritium* and *deuterium*—still requires temperatures on the order of 50-100 million kelvins! As you might imagine, matter could be only in a *plasma state*—separated nuclei and electrons—under these conditions. One method being investigated to produce such high-temperature plasma involves aiming a bank of lasers at the material to be fused and heating it rapidly to very high temperatures by bursts of laser light.

Not only is there the challenge of producing the plasma, but another significant technological challenge is that of maintaining and containing such an extremely hot plasma. Certainly, contact with any physical container by the plasma would either melt and vaporize the container or cool the plasma to such an extent that it would no longer be a plasma. Which event occurs would depend on the relative masses of the plasma and the container. Even without actual contact of the plasma with solid matter, there are significant and rapid losses of heat energy through radiation, resulting in cooling and loss of the plasma state. However, since a plasma is composed of charged particles, it can theoretically be contained with electrical and magnetic fields in what might be termed a "magnetic bottle." Because putting this theory into practice is difficult, however, sustained fusion is not yet commercially feasible. Nevertheless, though power production through fusion appears to be a long way off, physicists have recently made some encouraging advances as they strive to harness this "energy of the future" to meet our future needs.

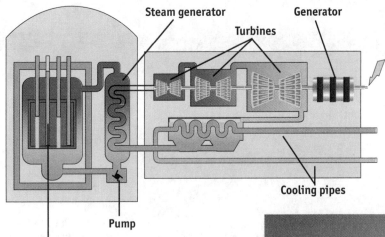

Fig. 6-26 How a nuclear reactor works. The uranium fuel in the core of a nuclear reactor produces intense heat. The primary coolant water (red), which circulates through the reactor, is heated as it flows around the nuclear fuel. The superheated primary coolant heats a second water system (blue) to produce steam. This steam rotates a turbine, which turns an electrical generator. The steam is condensed on cooling pipes and is then recycled through the system.

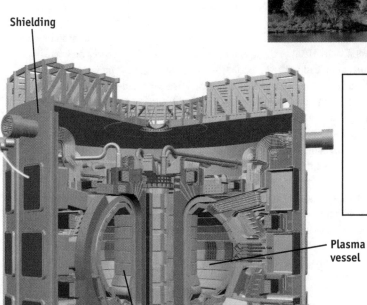

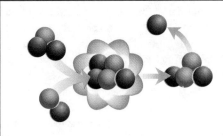

Fig. 6-27 The ITER fusion reactor is designed to test the practicality of producing electricity from fusion reactions. Lasers heat the deuterium and tritium to about 100 million degrees Celsius, causing them to undergo fusion. Compare the size of this reactor with the man standing at the lower right.

The Manhattan Project

Many scientists are motivated to work because of the thrill of discovery and their desire to see the world become a better place through the knowledge of God's creation. Putting a man on the moon, the polio vaccine, automobiles—thousands of discoveries have given mankind a longer and more comfortable life. However, fear is also a great motivator, and nothing caused more Americans to tremble than the possibility of losing World War II. In 1942, Germany and Japan were both at war with the United States, and the war in the Pacific was claiming thousands of American lives. Each combatant realized that to win, America must utterly defeat the foe. Surrender was not an option. President Roosevelt realized that to win the war the United States must begin another battle—in the laboratory.

The Manhattan Project was a top-secret program that would employ the best and brightest scientists in America to build an atomic bomb. The mission: to create an instrument so powerful that the instantaneous destruction of buildings and loss of life would be unfathomable. It would, without question, force the Japanese and Germans to surrender and bring peace once again to the world. However, the Manhattan Project also ushered in the atomic age and a nuclear arms race that keeps civilization under the constant threat of a nuclear holocaust.

In 1939, with the specter of war hanging over Europe, Albert Einstein wrote Roosevelt a letter in which he outlined the possibilities: "[A] chain reaction (of uranium) could now almost certainly be induced artificially; this chain reaction could lead to the construction of a devastatingly powerful bomb; . . . the President should promptly assign some eminent personage to coordinate the requirements for such a weapon with the U.S. defense establishment."

Germany had also researched nuclear fission, but it had neither the manpower nor the resources needed to build such a terrifying weapon. The Manhattan Project would employ thousands of Americans in labs across the country to synthesize uranium-235 and build the bomb. The center of the activity was the Los Alamos National Laboratory in New Mexico, and the project director was a young scientist named Robert Oppenheimer. As the secrets of radioactive decay were being

unraveled, it became clear that a baseball-sized amount of uranium-235 going through uncontrolled fission would release an explosive blast equivalent to that of 20,000 tons of TNT.

On July 16, 1945, the first atomic bomb was detonated in Los Alamos, New Mexico, at the remote Trinity test site. The bomb was placed on a reinforced steel tower high above the desert, and cameras were mounted in various places to record the nuclear explosion as it happened. The scientists who had worked so hard on this project knew the capabilities but were totally unprepared for the sight they saw that morning. The 100-foot steel tower was totally vaporized. Other buildings assembled a few thousand feet from ground zero were also obliterated. As the bright glow filled the pre-dawn sky and the mushroom cloud rose higher and higher, each observer knew that they were witnessing the greatest technological achievement in history and that the end of World War II was near. But they also knew that the next time the bomb was used would be over the skies of Japan and that thousands would perish. The rest of America would find out about the bomb in just a few weeks.

By August 1945, the war in Europe was over, but the war in the Pacific was still going on. Roosevelt died in April, so project leaders immediately briefed President Truman about the status of the atomic bomb, which until then he never knew existed. He would have to make the agonizing decision to drop the bomb. U.S. intelligence knew that the Japanese were preparing for an allied ground assault by digging in and that they would fight to the last man. U.S. forces dropped leaflets over Japan, warning the people to surrender or face certain destruction from the air. The Japanese High Command ignored the warning, unaware that a fully operational atomic weapon was already on its way. Truman had made his decision. On August 6, 1945, the first atomic bomb was dropped on the city of Hiroshima, a strategic military center for the Japanese. Seventy thousand people died instantly. Stunned, the Japanese military did not know what had hit them until President Truman informed the world later that day from the White House and implored the enemy to surrender. "If they do not now accept our terms, they may expect a rain of ruin, from the air, the like of which has never been seen on this earth."

Incredibly, the Japanese did not surrender, and on August 9 a second

bomb was dropped on the city of Nagasaki with similarly devastating results. On August 14, Japan finally relented and accepted the Allies' terms for peace.

Since then, other countries have developed nuclear weapons. The United States has expanded its atomic arsenal to include short-range nuclear missiles and the fearsome Intercontinental Ballistic Missiles (ICBM), which have multiple warheads that are hundreds of times more powerful than the Hiroshima or Nagasaki weapons. After World War II, an uneasy Cold War between the United States and Soviet Union developed. Both countries possessed huge nuclear stockpiles, and each feared the other's nuclear weapons. The superpowers avoided war because of the certainty of mutual annihilation.

The Manhattan Project not only brought nuclear weapons on the scene but also brought more information about how fission could be used for producing electrical power. Today many cities receive power from nuclear power plants. Nuclear-powered submarines can travel around the world without refueling, and plutonium-powered space probes now reach into deep space. Critics think that nuclear energy is too dangerous and that the risks far outweigh any benefits. They also contend that nuclear weapons will eventually result in the destruction of mankind and should be voluntarily banned by all countries. With the breakup of the Soviet Union and the rise of China in the Far East, that ban seems unlikely. Christians know that the heart of the king is in the Lord's hand and that the Lord is in control of human events (Dan. 5:21). We also know that this earth will eventually be destroyed and the Lord will bring ultimate judgment (Rev. 21:1). Will nuclear weapons play a role in this? We do not know for sure, but Christians can be confident that God has a plan for the end times.

1. Define an isotope.

2. Krypton and potassium have the atomic numbers 36 and 19 respectively. Using isotopic notation, write the notation for each of the following isotopes: a) krypton with 37 neutrons in its nucleus; b) potassium with 21 neutrons in its nucleus.

3. What is the most penetrating type of radiation?

4. How do fusion and fission differ?

CHAPTER REVIEW

SCIENTIFICALLY SPEAKING

law of definite proportions

electrons

nucleus

protons

neutrons

energy levels

planetary model

quantum model

orbitals

atomic mass

atomic mass unit (amu)

atomic number

mass number

isotopes

isotopic notation

nuclear chemistry

radioactivity

alpha particles

beta particles

gamma rays

alpha decay

beta decay

radioactive dating

nuclear bombardment reaction

fission

chain reaction

theory of relativity

fusion

CHAPTER REVIEW QUESTIONS

1. An atom of potassium (K) contains 19 protons, 19 electrons, and 20 neutrons. What is the atomic number of this atom? What is its mass number?

2. Why does an atom in its normal state have a total electrical charge of 0?

3. $^{36}_{16}$S—What is this atom's atomic mass? Atomic number? Number of protons? Number of neutrons? Number of electrons?

4. What law is represented by the fact that x grams of a given compound will always produce $0.2x$ grams of one element and $0.8x$ grams of another?

5. How did J. J. Thomson visualize the atom?

6. How many protons, neutrons, and electrons are in an atom of uranium-238?

7. What atomic particle determines specific isotopes?

8. Why do nuclear changes, such as nuclear fission, result in such large amounts of energy?

9. Compare and contrast the Bohr model of the atom and the quantum model of the atom.

10. Describe alpha decay and beta decay. Include the numbers and types of particles involved.

11. Contrast nuclear decay with fission and fusion.

FACET REVIEW QUESTIONS

1. How did Boyle's work affect the medieval practice of alchemy?

2. Give some of the physical "impossibilities" of the atom and give a scriptural explanation of how the atom can exist.

3. Name at least two of the long-term radioactive dating methods.

4. Of all the dating methods, which one is the most useful for determining the ages of living things?

5. What radioactive isotope did the first atomic bomb contain?

WHAT DID YOU LEARN?

1. Scientists are sometimes reluctant to discard scientific models because they thought of them as reality instead of representations. On the other hand, some new models are embraced for a time but later discovered to be a poor description. Do you think that there will be more atomic models developed in time, or is the quantum model "the last word" on atomic structure?

2. Since the discovery of nuclear fission, it has been considered a scientific "mixed blessing." What are some of the advantages and disadvantages of nuclear research?

3. If fusion has so many advantages as a source of electrical power, why has its potential not yet been tapped?

The Periodic Table of Elements

Chapter

7

How would you like to memorize all the physical and chemical properties of every element? If you were a student taking chemistry in the early nineteenth century, you would have to do just that. Just like today, chemists and chemistry students needed to know what the properties were so that they could predict how the elements would behave. By 1860 scientists had identified a jumble of more than sixty elements, but no one had been able to classify them into a useful order.

Your list of properties would seem endless. Some elements would be gases, some would be liquids, and many would be solids.

There would be metals and nonmetals and some elements with characteristics of both. You would have to remember which elements reacted explosively with water, which combined easily with other elements, and which ones failed to react at all. And your task would keep growing, because new elements were being discovered all the time. (We now know of more than 115.)

Nineteenth-century scientists knew that they had to find a way to organize the elements. Sorting them into groups of elements that acted alike would make them much easier to study. Finally, after various attempts by a number of scientists, a Russian scientist named Dmitri Mendeleev (MEN duh LAY ef) succeeded. He organized the elements into a useful chart very much like the periodic table we use today. The periodic table has become one of the most useful tools of science. What is a periodic table? How does it help scientists (and students) remember the chemical properties of elements? A good path to understanding the periodic table is understanding how it developed.

Fig. 7-1 Dmitri Mendeleev

Grouping Atoms Together

A German chemist named Johann Döbereiner was one of the first to classify elements by their properties. Döbereiner found several small groups of elements with similar properties. Since almost every group contained three elements, he called them triads. Unfortunately, not all the known elements fit into Döbereiner's system of triads, and it was not generally accepted by the scientific world.

Classification by Atomic Mass

In 1866 an English chemist named John Newlands proposed another system of classification. He arranged the elements in order of their increasing atomic masses, pointing out that in most cases every eighth element had similar properties. He called these groups *octaves*—a term he borrowed from music, where it refers to the interval between repeating notes in a musical scale consisting of seven notes and repeating on the eighth note. He placed forty-nine of the elements in seven rows of seven each and called his system the *law of octaves.*

Fig. 7-2 John Newlands organized the elements into octaves similar to the scales on a piano.

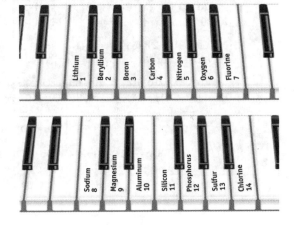

In Newlands's octaves the eighth element had properties similar to the first, the ninth to the second, and so forth. This system worked better than Döbereiner's had, but still not everyone was satisfied.

Just three years after John Newlands proposed his system, Dmitri Mendeleev proposed a similar idea. The Russian chemist also based his classification system on the atomic masses of the elements, but he did not believe that the properties of the elements always repeated every eight elements. He wrote all the elements and their properties on cards and filed them according to their atomic masses. Then he arranged the cards in different ways until he had grouped elements with similar properties in columns, which he then placed next to one another to form rows. Mendeleev placed hydrogen alone in the first row. In the next two rows he placed seven elements, and in the fourth row he placed fourteen elements and three blank spaces.

Mendeleev's table had one important unique feature: blank spaces. As he arranged his cards to group the similar elements, Mendeleev came across elements that did not fit. However, he realized that if he left a blank space and skipped to the next column each time he found a "misfit," all the elements lined up exactly. He predicted that the gaps would be filled by new elements as they were discovered. He even listed their possible chemical and physi-

Fig. 7-3 Mendeleev predicted the existence of an element he called ekasilicon. The chart below compares Mendeleev's ekasilicon to the germanium discovered by Clemens Winkler in 1866.

Ekasilicon
atomic mass 72 amu
high melting point
density 5.5 g/cm^3
dark gray metal

Germanium
atomic mass 72.60 amu
melting point 958 °C
density 5.5 g/cm^3
gray metal

Fig. 7-4 This is Mendeleev's early periodic table, which was published in 1872. Notice the blank places in the table. Why did Mendeleev leave these spaces?

TABELLE II

REIHEN	Gruppe I. — R^2O	Gruppe II. — RO	Gruppe III. — R^2O^3	Gruppe IV. RH^4 RO^2	Gruppe V. RH^3 R^2O^5	Gruppe VI. RH^2 RO^3	Gruppe VII. RH R^2O^7	Gruppe VIII. — RO^4
1	H=1							
2	Li=7	Be=9,4	B=11	C=12	N=14	O=16	F=19	
3	Na=23	Mg=24	Al=27,3	Si=2	P=31	S=32	Cl=35,5	
4	K=39	Ca=40	—=44	Ti=4	V=51	Cr=52	Mn=55	Se=56,Co=59, Ni=59, Cu=63.
5	(Cu=63)	Zn=65	—=68	—=72	As=75	Se=78	Br=80	
6	Rb=85	Sr=67	?Yt=86	Zr=90	Nb=94	Mo=96	—=100	Ru=104,Rh=104 Pd=106, Ag=108.
7	(Ag=108)	Cd=112	In=113	Sn=118	Sb=122	Te=125	J=127	
8	Cs=133	Ba=137	?Di=138	?Ce=140	—	—	—	— — —
9	(—)	—	—	—	—	—	—	
10	—	—	?Er=178	?La=180	Ta=182	W=184	—	Os=195,Ir=197, Pt=198, Au=199.
11	(Au=199)	Hg=200	Tl=204	Pb=207	Bi=208	—	—	
12	—	—	—	Th=231	—	U=240	—	— — —

cal properties! Because this arrangement was orderly, he thought he could predict these properties from those of the elements near the "unknowns" on the table.

At first his predictions shocked a skeptical scientific world, but soon researchers began to discover the elements that Mendeleev had predicted. In Mendeleev's chart the elements in the *rows* were arranged by increasing atomic mass, but each *column* of elements had similar properties. His table clearly showed that the properties of the elements repeat in an orderly pattern. We call his table of the elements a **periodic table** because the properties of the elements repeat in a periodic or recurring pattern, based on their atomic masses. Mendeleev called this principle the *periodic law.*

Classification by Atomic Number

There was a problem with Mendeleev's table, however. When the elements were arranged strictly according to their atomic masses, the elements tellurium and iodine seemed to be placed in the wrong columns (or families). However, if their positions were switched, they were placed in columns with elements of similar properties.

Time only added confusion to the issue. Soon scientists discovered several more pairs that seemed to have reversed positions on the periodic table. It was not until 1914 that Henry Moseley solved these mysteries. When the elements were arranged according to their *atomic numbers* (the number of protons in the nucleus), the order was corrected: iodine followed tellurium and was placed in the appropriate column. The other pairs that appeared to be out of order also fit properly when this correction was made.

As a result of Moseley's work, the periodic law was revised. It is now based on atomic numbers instead of atomic masses. Today's

Mass order			Property order	
O 15.99	F 18.99		O 15.99	F 18.99
S 32.06	Cl 35.45		S 32.06	Cl 35.45
Se 78.96	Br 79.90		Se 78.96	Br 79.90
I 126.90	Te 127.60		Te 127.60	I 126.90

Fig. 7-5 The elements I and Te seemed to fall into the wrong columns when they were arranged strictly according to their atomic masses. But if they were switched, the element I would be in a column with the similar elements F, Cl, and Br.

God's Order

Few examples in science exhibit God's purposeful design and fundamental orderliness more evidently than the periodic repetition of the properties of the elements. The scientists of the nineteenth century found a recurring pattern among the elements because it had been placed there by the Creator Himself. *The periodic law reflects the orderliness of God.*

In your study of science you will see the attributes of God, such as orderliness, in the physical universe. The famous English essayist Francis Bacon wrote that no man "can search too far or be too well studied in the book of God's Word or in the book of God's works." The book of God's Word is, of course, the Bible. In science, as well as in all our other studies, His Word must be our base—our underlying guide. The "book of God's works" is the world, which God has made. In your study of God's creation, take time to reflect and see the physical evidence He has placed there to testify of His wisdom and power.

statement of the **periodic law** is this: *the chemical properties of the elements are periodic functions of their atomic numbers.* When the elements are arranged according to their atomic numbers, the properties of the elements repeat.

But what is the underlying basis for the periodic variation in the properties of the elements? While it is true that the properties of the elements vary as a function of their atomic number, it is also true that the number of electrons in an electrically neutral atom is related to that atomic number. There must be an equal number of negatively charged electrons and positively charged protons in order for there to be no net charge on the atom. Thus, an atom that has 19 protons in its nucleus (atomic number 19) must have 19 electrons surrounding that nucleus if the atom is to be electrically neutral. In the next section we will deal with the electron structure—that which determines the periodically varying chemical properties.

Fig. 7-6 When the elements were arranged by atomic number, they fell into the proper columns.

Atomic number order	
$_8O$	$_9F$
$_{16}S$	$_{17}Cl$
$_{34}Se$	$_{35}Br$
$_{52}I$	$_{53}Te$

Fig. 7-7 Henry Moseley was in his twenties when he discovered the connection between atomic numbers and the periodic placement of elements.

1. Who is associated with grouping the elements by groups of three?
2. Compare and contrast Newlands's classification system with Mendeleev's "periodic table."
3. Who arranged the elements according to their atomic numbers?

Electron Levels

An atom of hydrogen has only one electron whirling rapidly about its nucleus. That one electron is relatively simple to locate. But an atom of uranium has ninety-two electrons orbiting its nucleus.

Scientists have discovered that these electrons are arranged about the proton-containing nucleus in certain patterns. The placement of the electrons is very important, for it determines the chemical and physical properties of the atom.

Energy Levels

The electrons orbiting an atom possess different amounts of energy. Niels Bohr calculated that these energies were the result of the electrons orbiting at different distances from the nucleus; that is, they occupied different energy levels. The *less* energetic electrons would orbit *closer* to the nucleus, while the *more* energetic electrons would orbit in pathways *farther away* from the nucleus.

As you saw in the last chapter, Bohr believed that these pathways were definite orbits, much like those in which the planets move. However, modern researchers have found evidence that, rather than occupying specific paths, the electrons move in general three-dimensional regions. Since the electron is so very tiny and moving so rapidly, it is impossible to know its specific location accurately. Instead, the model we often use pictures three-dimensional "layers" in which the electrons can be found, similar to the layers of an onion. These "layers," called energy levels, represent the regions where an electron with a certain amount of energy is *most likely* to be found; hence, the energy levels do not have well-defined boundaries.

The electrons with the lowest amounts of energy occupy the first level, which is closest to the nucleus. Those with more energy are located in higher levels, ranging from the second, to the third, all the way to the seventh, which is the energy level farthest from the nucleus. The number of levels occupied depends on the number of electrons in the atom.

Filling Order

Scientists have determined that electrons fill these energy levels in a specific order. The filling order is determined by two simple rules:

1. Each of the energy levels has a limit on the number of electrons it can hold. The first energy level can hold only 2, the second can hold 8, the third can hold 18, and the fourth can hold 32.

2. The maximum number of electrons in the outermost energy level of an atom is 8. This is called the *octet rule*. Once 8 electrons have entered an energy level, the next 2 electrons must enter a higher energy level before any unfilled lower energy level may be filled.

It should be noted here that the rules given above are not laws that *must* be obeyed. For reasons not covered here, some elements do not strictly follow the rules. However, the elements that are discussed below do follow the rules given here. Since it is nearly impossible to draw both the energy levels and all the electrons in an atom as three-dimensional layers, Bohr's planetary models will be used for sake of clarity.

For example, the 8 electrons in an oxygen atom fill the first level with 2 electrons and the second energy level with the remaining 6.

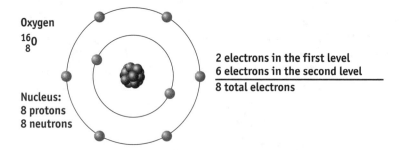

Oxygen
$^{16}_{8}O$

Nucleus:
8 protons
8 neutrons

2 electrons in the first level
6 electrons in the second level
—————————————
8 total electrons

The 16 electrons in sulfur fill 2 in the first level, 8 in the second level, and 6 in the third level. A Bohr model of sulfur would look like this:

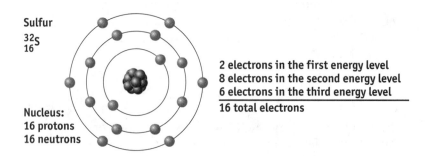

Sulfur
$^{32}_{16}S$

Nucleus:
16 protons
16 neutrons

2 electrons in the first energy level
8 electrons in the second energy level
6 electrons in the third energy level
—————————————
16 total electrons

Calcium has a mass number of 40 and an atomic number of 20; therefore, it has 20 protons and 20 neutrons. To be electrically neutral, it must also have 20 electrons. These electrons are positioned in this order: 2 in the first energy level (it is now filled), 8 in the second level (it is now filled), 8 in the third level (no more can fill this level until 2 electrons are placed in a higher level), and 2 in the fourth level. The Bohr model would look like this:

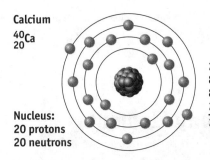

Calcium
$^{40}_{20}Ca$

Nucleus:
20 protons
20 neutrons

2 electrons in the first energy level
8 electrons in the second energy level
8 electrons in the third energy level
2 electrons in the fourth energy level
20 total electrons

The order in which the electrons fill the energy levels in an atom gives it a unique arrangement known as its **electron configuration—** *the number of electrons in each energy level.*

Let us determine the electron configuration for an atom of titanium (Ti), wherein we will need to use the second rule given above. An atom of titanium has 22 electrons. The first level will fill with 2 electrons, the second will fill with 8, both of which are now filled to capacity, leaving 12 more electrons to place. The third level can hold a maximum of 18 electrons but it does not accept all of them at once. After 8 electrons have been placed in the third level, the fourth level will immediately get 2 electrons (according to the octet rule). This will use up a total of 20 electrons, leaving the last 2 to be placed in the third level. Thus, the electron configuration for titanium is 2 electrons in the first level, 8 in the second, 10 in the third, and 2 in the fourth.

Using a similar procedure for an atom of bromine (Br), atomic number 35, leads us to the following electron configuration: 2 electrons in the first level, 8 in the second, 18 in the third (it is filled), and 7 in the fourth.

The electrons in the outermost energy level are known as the **valence electrons.** The ability of an atom to lose or gain these electrons is what gives the atom its chemical properties, as you will learn later in this chapter. Thus, for the above examples, both oxygen and sulfur have 6 valence electrons, both calcium and titanium have 2, and bromine has 7 valence electrons.

SECTION REVIEW QUESTIONS 7B

1. The closer an electron is to the nucleus, the _____ its energy.

2. How many electrons are required to fill the second energy level? The third?

3. What is the electron configuration for an atom of sodium (atomic number 11)? An atom of arsenic (atomic number 33)? Draw the Bohr model for these two atoms.

4. Define the term *valence electron*. How many valence electrons are in an atom of aluminum? An atom of helium?

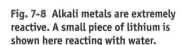

Relationships Among Elements

As you have learned, the elements of the periodic table are arranged according to their properties and in order of increasing atomic number. Since the number of protons (the atomic number) is equal to the number of electrons in a neutral atom, the arrangement in the periodic table is on the basis of increasing number of electrons and the electron configuration.

Families

All of the elements in a vertical *column* of the periodic table have the same number of *valence electrons*. For example, you have already seen that both oxygen and sulfur have 6 valence electrons.

Fig. 7-8 Alkali metals are extremely reactive. A small piece of lithium is shown here reacting with water.

You will note that they are located in the same column. Further, an atom of calcium has 2 valence electrons. Magnesium, the element listed above it in the periodic table, has atomic number 12 and therefore 12 electrons. Its electron configuration would consist of 2 electrons in the first level, 8 electrons in the second, and the remaining 2 electrons in the third. Hence, both magnesium and calcium have 2 valence electrons.

Because elements with the same number of valence electrons act very much alike, physically and chemically, each column is called a **family** or **group.** This is analogous to the fact that the members of a human family have certain similarities, though they also have their differences.

Group 1 (IA), for instance, contains six elements: lithium, sodium, potassium, rubidium, cesium, and francium. This family is known as the **alkali metals** (AL kuh lye), and each of them has 1 electron in its outermost energy level.

Since members of the same family or group have similar properties and the same number of valence electrons, it follows that the electron configuration must determine the properties of elements. The alkali metals (Group 1), for example, have similar properties because each of them has a single valence electron. Because this lone electron can be removed easily, these elements are extremely reactive. If you drop a small piece of an alkali metal into water, it will react violently as it forms a compound (see Fig. 7-8). In fact, alkali metals are so reactive that if are not stored in a container of oil (such as kerosene), they will react with oxygen in the air.

Two of the alkali metals, sodium and potassium, are an essential part of our diet. In the body they are involved with the movement of fluids, transmission of nerve impulses, and control of muscles. Common table salt (sodium chloride) is the main source of sodium in our diets. Important sources of potassium include bananas, grapefruit, oranges, carrots, potatoes, and celery.

Beryllium, magnesium, calcium, strontium, barium, and radium make up Group 2 (IIA), the **alkaline-earth metals.** They are "close cousins" of the alkali metals, but they each have 2 valence electrons. This added electron makes them slightly less reactive than the alkali metals but not stable enough to remain free (uncombined) in nature. Instead, they are found in many common minerals.

Beryllium is used to harden metal **alloys** (mixtures). A copper alloy that contains 2 percent beryllium is six times as strong as pure copper. Because it is so light, magnesium is mixed into metals that are used in airplanes. Calcium is also used for structural purposes, both in people and in building. Teeth, bones, and many modern construction materials—concrete, mortar, plaster, and plasterboard (also known as Sheetrock or drywall)—get their strength from calcium compounds. Calcium is also a vital part of stucco and glass.

Some of the alkaline-earth metals have important medicinal uses. You may have benefited from milk of magnesia if you needed a mild laxative. This chalky medicine is primarily magnesium hydroxide. When a doctor needs to examine a patient's digestive

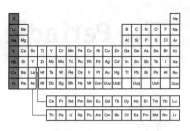

Fig. 7-9 Each of the elements in a family has the same number of outer-level electrons. The alkali metals (shown on the periodic table) all have 1 outer-level electron. These elements in the family (below) demonstrate the principle.

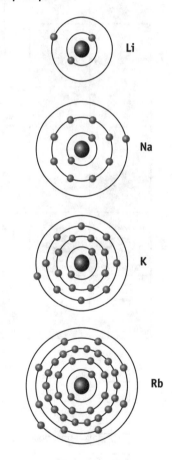

The Periodic Table of Elements

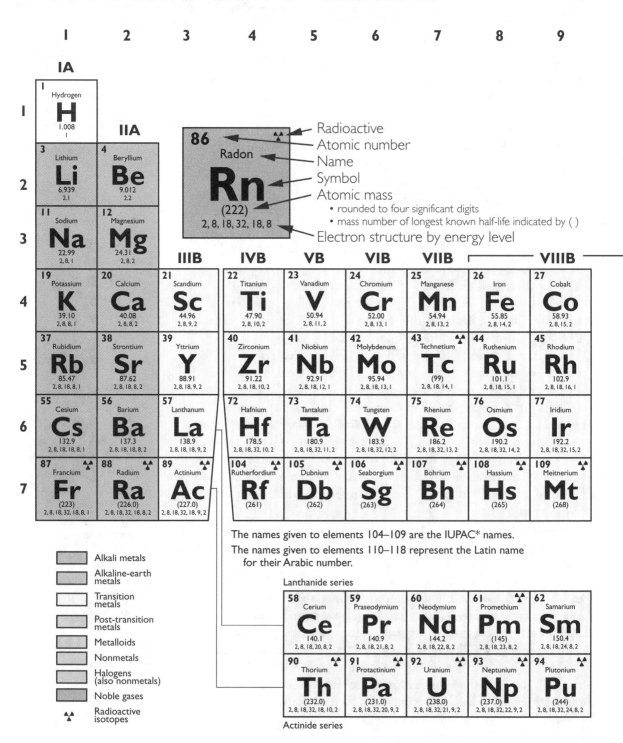

	1	2	3	4	5	6	7	8	9

IA

1 — Hydrogen — **H** — 1.008 — 1

IIA

86 — Radioactive
86 — Atomic number
Radon — Name
Rn — Symbol
(222) — Atomic mass
• rounded to four significant digits
• mass number of longest known half-life indicated by ( )
2, 8, 18, 32, 18, 8 — Electron structure by energy level

2
3 — Lithium — **Li** — 6.939 — 2, 1
4 — Beryllium — **Be** — 9.012 — 2, 2

3
11 — Sodium — **Na** — 22.99 — 2, 8, 1
12 — Magnesium — **Mg** — 24.31 — 2, 8, 2

IIIB | IVB | VB | VIB | VIIB | VIIIB

4
19 — Potassium — **K** — 39.10 — 2, 8, 8, 1
20 — Calcium — **Ca** — 40.08 — 2, 8, 8, 2
21 — Scandium — **Sc** — 44.96 — 2, 8, 9, 2
22 — Titanium — **Ti** — 47.90 — 2, 8, 10, 2
23 — Vanadium — **V** — 50.94 — 2, 8, 11, 2
24 — Chromium — **Cr** — 52.00 — 2, 8, 13, 1
25 — Manganese — **Mn** — 54.94 — 2, 8, 13, 2
26 — Iron — **Fe** — 55.85 — 2, 8, 14, 2
27 — Cobalt — **Co** — 58.93 — 2, 8, 15, 2

5
37 — Rubidium — **Rb** — 85.47 — 2, 8, 18, 8, 1
38 — Strontium — **Sr** — 87.62 — 2, 8, 18, 8, 2
39 — Yttrium — **Y** — 88.91 — 2, 8, 18, 9, 2
40 — Zirconium — **Zr** — 91.22 — 2, 8, 18, 10, 2
41 — Niobium — **Nb** — 92.91 — 2, 8, 18, 12, 1
42 — Molybdenum — **Mo** — 95.94 — 2, 8, 18, 13, 1
43 — Technetium — **Tc** — (99) — 2, 8, 18, 14, 1
44 — Ruthenium — **Ru** — 101.1 — 2, 8, 18, 15, 1
45 — Rhodium — **Rh** — 102.9 — 2, 8, 18, 16, 1

6
55 — Cesium — **Cs** — 132.9 — 2, 8, 18, 18, 8, 1
56 — Barium — **Ba** — 137.3 — 2, 8, 18, 18, 8, 2
57 — Lanthanum — **La** — 138.9 — 2, 8, 18, 18, 9, 2
72 — Hafnium — **Hf** — 178.5 — 2, 8, 18, 32, 10, 2
73 — Tantalum — **Ta** — 180.9 — 2, 8, 18, 32, 11, 2
74 — Tungsten — **W** — 183.9 — 2, 8, 18, 32, 12, 2
75 — Rhenium — **Re** — 186.2 — 2, 8, 18, 32, 13, 2
76 — Osmium — **Os** — 190.2 — 2, 8, 18, 32, 14, 2
77 — Iridium — **Ir** — 192.2 — 2, 8, 18, 32, 15, 2

7
87 — Francium — **Fr** — (223) — 2, 8, 18, 32, 18, 8, 1
88 — Radium — **Ra** — (226.0) — 2, 8, 18, 32, 18, 8, 2
89 — Actinium — **Ac** — (227.0) — 2, 8, 18, 32, 18, 9, 2
104 — Rutherfordium — **Rf** — (261)
105 — Dubnium — **Db** — (262)
106 — Seaborgium — **Sg** — (263)
107 — Bohrium — **Bh** — (264)
108 — Hassium — **Hs** — (265)
109 — Meitnerium — **Mt** — (268)

The names given to elements 104–109 are the IUPAC* names.

The names given to elements 110–118 represent the Latin name for their Arabic number.

Lanthanide series

58 — Cerium — **Ce** — 140.1 — 2, 8, 18, 20, 8, 2
59 — Praseodymium — **Pr** — 140.9 — 2, 8, 18, 21, 8, 2
60 — Neodymium — **Nd** — 144.2 — 2, 8, 18, 22, 8, 2
61 — Promethium — **Pm** — (145) — 2, 8, 18, 23, 8, 2
62 — Samarium — **Sm** — 150.4 — 2, 8, 18, 24, 8, 2

90 — Thorium — **Th** — (232.0) — 2, 8, 18, 32, 18, 10, 2
91 — Protactinium — **Pa** — (231.0) — 2, 8, 18, 32, 20, 9, 2
92 — Uranium — **U** — (238.0) — 2, 8, 18, 32, 21, 9, 2
93 — Neptunium — **Np** — (237.0) — 2, 8, 18, 32, 22, 9, 2
94 — Plutonium — **Pu** — (244) — 2, 8, 18, 32, 24, 8, 2

Actinide series

Key:
- Alkali metals
- Alkaline-earth metals
- Transition metals
- Post-transition metals
- Metalloids
- Nonmetals
- Halogens (also nonmetals)
- Noble gases
- Radioactive isotopes

								VIIIA
10	**11**	**12**	**13**	**14**	**15**	**16**	**17**	**18**

			IIIA	IVA	VA	VIA	VIIA	**2** Helium **He** 4.003 2
			5 Boron **B** 10.81 2, 3	**6** Carbon **C** 12.01 2, 4	**7** Nitrogen **N** 14.01 2, 5	**8** Oxygen **O** 16.00 2, 6	**9** Fluorine **F** 19.00 2, 7	**10** Neon **Ne** 20.18 2, 8
	IB	IIB	**13** Aluminum **Al** 26.98 2, 8, 3	**14** Silicon **Si** 28.09 2, 8, 4	**15** Phosphorus **P** 30.97 2, 8, 5	**16** Sulfur **S** 32.06 2, 8, 6	**17** Chlorine **Cl** 35.45 2, 8, 7	**18** Argon **Ar** 39.95 2, 8, 8
28 Nickel **Ni** 58.71 2, 8, 16, 2	**29** Copper **Cu** 63.55 2, 8, 18, 1	**30** Zinc **Zn** 65.38 2, 8, 18, 2	**31** Gallium **Ga** 69.72 2, 8, 18, 3	**32** Germanium **Ge** 72.59 2, 8, 18, 4	**33** Arsenic **As** 74.92 2, 8, 18, 5	**34** Selenium **Se** 78.96 2, 8, 18, 6	**35** Bromine **Br** 79.90 2, 8, 18, 7	**36** Krypton **Kr** 83.80 2, 8, 18, 8
46 Palladium **Pd** 106.4 2, 8, 18, 18	**47** Silver **Ag** 107.9 2, 8, 18, 18, 1	**48** Cadmium **Cd** 112.4 2, 8, 18, 18, 2	**49** Indium **In** 114.8 2, 8, 18, 18, 3	**50** Tin **Sn** 118.7 2, 8, 18, 18, 4	**51** Antimony **Sb** 121.8 2, 8, 18, 18, 5	**52** Tellurium **Te** 127.6 2, 8, 18, 18, 6	**53** Iodine **I** 126.9 2, 8, 18, 18, 7	**54** Xenon **Xe** 131.3 2, 8, 18, 18, 8
78 Platinum **Pt** 195.1 2, 8, 18, 32, 17, 1	**79** Gold **Au** 197.0 2, 8, 18, 32, 18, 1	**80** Mercury **Hg** 200.6 2, 8, 18, 32, 18, 2	**81** Thallium **Tl** 204.4 2, 8, 18, 32, 18, 3	**82** Lead **Pb** 207.2 2, 8, 18, 32, 18, 4	**83** Bismuth **Bi** 209.0 2, 8, 18, 32, 18, 5	**84** Polonium **Po** (209) 2, 8, 18, 32, 18, 6	**85** Astatine **At** (210) 2, 8, 18, 32, 18, 7	**86** Radon **Rn** (222) 2, 8, 18, 32, 18, 8
110 Unununilium **Uun** (269)	**111** Unununium **Uuu** (272)	**112** Ununbium **Uub** (269)		**114** Ununquadium **Uuq** (285)		**116** Ununhexium **Uuh** (289)		**118** Ununoctium **Uuo** (293)

63 Europium **Eu** 152.0 2, 8, 18, 25, 2	**64** Gadolinium **Gd** 157.3 2, 8, 18, 25, 9, 2	**65** Terbium **Tb** 158.9 2, 8, 18, 27, 8, 2	**66** Dysprosium **Dy** 162.5 2, 8, 18, 28, 8, 2	**67** Holmium **Ho** 164.9 2, 8, 18, 29, 8, 2	**68** Erbium **Er** 167.3 2, 8, 18, 30, 8, 2	**69** Thulium **Tm** 168.9 2, 8, 18, 31, 8, 2	**70** Ytterbium **Yb** 173.0 2, 8, 18, 32, 8, 2	**71** Lutetium **Lu** 175.0 2, 8, 18, 32, 9, 2
95 Americium **Am** (243) 2, 8, 18, 32, 25, 8, 2	**96** Curium **Cm** (247) 2, 8, 18, 32, 25, 9, 2	**97** Berkelium **Bk** (247) 2, 8, 18, 32, 26, 9, 2	**98** Californium **Cf** (251) 2, 8, 18, 32, 28, 8, 2	**99** Einsteinium **Es** (254) 2, 8, 18, 32, 29, 8, 2	**100** Fermium **Fm** (257) 2, 8, 18, 32, 30, 8, 2	**101** Mendelevium **Md** (258) 2, 8, 18, 32, 31, 8, 2	**102** Nobelium **No** (259) 2, 8, 18, 32, 32, 8, 2	**103** Lawrencium **Lr** (260) 2, 8, 18, 32, 32, 9, 2

*IUPAC – International Union of Pure and Applied Chemistry

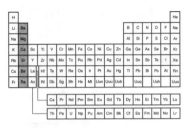

Fig. 7-10 **The alkaline-earth metals (above); the transition metals (below).**

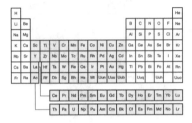

Fig. 7-11 **The alloy in this photomicrograph was found in a moon rock. Areas of the different metals that make up the mixture are clearly visible.**

tract, he orders a series of X rays. The patient drinks a liquid containing barium sulfate. This compound absorbs the X rays and highlights details of the intestines.

Radium compounds—all of which are radioactive—were formerly used in luminescent paints for "glow-in-the-dark" applications, such as watches and clocks. They have been replaced with safer alpha-emitters, however. Strontium compounds give fireworks and flares their brilliant crimson color. Due to its similarity in properties, strontium can replace calcium in bones. It is this fact that makes fallout from nuclear explosions so dangerous. The radioactive isotope, strontium-90, is produced in nuclear explosions. Once incorporated into bones, it continues to decay and produce radiation from within the body.

The families in the middle of the periodic table, labeled 3-12 (Groups IB through VIIIB), are sometimes called subgroups. They are all clearly from the same clan: they have either 1 or 2 electrons in their outer energy level and thus quite similar properties. These strong metals are called the **transition elements.** Very few of these metals are used in their pure form. Pure copper is used in electrical wiring; mercury is used in thermometers and electrical switches; and platinum is used as a catalyst in the petroleum industry and in the pollution control devices on cars. The most common uses of transition metals, however, are metal mixtures called alloys. Sterling silver is a mixture of copper and silver; gold in jewelry is a mixture of gold, silver, and copper; and 92 percent of steel is a simple mixture of iron and carbon.

Group 13 (IIIA) contains such elements as aluminum and boron. These elements have 3 valence electrons. Aluminum is the most abundant metal in the earth's crust. This plentiful element is used for a variety of products, ranging from pots and pans to engine blocks.

Carbon heads Group 14 (IVA) on the periodic table and gives the family its name; all elements with 4 valence electrons are members of the *carbon family.*

Group 15 (VA) is headed by nitrogen, the major component of our atmosphere. Air is nearly 79 percent diatomic nitrogen, N_2. Both nitrogen and a second member of group 15, phosphorus, are necessary for plant growth. Both are found in DNA, the substance of genes.

Group 16 (VIA) is called the *oxygen family.* Each atom has 6 electrons in its outer energy level. Oxygen, in its diatomic form, O_2, is essential for life. Without the oxygen in the atmosphere, most life on earth could not exist. Not only do animals breathe oxygen, but the ozone layer (a triatomic form of oxygen,

O_3) in our atmosphere protects the earth from harmful ultraviolet radiation.

All the elements in the **halogen** (HAL uh jun) family (Group 17 or VIIA) have 7 valence electrons. These electrons give the halogens very distinctive properties. They are very reactive chemically and exist in their pure form only as diatomic molecules. As is true for any of the families of the periodic table, the atoms of each halogen are larger than the atoms of the one above it in the column, and the physical properties change with the atom's size. As the atomic number of the halogen increases, its color gets darker and the material becomes denser. Fluorine, the first member of the halogens, is light yellow. Progressing down the family to the larger atoms, we find greenish-yellow chlorine, red bromine, and purplish-gray iodine. Their physical state also changes with their atomic size. Fluorine and chlorine are gases at room temperature, bromine is a liquid, and iodine is a solid.

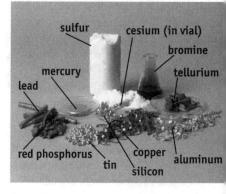

Fig. 7-13 Source of Halogens

Halogen	Source
Fluorine	The minerals fluorite (CaF_2) and cryolite (Na_3AlF_6)
Chlorine	Seawater and underground salt beds
Bromine	Seawater
Iodine	Sodium iodide in seaweed
Astatine	A radioactive decay product of francium-87

In high concentrations halogens are very dangerous. Chlorine was used as a poisonous gas in World War I. In smaller concentrations, however, the halogens can serve us well. Chlorine is dissolved in swimming pools to disinfect the water. On a larger scale, it is used in city water supplies for the same purpose. Before 1900, typhoid fever epidemics raged through cities because of unclean water. Now 1/2 kilogram of chlorine in 1,000,000 kilograms of water kills the harmful micro-organisms and keeps city water supplies healthful.

Fig. 7-14 The halogens

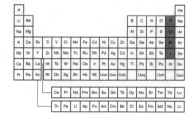

Chlorine is not the only halogen that is used to ensure good health. The element fluorine, in the form of the compound sodium fluoride, is added to many community water supplies to help prevent tooth decay. Iodine is another essential nutrient. If it is missing from your diet, a disease known as hypothyroidism could cause the thyroid gland in your neck to swell, forming a goiter. Years ago researchers wondered why people who lived near the sea never had goiters. Eventually their good health was traced to their diets. People who lived in coastal villages often ate saltwater

Adding to the Periodic Table

In 1939 the periodic table showed only ninety-two elements. Uranium was the most complex element that could be found on the face of the earth, and it held the highest position on the table. No matter how carefully scientists analyzed mineral ores, they could not find any atoms that had more than 92 protons. Had they discovered the limit, or were higher elements possible? They thought that new elements might still be added—and the study of nuclear reactions would be the key.

Scientists knew that elements 84 through 92 were radioactive. It seemed that the "heavier" the atom, the more unstable its nucleus. They also knew that neutrons could break up to form a proton and an electron, or beta particle. When this happened, the proton stayed in the nucleus and the electron was emitted. An extra proton in the nucleus would give the atom a higher atomic number and make it a higher element. What would happen if a neutron in a uranium atom split into a

fish that contained large amounts of iodine. Now potassium iodide is commonly added to table salt in the amount of 1 to 2 percent to prevent goiters.

The final family of the periodic table, Group 18 (VIIIA), has 8 valence electrons, except for the first member, helium, which has 2. The filled outermost energy levels of these elements make them very unreactive and allow them to exist as pure substances. In fact, they combine with other elements only when forced to do so under high temperature and extreme pressure. This "aristocratic"

proton and an electron (a process called beta decay)? The new proton would raise the atomic number to 93. It might be possible to make an entirely new element this way!

The idea of forming new elements fascinated scientists. But to make uranium emit a beta particle, they had to find a way to upset its nucleus. They could do that by adding extra neutrons to the nucleus. In 1940 scientists bombarded a uranium sample with neutrons and then painstakingly analyzed the resulting atoms. They found a new element! It had an atomic number of 93, and they named it "neptunium." Only a tiny number of neptunium atoms had been made, but they were a start. The next year, using the same technique, scientists were able to produce an even higher element, plutonium (atomic number 94).

After the first two **transuranium** ("beyond uranium") **elements** had been made, projectiles bigger than neutrons had to be used. In 1944 helium ions were fired at uranium: americium resulted. When helium ions were aimed at samples of the

new transuranium elements, even higher elements were made—curium (1944), berkelium (1949), and californium (1949).

Several years later, groups of scientists from the University of California at Berkeley and Argonne National Laboratories published sketchy reports about two new elements. At the end of all the reports, appended notes said that not all the data about the newer elements could be printed. Why had some information been held back? What were the new elements like? How had they been made? All these questions remained unanswered for a full two years.

In 1954 the reason for all the secrecy became obvious. The new elements had been formed inside the fireball of an experimental hydrogen bomb that was exploded in 1952. Until the secrecy that shrouded the test was lifted, only the barest details could be given to the public. It turned out that when tremendous streams of neutrons hit uranium during the explosion, 7 to 8 protons were added to the nucleus. The two elements were

named "einsteinium" and "fermium" to honor two great physicists, Albert Einstein and Enrico Fermi.

The quest for new elements continues. These higher elements are expensive because the small amounts that can be produced decay quickly. Even as you read this sentence, scientists are on the verge of discovering elements with higher and higher atomic numbers.

Fig. 7-15 The noble gases

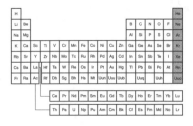

Fig. 7-16 Bright neon lights are a popular way to advertise.

behavior—being too "high class" to associate with others—gives them their family name. Helium, neon, argon, krypton, xenon, and radon are called the **noble gases.** All of these gases are present in the air we breathe, but only in very small amounts. Argon, making up about 1 percent of the atmosphere, is the most abundant. Although helium is the second most abundant element in the universe (it makes up a large part of stars), there is very little of it on earth. Some helium is found in the air, but the main source of this extremely light element is natural gas, which is 1 to 2 percent helium. The other noble gases are extremely hard to find.

Although they behave "royally," the noble gases do perform some important tasks. In fact, it is their inert (unreactive) qualities that make them useful. When dirigibles (lighter-than-air crafts) were first made, hydrogen gas was used to give them lift. The hydrogen gas was very light, but it also burned very easily. The slightest spark could transform the whole dirigible into a seething mass of flames. Helium gas solved this problem. It is also much lighter than air, and it eliminated the chance of fire. Because it is a noble gas, it does not burn. Helium is still used today in airships called blimps and, of course, in filling party balloons. Neon and xenon are used in advertising signs and fluorescent lighting; helium and argon are used to provide unreactive atmospheres for operations such as the cutting or welding of certain metals.

There is a quick and easy way to determine the number of valence electrons in a given element in groups 1 (IA), 2 (IIA), and 13-18 (III-VIIIA). We simply determine the group in which a given element belongs (by using the periodic table) and then use that number to indicate the number of its valence electrons. If it falls in groups 13-18, simply use the last digit to determine the number of valence electrons. For example, since germanium (Ge) is in Group 14, it has 4 valence electrons; krypton (Kr), being in Group 18, has 8 valence electrons.

Most of the 3-12 groups (or B group elements) have 2 valence electrons, though some have 1. However, knowing which number is correct requires a bit of memorization and a deeper understanding of filling order and electron configuration than will be covered here.

Periods

The *horizontal rows* of the periodic table are called **periods,** or **series.** The elements within the same period do not have similar properties. Though they are arranged in order of increasing atomic number, their properties change across each row. For example, on the left side of the periodic table, the elements are metals. Going across the table from left to right, the elements are less and less metallic, progressing to the point where the elements on the far right side of the table are classified as nonmetals. It is the electron configurations (number of electrons in each energy level) of the elements in a period that bring about the changes in a property. As you read across a period from left to right, the number of electrons in the outer level increases from 1 to 8 (except for the first period).

The number of valence electrons is a major factor in determining the chemical properties as well as many of the physical properties of an element. When the outer level of an element contains 8 electrons, according to the octet rule, it is filled; this marks the end of a period. (Helium is an exception; its outer level is completed with only 2 electrons.) The next element in sequence has one more proton and hence needs one more electron. This electron must occupy the next higher energy level. It therefore begins a new period, and the cycle begins again.

You can easily determine the total number of energy levels that are occupied by electrons for a given element by noting the row (that is, the period) in which you find the element. Further, the period in which an element is found tells you the energy level of the valence electrons. For example, sulfur (S) is in the third

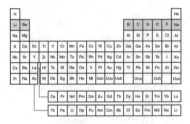

Fig. 7-17 The second period of the periodic table begins with the element lithium. Each succeeding element in the period has one more valence electron.

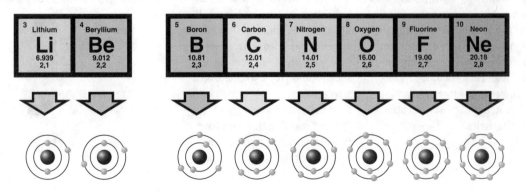

horizontal row; that is, it is in the third period. It therefore has three energy levels that are occupied by electrons, with its valence electrons occupying the third main energy level. The same things could be said of argon (Ar) since it is also in the third period. The element following argon—potassium (K)—is in the fourth row and therefore the fourth period; it therefore contains four occupied energy levels, with the valence electrons of its atoms occupying the fourth main energy level in each.

FACETS of the physical world

Unusual Elements

Scientists like to describe their observations using laws and theories. Although a scientific law may be "set in stone," almost always there are a few notable exceptions. For example, biologists know that all living things are made of cells. But what about viruses? They are not made of cells, but they show some characteristics of living things. Everybody also knows that mammals do not lay eggs—that is, 99% of them do not. The duck-billed platypus and spiny anteater are the lone hold-outs, and they do indeed lay eggs. Elements in the same family share the same characteristics—that is, most of them do anyway. There are a few elements that do not seem to "fit" the pattern. For example, all the metals are solids at room temperature—except for mercury, which is a liquid. Let's examine some other elements with some quirky, different, or just downright bizarre characteristics.

Francium (Fr) Z = 87: an alkali metal

(The letter Z is sometimes used as a symbol for the atomic number.) Mendeleev predicted the existence of francium, but it was not until 1939 that it was discovered at the Curie Institute in France. Of the first 101 elements, francium is by far the least stable. It is formed by the radioactive decays of actinium (Z = 89). Francium is so rare that scientists have estimated that only about 30 grams exist in the entire earth's crust at any given time. Francium decays so quickly that scientists have been unable to measure any quantities or isolate it in its pure form. The most stable isotope is francium-223, which has a half-life of only 22 minutes. Only minute traces of this isotope have ever been found, mainly in uranium deposits.

Technetium (Tc) Z = 43: a transition element

Most radioactive elements are "heavy," meaning that they have fairly large atomic numbers and masses. But technetium is a rarity.

Right in the middle of the transition metals, this radioactive element seems to be out of place. Unlike the other transition metals, it has no stable isotopes. It is not found naturally on the earth but is formed by bombarding molybdenum (Z = 42) with hydrogen nuclei. In fact, it was the first element to be "artificially" formed in a laboratory from another element (the Greek word *tekhnetos* means "artificial") in 1937. Unlike francium, technetium can be produced in large quantities and does have several uses. Physicians inject technetium into a patient's veins, where it concentrates in body tissues. As the technetium isotope decays, it gives off small amounts of

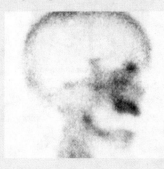

7 The Perodic Table of Elements

From the previous discussion, you can see how the periodic table can be used to determine both the number of valence electrons and the main energy level in which they are found. For example, sulfur has 6 valence electrons in the third main energy level (Group 16, period 3); argon has 8 valence electrons in the third main energy level (Group 18, period 3); and potassium has 1 valence electron in the fourth main energy level (Group 1, period 4).

gamma radiation, allowing an image similar to an X ray to be obtained using special equipment.

Manganese (Mn) Z = 25
Manganese, located in the middle of the transition elements, is a very important exception to the general description of metals. Chemically, manganese is a metal because it has electrons which are easily removed in its outermost energy level. But in its stable form it is a gray-white, brittle substance that is too weak to be used in engineering. Not ductile, not malleable, and without luster, it seems to be an outcast among the transition elements. Manganese behaves like the other transition elements only when it is alloyed with other metals. Then it gains strength and flexibility. In fact,

there are approximately 33 kilograms of manganese in every metric ton of special structural steel. Manganese in powdered form is a fire hazard, and compounds of manganese sometimes burn with terrific intensity. Not only does manganese strengthen steel, but biologists have also found that many living things need a small amount of manganese as part of their diet. It is a trace mineral—a substance that the body needs to survive (but only in very small amounts). In fact, the human body contains only about 0.01 gram of manganese.

Hydrogen (H) Z = 1
With 1 proton, 1 electron, and no neutrons, hydrogen bears no family resemblance to any group on the periodic table. It is often grouped with the alkali metals, but this colorless, odorless gas is anything but metallic. Hydrogen exists only in the gaseous state. To be a solid or liquid it would have to be lowered to a temperature near absolute zero. Since the first energy level needs only 2 electrons to be filled, hydrogen needs to gain only 1 electron to be satisfied. This would seem to place it as a distant relative of the halogens, which precede the noble

gases on the periodic table. But it does not have properties resembling the halogens either.

Hydrogen is probably the most abundant element in the entire universe. Astronomers have estimated that 90% of the atoms in existence are hydrogen atoms. Yet here on the earth hydrogen ranks only tenth in order of abundance and makes up less than 1/1,000,000 of the volume of our atmosphere. Hydrogen is the lightest element of all; in the past it was used to fill up blimps. However, the extremely flammable properties of hydrogen ended that practice. There are so many hydrogen compounds that it would be a major challenge to list them all, but the most common is plain old H_2O—water.

Relationships Among Elements

153

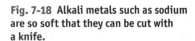

SECTION REVIEW QUESTIONS 7C

1. Name one element to represent each of these groups: alkali metals, alkaline-earth metals, transition elements, halogens, noble gases.

2. How many valence electrons does an atom of a halogen contain?

3. Give the group and period numbers for the element lead.

4. In what energy level are the valence electrons in an atom of silver?

7D

Section

Periodic Trends

A quick glance at the periodic table tells you that most of the elements are classified as metals, some are labeled nonmetals, and a very few have the distinction of being *metalloids.* There seem to be clear differences among these three classes of elements. Metals are on the left side of the table, nonmetals are on the right side of the table, and the metalloids are in a region between them. There also seems to be a clear trend from metals to nonmetals as you cross the periodic table. What causes this trend? What makes metals metallic, nonmetals nonmetallic, and metalloids not quite either?

Metals

Almost three-fourths of the elements are classified as **metals.** We use metals in our cars, bridges, ships, planes, cooking utensils, and home appliances. Our modern way of life depends on metals. The metals we most commonly use are hard, strong, and dense. And because these metals are most familiar, many people think that *all*

Fig. 7-18 Alkali metals such as sodium are so soft that they can be cut with a knife.

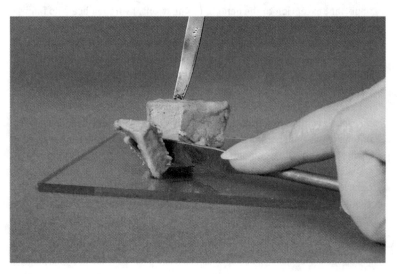

Common Characteristics of Metals

1. Most metals have a silvery **luster** if their surfaces are clean.

2. Most metals are solids at room temperature; only mercury (Hg) is a liquid.

3. Most metals are **malleable** (can be rolled or hammered into a shape).

4. Most metals are **ductile** (can be drawn into wire).

5. Most metals are good conductors of electricity and heat.

6. Metals tend to be reactive; they give up electrons in chemical reactions.

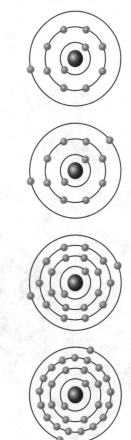

Fig. 7-19 Most metals have either 1 or 2 valence electrons. These configurations represent sodium, magnesium, titanium, and copper. Can you match the element to its configuration?

metals have these qualities. Yet many pure metals are so soft that they can be cut with a knife! Some are very weak; some are lightweight. In fact, most metals do not have physical properties anything like the familiar metals that we use every day.

Then how can we identify metals? They have common properties that give us clues to their identity.

All of these properties are related to the electron structure of metals. Metals belong to families with relatively few electrons in their outer energy level. They do not hold these valence electrons very strongly and can easily give them up. (We will see the reason for this in the next chapter.) That is why all metals have such similar chemical and physical properties. If it were not for these "loose" electrons, metals would not have a silvery luster, be malleable and ductile, or conduct electricity.

Metalloids

Across the periodic table from left to right, the properties of the elements become less and less metallic. Toward the right side of the periodic table, a heavy zigzag line divides the metals from the nonmetals. Touching either side of this line are some *elements that have both metallic and nonmetallic properties.* These elements are called **metalloids.**

Having properties that are between metals and nonmetals makes these elements especially useful. Metalloids do not conduct electricity as well as metals, but since they are slightly conductive, they are called *semiconductors.* Silicon is probably the most widely used semiconductor. Scientists have learned to use this limited conducting ability to control the amount of electricity that flows through electronic instruments. At room temperature, metalloids are poor conductors, but at higher temperatures they become better conductors. Without semiconductors, we would not have electronic watches, pocket calculators, computers, or a host of other common items.

Fig. 7-20 The metalloids

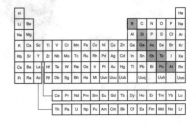

Periodic Trends

Fig. 7-21 Silicon is a metalloid that is used to make computer chips and other electronic products.

7 The Perodic Table of Elements

Nonmetals

Hydrogen and the elements on the right side of the periodic table are called **nonmetals.** The halogens and noble gases make up a significant portion of the nonmetals. These elements hold their electrons tightly, so their properties are very different from those of the metallic elements. Compare their physical properties, given below, with those of the metals.

You may have noted that the metals have many more properties in common with each other than do the nonmetals. Just as *similar* electron structures account for the similar properties among metals, so the *dissimilar* electron structures among the nonmetals can account for their significant differences in properties. Whereas most metals have 1 or 2 valence electrons, the number of valence electrons in the nonmetals ranges between 4 and 8.

Common Characteristics of Nonmetals

1. Nonmetals do not have a silvery luster. They exist in a variety of colors. Sulfur is yellow, bromine is reddish brown, iodine is purple, and carbon is black.
2. Nonmetals exist as solids, liquids, and gases at room temperature, but the gaseous state is the most common. (Eleven of the nonmetals are gases at room temperature.)
3. Solid nonmetals exist as brittle crystals that shatter easily.
4. Nonmetals are poor conductors of heat and electricity.
5. The noble gases are nearly inert chemically—they usually do not react.
6. Nonmetals tend to gain or share electrons in chemical reactions.

SECTION REVIEW QUESTIONS 7D

1. Would you classify the element aluminum as a metal, nonmetal, or metalloid?
2. If an element has the properties of being a reddish liquid that does not conduct electricity, it is most likely classified as a _____.
3. An element that has few valence electrons and gives them up easily would most likely be classified as a _____.
4. The heavy zigzag line in the periodic table separates what two elemental classifications? What are the names of these "dividing" elements?

CHAPTER REVIEW

SCIENTIFICALLY SPEAKING

periodic table	noble gases
periodic law	periods
electron configuration	series
valence electrons	metals
family	luster
group	malleable
alkali metals	ductile
alkaline-earth metals	metalloids
alloys	nonmetals
transition elements	
halogens	
transuranium elements	

CHAPTER REVIEW QUESTIONS

1. What was the problem with Mendeleev's original periodic table?

2. What is the meaning of the word *periodic* as used in the term *periodic table?*

3. Why do elements in the same family have similar properties?

4. What is it about the atom that gives it metallic, nonmetallic, or metalloid properties?

5. What makes Group 18 gases "noble"?

6. Give two uses for the halogens and two uses for the noble gases.

7. Give three examples of metalloids (use names and symbols).

FACET REVIEW QUESTIONS

1. Describe how transuranium elements were developed.

2. Explain how the element technetium got its name.

WHAT DID YOU LEARN?

1. How was Mendeleev able to predict the discovery of new elements and their properties?

2. Why is the periodic table a powerful testimony for a Creator?

3. Suppose you discovered a new element that you decided to name sciencium. If sciencium were very reactive—so reactive that you had to store samples of it under oil to prevent it from reacting with the air—and it easily gave up one electron in a chemical reaction, in what family would you classify it?

4. Could an atom have the following electron configuration: 2 electrons in the first energy level, 8 in the second level, and 10 in the third, for a total of 20 electons? Why or why not?

Forces Between Atoms

8A **Chemical Bonding with Electrons**

8B **Ionic Bonding**

8C **Covalent Bonding**

8D **Metallic Bonding**

We have spent much time examining the composition of matter. The basic principles of matter are actually quite simple. Every physical "thing" is made of atoms. There are about 115 different types of atoms that we call elements, and they are arranged on a useful diagram we call the periodic table. These elements can be found in pure form, blended together in mixtures, or chemically bonded together as molecules and compounds. We have also discussed the composition of the atom—especially the tiny electrons which surround the nucleus. What you may not know is that the electrons play a vital role in determining how atoms bond to each other. Some atoms bond to each other quickly, just by putting them together. Other elements refuse to form compounds with each other under any circumstances. We can trace this behavior back to the number and position of the electrons in each individual atom. In this chapter, we will explore the reasons that this is so and predict how elements will react with one another.

Chemical Bonding with Electrons

Could any two substances appear more different than graphite and diamond? Yet both of these substances are made of the same element: carbon. *Graphite*—much like soot in its appearance—is an inexpensive, black, soft and slippery substance used in lubricants, pencil leads, and dry-cell electrodes. Diamond, in contrast, is of great value, transparent, generally colorless to blue-white, and the hardest of all natural substances.

What makes these two forms of carbon so radically different? The answer lies in the way their atoms are joined together—their **chemical bonds.** Graphite and diamond illustrate the fact that the same element can often bond in more than one way.

Using one type of bonding, carbon atoms can link together to form six-member rings that join to form sheets. Each carbon atom in the sheet is thus bonded to three other carbon atoms. Though the bonding within each sheet is strong, the sheets are not strongly attracted to each other, allowing them to slide over one another. This is the type of bonding found in graphite.

In diamond, carbon atoms bond to each other in such a way that they form a structure composed of connected pyramids *(tetrahedra)* extending in three dimensions. Each carbon atom is surrounded by four other

Fig. 8-1 Both diamonds and graphite are made of carbon atoms.

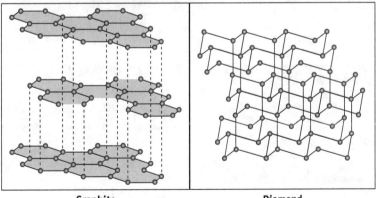

Graphite   Diamond

carbon atoms, thereby forming a three-dimensional network of carbon atoms that results in a very hard and strong structure.

What is true of carbon is true of most of the other elements. Aluminum can bond to chlorine in one way to make a white, water-absorbing crystal that is the active ingredient in many deodorants (aluminum chlorohydrate). It can also bond in a different way with magnesium to form *magnalium,* a lightweight alloy used in aircraft.

One thing seems clear. When two elements join, their chemical union determines the characteristics of the resulting compound. Therefore, scientists are very interested in how substances bond (join together). Their studies have led them to conclude that *chemical bonds involve mainly the valence electrons*—those in the outermost energy level. The need that most individual atoms have for increased stability causes them to bond together.

Though there are some exceptions (such as hydrogen), *atoms generally are most stable when they have a full octet (8 electrons) in their valence level.* You saw this octet rule in the last chapter, where it was used to determine electron configurations. In this chapter it will be applied to bonding between atoms. But how does an atom with fewer than 8 electrons fill its valence level? By bonding with other atoms to form *compounds.* In this way, groups of atoms "cooperate" to fill each other's electron needs.

Atoms can react in several ways to achieve this greater stability. One possibility is for atoms to *lose or gain electrons.* When certain elements bond together, the atoms of one type may forcibly remove electrons from atoms of another type. The atoms that lose their electrons are stable with the full level that remains beneath their lost electron(s). Further, the atoms that gain electrons are stable with their now-full outer energy level. In other bonding situations, separate atoms *share* electrons with one another so that they can each have filled outer energy levels. No matter which method is used, the ultimate goal of bonding is the same: atoms tend to be more stable with an octet of electrons in their valence shells.

Sharing electrons:
Similar electronegativity

Losing electrons:
Low vs. high electronegativity

Electronegativity

The method by which an atom fills its outer level depends on how strongly it attracts and holds electrons. A scale has been devised which gives *the relative ability of an atom to attract electrons in a chemical bond.* This ability is known as an element's **electronegativity.** It is a periodic function of the elements, based on their group number. As it turns out, atoms that have nearly filled valence levels tend to have high electronegativities. Atoms whose outer levels are nearly empty have very low electronegativities.

8 Forces Between Atoms

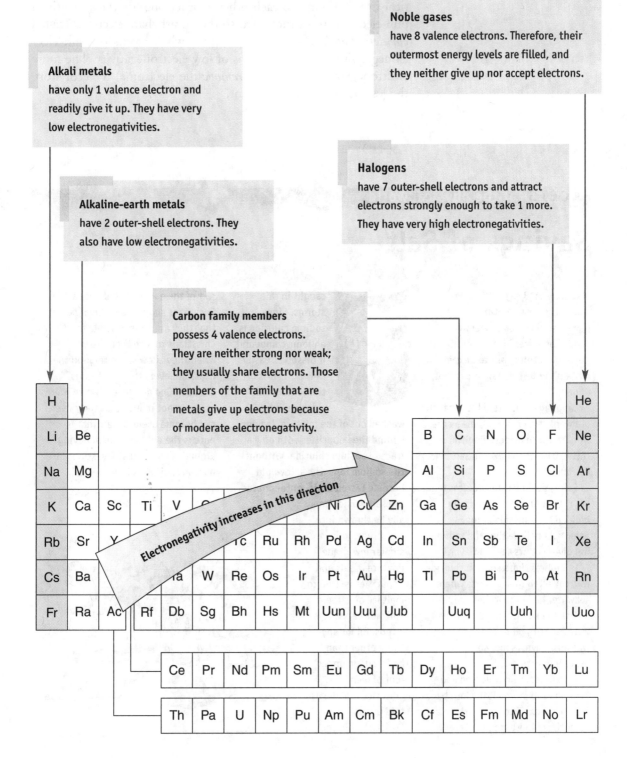

Alkali metals
have only 1 valence electron and readily give it up. They have very low electronegativities.

Alkaline-earth metals
have 2 outer-shell electrons. They also have low electronegativities.

Carbon family members
possess 4 valence electrons. They are neither strong nor weak; they usually share electrons. Those members of the family that are metals give up electrons because of moderate electronegativity.

Noble gases
have 8 valence electrons. Therefore, their outermost energy levels are filled, and they neither give up nor accept electrons.

Halogens
have 7 outer-shell electrons and attract electrons strongly enough to take 1 more. They have very high electronegativities.

Electronegativity increases in this direction

When atoms that have electronegativities that are close or identical in value bond to each other, neither one has the strength to pull electrons from the other, so they must share electrons (called *covalent bonding*). *Ionic bonds* form when atoms of high electronegativity bond with atoms of low electronegativity. The more electronegative element can *remove* the electron(s) it needs from the less electronegative element.

Sayings of Salt

Matthew 5:13 says, "Ye are the salt of the earth: but if the salt have lost his savour, wherewith shall it be salted? it is thenceforth good for nothing, but to be cast out, and to be trodden under foot of men."

Language scholars tell us that the old word *savour* is the same as the word *flavor* in modern English. If this is true, then how can salt lose its *flavor*?

Salt is sodium chloride. It is made up of a sodium cation ionically bonded to a chloride anion. Scientists believe that the sodium ion gives salt its special flavor.

In biblical times sodium chloride was collected from deserts where seawater had evaporated and left salt deposits. These deposits were not very pure. The salt was mixed with sand, soil, and other impurities.

The traders who collected and sold this salt stored it in cloth bags for the long trip to the marketplace. Sometimes these traders were caught in rainstorms. Since sodium chloride is an ionic compound, it dissolves easily in water. Most of the sodium chloride would be washed out of the mixture, leaving behind the impurities with only a trace of sodium chloride. Without the sodium ions, the salt would become tasteless. If contaminated, the salt would literally be thrown into the street. Today a similar low-grade mixture of salt and impurities is used to melt ice on streets and sidewalks. It is not useful for anything other than to be "trodden under foot of men."

Notice that Jesus told us that Christians are the salt of the earth. He did not say Christians *should be* or *could be* but that they are. It is possible for Christians to lose their "flavor" when they allow sin to reign in their lives. Believers that put things ahead of God and go their own way often do not realize that their lives can become useless. Salt that is pure is the only salt worth having around; so also must Christians be pure in their lives to serve God.

1. Which electrons are involved in chemical bonds?

2. How many electrons do most atoms need in their outermost energy level to be stable in a compound?

3. As you move from left to right on the periodic table, what happens to the electronegativity of the elements?

Ionic Bonding

Sodium is a soft, silvery metal that reacts explosively with water. Fluorine is a pale, greenish yellow gas that is extremely corrosive. Both are very poisonous and should never be taken internally. Yet when atoms of fluorine and sodium bond, they form a white crystalline compound that is used in toothpaste to prevent cavities. Why do the properties of sodium and fluorine change when they bond?

An **ionic** (eye AHN ik) **bond** forms when *one or more electrons are transferred from one atom to another.* If an atom gains or loses electrons, it is no longer electrically neutral because the number of electrons is not equal to the number of protons. Such *a particle that has a negative or positive charge* is known as an **ion.** If an atom gains electrons, it will have more electrons (negative charges) than protons (positive charges), resulting in an atom that will be negatively charged. Such a *negative ion* is called an **anion** (AN EYE on). If an atom loses electrons, it will have more protons than electrons. With more positive charges than negative charges, that atom would then be positively charged. A *positive ion* is called a **cation** (CAT EYE on). Ionic bonds form as a result of the attraction between these two oppositely charged types of particles.

Fig. 8-2 Toothpaste contains sodium and fluorine, but not as pure elements. They are bonded to form sodium fluoride, a safe and effective cavity fighter.

Electron Transfer in Ionic Bonds

For electrons to be transferred from one atom to another, they must be pulled. The electronegativities of the elements help us to determine which ones pull and which ones get pulled. Highly electronegative nonmetals, such as fluorine, can pull electrons away from weakly electronegative elements, such as sodium. For that reason, when highly electronegative nonmetals in Group 17 (VIIA) come near weakly electronegative metals in Group 1 (IA), we can expect electrons to be transferred and ionic bonds to form.

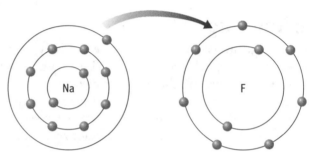

Before:	11 protons, 11 electrons	Before:	9 protons, 9 electrons
After:	11 protons, 10 electrons	After:	9 protons, 10 electrons
	Sodium becomes a cation.		Fluorine becomes an anion.

With 7 valence electrons, the outer energy level of the nonmetal fluorine is almost full. Consequently, it has a very strong pull for 1 more electron. The metal sodium has only 1 loosely held valence electron. It is easy prey for the very electronegative fluorine.

After fluorine takes the electron from sodium, its outer level is full. What happens to the sodium atom? Now it too has a full outer level. After the lone electron in the third level is taken, the 8 electrons in the second level serve as a complete octet which is now in the outermost energy level. Both atoms are satisfied, and the compound sodium fluoride is formed.

What force holds this compound together? You have probably heard the phrase "opposites attract." Well, when sodium loses its valence electron, it becomes a cation. Only 10 negatively charged electrons $(11 - 1)$ offset 11 positively charged protons. When the fluorine atom receives the electron, it also becomes electrically unbalanced. A -1 charge results when 10 electrons $(9 + 1)$ oppose only 9 protons. This is how a sodium ion is bonded to a fluoride ion. The sodium ion that has a $+1$ charge attracts the fluoride ion that has a -1 charge. This ionic attraction, called ***electrostatic force***, forms a very strong bond.

Illustrating Electron Transfer

In the example below, Bohr models of the atoms were used to show ionic bonding. Since only the outermost electrons are available to interact with other atoms, scientists have devised a shortcut to illustrate the bonding process, showing only the valence electrons. The other electrons, which do not actively participate in bonding, are omitted. These shortcut representations, called **Lewis dot structures** (sometimes called *electron dot notation*), use the element's symbol and a pattern of dots to represent valence electrons. They are named for Gilbert N. Lewis from the University of California, Berkeley, who devised them.

As you should recall from Chapter 7, the number of valence electrons in an atom is revealed by its position on the periodic chart. For example, all elements in Group 1 (IA) have only 1 electron in their highest energy level. In electron dot diagrams, they have one dot beside their symbols. All halogens, Group 17 (VIIA) have 7 valence electrons. Thus, their symbols are surrounded by a pattern of seven dots. Look at the electron dot structures for the elements of the other groups and note how the number of valence electrons increases as you move across the groups.

```
    6   3
  4           2
     Symbol
  7           1

    8   5
```

Fig. 8-3 This is the commonly accepted pattern for placing electrons in electron dot diagrams. This is not a fixed order. Sometimes the placement of the dots will change to illustrate bonding.

Group	IA	IIA	IIIA	IVA	VA	VIA	VIIA	VIIIA
Valence Electrons	1	2	3	4	5	6	7	8
Bohr model								
Electron dot structures	Na.	Mg:	Al:	·Si:	·P:	·S:	:Cl:	:Ar:

Now you are ready to depict sodium and fluorine using electron dot structures:

Na.   :F:

Using the principle of electronegativity and electron dot structures, we can show what happens to the electrons when sodium and fluorine react together. Remember that the fluorine atom exerts a tremendous "pull" on the lone sodium valence electron. The product of the reaction is NaF, or sodium fluoride. The bond between the sodium and fluorine atom is possible because the atoms have opposite charges.

$$\text{Na} \cdot \overset{\cdot\cdot}{:}\underset{}{\text{F}}\overset{\cdot\cdot}{:} \longrightarrow \text{Na}\, \overset{\cdot\cdot}{:}\underset{\rightarrow}{\text{F}}\overset{\cdot\cdot}{:} \longrightarrow \text{Na}^+ \longleftrightarrow \overset{\cdot\cdot}{:}\underset{\cdot\cdot}{\text{F}}\overset{}{:}^-$$

| Electron dot structures of atoms | Electron transfer | Electron dot structures of the ions |

It is important to show the charges on the ions, both by their *sign* (positive or negative) and their *magnitude* (how many there are). Such information is needed in order to decide which ions can react and how many of each will be in the compound.

Multiple Electron Transfers

The formation of sodium fluoride from sodium and fluorine atoms involves one of the simplest electron transfers: a single electron is transferred from a sodium atom to a fluorine atom. Some bonds involve the transfer of 2 or 3 electrons. When magnesium bonds with sulfur, 2 electrons are transferred. Sulfur has 6 valence electrons; it needs 2 more to complete its octet. Magnesium has 2 valence electrons. Its low electronegativity allows the more electronegative sulfur to take those 2 electrons. Each ion that forms will then have a full octet in its outer level.

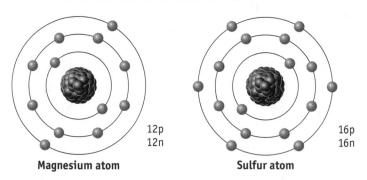

| 12p 12n | 16p 16n |
| Magnesium atom | Sulfur atom |

The electron dot structures for the transfer would look like this:

$$\text{Mg} : + \overset{\cdot\cdot}{\cdot}\text{S}: \longrightarrow \text{Mg} : + \overset{\cdot\cdot}{\underset{\curvearrowright}{}}\text{S}: \longrightarrow \text{Mg}^{2+} \quad \overset{\cdot\cdot}{:}\underset{\cdot\cdot}{\text{S}}:^{2-}$$

| Electron dot structures of the atoms | Two electrons are transferred. | Electron dot structures of the ions |

Magnesium loses 2 electrons and has a +2 charge. Sulfur gains 2 electrons and has a –2 charge. The 2 ions are held together by their opposite charges.

Ionic bonds can also include more than 2 ions. In magnesium fluoride, 2 fluorine atoms meet their need for electrons by each taking 1 electron from a magnesium atom's highest level.

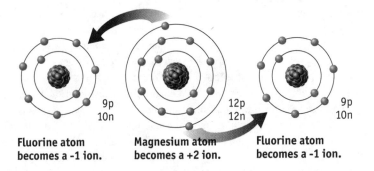

Fluorine atom becomes a -1 ion.   **Magnesium atom becomes a +2 ion.**   **Fluorine atom becomes a -1 ion.**

For every +2 magnesium ion, there are two –1 fluorine ions. *In every ionic bond, the total of the negative charges on the anions must be equal to the total of the positive charges on the cations.* The electron dot diagram would look like this:

$$Mg: + : \ddot{F}: + : \ddot{F}: \longrightarrow Mg: + : \ddot{F}: + : \ddot{F}: \longrightarrow Mg^{2+} : \ddot{F}:^{1-} + : \ddot{F}:^{1-}$$

In another variation of ionic bonding, more than one metal atom may be needed to provide the electrons for a single nonmetal atom. For example, in sodium sulfide, sulfur acquires the 2 electrons it needs from 2 sodium atoms. Each sodium atom donates 1 electron.

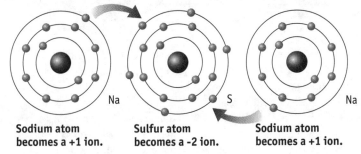

Sodium atom becomes a +1 ion.   **Sulfur atom becomes a -2 ion.**   **Sodium atom becomes a +1 ion.**

You would write the electron dot structures for the reaction this way:

$$Na \cdot + Na \cdot + \cdot \ddot{S}: \longrightarrow Na \cdot + Na \cdot + \cdot \ddot{S}: \longrightarrow Na^{1+} + Na^{1+} + : \ddot{S}:$$

In every case of ionic bonding, highly electronegative nonmetals pull electrons away from weakly electronegative metals. Ionic bonding will occur any time a *nonmetal* has enough attraction to pull away the valence electrons of a *metal.* Two atoms with similar

The Shocking Story of Electrolytes

Most people do not realize the fact that pure water is not a very good conductor of electricity. If pure water does not conduct electricity, then why are water and electricity such a dangerous combination? Why

transport electrical charges through a solvent.

The strength of an electrolyte can be tested by a conductivity apparatus such as the one pictured. The two electrodes can complete an electrical circuit only if the solution between them can conduct electricity. When the circuit is complete, the light bulb glows.

If a substance does not ionize in solution, it cannot conduct electricity. Such substances are classified as nonelectrolytes. Sugar is an

strong electrolyte. If the bulb glows dimly when the electrodes are immersed in a solution, we can conclude that the solute does not ionize thoroughly. Vinegar is a good example of such a solution. Vinegar is composed of acetic acid dissolved in water. Since acetic acid does not easily break up into ions, it is classified as a weak electrolyte.

The importance of eating and drinking foods with electrolytes (namely sodium chloride, calcium, and potassium compounds) cannot

  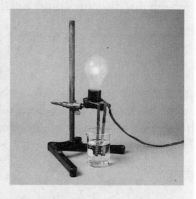

are we warned to keep radios, hair dryers, and other electrical appliances safely away from bathtubs and sinks? True, water cannot conduct electricity, but some of the solutes in it can. These substances are called electrolytes. Unless the water is distilled, almost all tap water, seawater, and fresh water contain dissolved electrolytes. Electrolytes break up into ions (ionize) as they are dissolved. Electrolytes are ionic compounds that disassociate in water, leaving free positive and negative ions to act as ferryboats to

example of a nonelectrolyte. Substances that do ionize are classified according to the number of ions they produce: the more ions there are, the more electricity will be conducted through the solvent. Substances that ionize thoroughly to produce many ions are called strong electrolytes. The light bulb in the conductivity apparatus glows brightly when its electrodes are immersed in such a solution. Table salt (sodium chloride) is a good example of a solute that ionizes well; sodium chloride is a very

be underestimated. Nerve impulses to muscles are generated using electrical current. Since ions are charged atoms, nerve cells use them to carry nerve impulses to muscle cells. Inadequate levels of potassium and calcium ions can sometimes cause cramping and other health problems. Electrolytes help maintain the body's fluid levels. Sport drinks often contain electrolytes that help keep water present within body cells so that dehydration does not occur during strenuous exercise.

electronegativities cannot bond ionically because neither can pull electrons away from the other. Therefore, ionic bonding unites elements from *opposite sides* of the periodic chart.

Structure and Properties of Ionic Compounds

Ionic compounds are composed of vast numbers of ions. Just think about how many atoms are present in just a pinch of salt! In the case of the ionic compound sodium chloride, each sodium atom donated an electron to each chlorine atom. The resulting sodium and chlorine ions then attracted each other to form an ionic bond:

But the attraction between positive and negative charges does not stop there. Other units of sodium chloride can be attracted to another unit,

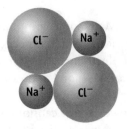

or three units can form, and so on,

until *a regular and repeated three-dimensional pattern of arrangement of positive and negative ions* is formed. Such a structure is a **crystal lattice** (LAT iss). Ionic solids exist as crystal lattices of anions and cations.

Since each individual ion in the lattice is bonded to all of its oppositely charged neighbors, the particles of an ionic solid are held strongly in place. This explains the fact that ionic compounds are solids with high melting points. For example, sodium chloride melts at 801°C, and sodium fluoride melts at 988°C. Such a lattice structure also explains why chemists prefer to use the term **formula unit** to

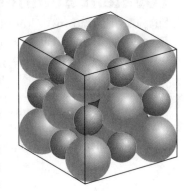

refer to *the basic or simplest repeating unit of an ionic solid.* Ionically bonded compounds are generally not referred to as molecules.

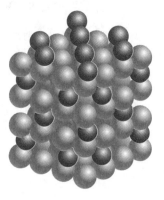

Many ionic compounds, like table salt, dissolve in water. When an ionic solid is melted or dissolved, it is an excellent conductor of electricity. An **electrolyte** (ih LEK truh LYT) is a substance that produces ions upon dissolving. The positive and negative charges on these ions help to conduct current through the water. As a solid, however, salt cannot conduct because the ions are held in place in the crystal lattice by the firm grip of the ionic bond.

SECTION REVIEW QUESTIONS 8B

1. What happens to valence electrons in the formation of an ionic bond?

2. What do we call ions that have a positive charge? Negative?

3. Write the electron dot structure for an atom of selenium (Se).

Covalent Bonding

Suppose two atoms with similar electronegativities react. Both have fewer than 8 valence electrons, and both need to fill their outer levels; but since their pulls are of similar strengths, neither one can actually remove any electrons from the other. Ionic bonding is therefore impossible. The only way for both atoms to get a full octet is to share valence electrons. Such a bond that *involves sharing of one or more pairs of electrons between two atoms* is called a **covalent** (ko VAY lunt) **bond.**

Diatomic Molecules

What combinations of elements put atoms with similar electronegativities together? Obviously, two atoms of the same element have identical strengths; they must use covalent bonding if they are to bond to each other. Sometimes only *two atoms are bonded together to form a unit* known as a **diatomic molecule.** Many gases consist of diatomic molecules composed of two of the same type of atom; seven of the nonmetallic elements exist as diatomic molecules.

As an example of how two atoms bond covalently, visualize how two chlorine atoms might combine. Both atoms have 7 valence electrons. Thus, each needs 1 more electron to complete its octet. You could use the Bohr model to represent these atoms as follows:

Diatomic Nonmetals	
Hydrogen	H_2
Oxygen	O_2
Nitrogen	N_2
Fluorine	F_2
Chlorine	Cl_2
Bromine	Br_2
Iodine	I_2

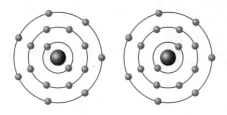

Using Lewis dot structures is very useful in showing ionic and covalent bonding.

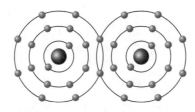

You should recall the electron dot diagram for chlorine as follows:

$$: \overset{\displaystyle ..}{\underset{\displaystyle .}{Cl}} :$$

Even if one chlorine atom could pull an electron from the other, a stable bond would not form. While one atom would have an octet, the atom that lost the electron would have only 6 valence electrons, not a stable octet. The solution to this apparent dilemma is *sharing.* By contributing 1 electron apiece to form a shared pair, both atoms can have partial use of a full octet of valence electrons.

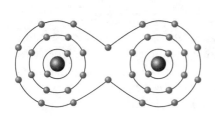

Both positively charged nuclei are held together as a unit by their mutual attraction for the same pair of negatively charged electrons. Both atoms have now attained chemical stability.

Fig. 8-4 Chlorine helps to keep bacteria levels low in swimming pools.

Note that to show the bond between two atoms in electron dot diagrams, their symbols are written very close together. The shared pair of electrons, represented by two dots between the symbols, is considered to be part of each atom's electron cloud. Instead of a pair of dots to represent a shared electron pair in a covalent bond, a line is often used. No ions are formed in this sharing of electrons, so no charges are shown. The result of this covalent bond between chlorine atoms is a diatomic molecule (Cl_2) that appears as a greenish yellow gas that is used, among other things, to disinfect swimming pools.

$$:\ddot{C}l: \ + \ :\ddot{C}l: \ \longrightarrow \ :\ddot{C}l:\ddot{C}l:$$

Electron dot structures of the uncombined elements   **Electron dot structure of the covalently bonded molecule**

Hydrogen is another element that exists naturally as a diatomic molecule. Each hydrogen atom has 1 valence electron, but it needs to have 2 electrons in its valence shell in order to be a stable molecule. Thus, two hydrogen atoms share their single electrons with each other in a covalent bond. This could be represented in either of the following ways:

$$H : H$$
$$H - H$$

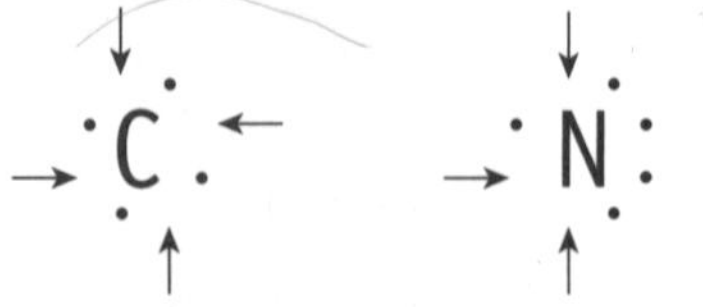

Oxygen is a diatomic molecule as well. Oxygen has six valence electrons, so each atom must *share two electrons* in order to bond. We call this a **double bond.** Double bonds, as you might guess, are stronger than single bonds. We could also represent a double bond with two lines instead of the Lewis structures. A **triple bond** exists when each atom must *share three* electrons in order to bond.

·Ċ· →   · N̈ :

4 valence   5 valence

Fig. 8-5 Nitrogen has three possible sites for bonding; carbon has four.

Diatomic nitrogen is one such compound. Remember that when using the pattern for electron dot notation, each lone electron represents a possible bond with another atom. So oxygen has two possible bonding sites, nitrogen three, carbon four, and hydrogen one.

Diatomic Element	Lewis structures			Structural formula	Type of Covalent Bond
(H$_2$) hydrogen	H $\cdot$ + H $\cdot$	$\longrightarrow$	H : H or	H – H	single bond
(O$_2$) oxygen	$\cdot \ddot{O} :$ + $\cdot \ddot{O} :$	$\longrightarrow$	$: \ddot{O} :: \ddot{O} :$ or	O = O	double bond
(N$_2$) nitrogen	$\cdot \ddot{N} :$ + $\cdot \ddot{N} :$	$\longrightarrow$	$\ddot{N} ::: \ddot{N}$ or	N $\equiv$ N	triple bond

Polyatomic Molecules

The electronegativities of nonmetals are all relatively high; therefore, you might expect that bonds between *different* nonmetals are also covalent. There are numerous common examples of simple molecules composed of nonmetals that are held together by covalent bonds. Water (composed of hydrogen and oxygen), ammonia (composed of hydrogen and nitrogen), and methanol (composed of hydrogen, oxygen, and carbon) are three such compounds. Since they all contain only nonmetals, the bonds within each molecule must be covalent. Molecules composed of two or more different elements are called *polyatomic molecules.* The prefix *poly-* means many.

A water molecule (H$_2$O) is composed of 3 atoms: an oxygen atom and 2 hydrogen atoms. An oxygen atom (Group 16 or VIA) has 6 valence electrons, 2 short of an octet. The 2 hydrogen atoms (Group 1 or IA) have 1 valence electron apiece; each needs 1 more electron to fill its first energy level. When these three atoms chemically combine, oxygen forms 2 covalent bonds with hydrogen. In this way, each atom has access to enough electrons to fill its outer energy level.

Fig. 8-6 Every water molecule is comprised of only three atoms (two hydrogen and one oxygen).

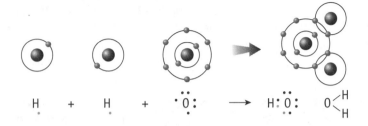

$$H \quad + \quad H \quad + \quad \cdot \ddot{O} : \quad \longrightarrow \quad H : \ddot{O} : \qquad O \!\!<\!\!\!\begin{array}{c} H \\ H \end{array}$$

You should understand that the electrons from one atom are no different from any other atom's electrons. In these representations, however, the electrons in the electron dot diagrams are colored differently to more easily show the source of each.

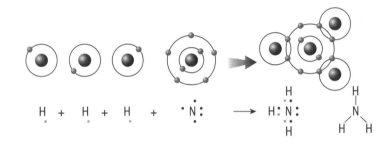

$$H \; + \; H \; + \; H \; + \; \cdot \ddot{N} : \quad \longrightarrow \quad H : \!\!\underset{\displaystyle H}{\overset{\displaystyle H}{N}} : \qquad \underset{H \quad H}{\overset{\displaystyle H}{N}}$$

Before nitrogen atoms react with hydrogen atoms to form ammonia (NH_3), each nitrogen atom (Group 15 or VA) has 5 valence electrons. It needs 3 more electrons to achieve an octet. To do this, it shares each of its 3 unpaired electrons with 3 hydrogen atoms. Each hydrogen atom contributes 1 electron, resulting in 3 shared pairs or 3 covalent bonds.

The third example—a molecule of methanol (CH_3OH)—is a bit more complicated. Methanol, used in the production of many important chemicals, is known as an *organic compound* since it contains carbon. Since each carbon atom (Group 14 or IVA) has 4 valence electrons, it needs 4 more to attain an octet. You already know that oxygen needs 2 more electrons to achieve an octet and hydrogen needs 1 more electron to achieve its full shell.

In a molecule of methanol, carbon shares 3 of its electrons with 3 hydrogen atoms and 1 electron with an oxygen atom, forming a total of 4 covalent bonds. The second covalent bond needed by oxygen forms when it shares a pair with another hydrogen atom. The final result is that all 6 atoms end up with the number of electrons needed for stability—oxygen and carbon with octets and each hydrogen with two. Remember that each shared electron pair is represented by a pair of dots or by a line.

Properties of Covalent Compounds

Whereas the basic unit of an ionic solid is the formula unit, *the basic unit of a covalent compound* is the **molecule.** These molecules *are separate, distinct particles formed by the bonding of a limited but specific number of atoms.* Although there is some attraction between the molecules in a covalent solid, there are still distinct units—molecules—in the solid.

The attraction between the molecules composing a covalent compound is generally not as strong as the attraction between the ions in ionic compounds. This has a significant effect on the physical properties of covalent compounds, causing most of them to have relatively low melting points. All pure compounds that exist as gases at room temperature are covalent compounds (for example, trace CO_2 in the air you breathe). This is also true for most of the compounds that exist as liquids at room temperature.

As with any generality there are exceptions. Many of the molecules that are involved in living organisms are very large molecules called *macromolecules,* with properties quite different from "ordinary" covalent molecules. For example, the proteins, fats, and starches that you eat or that are part of your body are all solid covalent compounds that have reasonably high melting points.

God's design is very evident in the covalent compounds He created to form our bodies. Ionic compounds would tend to be brittle and soluble in water. Metallic solids (see the next section) would be extremely heavy and prevent flexible movement. But the covalent compounds that form the structures of our bodies are strong, lightweight, and flexible. They do not dissolve easily in water (insoluble) and are perfectly suited for maintaining the life God gave us.

SECTION REVIEW QUESTIONS 8C

1. Give three examples of diatomic molecules and draw the Lewis dot structures for each.
2. State a definition for covalent bonding.
3. What kind of molecule is composed of two or more elements?

8D

Section

Metallic Bonding

How do metals "stick together"? What holds the atoms together in pieces of pure aluminum, for example? Each aluminum atom has three valence electrons. To form an ionic bond, it would have to give away all three of these electrons from the third energy level in order to have a filled outermost energy level—the second energy level—located beneath it. But in order for some atoms to give them up, there would have to be others that would accept them. It is hard to imagine why identical atoms would behave differently concerning their attraction for electrons! Some would have to become anions, and others would become cations. There is no simple way to imagine aluminum atoms forming ionic bonds with other aluminum atoms.

Would aluminum atoms form covalent bonds? Again, the answer is no. There is no apparent way that aluminum atoms could share electrons with other aluminum atoms so that all atoms would end up with stable octets.

Fig. 8-8 Aluminum is one of the most common metals used in manufacturing.

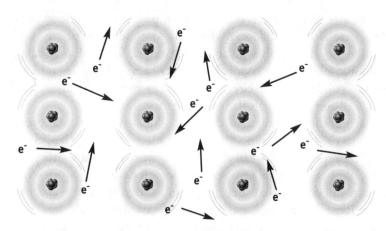

A number of theories have been developed to handle this problem. The one that seems to provide the best explanation for observations is called the **free electron theory.** According to this theory, *all* of the valence electrons in a metal are shared by *all* of the atoms. This differs from sharing of electrons between individual atoms (covalent bonding), which cannot explain the behavior of metals. The sharing in metals is on a grand scale rather than on the level of two, three, or four atoms. You may visualize the **metallic bonds** in a metal such as aluminum as *positive metal ions embedded in a sea of negative electrons.* Many of these valence electrons are free to roam about the entire structure. All the valence electrons are shared by all the nuclei.

Three Types of Bonding

Characteristic	Ionic	Covalent	Metallic
1. Valence electrons	Transferred electrons	Shared electrons	Free electrons
2. Electronegativity	Between elements with very different electronegativities	Between elements with similar high electronegativities	Between elements with similar low electronegativities
3. Types of elements	Between metals and nonmetals	Between nonmetals	Between metals
4. Melting point	Form solids with high melting points	Form solids with low melting points	Form solids with relatively high melting points
5. Solubility	Mostly soluble in water (dissolves easily)	Mostly insoluble in water	Insoluble in water
6. Conductivity	Compounds conduct electricity when melted or dissolved in water.	Compounds do not usually conduct electricity.	Pure metals and alloys conduct electricity in all phases.

IF WATERMELONS GREW ON TREES, SIR ISAAC NEWTON MIGHT NEVER HAVE DISCOVERED GRAVITY.

Wha..Wha What Happened!?!

Fig. 8-10 An ionic bond cannot produce metallic properties any more than an apple tree can produce watermelons.

The free electrons account for several properties unique to metals. These electrons allow solid metals to conduct electricity well because they drift easily with an applied electric force. Most covalent and ionic solids do not conduct electricity because their electrons are held in bonds. The free electrons also allow metals to conduct heat very well and give metals their characteristic shiny luster.

Each of the three types of chemical bonds gives particular properties to the substance in which it is found. Observing the behavior or properties of a substance can reveal its inner structure. Though it is impossible to "see" the ionic bonds in a compound, we can still deduce that they are present if that substance acts like other ionic compounds. Nor can we see covalent bonds; however, if a material has a relatively low melting point and does not dissolve in water, we might predict that it has covalent bonds. We cannot see metallic bonds either, but if a material is hard and shiny and conducts electricity well, metallic bonds are probably present. An ionic bond that results in metallic properties is just as unlikely as an apple tree that grows watermelons!

SECTION REVIEW QUESTIONS 8D

1. What allows a metal to conduct electricity so well?
2. Why is it not possible for aluminum atoms to form covalent bonds with other aluminum atoms?

CHAPTER REVIEW

SCIENTIFICALLY SPEAKING

chemical bonds
electronegativity
ionic bond
ion
anion
cation
Lewis dot structures
crystal lattice
formula unit

electrolyte
covalent bond
diatomic molecule
double bond
triple bond
molecule
free electron theory
metallic bonds

CHAPTER REVIEW QUESTIONS

1. Tell whether each element has a high or low electronegativity: bromine, chlorine, potassium, lithium.

2. Define the *octet rule*. Why is hydrogen an exception to this rule?

3. An element that has a full octet of valence electrons would neither give up nor accept electrons. What group on the periodic table does this describe?

4. What do we call a substance that produces ions as it dissolves in water?

5. Use Lewis dot structures to show the reaction between a calcium atom and two chlorine atoms (calcium chloride, or $CaCl_2$).

6. What do we call the basic unit of a covalent compound?

7. Describe the theory that explains metallic bonds.

FACET REVIEW QUESTIONS

1. How are electrolytes important to the human body?

2. How does Matthew 5:13 explain some of the properties of ionic compounds?

WHAT DID YOU LEARN?

1. Why should ionic compounds be described as composed of formula units instead of molecules?

2. In the upper atmosphere, a layer of triatomic oxygen (three oxygen atoms bonded together) called ozone protects the earth from harmful ultraviolet radiation. What type of bonding would you expect to be present in ozone molecules? Why?

3. Draw the electron dot structure for a molecule of the anesthetic chloroform, which contains 1 carbon atom, 1 hydrogen atom, and 3 chlorine atoms.

4. Helium and chlorine are both gases, yet one is extremely poisonous if inhaled by humans and the other is harmless. Using what you know about electronegativity, determine which gas is the poisonous one and why it causes so much harm to lung cells.

447-7234

Chemical Applications

Chemical Reactions

9A Chemical Formulas

9B Equations

9C Types of Reactions

A large crowd has gathered some distance from a tall, old building in the downtown section of a city. The lot surrounding the building has had a chainlink fence erected around it to keep people at a distance. What could be attracting everyone's attention? The answer is not long in coming. BOOOOM! With a deep roar, clouds of smoke and dust shoot out from the top floors of the building, and then middle floors, and eventually the ground level. Accompanying these clouds are tons of block and mortar that once composed the walls of the structure. In a matter of seconds, a building that stood for decades and took many months to build collapses on itself, reduced to a pile of rubble by carefully placed and timed explosive charges.

People are fascinated by dramatic, awe-inspiring chemical reactions such as those that produce explosions and flames. But the heat, light, and sound you observe in the examples mentioned are just several of the indications that a chemical change has taken place. Most chemical reactions are not so spectacular or destructive.

As you should recall from Chapter 4, a chemical change takes place when substances react to form new substances. Chemical changes may be as different as the rusting of iron, the blast of dynamite or plastic explosives, or combustion within a jet engine. Other chemical changes, such as photosynthesis and the digestion of foods, are common chemical changes that are necessary for our survival. Industry also uses chemical changes to produce plastics, textile fibers, and a vast array of other materials. Many of these reactions play a vital role in our daily lives.

In a chemical change, the participating elements do not change into other elements; their atoms are simply rearranged. Therefore, a chemical change is really a change in the composition or makeup of the substances involved. When nitroglycerine ($C_3H_5N_3O_9$)—used in some dynamites—explodes, the carbon, hydrogen, nitrogen, and oxygen atoms are not destroyed. Instead, the existing bonds between them are broken and new ones are made to form totally different substances: carbon dioxide (CO_2), water (H_2O), nitrogen (N_2), and oxygen (O_2).

How do we know that different substances were formed? Though we cannot watch the individual atoms and molecules change as they react, we can observe indications that a chemical change or reaction has occurred. If a chemical reaction takes place, one or more of the following usually occurs:

1. A solid separates from a liquid.

2. A gas is produced.

3. The colors of the chemicals change permanently.

4. The temperature of the substances changes.

5. Light or sound is produced.

Several of these observations can be made in the explosion of dynamite: gases are produced, colors change, and sound is produced.

Scientists represent chemical changes with two very important tools: the chemical formula and the chemical equation. *Chemical formulas* represent the chemical composition of substances. *Chemical equations* represent the changes that take place in those compositions as the substances react. Let us look at each of these in more detail.

Chemical Formulas

A **chemical formula** is a shorthand way to represent the composition of a pure substance. It specifies the elements present in a compound as well as the actual or relative number of atoms of each. For example, a molecule of methane—present in natural gas—is composed of 1 carbon atom bonded with 4 hydrogen atoms. In formulas, the symbols of the elements are used to tell which kinds of atoms are present. **Subscripts** (numbers below the line) tell how many of each kind of atom are present. If no number is written, a 1 is understood. The formula of methane would therefore be CH_4, not C_1H_4. One simple formula completely describes the chemical makeup of methane.

As is true for any pure substance, methane has a definite composition. Each molecule consists of the same arrangement of 1 carbon atom and 4 hydrogen atoms. A molecule with any other combination of carbon and hydrogen would not be methane.

Molecular models are three-dimensional representations that are used throughout the book to show the relative sizes of atoms or ions in chemical bonding. There are the space-filling model and the ball-and-stick type.

Empirical formulas show only the relative proportion of atoms in a molecule. The chemical formula or molecular formula for glucose is $C_6H_{12}O_6$, and it shows the exact amount of atoms in the molecule. But the empirical formula for glucose is CH_2O.

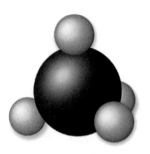

Fig. 9-1 Methane

Oxidation Numbers

How do we know that the formula for table salt is NaCl and not Na_2Cl, $NaCl_2$, or some other ratio of atoms? That is, how do we know that each formula unit of table salt has exactly 1 sodium atom and 1 chlorine atom?

To answer these questions, we could send a sample of table salt to an *analytical chemist.* The analytical chemist would decompose the sample, measure the amounts of its individual elements, and give us an exact formula for it. But this process is time-consuming and expensive. Scientists have developed a shorter, less expensive method that allows them to predict chemical formulas based on the oxidation numbers of the elements. **Oxidation numbers** tell how many electrons an element is likely to gain, lose, or share as it bonds to other atoms.

Oxidation numbers may be positive or negative. As you learned in Chapter 8, atoms may gain, lose, or share electrons with other atoms in order to have 8 valence electrons. The atoms of some elements, such as most metals, have low electronegativity and tend to lose electrons as they bond with other atoms. After losing electrons, these atoms are positively charged. Therefore, these atoms are assigned positive oxidation numbers. Elements whose atoms have high electronegativity tend to gain electrons. Since gaining electrons gives these atoms negative charges, they are assigned negative oxidation numbers.

How are specific numbers assigned? A look at the families of the periodic table can help us answer this question. Each of the *alkali metal* atoms (Group 1 or IA) has 1 valence electron. When an alkali metal atom bonds, it loses this electron and acquires a charge of 1+; therefore, each alkali metal is assigned an oxidation number of +1. The *alkaline-earth metal* atoms (Group 2 or IIA) each have 2 valence electrons. Since they readily lose these electrons as they bond, they are each assigned an oxidation number of +2. Aluminum is in Group 13 (IIIA). It has 3 easily removed valence electrons and has an oxidation number of +3.

The *noble gases* (Group 18 or VIIIA), on the opposite side of the periodic table, have 8 valence electrons in each atom—a complete octet. They do not normally gain, lose, or share electrons. Therefore, they are each assigned an oxidation number of 0. However, their neighbors, the *halogens* (Group 17), have a great tendency to gain 1 electron per atom in order to complete their valence octets. Strongly electronegative elements such as the halogens, which gain control of electrons as they bond, have negative oxidation numbers. When a halogen atom gains an electron, its oxidation number is -1. Atoms of the *oxygen family* (Group 16) have 6 valence electrons—2 fewer than a complete octet. As you should be able to predict, elements in this family are normally assigned oxidation numbers of -2.

From this discussion, you can see that the metals in Groups IA, IIA, and IIIA generally have positive oxidation numbers of the same magnitude as their group numbers. Furthermore, when nonmetals combine with metals, they have a negative oxidation number whose magnitude is found by subtracting the group Roman numeral from 8. Transition metals usually have +1 or +2 oxidation numbers.

A number of elements have more than one oxidation number. For example, nitrogen atoms (Group 15) have 5 valence electrons. In compounds in which nitrogen atoms combine with *less* electronegative elements, they attract the 3 electrons they need to complete their octets. In such cases they are assigned an oxidation number of -3. Yet in other compounds with *more* electronegative elements, nitrogen atoms share, and thereby lose control of, all 5 of their valence electrons. In such cases, nitrogen is assigned an oxidation number of +5.

Iron is another element with multiple oxidation numbers. In rust it has an oxidation number of +3. But how do we know this? We can find the oxidation number of any element in any compound for which we know the formula. Though actually somewhat more complicated, the formula for rust is often given as Fe_2O_3. *The sum of the oxidation numbers of all the atoms in any formula must be 0.* Do you remember the oxidation number of oxygen? It is usually -2. Since there are 3 oxygen atoms in the formula for rust, the sum of their oxidation numbers is -6. In order to produce a total of 0, the oxidation numbers of the iron atoms must total +6. Since there are 2 iron atoms, each has an oxidation number of +3. Iron can also carry an oxidation number of +2. In iron (II) oxide (FeO), for example, the Fe carries a +2 oxidation number to balance the -2 from the one oxygen atom.

Writing Formulas

You can determine the formula for a compound if you know the oxidation numbers of the elements composing it. Table 9-2 gives the common oxidation numbers for a number of elements. Using this information, let us determine the formula for a compound composed of the elements magnesium and chlorine.

The War on Rust

America has an unquenchable desire for the automobile. Despite the rise of air travel, subways, and public transportation, the number of cars in this country is staggering. But where there is iron and steel there is also rust. Car manufacturers have made great strides in reducing the effects of rust on their automobiles. In the past, it was very common to see vehicles on the road that were literally falling apart from rust. Unfortunately, some of those cars were only a few years old. Today, the war on rust is being won by a combination of scientific research and a better understanding of the environment.

The chemical reaction that produces rust is actually very complex, but the basic idea is that oxygen and iron combine to form iron oxide. Rust is simply a common name for iron oxide. The presence of water is a key factor for this chemical reaction to take place, as is the presence of salt. That is why those that live in dry areas, such as the Southwest, have very few problems with rust. The air is not humid, and the rain is not as frequent. Those in humid climates or those who live in places where roads are salted to melt snow have cars that are prime candidates for rust.

What are some ways to combat rust? Automakers are now coating the steel bodies of vehicles with a zinc coating that forms a strong barrier to rust formation. This process is called *galvanization*. In addition, spraying a tarlike coating underneath vehicles protects those hard-to-reach places where rust is hard to prevent. Of course, paint is still the first and most important barrier. In addition to adding beauty to a vehicle, paint must also protect from the battering effects of sunlight, acid rain, and dirt. Some entrepreneurs have capitalized on our fear of rust by offering "rust-proofing" services. It is very difficult to judge the effect of rust-proofing for two reasons. First, carmakers have already done much to make the car as rust resistant as possible before it rolled off the assembly line. Second, the life span of a car varies according to driving habits and climate. It is hard to say whether the money spent on rust-proofing actually extends the life of the car all that much. Most of these techniques probably have some benefit, depending on the use.

The simplest way to protect a car against rust is to keep it out of the weather as much as possible and to wash and wax it regularly. That is probably the best advice (and the most scientific)!

Step 1: First, write the symbols of the two elements next to each other. *Always put the less electronegative element first,* that is, the element that is farther toward the left or bottom of the periodic table.

MgCl

The metal magnesium has a low electronegativity.

The halogen chlorine has a high electronegativity.

Step 2: Now use the periodic table (or Table 9-2) to find the oxidation numbers of the two elements. The oxidation number of magnesium (Group 2) is +2; that of chlorine (Group 17) is -1. Write these numbers above the symbols.

+2 -1
Mg   Cl

One clue tells us immediately that MgCl is not the correct formula: the sum of the formula's oxidation numbers is not zero. *In a neutral compound (one without a net charge), the sum of all the oxidation numbers must be zero.*

Step 3: To remedy the problem, we must add another chlorine atom. The presence of 2 chlorine atoms is indicated by a subscript.

$MgCl_2$

TABLE 9-2 The Oxidation States of the Common Elements

Periods	Group IA	Group IIA	Typical Transition Metals			Group IIIA	Group IVA	Group VA	Group VIA	Group VIIA	Group VIIIA
1	H +1 -1										He 0
2	Li +1	Be +2				B +3	C +4 -4 +2	N -3 +5	O -2	F -1	Ne 0
3	Na +1	Mg +2				Al +3	Si +4	P +5 +3 -3	S -2 +4 +6	Cl -1	Ar 0
4	K +1	Ca +2	Fe +2 +3	Cu +1 +2	Zn +2			As +5		Br -1	Kr 0
5		Sr +2		Ag +1	Cd +2			Sn +4 +2		I -1	
6		Ba +2		Au +1	Hg +1			Pb +2 +4			

There is no subscript beside the Mg. This indicates that there is only 1 magnesium atom in the formula unit. The +2 oxidation number of this single magnesium atom is now balanced by the two -1 oxidation numbers of the chlorine atoms.

$$+2 \quad 2(-1)$$
$$MgCl_2$$

You can use the same process to write the formula for a compound of sodium and sulfur.

The symbols: Na   S

The oxidation numbers: +1   -2
                                Na   S

The balanced formula: 2(+1)   -2
                                Na_2S

The sum of the two +1 oxidation numbers from sodium and the -2 oxidation number from the sulfur atom is 0.

So far we have determined formulas for compounds in which only one of the elements has a subscript. In some compounds, the oxidation numbers of the elements cannot be balanced by simply adding more atoms of one element. In rust, for example, iron (oxidation number +3) is bonded to oxygen (oxidation number -2). After Step 2 of our process, you might run into a roadblock:

The symbols: Fe   O

The oxidation numbers: +3   -2
                                Fe   O

The balanced formula: Fe_2O_3

Whether you put 2 oxygen atoms or 2 iron atoms into the formula, the sum of the charges still will not balance. You could use the trial-and-error method and place a series of different subscripts into the formula until you find two that work, but that process would be time consuming and definitely unscientific! Scientists use a common mathematical tool—the *least common multiple* of the two oxidation numbers—to balance the formula. The least common multiple (LCM) is the smallest number that is a multiple of all the numbers being considered. The LCM of 2 and 3 is 6. Once you have found the LCM of the elements' oxidation numbers, the final step of balancing the formula is short and simple. To find the subscript for each element, divide the LCM by that element's oxidation number, ignoring its sign. The oxidation number of iron is +3.

$$\frac{\text{LCM}}{\text{oxidation number}} = \frac{6}{3} = 2$$

This tells you that the subscript of iron is 2. The oxidation number of oxygen is -2.

$$\frac{\text{LCM}}{\text{oxidation number}} = \frac{6}{2} = 3$$

This tells you that the subscript for the oxygen atom is 3. You can check the subscripts by totalling the oxidation numbers. (Be sure to include the sign in this process!) The sum must equal 0.

$$\begin{array}{rcl} \text{Fe} \quad 2(+3) &=& +6 \\ \underline{\text{O} \quad 3(-2)} &=& \underline{-6} \\ & & 0 \end{array}$$

Since the sum of the oxidation numbers is 0, this formula for rust (Fe_2O_3) must be balanced.

One of the compounds used in safety matches is composed of phosphorus (oxidation number +5) and sulfur (oxidation number -2). How would you determine the formula of this compound?

The symbols: P   S

The oxidation numbers: +5   -2
                          P   S

The LCM of 2 and 5 is 10. If you then divide 10 by the magnitude of each oxidation number, you will find that you need 2 P atoms ($\frac{10}{5} = 2$) and 5 S atoms ($\frac{10}{2} = 5$). These numbers would be indicated by using them as appropriate subscripts in the formula, as shown.

The balanced formula: P_2S_5

Is this formula correct? You should be able to determine this by finding the total of the positive and negative charges to see whether it equals zero.

Polyatomic Ions

There are numerous examples of *ions composed of two or more atoms that are covalently bonded and act as a single particle.* Such ions are known as **polyatomic ions.** They often bond with other ions to form compounds and therefore play an important role in many chemical formulas. Table 9-4 lists some common polyatomic ions. Note that the charge on an ion is equal to its oxidation number.

Milk of magnesia is a compound that contains a polyatomic ion. This common product consists of magnesium ions and hydroxide ions. Its formula can be found by using the three steps previously discussed:

The symbols: Mg^{2+} OH^-

The oxidation numbers: $+2$ -1
Mg OH

The balanced formula: $+2$ $2(-1)$
$Mg(OH)_2$

A polyatomic ion must always be enclosed in parentheses when it has a subscript. Also, when the final formula is written, the ion's charges should be omitted so they do not appear in the formula.

Another common product that contains a polyatomic ion is *baking soda*. Baking soda is the common name for the chemical sodium bicarbonate. Its formula can be determined by the now-familiar three steps:

Fig. 9-3 Various compounds made up of polyatomic ions

The symbols: Na^+ HCO_3^-

The oxidation numbers: $+1$ -1
Na^+ HCO_3^-

The balanced formula: $+1$ -1
$NaHCO_3$

TABLE
9-4 **Polyatomic Ions**

Name	Formula	Oxidation Number
ammonium	NH_4^+	+1
acetate	$C_2H_3O_2^-$	-1
bicarbonate	HCO_3^-	-1
carbonate	CO_3^{--}	-2
hydroxide	OH^-	-1
nitrate	NO_3^-	-1
phosphate	PO_4^{---}	-3
sulfate	SO_4^{--}	-2
sulfite	SO_3^{--}	-2

The first part of every formula should be the element or polyatomic ion that has the positive oxidation number. Ammonium chloride illustrates this principle. The NH_4^+ (oxidation number +1) goes before the highly electronegative halogen Cl^- (oxidation number -1). The compound's formula, based upon these oxidation numbers, is NH_4Cl. As another example, cement contains a compound of both calcium and carbonate ions commonly known as *limestone.* From the periodic table you know that when calcium forms compounds, it becomes a +2 ion. (It is in Group 2.) From Table 9-4 you can see that the formula of the carbonate ion is CO_3^{2-}. Since calcium has a positive oxidation number, it will be written first in the formula. One of each ion will result in no net charge, so the correct formula for limestone is $CaCO_3$.

Naming Compounds

Binary compounds, or *compounds with only two elements,* have both a first and a last name. The first name is simply the name of the first element in the formula (the element with the positive oxidation number). The last name is the name of the second element (the one with the negative oxidation number) with its ending changed to *-ide.*

How would you name common table salt, whose formula is NaCl? The Na represents sodium; therefore, the first name is *sodium.* The Cl represents chlorine, but since it is the second element of a binary compound, the ending (*-ine* in this case) is changed to *-ide.* The last name for NaCl is thus *chloride.* Putting both names together, the correct name for table salt is *sodium chloride.*

The other halogens are treated in the same way as chlorine, where the *-ine* ending is changed to *-ide.* Some other nonmetals that appear frequently in binary compounds undergo name changes that are not quite as straightforward as those for the halogens. For example, sulfur becomes *sulfide,* oxygen becomes *oxide,* phosphorus becomes *phosphide,* and nitrogen becomes *nitride.* You can see

TABLE 9-5 Some Binary Compounds

Formula	Name
NaF	sodium fluoride
K_2S	potassium sulfide
Ag_2O	silver oxide
Zn_3N_2	zinc nitride
$AlBr_3$	aluminum bromide

some examples of binary ionic compounds and their names in Table 9-5. Note that binary compounds do not necessarily contain only two *atoms;* rather, they contain two different elements.

Sometimes two elements can combine in more than one way to form more than one compound. For example, carbon and oxygen can form CO or CO_2. The first compound, CO, is a deadly gas that is formed by the incomplete burning of fuel. Not only is it given off in the exhaust of gasoline engines but it is also formed by improperly adjusted furnaces and kerosene heaters in homes. Breathing carbon monoxide affects your blood so that it cannot carry life-supporting oxygen throughout your body. The second compound, CO_2, is a harmless gas that plants use as they grow. It is also the gas that bubbles out of soft drinks (carbonated beverages). Clearly, there is quite a difference between the two compounds!

To prevent confusion which could have serious consequences, a system of prefixes is used to specify the formula of a binary compound of nonmetals. A prefix placed before one or both of the names in a compound indicates how many atoms of that element are present in each molecule of the compound. Prefixes allow us to distinguish easily between the deadly gas carbon monoxide (CO) and carbon dioxide (CO_2), the gas in soft drinks. Some common prefixes and examples of their uses are listed in the table below.

Note that the prefix *mono-* is needed if there is a single atom of the second element in the formula but is not needed for the first element in the formula. Other prefixes (*di-, tri-,* etc.) are always needed. Thus, both "monocarbon monoxide" and "carbon oxide" are incorrect names for the formula CO.

Sometimes the common name of a compound is used more often than its scientific name. You will probably never hear water (H_2O) called "dihydrogen monoxide"! Nor will you ever hear someone refer to ammonia (NH_3) as "nitrogen trihydride."

TABLE 9-6 Using Prefixes

Prefix	Number	Example
mono-	1	CO carbon monoxide
di-	2	CO_2 carbon dioxide
tri-	3	BCl_3 boron trichloride
tetra-	4	CCl_4 carbon tetrachloride
penta-	5	P_2O_5 diphosphorus pentoxide
hexa-	6	SF_6 sulfur hexafluoride

Chemical Formulas

Fig. 9-7 Transferring Mr. Simons from teaching chemistry to teaching cooking was a big mistake.

However, the common name of a compound does not give us any clues about its chemical formula. Therefore, scientists and students have to memorize the formulas of common substances, such as water and ammonia.

It should be noted that this system of prefixes to name binary compounds is used only for compounds of the nonmetals. Compounds containing metals and nonmetals do not use prefixes in their names. Due to the more complex nature of naming compounds containing metals that can exist in more than one oxidation number, they will not be discussed here.

Compounds that contain polyatomic ions will necessarily be *composed of three or more different elements.* These compounds are named much like binary compounds simply by naming the ions composing them. The first name of the compound is the name of the cation (positive ion) that begins the formula. The last name is derived from the name of the anion. If the anion is a single element, an *-ide* ending is added. If the anion is a polyatomic ion, the ending is never changed to an *-ide* ending. (Hydroxide already has such an ending as part of its name.) *No prefixes indicating the number of each ion are used.* The following table gives examples of names of compounds that contain polyatomic ions.

TABLE
9-8

Compounds with Polyatomic Ions

Formula	Name
NH_4Cl	ammonium chloride
NaOH	sodium hydroxide
K_2CO_3	potassium carbonate
$(NH_4)_3PO_4$	ammonium phosphate
$BaSO_4$	barium sulfate

SECTION REVIEW QUESTIONS 9A

1. Predict the oxidation numbers of the following elements.

   (a) strontium (b) lithium (c) selenium (d) iodine

2. List three of the indications that a chemical reaction has occurred.

3. Give names for the following compounds.

   (a) SO_2 (b) Mg_3N_2 (c) NH_4NO_3

9B

Section

Equations

Scientists use **chemical equations** to describe the changes that take place during a reaction. Do you remember the *law of conservation of matter?* That law states that matter is neither created nor destroyed during a chemical change. The total amount of matter is conserved. That is why chemical reactions can be described by equations. The total amount of matter present before a reaction must be equal to the total amount of matter present after the reaction.

Word and Formula Equations

The following equation describes the reaction between zinc and oxygen:

zinc plus oxygen produces zinc oxide

Equations written out in this way are called *word equations.* Word equations can be useful, but they do not clearly show the conservation of matter during a chemical reaction. To illustrate conservation of matter, scientists use *formula equations.* The formula equation for this reaction is written this way:

$$2Zn + O_2 \rightarrow 2ZnO$$

The symbols in a formula equation show how the atoms of each element are both rearranged and conserved during the reaction. *The formulas on the left side of the arrow* represent the substances known as **reactants.** They show the arrangement of the atoms before the chemical change takes place. *The formulas on the right side of the arrow* represent the **products** of the reaction. These formulas show the arrangement of the atoms after the chemical change. The arrow indicates the direction of the chemical change from the reactants to the products. *The numbers in front of the formulas* are called **coefficients** (KO uh FISH unts). They indicate the number of formula units or molecules of reactants and products needed to balance the equation. According to the law of conservation of matter, the number of atoms of each element must be the same on both sides of the equation. If they are, the equation is said to be balanced. If the number of atoms is not the same, coefficients can be added to balance the equation. *Never change a formula to balance an equation!* The following equation is labeled to show the various parts of a formula equation:

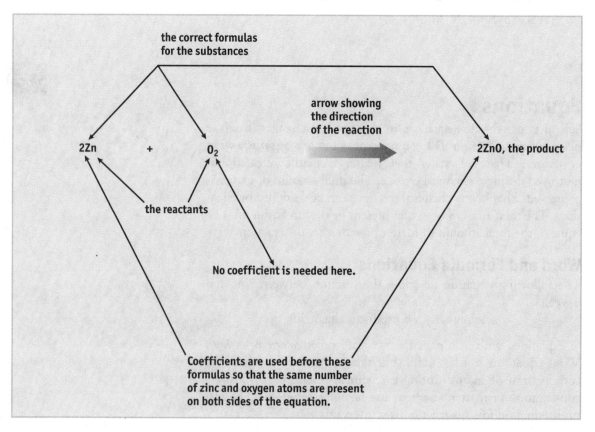

the correct formulas for the substances

arrow showing the direction of the reaction

2Zn + O₂ → 2ZnO, the product

the reactants

No coefficient is needed here.

Coefficients are used before these formulas so that the same number of zinc and oxygen atoms are present on both sides of the equation.

Writing Formula Equations

By following three simple steps, you can write formula equations correctly. Carefully study these steps in the following example.

Example one: How to write balanced equations

Carbon reacts with oxygen to produce carbon dioxide. Write the formula equation for this process.

Step 1: *Write the word equation for the reaction.*

carbon plus oxygen produces carbon dioxide

Step 2: *Write the formula equation for the reaction.* As you write the formula equation, make sure that each formula for carbon is simply C and that the formula for oxygen is O_2. (Remember that free oxygen normally exists as diatomic molecules—two atoms of the same element bonded together.) The formula for carbon dioxide is determined by its name: one carbon and two *(di-)* oxygen atoms, or CO_2.

Now we are ready to write the formula equation:

$$C + O_2 \rightarrow CO_2$$

Step 3: *Balance the formula equation with coefficients, if necessary.* Chemical equations follow the law of conservation of matter; therefore, the same number of atoms of each element must be present on both sides of the equation. Check whether each type of atom is balanced in our equation for the production of carbon dioxide.

There are 2 oxygen atoms on each side.

$$\downarrow \qquad \downarrow$$
$$C + O_2 \rightarrow CO_2$$
$$\uparrow \qquad \uparrow$$

There is 1 carbon atom on each side.

This equation is balanced. No coefficients are necessary.

Example two: How to write balanced equations

Water is formed by the chemical union of hydrogen and oxygen. What equation describes this chemical change?

Step 1: *Write the word equation for the reaction.*
hydrogen plus oxygen produces water

Step 2: *Write the formula equation for this reaction.* Hydrogen and oxygen are both diatomic molecules; therefore, their formulas are H_2 and O_2. The correct formula for water is H_2O. Now we are ready to write the equation for this reaction:

$$H_2 + O_2 \rightarrow H_2O$$

Step 3: *Balance the formula equation with coefficients, if necessary.* Is this equation balanced? There are 2 oxygen atoms on the left side of the equation. How many are on the right side? What coefficient must be added to balance the oxygen atoms? Placing a 2 before the H_2O shows that there are 2 water molecules and, therefore, 2 oxygen atoms in the product. This balances the oxygen atoms.

Note that a coefficient multiplies each atom in the formula, just as a coefficient in an algebraic equation does. Therefore, if you add a 2 in front of the fictitious compound Z_2, you have 4 atoms of Z. A 3 in front of Z_2 would represent 6 atoms of Z, and so forth.

$$H_2 + O_2 \rightarrow 2H_2O$$

Now are the hydrogen atoms balanced? There are 4 hydrogen atoms on the product side of the equation but only 2 on the reactant side. Adding the coefficient 2 to the hydrogen in the reactants balances the hydrogen atoms. We now have the balanced equation for the reaction between hydrogen and oxygen:

$$2H_2 + O_2 \rightarrow 2H_2O$$

Example three: How to write balanced equations

Now let's review the steps for writing formula equations by determining the balanced equation for the formation of rust, Fe_2O_3. Rust is formed by the chemical action of oxygen on iron. (The actual chemical reaction is more complex than this, however.) Oxygen bonds with the iron to form the reddish brown compound known as rust. You can determine the equation that describes this process by applying the three steps that you learned in the previous examples.

Step 1: *Write the word equation for the reaction.*
iron plus oxygen produces rust (iron oxide)

Step 2: *Write the formula equation for this reaction.* Iron is a metal whose symbol is Fe. Oxygen is a diatomic element; therefore, it must be written O_2. The balanced formula for rust was given earlier in this chapter as Fe_2O_3. Can you write the unbalanced formula equation for this reaction?

$$Fe + O_2 \rightarrow Fe_2O_3$$

Step 3: *Balance the formula equation with coefficients.* This equation is not balanced as it stands. There are 2 oxygens on the left side of the equation and 3 oxygens on the right side of the equation. To balance these we must use the least common multiple (LCM) of 2 and 3, or 6. Therefore, you should place a 3 in front of the O_2 and a 2 in front of the Fe_2O_3.

$$Fe + 3O_2 \rightarrow 2Fe_2O_3$$

Sometimes students try to place the 2 in the middle of the rust formula: $Fe_2\ 2O_3$

Never break up a formula with a coefficient. Coefficients always go *before* a formula.

Now the number of oxygen atoms in the reactants ($3 \times 2 = 6$) is equal to the number of oxygen atoms in the products ($2 \times 3 = 6$).

Now you must balance the iron atoms. There is still only 1 iron atom on the left side of the equation, but now there are 4 iron atoms on the right side of the equation ($2 \times 2 = 4$). Placing the coefficient 4 in front of the iron on the left side of the equation will balance the iron atoms. The entire equation is now balanced.

$$4Fe + 3O_2 \rightarrow 2Fe_2O_3$$

In these examples we began the operation of balancing the equation by balancing the oxygen atoms. Since balancing a diatomic molecule (such as oxygen) in an equation often requires the use of a least common multiple, this is often a wise first step. When balancing equations it is often easiest *to first balance the elements that occur in only one substance on each side of the equation.*

SECTION REVIEW QUESTIONS 9B

1. Explain the difference between products and reactants.

2. Balance the following equation for the burning of propane:
$C_3H_8 + O_2 \rightarrow CO_2 + H_2O$.

3. What do we call the numbers we place in front of chemical formulas in order to balance a chemical reaction?

Types of Reactions

Some chemical reactions combine two or more substances into one more complex compound. Other reactions take apart compounds. Some reactions replace one element in a compound with another element, while still other reactions trade elements between two different compounds. These distinctions are the key to classifying chemical reactions. Being able to classify chemical reactions into one of the four general types discussed here can allow you to predict the products of a reaction.

Combination Reactions

Reactions that combine two or more substances into one more complex compound are called **combination reactions.** (They are also sometimes called *synthesis* or *composition reactions.*) A generalized chemical equation for composition reactions shows two reactants, represented by letters, forming one product.

$$X + Y \rightarrow XY$$

The substances that combine can be two elements. For instance, zinc and sulfur combine to form zinc sulfide.

$$Zn + S \rightarrow ZnS$$

Combination reactions may also involve compounds that combine to form a more complex compound. Soft drinks are carbonated by bubbling carbon dioxide under pressure through these beverages. Some of the carbon dioxide reacts with the water in the soft drinks and produces carbonic acid.

$$CO_2 + H_2O \rightarrow H_2CO_3$$

The carbonic acid in the soft drinks gives them their sharp taste.

The trademark of all composition reactions is a single product. A composition reaction may begin with two, three, or even more reactants, but it will always result in only one compound as a product.

Decomposition Reactions

Reactions that decompose, or take apart, the formula units or molecules of a substance are called **decomposition reactions.** The generalized chemical equation of a decomposition reaction shows one reactant breaking apart to form two products.

$$XY \rightarrow X + Y$$

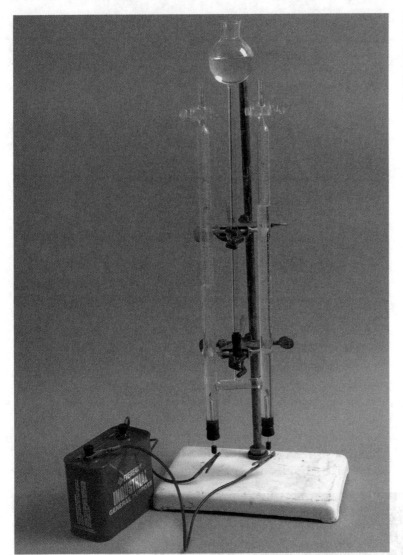

Fig. 9-9 The electrolysis of water is a decomposition reaction. If you look carefully, you can see hydrogen gas trapped in the left column and oxygen gas trapped in the right column. Note that there is twice as much hydrogen as oxygen. The perfect proportion (H_2O) is conserved.

Usually, energy in the form of electricity or heat is necessary to decompose molecules. In the case of water, an electrical current can pull apart its molecules. This type of reaction is called **electrolysis**[1] (ih lek TRAHL uh sis).

$$2H_2O \rightarrow 2H_2 + O_2$$
$$XY \rightarrow X + Y$$

Note: you must have 2 molecules of water on the left to balance the 2 oxygens on the right.

[1] (*electro* = electricity; *lysis* = splitting)

Fig. 9-10 Carbon dioxide is produced when baking soda is heated, making pancakes "fluffy."

Heat can also decompose molecules. For example, when limestone (calcium carbonate) is heated enough, it breaks down into calcium oxide *(quicklime)* and carbon dioxide. Can you write the equation for this reaction?

$$CaCO_3 \xrightarrow{\Delta} CaO + CO_2$$

The Greek letter *delta* (Δ) over the arrow indicates that the reactant must be heated for the reaction to occur.

Another similar reaction occurs when dough or batter containing baking soda (sodium bicarbonate, $NaHCO_3$) is subjected to the heat of an oven or griddle. Gaseous carbon dioxide is produced, which makes the dough or batter "rise":

$$2NaHCO_3 \xrightarrow{\Delta} Na_2CO_3 + CO_2 + H_2O$$

The main reaction in oil refineries is a decomposition reaction. The crude oil that is pumped from oil wells consists of long-chained molecules. Oil refineries heat these large molecules until they break down into smaller, more useful molecules, such as those in gasoline.

Single-replacement Reactions

In a **single-replacement reaction,** one element in an existing compound is replaced by another element. The general chemical equation for single-replacement reactions shows this exchange.

$$XY + Z \rightarrow ZY + X$$

This type of reaction is characterized by an element and a compound on both sides of the arrow.

If a piece of copper is dropped into a silver nitrate solution, copper and silver atoms will exchange places. The copper atoms will become ions and the silver ions will become atoms, resulting in a different uncombined ("free") element on either side of the equation.

$$2AgNO_3 + Cu \rightarrow Cu(NO_3)_2 + 2Ag$$

Note that you need 2 silver nitrates on the left [$2AgNO_3$] to balance the 2 nitrates in copper nitrate [$(NO_3)_2$] on the right.

Copper replaces silver in its compounds because it is said to be "more active" than silver. That is, copper has a greater tendency to be bonded in a compound than silver has. This is because copper loses its valence electrons more readily than silver does.

Many metals react with acids because those metal atoms are more active than the hydrogen atoms in acids. The *more* active metal atoms replace the less active hydrogen atoms. For example, when the metal magnesium is placed in hydrochloric acid, magnesium atoms take the place of the hydrogen in the acid, releasing hydrogen gas. Can you write the balanced formula equation for this reaction?

$$Mg + 2HCl \rightarrow MgCl_2 + H_2$$

Remember that hydrogen exists as diatomic molecules when it is a free, uncombined element.

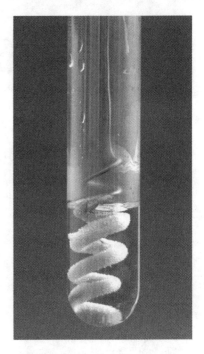

Fig. 9-11 Notice the silver collecting on the copper wire when silver nitrate and copper react.

Fig. 9-12 Hydrogen gas is produced when hydrochloric acid and magnesium react.

Atoms of very active metals, such as sodium and potassium, can even replace one of the hydrogen atoms in a water molecule. This fact can be seen better if the formula for water, H_2O, is written HOH. You can also more easily see how this reaction is classified as a single-replacement reaction.

$$2Na + 2HOH \rightarrow 2NaOH + H_2$$

Again, hydrogen is given off as a diatomic gas.

The Aluminum Revolution

Scientists have tried to make various estimates about the abundance of elements in the earth's crust. As far as we can tell, oxygen is the most abundant element, followed by silicon. You may be surprised to learn that the third most abundant element is aluminum. In fact, 8% of the earth's crust, by weight, is composed of aluminum!

Today we consume over 4,000,000 tons of aluminum each year. But in 1855, aluminum was such a curiosity that a display of 1 kg ingots at New York's Crystal Palace Exhibition caused a sensation. Napoleon III ordered a baby's rattle for Prince LuLu and had one dozen amazingly light spoons manufactured for his wife. The king of Siam was presented with a watch chain of the light metal. The designer of the periodic table, Dmitri Mendeleev, received a vase made of the rare metal in recognition of his scientific contributions. The architects of the Washington Monument chose a 2.7 kg aluminum cap for America's tallest memorial.

What made aluminum so rare? What change allowed aluminum to become one of the most plentiful metals in the world? We can find the answer by exploring the woodshed of a young American chemist named Charles Martin Hall.

Charles Hall was twenty-two. He had just graduated from college in

Ohio and set up a simple laboratory in his woodshed. His college chemistry professor had challenged him to find a cheap way to purify aluminum metal from its ore. Until that time, aluminum had had many potential uses, but it could be separated from its ore only by a costly chemical process that made the metal too expensive to use widely. Hall decided to accept the challenge.

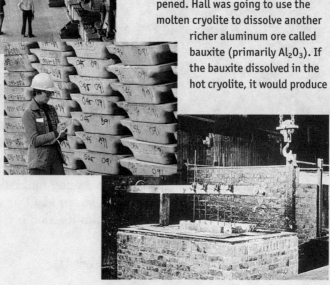

In his search for an inexpensive way to purify aluminum, Hall chose to experiment with *electrolysis*. Chemists had been able to separate many substances by passing an electrical current through a solution. One of the substances would be attracted to one of the current-producing electrodes.

On February 23, 1886, Charles Hall busily prepared to try a new idea. In nature, you cannot find aluminum in its pure state. It is part of compounds contained in minerals we call ores. Isolating metals from ore is called *smelting*. Others had tried to separate aluminum with electricity. Chemists had melted an aluminum ore called cryolite (primarily Na_3AlF_6), but when they passed a current through it, nothing happened. Hall was going to use the molten cryolite to dissolve another richer aluminum ore called bauxite (primarily Al_2O_3). If the bauxite dissolved in the hot cryolite, it would produce aluminum ions that should migrate to one of the electrodes.

Hall slowly added the powdered bauxite to the molten cryolite. It disappeared. Apparently it had dissolved! He then placed two carbon electrodes into the solution and switched on the current. If the experiment succeeded, Hall would find small pieces of aluminum metal on or near the negative carbon rod. After the mixture had cooled, Hall probed the bottom of the container—and found several small bits of pure aluminum! He had done it. He had made aluminum in a very inexpensive way. The process that would one day supply the world with aluminum was born. An exuberant Hall began to publicize his findings and was stunned to discover that a scientist in France had also laid claim to the exact process Hall had discovered. After much debate, it was soon decided that the two scientists had known nothing of each other's research and had arrived at their results independently—at almost the same time in February 1886. Both men were able to gain great wealth because they found several financial backers to help them develop this new way of purifying aluminum.

Charles Hall had used his knowledge of chemistry to develop an important industrial process. He had predicted that aluminum oxide could be separated into aluminum and oxygen. The equation for this process is as follows:

$$2Al_2O_3 \rightarrow 4Al + 3O_2$$

This simple chemical equation provided the key to the entire aluminum industry. Over the years, there have been many different ways devised for smelting aluminum, but all of them are based on the simple decomposition reaction that Charles Hall discovered. Today lightweight, economical aluminum is used in everything from cookware to airplanes. It is easily recyclable, never rusts or flakes, and conducts electricity and heat very well. Aluminum is at its strongest when small amounts of iron and silicon are added. Though it is strong, it is also quite *malleable*—capable of being rolled into coils, drawn out for wire, or even pressed into thin sheets as foil. Its uses are never-ending, and aluminum is getting even more popular as we start the twenty-first century.

Fig. 9-13 Bubbling chlorine through a sodium iodine solution yields iodine, seen here as the brown liquid.

Nonmetals can replace one another in compounds just as metals do. For example, when chlorine gas (Cl_2) is bubbled through a solution of sodium iodide, the more active chlorine atoms take the place of the iodine atoms. This reaction will form a solution of sodium chloride and free diatomic iodine. Write the balanced equation for this reaction.

$$2NaI + Cl_2 \rightarrow 2NaCl + I_2$$

Can you see why this is called a single-replacement reaction? Such a reaction will occur only if the more active element is present in its uncombined ("free") form as a reactant. The activity of the halogens decreases going down the group from fluorine to iodine. Thus, a reaction would not occur if chlorine were bubbled through a solution of sodium fluoride, for example, since chlorine is less active than fluorine.

Double-replacement Reactions

In **double-replacement reactions**, two ionic compounds swap cations and anions with each other. The general chemical equation for a double-replacement reaction shows how the compounds might trade parts. Remember that compounds are written with the positive part first and the negative part second.

$$WX + YZ \rightarrow WZ + YX$$

The order in which the products or reactants are written in the equation is not important, just as it makes no difference whether you add 4 to 6 or 6 to 4—the result is still 10.

Double-replacement reactions usually occur in water solutions. The ions of a compound that can be dissolved (soluble) in water are free to move around and react. The symbol *(aq)* after a formula indicates that the chemical is in a water solution. *Aq* is an abbreviation for *aqueous,* a word which comes from the Latin word for water.

Fig. 9-14 The reaction between lead nitrate and potassium chromate yields the brilliant yellow substance called lead chromate. This precipitate is used most often for paint pigment.

Many double-replacement reactions produce solids that cannot be dissolved in water (insoluble) and settle to the bottom of the solution. These solids are called **precipitates.** Such reactions are therefore often called *precipitation reactions.* The formation of such an insoluble solid (precipitate) is indicated by the symbol *(ppt)* after its formula.

In one double-replacement reaction, sodium chloride and silver nitrate exchange parts to become sodium nitrate and silver chloride. By now, you should be able to write the balanced chemical formula by yourself.

$$NaCl \; (aq) + AgNO_3 \; (aq) \rightarrow NaNO_3 \; (aq) + AgCl \; (ppt)$$

The silver chloride product has a *(ppt)* after its formula, indicating that it is insoluble in water.

In another example of a double-replacement reaction, solutions of sodium sulfate and barium chloride will form soluble sodium chloride and insoluble barium sulfate. You would first write the formulas for all the reactants and products, each followed by the appropriate symbol *(aq)* or *(ppt)*, and then balance the equation.

$$Na_2SO_4 \; (aq) + BaCl_2 \; (aq) \rightarrow BaSO_4 \; (ppt) + 2NaCl \; (aq)$$

Note that the formulas for the products are not dependent upon the subscripts used in the reactant formulas. That is, you would not write Na_2Cl_2 just because the subscripts for Na and Cl are both 2 as they appear in the reactants. Rather, sodium chloride has the balanced formula NaCl. Remember that the number of atoms of each element is balanced by using *coefficients* in the equation.

Exothermic and Endothermic Reactions

Another way to classify reactions is by whether or not they give off or require energy when they occur. Natural gas is used to dry clothes, cook food, heat water, and provide heat in many of our homes. Natural gas—largely methane, CH_4—provides the energy necessary to accomplish these tasks through a chemical reaction known as *combustion,* or burning. As natural gas burns, it combines with oxygen to produce carbon dioxide and water. This chemical reaction may be written as the following equation:

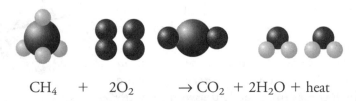

Fig. 9-15 An explosion is a perfect example of an exothermic reaction.

$$CH_4 \quad + \quad 2O_2 \quad \rightarrow CO_2 + 2H_2O + heat$$

Combustion reactions such as this are useful because they give off large quantities of heat. Reactions that give off heat energy are called **exothermic reactions.**[1] It is helpful for you to think of exothermic reactions as those which produce heat, that is, which have heat as a product. Sometimes the word *heat* is placed on the product side of the equation to represent this.

The chemical reaction that powers a car is exothermic. So much heat energy is produced by the combustion of fuel that cars need radiators to remove excess heat from the engine.

As another example, large amounts of heat energy are released as your body utilizes the food you eat. These exothermic reactions are used to keep your body temperature as high as it should be.

On the other hand, some reactions occur only if energy is continually added to the reactants. Reactions that absorb heat energy are called **endothermic reactions.**[2] Most decomposition reactions are endothermic in that they require the input of energy. Some examples discussed earlier include the electrolysis of water, the production of slaked lime, the decomposition of baking soda in batter, and the breaking down of crude oil.

In this case, heat is considered to be a reactant of sorts. Sometimes the word *heat* is written on the reactant side of the equation to represent this, as shown below.

$$CaCO_3 + heat \rightarrow CaO + CO_2$$

Chemical reactions play a big part in our everyday lives. Understanding these reactions is very important if we want to explore the world around us.

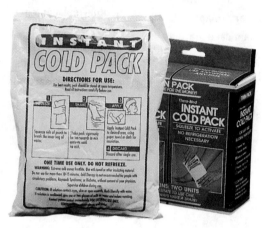

Fig. 9-16 This special ice pack is cold because of a chemical reaction. Two chemicals in separate compartments of the ice pack mix when a seal is broken. As they mix, an endothermic chemical reaction takes place, absorbing thermal energy and making the pack feel cold to the touch.

SECTION REVIEW QUESTIONS 9C

1. Classify each of the following reactions as combination, decomposition, single-replacement, or double-replacement.
   (a) $2Ag_2O \rightarrow 4Ag + O_2$
   (b) $Fe_3O_4 + 4H_2 \rightarrow 4H_2O + 3Fe$
   (c) $2HCl + Cu(OH)_2 \rightarrow 2H_2O + CuCl_2$
2. Explain what is meant by an endothermic reaction. Give an example.

[1]From the Greek *exo*, out, and *therme*, heat
[2]From the Greek *endo*, within, and *therme*, heat

CHAPTER REVIEW

SCIENTIFICALLY SPEAKING

chemical formula	decomposition reactions
subscripts	electrolysis
oxidation numbers	single-replacement reactions
polyatomic ions	double-replacement reactions
binary compounds	
chemical equations	precipitates
reactants	exothermic reactions
products	endothermic reactions
coefficients	
combination reactions	

CHAPTER REVIEW QUESTIONS

1. A clear, colorless solution in one beaker is added to a clear, pale yellow solution in another beaker. Immediately, a dark, reddish solid forms and begins to settle out of solution on the bottom of the beaker. At the same time, the temperature of the mixture rises several degrees. From these observations, list all the indications that would confirm that a chemical reaction has occurred.

2. Write the formula for each of the following compounds: (a) ammonium bicarbonate, (b) aluminum sulfate, (c) dibromine monoxide, (d) calcium phosphate.

3. Write a balanced formula equation for aluminum reacting with phosphoric acid (H_3PO_4) to produce hydrogen gas (a diatomic molecule) and aluminum phosphate.

4. Why is it important that compounds have distinctive names?

5. Dissolving calcium chloride in water will result in the temperature of the solution rising, whereas dissolving ammonium nitrate in water will result in a temperature decrease. Which process is endothermic, and which is exothermic?

6. Our bodies use glucose, $C_6H_{12}O_6$, as a primary source of energy in a complicated series of reactions. The overall reaction is given below. Balance the equation.
$$C_6H_{12}O_6 + O_2 \rightarrow CO_2 + H_2O + energy$$

Facet Review Questions

1. What is galvanization?
2. Describe the experiment Charles Hall performed to isolate aluminum metal from aluminum ore.

What Did You Learn?

1. Give an example of a chemical change that you depend on to do the following: (a) warm your house, (b) give your body energy, (c) get you to school.
2. Of all the elements, which group would most likely be found naturally in an uncombined state?
3. Using hydrogen for fuel is an excellent alternative to gasoline and coal. The simple product of combustion is water. What are some of the reasons you believe it is not used more in our society?
4. Why should you think twice before mixing chemicals found in household cleaners?

Solutions

Chapter

10

"**W**HEW! Is it ever hot today!" you exclaim as you complete your job of weeding the flower beds and vegetable garden. You wipe the beads of sweat from your forehead before they can accumulate to form rivulets that run into your eyes and make them sting. At that moment, your thoughtful mom appears with an insulated cup containing your favorite cola—ice cold! You move to the shade to enjoy this refreshing pause in your yard job.

Having completed the task of weeding, you spray the garden and flower beds with plant fertilizer contained in a hose-end sprayer. That done, you get out the lawn mower, fill the tank with gasoline,

and mow the grass. Slightly panting for air from the exertion, you find still more sweat being produced by your body in its efforts to cool you.

When Dad comes home and surveys your work, he is so pleased that he rewards you by taking you for a short drive in the car to the ocean where you have been longing to go all afternoon.

We live in a world that abounds in solutions, both within and around us. The example above had several: sweat, carbonated beverage, liquid fertilizer, gasoline, air, metal alloys in the automobile and lawn mower, and ocean water.

The oceans of the world are an excellent example of a solution. Ocean water as a solution is far more complex than most of us imagine. Although the main elements that are dissolved in the oceans are sodium and chlorine (from salt), as many as seventy-one other elements have been found. Even precious metals such as gold are present in seawater!

One element found in seawater is bromine. Its concentration there is very small—less than 0.2% of the total mass of dissolved solids—yet the sea is a profitable source of this halogen. The amount in one cubic kilometer of seawater is valued at almost $9 billion at current prices, and there are over a billion cubic kilometers of seawater! Yet bromine makes up only a fraction of the wealth in the oceans.

The ocean is not the only example of a solution with which you are familiar, however. As you can see from the examples given above, solutions can involve not only liquids, but solids and gases as well.

In this chapter we will answer some important questions about solutions. How do materials dissolve? How much material can

Introduction

dissolve? Why does water dissolve so many substances? How are the properties of pure water affected by dissolving something in it? But first we need to find out what a solution really is.

Types of Mixtures

To many people, a solution is an answer to a question or problem. To scientists, however, a solution is something that is all mixed up! A true solution is just that—a mixture. But what kind of mixture is it? In Chapter 5 two kinds of mixtures were identified: heterogeneous (a mixture that appears different in different parts) and homogeneous (a mixture that appears the same, or uniform, in every part). A **solution** may be defined as a homogeneous mixture of two or more substances.

The word *solution* is related to the word *dissolve.* Both words come from the Latin verb *solvere,* meaning "to loosen." In its simplest form, a solution is one substance dissolved in another. The substance that is dissolved is called the **solute** (SAHL yoot). The substance that does the dissolving is called the **solvent** (SAHL vunt). However, there are some cases where it is difficult to determine which substance is *being* dissolved and which one is *doing* the dissolving. For example, automobile antifreeze is a solution of water and ethylene glycol, both liquids. The question may be posed, "Which liquid is dissolving which?" Thus, another more complete definition is that *the solute is the substance in a solution that is present in the smaller amount, while the solvent is the substance present in the larger amount.*

Fig. 10-1 Scientists find it difficult to explain how all the elements found their way into the oceans and why the concentrations are what they are now. From the biblical record, we know there was a great Flood, which likely would have had a dramatic effect on the content of the oceans.

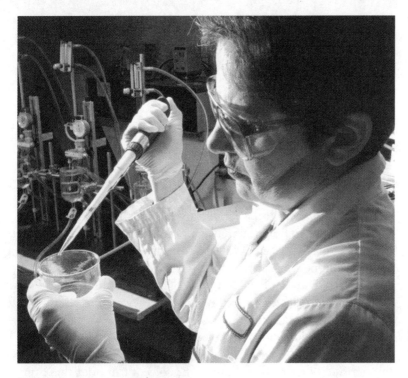

Fig. 10-2 A scientist can analyze a water sample and determine what substances are dissolved in the water.

Homogeneous Mixtures

Sometimes heterogeneous mixtures are mistakenly identified as solutions. People often refer to milk, orange juice, or even muddy water as "solutions." But these mixtures are not true solutions.

If you dissolved some table salt in water, you would not be able to filter out the salt particles from the water. If you examined the salt water under a microscope, it would appear to be homogeneous. These two characteristics (not filterable and homogeneous in appearance) apply to all true solutions.

The salt (solute) in the salt water would not settle out, either, even after a long period of time (assuming water has not evaporated from the mixture). The solutes in a true solution do not settle out.

If you boiled the salt water solution or simply allowed it to stand for some time to evaporate the water, only the salt would be left. Thus, physical changes such as evaporation can be used to separate the components in a solution.

You would also note that the salt water mixture is clear; that is, it is transparent to light. Liquid solutions may have color, but they are always clear (transparent).

Unless you added quite a bit of salt to the water initially, you would find that more could be added and still dissolve. Solutions such as salt water are of variable composition—they can have varying amounts of solute.

The characteristics discussed above apply to all true solutions. They can be summarized as follows:

1. Solutions are homogeneous.
2. Solutes cannot be filtered out.
3. Solutes do not settle out.
4. Components of a solution can be separated by physical means.
5. Liquid solutions are transparent.
6. Solutions are of variable composition.

You can identify true solutions by the size of the particles dissolved in the solvent. If the solute particles are too large, the solvent will not be able to hold them in solution; the solute will eventually settle out. Such a mixture is called a **suspension.** The particles in suspensions can be seen under a microscope (they are heterogeneous), can be filtered out, and will not allow light to pass through easily or without being reflected from the particles (they are not clear).

In a homogeneous mixture the particle size is very small, usually the size of individual ions or molecules. They are so small that they cannot be seen under a microscope, and they can pass right through the pores of filter paper. The solvent can hold these tiny particles in solution permanently. Further, the particles are too small for visible light to be reflected from them, so the mixture appears clear.

Types of Homogeneous Mixtures

When you hear the term *solution,* you probably think of liquids. Liquid solutions are the most common type, but solutions can occur in all three of the ordinary states of matter—solids, liquids, and gases. The state of the solution is normally determined by the state of the solvent, the component present in the larger amount. If the solvent is a gas, the solution is considered gaseous. If the solvent is a solid, the solution is considered solid.

For liquid solutions, the most common solvent is water. The solute may be a solid, a liquid, or a gas. In brine—saltwater solutions—the solute is the solid sodium chloride. Brine is used for everything from packing seafood to gargling for sore throats. In vinegar the solute is a liquid: acetic acid dissolved in water. And in carbonated beverages the solute is a gas: carbon dioxide dissolved in flavored water.

Although it may seem unusual to you, it is quite possible to form solid solutions. Gases, liquids, and other solids can be dissolved in a solid solvent. Hydrogen gas will dissolve into metals such as platinum (Pt) and palladium (Pd). When hydrogen gas is produced industrially, it is purified with palladium. This metal allows hydrogen gas to pass through it but stops all other gases. Certain liquids will also dissolve in solids. For instance, mercury easily dissolves in gold and silver. A *liquid-solid solution* such as this is called an **amalgam** (uh MAL gum). Dentists use a silver amalgam to fill cavities in teeth. Most *solid-solid solutions* are **alloys**—metals or other substances dissolved in a metal. Alloys are generally formed by pouring two molten metals together and letting the mixture cool. Brass is an alloy formed by mixing molten copper and zinc, and bronze is an alloy of copper and tin.

These metal mixtures are useful because the properties of the alloy often differ greatly from those of the ingredients. An alloy of lead, bismuth, tin, and cadmium is called *Wood's metal*. All the ingredient metals have melting points above 200°C, but the alloy melts at only 70°C. This unusual alloy plays a vital part in many automatic sprinkler systems. The water valves of the sprinkler system are made from Wood's metal. When a fire heats the alloy sufficiently, it quickly melts, releasing a shower of water. Many fires have been stopped quickly because of this alloy's unique properties.

Common Alloys

Name	Components	Typical Applications
Brass	Copper, zinc	Plumbing fixtures, musical instruments
Bronze	Copper, tin	Ball bearings, gears, valves
Boral	Aluminum, boron carbide	Neutron absorbers in nuclear reactors
Chromel	Nickel, chromium	Heat sensors (thermocouples)
Eighteen-karat gold	Gold, silver, copper, nickel	Jewelry
Dental amalgam	Silver, mercury	Dental fillings
Monel	Nickel, copper, iron, manganese	Kitchen appliances
Nichrome	Iron, nickel, chromium	Stove heating coils
Solder	Tin, lead	Electrical wire connections
Sterling silver	Silver, copper	Flatware, jewelry
Wood's metal	Bismuth, lead, tin, cadmium	Automatic sprinklers

In a *gaseous solution,* both the solvent and solute must be gases. Liquid or solid solute particles would settle out because they are too large and heavy to be kept suspended by the gaseous solvent. The most common example of a gaseous solution is air—composed of approximately 78 percent nitrogen, 21 percent oxygen, and 1 percent other gases. Since nitrogen is the major component, air could be considered to be a solution of oxygen and other gases (the solutes) dissolved in nitrogen (the solvent). While humid air

Fig. 10-3 Many chemicals are dissolved in the ocean. One ton (907 kg) of seawater contains 25 kg of sodium chloride (table salt), 1.2 kg of magnesium, 0.80 kg of sulfur, 0.36 kg of calcium, 0.34 kg of potassium, 0.06 kg of bromine, and even smaller amounts of the elements strontium, boron, fluorine, iodine, iron, copper, lead, zinc, uranium, silver, and gold.

does contain water as one of the solutes, under these conditions the water is in a gaseous state rather than a liquid state.

There would seem to be nine ways in which the three states of matter could be combined in simple solvent-solute combinations. But for reasons explained in the last paragraph, this number is reduced to seven since liquid-gas and solid-gas solutions cannot exist. The seven possible combinations and the examples given in the following table consist of a single solute in a single solvent, but solutions can be far more complex. Seawater, for example, is a very complex solution containing hundreds of different solids, liquids, and gases!

TABLE 10-4 Solutions

		solvent		
		gas	liquid	solid
solute	gas	gas-gas (O_2 in N_2 air)	gas-liquid (soft drink)	gas-solid (H_2 in Pd)
	liquid	does not exist	liquid-liquid (vinegar)	liquid-solid (amalgam, such as Hg in Ag)
	solid	does not exist	solid-liquid (salt water)	solid-solid (alloy, such as brass)

SECTION REVIEW QUESTIONS 10A

1. Define the term *solution* as used by chemists.
2. If a sample of an alloy contains 10 parts gold and 14 parts copper (10-karat gold), which metal is the solute and which is the solvent?
3. What physical features distinguish solutions and suspensions?

Solubility Factors

Of all the substances that God created, water comes closest to being a universal solvent. In fact, water dissolves so many materials that totally pure water is extremely rare, if not impossible to find. Even a beaker of "pure" water distilled in a laboratory has minute amounts of the components of glass dissolved in it! As it plummets through the sky, rain dissolves atmospheric gases. As it soaks into the ground or runs off rocks, roads, and structures, it dissolves still more substances. By the time water reaches the sea, many elements have been added to the solution we call the ocean.

Water is also the solvent for the complex mixture we know as our blood. Our bodies depend on the staggering array of substances that are both dissolved and suspended in the watery plasma of our circulatory system so they can be transported throughout the body. Some of these substances do not form true solutions, however, because of their size. Small proteins, minerals, sugars, amino acids, vitamins, hormones, and gases are some of the major categories of substances that are dissolved in our blood.

Fig. 10-5 Dirt dissolves easily in water, causing serious erosion problems in places where there is a lack of drainage and plant life to hold the soil together.

The Water Molecule

Water succeeds so well as a solvent because of its unique molecular structure. As you know, each water molecule consists of two hydrogen atoms covalently bonded to a central oxygen atom. But since covalent bonds are not unique to water and since many substances contain hydrogen and oxygen, what makes water special?

Water's unmatched performance as a solvent is due to the unique shape of its molecules. Water molecules are "lopsided": the two hydrogen atoms are bonded to one side of the oxygen atom at an angle of approximately 105° to each other.

The hydrogen atoms are bonded to the central oxygen atom by pairs of shared valence electrons—covalent bonds—which are not shared equally. The more electronegative oxygen atom pulls the shared negative electrons closer to itself than to the hydrogen atoms. This unequal sharing results in an unequal distribution of the negative charges (electrons), causing the molecule to have electrical poles. Oxygen thereby acquires a small negative charge, and hydrogen is left with a small positive charge. The resulting molecule is a **dipole** (DY pole)—not unlike a bar magnet—a molecule with two oppositely charged ends.

The unsymmetrical ("lopsided") shape of a water molecule is important in its role as a solvent. If the molecules were not in a bent shape, the negative charge would be distributed uniformly about the oxygen. It would be like a bar magnet with two north ends and a south center. But the bend in the molecule creates a positive pole and a negative pole. A molecule that has negative and positive poles, such as water, is said to be a **polar molecule**. Such polar molecules react to charges just as a bar magnet reacts to magnetic fields. Its negative side (the oxygen atom) will be attracted to positive charges, and its positive side (the hydrogen atoms) will be attracted to negative charges. These attractions play a key role in the dissolving action of water.

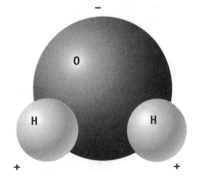

Fig. 10-6 The polarity of the water molecule is caused by the uneven distribution of electrons.

The Solution Process

When water dissolves a substance, it literally pulls the solute particles apart from each other! Consider what happens when an ionic solid such as table salt (sodium chloride) is dissolved in water. You should recall that ionic solids are simply alternating patterns of positive and negative ions. To dissolve the solid, water must break apart this pattern, for only relatively small particles can remain in solution; larger particles will settle out. Somehow, the water molecules must pull the individual ions of the ionic solid apart.

Water does this with its electrical poles. A water molecule's positive pole can attract and pull the negative ions out of the solid,

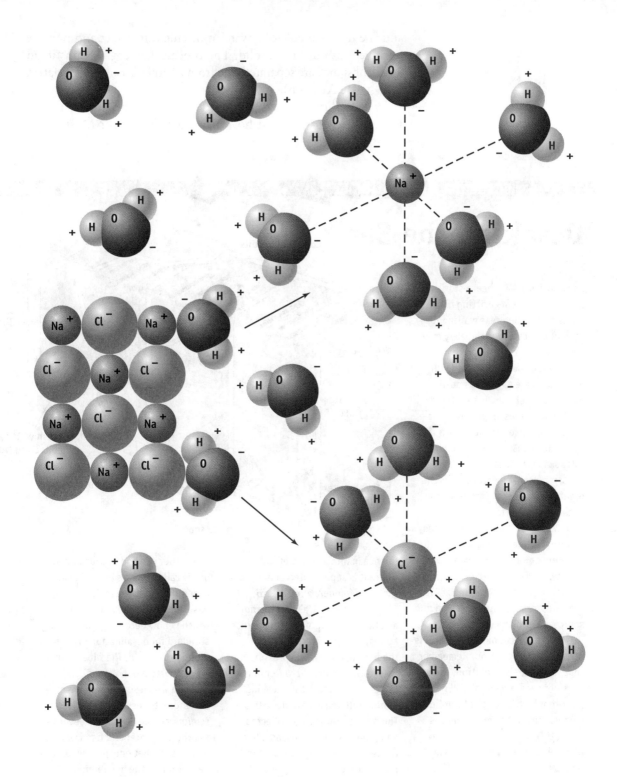

and the negative pole of a water molecule can attract and pull the positive ions out of the solid. The process whereby the ions in an ionic substance are separated one from another is called **dissociation** (dih SO see AY shun).

Water solutions play an important role in the diet of plants. Have you ever wondered how plants get their food? Most of the

Desalting the Sea

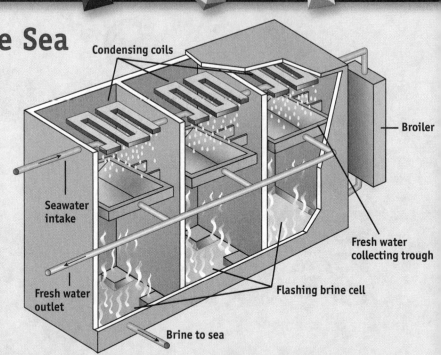

Condensing coils

Broiler

Seawater intake

Fresh water outlet

Fresh water collecting trough

Flashing brine cell

Brine to sea

No doubt you have heard stories of sailors on lifeboats drifting aimlessly on the high seas waiting for someone to rescue them. They may have survived the sinking of the ship—but if they do not get fresh water, they are as good as dead men. The cruel irony is that the billions and billions of gallons of seawater that surround them are unfit for human consumption. Drinking salty seawater does not quench thirst; it intensifies it. Perhaps the greater irony is that three-fourths of the earth's surface is covered with water yet there are vast areas of desert where finding even small amounts of water is an exercise in futility. Now more than ever, scientists are seeking ways to make "useless" oceans a profitable, life-giving source of fresh and clean water.

Getting the salt out of seawater is not an easy proposition. Remember that salt water is a solution. The salt does not separate out of still water, nor can it be filtered out by ordinary means. One of the earliest means (and still one of the most effective) of desalinating seawater is flash distillation. Water is pumped from

the ocean into a series of coils where it is superheated under pressure. The temperature rises to 121°C, which is 21°C over the normal boiling point of water (the more atmospheric pressure, the higher the boiling point). The pressure is then released and the water immediately flashes to steam, leaving behind salt and other impurities. The fresh water is then collected and piped to neighborhoods, businesses, and farms or is stored in large tanks.

Another method in widespread use is called *reverse osmosis,* sometimes abbreviated as RO. Dupont has developed the Permasep filter, which is now becoming the industry standard for desalination efforts around the world. The filter is made up of a system of hollow fibers through which seawater is forced under great pressure. A special *semipermeable membrane* separating the salt water and fresh water guarantees that only pure water can pass through the membrane, not

nutrients necessary for plants are water-soluble (they dissolve in water). As water passes through soil, it dissolves the many different minerals on a plant's daily menu. The plant feeds on these delicacies through its root system and transports them in solution to its stems and leaves. If these substances were not in solution, plants could not get their food.

salt. Under normal conditions, the pure water would flow through the membrane into the salt water, effectively diluting the salt water. This process is called *osmosis,* a naturally occurring phenomenon by which water flows from an area of high concentration (fresh water) to an area of lower concentration (salt water). In time, the salt water will become less and less concentrated as the fresh water "fills" the salt solution. Although this process of osmotic equilibrium is interesting, it does not get the salt out of the seawater—it just adds fresh water to it. But what if we could reverse the process so that pure water actually flows out of solution, leaving the salt behind? If pressure is applied to the salt water side, the flow is reversed so that the salt is left behind and fresh water flows through the membrane, hence the term reverse osmosis.

As the world's population grows, the availability of fresh water

becomes more crucial. Only recently have desalination efforts become profitable, widespread enterprises. One hundred and twenty countries now have some type of desalination program for salt water or brackish water. Desalination plants around the world now produce over 13.2 million m^3 of water *each day!* That is 5.3 billion gallons of water, enough to give every man, woman, and child on the planet a gallon of water every day, with another billion gallons to spare. Most desalination plants are located in the dry regions of the Middle East and North Africa, but they can also be found on many islands, the Florida Keys, and the California coast.

Desalination does have its drawbacks. Even though the demand is great, the vast majority of the world still gets its potable (drinkable) water from freshwater sources—lakes, reservoirs, rivers, and ground water. Of every hundred gallons of seawater pumped into a desalina-

tion plant, only fifteen to forty gallons become potable water. The extremely salty brine that is left over from the process is often dumped back into the ocean, a practice that irritates some conservationists. It takes electricity, manpower, and specialized equipment to run these plants, and they must be located close to the ocean—prime real estate that homeowners are reluctant to give up. For customers, desalinated water is more expensive than ground water, but the prices continue to go down as the technology for reverse osmosis becomes more advanced. Besides, if fresh water had to be shipped in from faraway sources, the cost would be even greater.

Since the beginning of time, man has settled in areas where fresh water was plentiful. Look on a map sometime and see how many cities are located along lakes and rivers. Even a small oasis in the desert is a welcome area because of the precious water that flows there. But as the population of coastal and desert areas continues to grow, it has become clear that converting seawater to fresh water is no longer a novelty but a necessity in some places on the earth.

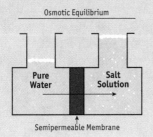

Osmotic Equilibrium

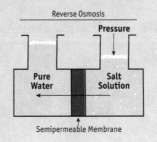

Reverse Osmosis

A substance is **soluble** (SAHL yuh bul) when it is able to be dissolved by a solvent. When water molecules come in contact with water-soluble materials, they attract them by opposite charges, force their way between clusters of solute particles, and break them apart. By so doing, they keep the solute particles from regrouping.

Water's ability to dissolve substances is astounding. For example, 100 mL of water at 100°C can dissolve 871 g of ammonium nitrate, a common fertilizer. This capacity is measured in terms of solubility. **Solubility** is the maximum amount of solute that will dissolve in a given amount of solvent at a given temperature. For water solutions, solubility is usually expressed in grams of solute per 100 mL of water. Here is a table of solubilities in water at room temperature for some common substances.

TABLE 10-7

Solubility of Common Substances		
Name	Formula	Solubility (g solute/100 mL of H_2O at 25°C)
Sodium bicarbonate (baking soda)	$NaHCO_3$	9.2
Calcium carbonate (chalk)	$CaCO_3$	0.0015
Carbon dioxide (gas)	CO_2	0.17
Ethyl alcohol (liquid)	C_2H_5OH	Infinitely soluble
Sucrose (sugar)	$C_{12}H_{22}O_{11}$	210
Sodium chloride (table salt)	NaCl	36

The Limits of Solubility

Some substances are infinitely soluble in each other. That means that they are soluble in one another in all proportions. In the chart above, ethyl alcohol (ethanol) is listed as being infinitely soluble in water. This is a very interesting case, for something unusual happens when water and ethyl alcohol mix. If 100 mL of ethyl alcohol is mixed with 100 mL of water, you would expect the total solution to measure 200 mL. But the resulting solution will actually measure only 198 mL—a loss of 1%. Where did the missing 2 mL go?

The rule that governs the solubility of substances is *"like dissolves like."* We call this **miscibility.** Alcohol dissolves well in water, so we

Water   **Ethyl alcohol**

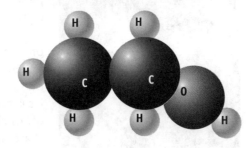

say that alcohol and water are miscible. If the two liquids do not form a solution, they are immiscible. One substance is likely to dissolve another substance if they have similar structures. Examine the structures of water and ethyl alcohol. They both have a special oxygen-hydrogen combination—the *OH* or *hydroxyl group.*

This similarity allows them to attract one another, flow freely over each other, and mix completely. In fact, water molecules can pack between the alcohol molecules. Such an arrangement is more tightly packed than the molecules of the alcohol alone. That is why the total volume of the solution is less than the sum of the individual volumes of the water and the alcohol.

Most substances have a limit on how much can be dissolved. This limit is based on the characteristics of both the solute and the solvent. Some substances, like the fertilizer ammonium nitrate, dissociate very easily. It does not take much effort for water to separate the ammonium and the nitrate ions and keep them in solution. Solubility also depends on temperature. If more solute is dissolved than can be contained by the solvent at a specific temperature, the excess will settle to the bottom as a solid **precipitate.** The remaining solution is said to be **saturated** at that temperature. Under special conditions, when more solute is dissolved than normal at a temperature, the solution is **supersaturated.** A supersaturated solution is very unstable, and if a

Fig. 10-8 Crystals can form in supersaturated solutions.

Fig. 10-9 Placing a piece of chalk in a glass of water proves that calcium carbonate is insoluble.

small seed crystal is suspended in the solution, the extra solute present will precipate onto the crystal.

Certain substances cannot be broken apart by water molecules. Because these will not go into solution, they are said to be **insoluble.** Look up the solubility of calcium carbonate in the chart on page 226. This amount is so slight that calcium carbonate is considered insoluble. You could test it by placing a piece of chalk in a glass of water. No matter how hard you stirred,

How to Get Squeaky Clean

Why do we use soaps to get things clean? The answer lies in a basic principle of solution chemistry: like dissolves like. Water is a polar molecule. Dirt and greasy oils are usually nonpolar molecules. They will have nothing to do with water. Since water cannot dissolve them, these oil and dirt particles would remain on our clothing and us unless there were

a go-between that could dissolve them and yet be soluble in water. Soap is the perfect middleman for the job!

Look at the structure of a typical soap molecule. The molecule itself resembles both polar and nonpolar molecules. It is actually slightly related to a fat molecule (oils are fats). In fact, your great-great-grandmother

probably made soap by mixing beef fat and lye in a giant kettle over a blazing kitchen fire. The part of the molecule that is like oils and dirt is the long chain of carbons. This nonpolar end pulls the dirt and oils off your skin and clothes. The opposite end has ionic charges. These charges make this end polar, and therefore soluble in water. Once the

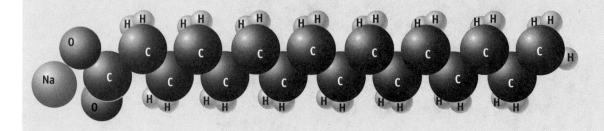

10 Solutions

you would not be able to get a noticeable amount of the calcium carbonate to dissolve.

A common combination of insoluble liquids is Italian (or oil-and-vinegar) salad dressing. The nonpolar oil molecules cannot mix with the polar water molecules of vinegar. The rule that like dissolves like can certainly be applied here. Shake the mixture and it appears for a few moments that the oil and vinegar have mixed, but the unlike liquids will soon separate into two distinct layers.

Fig. 10-10 Shaking mixes oil and vinegar for only a short time. They will soon separate into two layers.

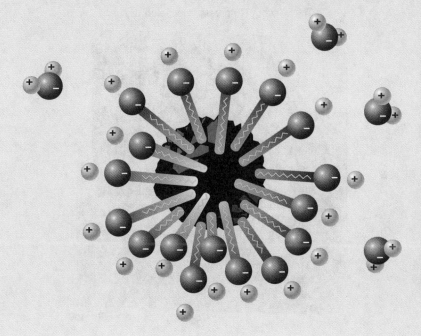

nonpolar end grabs the dirt and oils, all we have to do is rinse the soap molecules away with the water!

Soap is produced by combining lye (sodium hydroxide) with animal or vegetable fats, a process we call saponification. The first soaps were probably produced as early as 2000 B.C., but no one was really interested in them. In fact, the grand baths the Romans built were probably absent of soap. Even the great Cleopatra of Egypt was "soapless." She is said to have used very fine sand for its abrasive properties. It wasn't until the thirteenth century that soap making became an industry in Europe. In the early history of the United States, soap making in the home was as common as spring cleaning or crop harvesting. Common household items provided the materials. Lye was obtained from ashes, and the fat came from butchered animals. Animal fat and ashes were saved so that most homes had a fairly large quantity for making soap.

Factors That Affect Solubility

At 10°C, 100 mL of water can dissolve 118 g of ammonium nitrate, while 100 mL of boiling water can dissolve 871 g of the same fertilizer. *Temperature* obviously affects solubility. Though there are some exceptions, most solids become more soluble in liquids as the temperature increases. The weakened structure produced by heating the solid solute is more easily broken apart by the liquid solvent.

A temperature increase also affects the solvent by causing its molecules to move more rapidly and spread apart (see Chapter 4). This allows more room between the solvent molecules which solute particles can occupy. The result is an increase in the solubility of the solute.

The following chart shows the relationship between temperature and solubility in water for several ionic substances. Note that one of them is only slightly affected by temperature, while the solubility of others increases dramatically as the temperature rises.

Generally, solutions of two liquids follow the same trend as solid solutes in liquid solvents. But when gases are dissolved in liquids, an increase in temperature has the opposite effect. When a cold bottle or can of a carbonated drink is uncapped, most of the car-

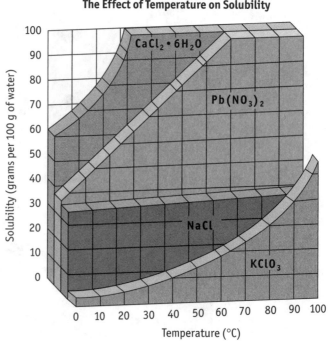

Table 10-11
The Effect of Temperature on Solubility

bon dioxide stays dissolved in the solution. But if you open a warm bottle or can of soft drink, you will have a mess on your hands—literally! As the gas escapes rapidly from the warm solution, it forces the liquid out of the container. As the temperature increases, the solubility of the carbon dioxide in water decreases; the gas remained in the solution only because the bottle was sealed. Once the seal is broken, the carbon dioxide escapes and you are left with a flat-tasting soda.

Fig. 10-12 These active bass get more oxygen from the water when it is very cold.

What is true for carbon dioxide is also true for oxygen. More oxygen dissolves in cold water than in warm water. Very active fish such as bass thrive better in cold streams because the water contains more of the oxygen that they need. Being forced to live in shallow water which has been warmed by the sun may result in their suffocation. You could observe the decreased solubility of air in water by allowing a cold glass of water to warm to room temperature. The small bubbles you see forming on the inside of the glass are a result of air coming out of solution.

Another factor that affects the solubility of a gas in a liquid is the pressure of the air or other gases that are touching the liquid. This relationship was studied by William Henry. In 1801 he formulated a law that we now call **Henry's law**. It states that *the greater the pressure on a liquid, the greater the mass of the gas that will remain dissolved at any given temperature.* That is why the gas remains in the soft drink while it is sealed. But as soon as the pressure is released, the gas begins to escape.

Fig. 10-13 The CO_2 gas escaping from the glass tells us the drink is lukewarm.

Factors That Affect Solubility
The nature of the solute and the solvent
All solutions: *Like dissolves like.* The more alike the solute and the solvent, the more soluble they will be.
Temperature
Solids in liquids: Solubility generally increases with a rise in temperature.
Liquids in liquids: Solubility generally increases with a rise in temperature.
Gases in liquids: Solubility decreases with a rise in temperature.
Pressure
Gases in liquids: Solubility increases with pressure.
Liquids or solids in liquids: No effect

Factors That Affect the Rate of Solution

It is important to understand the distinction between *solubility,* just discussed, and *rate of solution.* Three primary factors help dictate the rate at which a solute dissolves.

Temperature is one factor that has an effect on the rate at which a solute dissolves. Since the solvent molecules move faster at a higher temperature, more of them can come in contact with solute particles in a given amount of time, thereby speeding the solution process. Sweetened tea is often prepared by dissolving sugar in the tea while it is hot. The more energetic water molecules rapidly "attack" the sugar crystal, pulling it apart, distributing the molecules throughout the solution, and exposing fresh areas to solvent. When sugar is added to cooled tea, it does not dissolve as quickly; a large amount of sugar may remain at the bottom of the container.

If you add some sugar or other sweetener to a glass of tea or other beverage, you probably instinctively stir it to hasten its solution. *Stirring* is the second factor that has the effect of bringing more solvent molecules in contact with the solute more quickly and hastening its rate of solution.

The third factor affecting the rate at which a solute dissolves is the size of particles of the parent solute. For example, a sugar cube dissolves more slowly than an equal amount of granulated sugar at the same temperature. Why? Although the mass of the two sugar samples is the same, thousands of tiny granules have more surface area than does one large cube. As a result, there can be more collisions of the solvent with the solute in a given time; more rapid dissolution results. Thus, *grinding* or *crushing* the solute increases the rate of solution.

1. Which would you expect to be more soluble in water?
   Hints: water can be written as H_2O or HOH
   >   "like dissolves like"
   >   water is a polar molecule

   (a) propyl alcohol (C_3H_7OH) or butane (C_4H_{10})

   (b) cholesterol (a nonpolar solid) or glucose (a polar solid)

2. What happens to solvent molecules as the temperature increases?

3. How do you associate Henry's law with opening a soft drink can?

10C

Section

Concentration

Have you ever been served a glass of fruit punch that was too weak? Or perhaps you have been served lemonade that was too strong. Generally speaking, we could say that the fruit punch was too *dilute* and the lemonade was too *concentrated.* You may use these terms frequently, but do you understand what they mean? When you make orange juice you dilute the frozen concentrate; when you make lemonade you dilute the pure lemon juice or frozen concentrate; and when you make a powdered drink you add water to the concentrated powder. But what tells us whether the substance is dilute or concentrated?

Generally, the terms *dilute* and *concentrated* refer to the number of solute particles that are in solution. If there are just a few dissolved particles, the solution is dilute. If the solution is close to its saturation point (maximum amount of solute a solvent can hold), it is concentrated. As you can see, these terms are not very precise. They are relative terms that help us distinguish between solutions of the same substances but are not practical for solutes that differ greatly in their solubility. For example, 100 mL of a solution containing 0.0014 g of calcium carbonate (solubility at 25°C = 0.0015 g/100 mL) would be considered concentrated. But 100 mL of a solution containing the same amount of table salt (solubility at 25°C = 36 g/100 mL) would be very dilute! Scientists need a more precise way to measure the concentration of a solution.

Concentration Measurements

Scientists can specify the concentration of a solution in several ways. One is called *mass-percent,* or **percentage by mass.** You should understand that the word *percent* literally means "per hundred," since *cent* means "hundred." Thus, the number you are given as the concentration is the number of grams of solute needed for every 100 g of solution. Simply subtract it from 100 to obtain the amount of water you need to make the solution. If you are asked for some amount other than 100 g of solution, simply use proportional amounts of each.

Patients in the hospital often receive a solution of sodium chloride, known as *physiological saline.* The concentration of NaCl in it is 0.9%. To prepare it, you would dissolve 0.9 g NaCl in 99.1 g water (100.0 g − 0.9 g). This would give 100.0 g of solution. You could also dissolve 0.45 g NaCl in 49.55 g water if you wanted only 50.00 g of solution.

Another way to indicate the concentration of a solution is by **specific gravity.** Chemical manufacturers list specific gravities on product labels to specify the concentration of a prepared solution. Concentrated sulfuric acid, a very caustic chemical that is used in laboratories and industry, is labeled with a specific gravity of 1.84. Specific gravity is simply a comparison of the density of a solution to the density of water. If it has a number greater than 1, it is more dense than water. The density of water is 1 g/mL. A specific gravity less than 1 means it is "thinner" or less dense than water.

Automobile mechanics make use of specific gravity when they test car batteries. They use a device called a hydrometer to suck up a certain volume of acid from the battery. Inside the hydrometer is a calibrated floater which is buoyed up to a level that is related to the specific gravity of the battery acid solution. The greater the concentration of sulfuric acid, the greater the specific gravity of the solution and the higher the floater rides. As the battery loses its charge, the amount of acid in solution decreases, lowering the specific gravity of the liquid. As a result, the floater sinks deeper in the battery acid solution.

Specific gravity is also used to test the degree of protection afforded by an automobile's radiator antifreeze mixture. A hydrometer, much like that used for batteries but calibrated for use with antifreeze, is used to determine the concentration of ethylene glycol in the ethylene glycol-water mixture. The calibration is such that the freezing point of the mixture can then be determined.

Oftentimes the addition of a solute will affect the boiling point, the freezing point, or both. For example, dissolving salt in water makes the water boil at a higher temperature. This effect is true for all solid solutes and many liquid solutes and is called **boiling point elevation.** Some liquid solutes such as alcohol actually lower the boiling point of water.

Another effect of solution concentration is **freezing point depression.** You may have had the experience of using salt in an ice-cream freezer to lower the freezing point of the water surrounding the canister of ice-cream mix. The greater the concentration of salt, the more the freezing point was lowered.

When water freezes, the molecules must move into certain definite locations to form the regular patterns found in crystals of ice. Solute ions hinder the water molecules from getting to their proper places. The greater the concentration of the solute, the greater the hindrance, and the more the solution must be cooled to make it freeze.

The antifreeze used in cars is an important application of both boiling point elevation and freezing point depression. Adding antifreeze to the water in a radiator produces a mixture that has a considerably lower freezing point and a higher boiling point than water alone. The engine's coolant is now in little danger of freezing, expanding, and damaging the engine block when a car is left outside in below-zero weather. Nor is it as likely to boil over in hot summer driving.

Fig. 10-14 Salt lowers the freezing point of the water surrounding the ice cream.

SECTION REVIEW QUESTIONS 10C

1. How much glucose would you need to prepare 100.0 g of a 2.5% glucose solution? How much water?

2. Is the density (in g/mL) of a solution that has a specific gravity of 1.08 greater than or less than that of water?

3. Which has the lower freezing point, seawater or lake water?

CHAPTER REVIEW

SCIENTIFICALLY SPEAKING

solution	miscibility
solute	precipitate
solvent	saturated
suspension	supersaturated
amalgam	insoluble
alloys	Henry's law
dipole	percentage by mass
polar molecule	specific gravity
dissociation	boiling point elevation
soluble	freezing point
solubility	depression

CHAPTER REVIEW QUESTIONS

1. Identify the solute and the solvent in each of the following solutions.

   (a) 15 g baking soda and 100 mL water

   (b) 35 g silver and 30 g mercury

   (c) 1.00 L ethylene glycol and 875 mL water

   (d) 2 g zinc and 10 g copper

2. What is one way that salt could be taken out of a saltwater solution?

3. How would you prepare a 100 g solution of 1.9% $NaHCO_3$?

4. What do we call a molecule that has negative and positive poles?

5. Describe what usually happens to the boiling point and the freezing point of a solvent with the addition of a solute.

FACET REVIEW QUESTIONS

1. What are the two main methods of desalination?

2. Why are soaps and detergents so effective as cleaning agents?

WHAT DID YOU LEARN?

1. Make a list of everyday solutions in which water is the solvent. List as many as you can, including substances you may find in the kitchen, the medicine cabinet, and even the car.

2. Using the principles involved in the rule of thumb "like dissolves like," explain why some substances, such as oil and water, do not mix.

3. Scuba divers that ascend too quickly from deep dives can form bubbles of air in the bloodstream. We call this condition the "bends," and it is quite common, even among the most experienced divers. Why do these bubbles form, and do you think the "bends" is harmful?

Acids, Bases, and Salts

Chapter

11

Have you ever wondered what gives foods their distinctive flavors? Some foods are sour, others are bitter, and many are salty. Foods can be sour because of the presence of *acids*. Grapes contain tartaric acid; citrus fruits contain citric acid and ascorbic acid (vitamin C); carbonated beverages contain carbonic acid and sometimes phosphoric acid; apples contain malic acid; and many vegetables contain ascorbic acid.

Other foods are bitter because of the presence of *bases* in them. Unsweetened chocolate, raw almonds, and certain kinds of herbs are examples in this category.

Salt remains the most popular food seasoning. Look inside a restaurant and you will find it on every table. As you will learn in this chapter, there are many more salts than just table salt. Some of them are used for seasoning food, but many are not. Acids and bases can combine to form many different salts.

In the first two chapters of this unit, you studied how substances in general react and how they dissolve in solutions. In this chapter we will study three specific types of substances—acids, bases, and salts—and how to identify them by the unique ways they react in solutions.

Comparing Acids and Bases

What makes a fire ant's sting painful? The irritation is caused by an **acid.** When a fire ant stings you, it injects formic acid under your skin. As the formic acid dissolves in the water of your cells, its molecules produce a specific ion that irritates the cells and causes the sting to hurt.

The Acid Ion

So what makes formic acid an acid? A formic acid molecule (HCOOH), like all acids, is capable of donating hydrogen ions (H^+) to another substance, leaving "behind" its electron. The hydrogen atom is said to be ionizable, and the process whereby a molecule gives up an ion is called **ionization.**

When formic acid dissolves in water, its ionizable hydrogen atom breaks away from the rest of the formic acid molecule to form positive and negative ions. The less electronegative hydrogen atom leaves behind the entire electron pair it was sharing with the more electronegative oxygen atom. This leaves oxygen with an extra electron—the one that came from the hydrogen atom—to give it a negative charge. When it breaks off, hydrogen has no electrons, just a proton from its nucleus, leaving it with a positive charge.

Fig. 11-1 The pain from a fire ant's sting comes from the formic acid the ant injects into its victim's skin.

Formic acid molecule

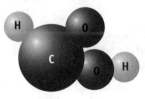

Ionized formic acid molecule

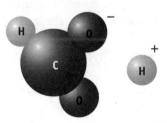

But can such a proton exist by itself? No. A hydrogen ion (proton) is too unstable to exist alone in solution; it is immediately donated to a water molecule. Two chemists in the 1920s pointed out that acids were *proton donors* and that bases were *proton acceptors*. We call this the **Brönsted-Lowry** definition of an acid.

1. Some molecules can behave as acids or bases depending on what the other reactants are.

2. Acid-base reactions do not always have to occur in aqueous solution.

3. A base is any molecule that accepts protons (H^+), not just OH^-.

The ion that is formed by the donation of a proton to one water molecule—H_3O^+—is called a **hydronium** (hye DRO nee um) **ion.** In actuality, investigations have shown that four water molecules are usually needed for this reaction, but for simplicity only one is generally written.

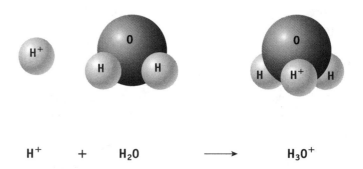

$$H^+ \quad + \quad H_2O \quad \longrightarrow \quad H_3O^+$$

Hydronium ions can be powerful irritants under the proper conditions. Ant stings hurt because formic acid produces hydronium ions in the water solutions of your cells.

You may have seen a product called *muriatic acid* in a hardware or building supply store. The chemical name for this cleaning agent is *hydrochloric acid,* which has the formula HCl—an aqueous solution of hydrogen chloride gas. Hydrochloric acid has many industrial uses, including cleaning metals and brick, refining sugar, and producing corn syrup. Your body uses it about three times a day (more if you eat snacks!). How? Hydrochloric acid is a key ingredient in your stomach's digestive juices.

How is hydrogen chloride an acid according to the definition for acids? That is, how does it produce hydronium ions in water solution? When hydrogen chloride molecules (HCl) dissolve in water, the water molecules pull apart (ionize) the HCl molecules into hydrogen ions (protons) and chloride ions. The hydrogen ions are thus attached to water molecules and form hydronium ions while the chloride ions remain in solution. The following equation describes the process:

$$HCl + H_2O \rightarrow H^+ + Cl^- + H_2O \rightarrow H_3O^+ + Cl^-$$

We can see by this reaction that hydrogen chloride produces hydronium ions in water and is thus an acid by our definition.

TABLE

11-2 Acids in Common Substances

Acid	Substance
Acetic acid	Vinegar
Citric acid	Citrus fruit
Ascorbic acid	Vitamin C, vegetables
Carbonic acid	Soft drinks
Lactic acid	Sour milk
Formic acid	Ant stings
Oxalic acid	Rhubarb

Properties of Acids

What taste is common to lemons, grapefruit, and dill pickles? Sourness. Each of these foods tastes sour because it contains an acid. Grapefruit and lemons contain *citric acid,* and dill pickles contain *acetic acid,* which they absorb from the vinegar used to pickle them. Sourness is the typical taste of an acid. Though the sour or tart taste of foods can be traced to the presence of the hydronium ion, *it is NEVER advisable to touch or taste any chemicals in a laboratory to see if they are acids!*

Acids have a number of other characteristic properties. One of the first properties of acids to be discovered was the ability of acid solutions to conduct electricity. In the late nineteenth century, a Swedish chemist named Svante Arrhenius discovered that solutions of certain substances conducted electricity. He called these substances *electrolytes* because of this property, concluding that electrolytes conduct electricity because of the ions that they produce in solution. All acids are electrolytes, as are bases and salts, the other compounds discussed in this chapter; these three groups of compounds are classified according to the type of ions each produces in solution. The **Arrhenius** concept of acids says that an acid is a substance that, when dissolved in water, increases the concentration of the hydrogen ion (H^+). The Arrhenius concept of a base is a substance, dissolved in water, which increases the concentration of the hydroxide ion (OH^-). The ability of acids and bases to form ions in solution is very important. It means that electrical charges can be stored and transported through a solution. Do you realize that starting a car depends upon the property that acids are electrolytes? The sulfuric acid solution in a car battery conducts the electrical current needed to start the car's engine.

One of the best-known properties of an acid is its ability to *corrode metals*. Again, the ionizable hydrogen of acids plays the leading role in the reaction of acids with metals. The corrosion reaction is actually a *single-replacement reaction:* the metal switches places with the hydrogen in the acid.

Consider the reaction between zinc metal and hydrochloric acid. By losing its outermost two electrons to become Zn^{2+}, a zinc atom can achieve an octet in its remaining outer energy level. Being more electronegative than zinc, hydrogen ions each attract one electron from the zinc to become atoms; two of these will join to form a gaseous hydrogen molecule (H_2) in which each atom will

The King of Chemicals

Chemical companies in the United States produce more sulfuric acid than any other single chemical. Production of sulfuric acid in America began in Philadelphia thirty-one years after the signing of the Declaration of Independence. By the time of the Civil War, sulfuric acid had become one of the most important chemical products of our nation.

11 Acids, Bases, and Salts

have a shared duet. As the zinc atoms become ions, they dissolve into the acid solution and the metal appears to be "eaten away."

$$Zn + 2HCl \rightarrow ZnCl_2 + H_2$$

Fig. 11-3 Hydrochloric acid readily reacts with zinc.

Acids are also able to cancel the chemical action of bases, which you will learn about in the next section. When equal numbers of H_3O^+ ions and OH^- ions are combined, they will *neutralize* each other. The resulting solution is neither acidic nor basic—it is *neutral.*

Today this acid is used in almost every industrial process. In fact, economists consider sulfuric acid so essential to industry that they sometimes measure the economic condition of a country by how much sulfuric acid it uses. Generally, when a nation's usage of sulfuric acid drops, its whole economy is headed for a downturn.

You can easily understand why sulfuric acid is often referred to as the "king of chemicals." Its properties make it extremely useful. A dense, oily substance with a high boiling point, concentrated sulfuric acid is highly caustic and can eat through metals in a matter of minutes! Most importantly, sulfuric acid can react with numerous other chemicals to produce thousands of useful products. More than 40 percent of the sulfuric acid used in the United States goes into the manufacture of phosphate fertilizers. The second largest consumer of sulfuric acid is the chemical industry. Chemists use sulfuric acid to pro-duce paints, dyes, plastics, fibers, and a vast array of other chemical products.

Sulfuric acid is sometimes produced naturally, usually with dangerous results. Pyrite is an iron compound that contains sulfur. It can be found in coal mines or other areas in which mining or excavation is taking place. When exposed to water and oxygen, sulfuric acid is produced and can be swept into streams and lakes. Since it is such a strong acid, it is lethal to wildlife.

Fig. 11-4 Limestone and hydrochloric acid

Another useful chemical property of acids is that they react with carbonates and bicarbonates to form carbon dioxide gas. For example, the acetic acid ($HC_2H_3O_2$) in vinegar reacts with sodium bicarbonate (baking soda) to result in a great deal of bubbling (called effervescence), according to the following equation:

$$HC_2H_3O_2 + NaHCO_3 \rightarrow NaC_2H_3O_2 + H_2O + CO_2$$

Antacid tablets such as Alka-Seltzer utilize a reaction of this type, where citric acid within the tablet makes the acidic solution in which the bicarbonate reacts.

An additional application of this type of reaction is the test to confirm the presence of a carbonate in a rock sample. Limestone and marble contain calcium carbonate, which reacts with any acid to form bubbles. Applying a few drops of an acid such as HCl (or vinegar) to the suspected carbonate rock will result in noticeable bubbling, thereby giving a positive test:

$$CaCO_3 + 2HCl \rightarrow CaCl_2 + H_2O + CO_2$$

Bases

A variety of bases is lurking in your kitchen! Many of the floor cleaners, window cleaners, and oven cleaners that are commonly stored under kitchen sinks contain the base *ammonium hydroxide* (more correctly called *aqueous ammonia*). Sometimes the solution is known as *household ammonia.* Another base that you may find among your household chemicals is *lye,* or sodium hydroxide (NaOH). The commercial preparations used to open clogged drains usually contain lye.

There is a good chance that bases are concealed in your bathroom as well. *Milk of magnesia,* which is used as an antacid or a laxative (depending on dosage), is a water suspension of the base magnesium hydroxide [$Mg(OH)_2$]. Other antacid products such as Maalox, Rolaids, and Mylanta contain bases that neutralize stomach acids.

The Base Ion

All three substances mentioned so far have one thing in common: they result in the formation of a **hydroxide ion** (OH^-) in water solution. The classical (or Arrhenius) definition of a **base** is any substance that produces hydroxide ions when it is dissolved in water. Such a solution is referred to as basic or alkaline. You can see how ammonia reacts in water to qualify as a base in the following equation:

$$NH_3 + H_2O \rightarrow NH_4^+ + OH^-$$

Note how this equation is *balanced.* Count and see how many H's are on each side. How many N's? O's?

When ammonia (NH_3) molecules dissolve in water, some of them remove a proton from water molecules, resulting in NH_4^+ and OH^- ions. That is why it is often referred to as "ammonium hydroxide." The other two bases listed here—sodium hydroxide and magnesium hydroxide—contain hydroxide ions already. Both will *dissociate* (see Chapter 10) into the ions that compose them: sodium hydroxide into sodium and hydroxide ions, and magnesium hydroxide into magnesium and hydroxide ions. Thus, all three of these substances produce the hydroxide ion when dissolved in water.

H : N : H   ←   Pair of nonbonded electrons

H

The reaction between ammonia and water given above is possible because of the structure of the ammonia molecule. A pair of nonbonded electrons on the nitrogen atom in ammonia attracts protons and bonds with them.

This nonbonded electron pair can pull a hydrogen ion (proton) from a water molecule and thereby become an ammonium ion; as a result, a hydroxide ion is also produced.

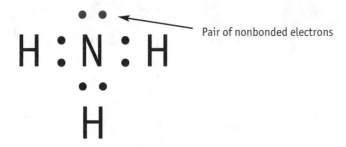

Fig. 11-5 The nonbonded pair of electrons in the ammonia molecule makes it an excellent proton acceptor.

Properties of Bases

If you have ever tasted soap, you know that bases have a bitter taste. They also have a *slippery feel.* This is because bases react with the oils of your skin. The same caution given you in the section on acids applies here too: *NEVER touch or taste a chemical to see if it is a base unless you are instructed to do so by your teacher, or unless the chemical's label states that it is safe to do so!* Many strong acids and bases can cause severe burns; and if eaten or drunk, they can act as poisons!

Just as acids can neutralize bases, bases can neutralize acids. You can see how the characteristic ion of an acid (hydronium) and the characteristic ion of a base (hydroxide) react to form water by carefully examining the following equation.

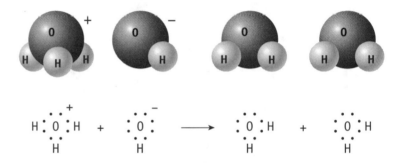

This reaction is the heart of the neutralization process, which you will learn more about in a later section.

SECTION REVIEW QUESTIONS 11A

1. What is common to all acids, according to the classical (Arrhenius) definition?

2. Show how hydrogen bromide, HBr, is an acid by writing an equation for its reaction with water.

3. List three of the properties of acids and two of the properties of bases.

The pH Scale

The sulfuric acid in a car battery can corrode painted surfaces and burn holes in clothing. Yet we touch and eat other acids every day. The aspirin that you take for a headache is an acid; the sharp flavor of soft drinks is caused by an acid; and several of the vitamins that you take or that are found in foods are actually acids. What makes some acids strong, caustic, and dangerous and other acids weak and quite harmless? Similarly, some bases are very damaging to clothing and tissue; others are used in cleaning solutions and need no particular safeguards. What makes the difference?

Acid Strength

Acids are classified as strong or weak according to the number of hydronium ions that they produce in a water solution. This is directly related to the *degree of ionization* of the acid molecule. The greater the degree of ionization, the more hydronium ions are produced in solution and the stronger the acid. Thus, *strong acids ionize to a large extent,* even 100%, and *weak acids ionize only slightly.*

The number of ionizable hydrogens does not necessarily indicate whether or not an acid will be strong. If it did, you might expect that acids that have two or more ionizable hydrogen atoms would be stronger acids than those that have only one. This is not the case. For example, hydrochloric acid (HCl), a *monoprotic acid* (having only one hydrogen), is virtually 100% ionized and is therefore a very strong acid. Though it has two ionizable hydrogens, sulfuric acid (H_2SO_4)—a *diprotic* acid—is not as completely ionized as HCl, so it is not as strong an acid. It is still classified as a strong acid, however, since it ionizes to a large extent. Phosphoric acid (H_3PO_4) ionizes only moderately and is therefore only a moderately strong acid, even though it has three ionizable hydrogens—it is *triprotic*. Citric acid ($H_3C_6H_5O_7$), also triprotic, is a very weak acid because it ionizes only slightly.

Another observation that you can make from Table 11-6 is that acids with the same number of ionizable hydrogens do not necessarily have the same strength. Among the monoprotic acids, you can see that they range from very strong ($HClO_4$) to very weak (HCN). *The stronger an acid "holds" its ionizable hydrogens, the weaker its strength is.*

11-6 The Strength of Some Important Acids

Chemical name	Formula	Ability to produce hydronium ions in water solutions	Strength
Perchloric acid	$HClO_4$	very good	very strong
Hydriodic acid	HI	very good	very strong
Hydrobromic acid	HBr	very good	very strong
Hydrochloric acid	HCl	very good	very strong
Nitric acid	HNO_3	very good	very strong
Sulfuric acid	H_2SO_4	good	strong
Sulfurous acid ($SO_2 + H_2O$)	H_2SO_3	medium	moderate
Phosphoric acid	H_3PO_4	medium	moderate
Hydrofluoric acid	HF	poor	weak
Nitrous acid	HNO_2	poor	weak
Benzoic acid	$HC_7H_5O_2$	poor	weak
Acetic acid	$HC_2H_3O_2$	very poor	very weak
Carbonic acid ($CO_2 + H_2O$)	H_2CO_3	very poor	very weak
Hydrosulfuric acid	H_2S	very poor	very weak
Boric acid	H_3BO_3	very poor	very weak
Hydrocyanic acid	HCN	very poor	very weak

Base Strength

Bases have varying strengths just as acids do. There are *strong base*s that ionize completely in solution and produce many hydroxide ions, and there are *weak bases* that do not ionize easily and produce few hydroxide ions in solution. A substance that produces a large amount of hydroxide ions can be very corrosive. For this reason, strong bases should be handled with great care; if they are misused, they can cause severe burns.

What kinds of substances act as strong bases? Scientists have found that when the ions of the alkali metals and the alkaline-earth metals (Groups 1 and 2) combine with hydroxide ions, the resulting compounds are capable of releasing large amounts of hydroxide ions in solution. Compounds such as sodium hydroxide (NaOH), potassium hydroxide (KOH), and calcium hydroxide [$Ca(OH)_2$] readily dissociate into metal ions and hydroxide ions. The following equation shows you how the strong base NaOH dissociates into solvated ions when it is dissolved in water. (To simplify the equation, the water involved in the hydration is shown simply as H_2O over the arrow.)

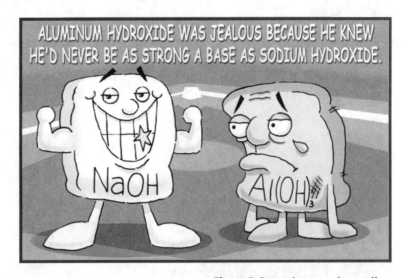

Fig. 11-7 Strong bases, such as sodium hydroxide, produce more hydroxide ions than do weak bases, such as aluminum hydroxide.

$$NaOH \xrightarrow{H_2O} Na^+ (aq) + OH^- (aq)$$

Though calcium hydroxide is not very soluble in water, the formula units that do dissolve dissociate completely. The bond between hydroxide ions and these active metals can easily be broken by water molecules, making these compounds strong bases.

What makes some substances, such as ammonia, weak bases? As you learned already, the strength of a base is measured by the number of hydroxide ions the base produces in a solution. Ammonia is a weak base because it produces relatively few hydroxide ions in a water solution when it "rips apart" water molecules. Because it is weak, it is reasonably safe to use in cleaning solutions. Other metal hydroxides, such as $Al(OH)_3$, are very weak bases because they are so insoluble in water that very few OH^- ions are released into solution.

TABLE 11-8 The Strength of Some Common Bases

Chemical name	Formula	Ability to produce hydroxide ions in water solutions	Strength
Sodium hydroxide	NaOH	very good	strong
Potassium hydroxide	KOH	very good	strong
Calcium hydroxide	$Ca(OH)_2$	good	strong
Ammonium hydroxide	NH_4OH	poor	weak
Aluminum hydroxide	$Al(OH)_3$	very poor	very weak

The pH Scale

In Chapter 10 you learned that the concentration of a solution is a measure of the amount of solute that is dissolved in the solution. Sometimes people use the terms "strong" or "weak" to refer to a concentrated or dilute solution, respectively. However, the *strength* of an acid or base in solution—the number of ions produced—must not be confused with the *concentration* of the solution. It is possible to have a concentrated solution of a weak acid or base and a dilute solution of a strong acid or base. Because of the possibility of confusion, *it is best to refer to solution concentrations as dilute or concentrated rather than weak or strong.*

FACETS of the physical world

pH Measurement

The indicators that are mentioned in this chapter change colors over a relatively narrow range of pH values. Some change in the acid range, and some change very close to neutral; still others change in the basic range. Indicator molecules can exist in either an acid form or a base form in solution, each a different color. In a solution that has more protons than hydroxide ions—an acidic solution—the indicator molecules pick up protons and become "protonated." This acid form of the indicator exhibits one color. In a basic solution, some of the excess OH⁻ ions will remove protons from the indicator molecules, making them "unprotonated." This base form of the indicator exhibits the other color. How readily the loss or gain of protons occurs depends on the specific indicator and is reflected in the pH at which the color change occurs.

Phenolphthalein is colorless below pH 8 and red above about pH 10. Thus, the acid form (colorless)

predominates below pH 8 and the base form (red) predominates above pH 10. Between pH 8 and pH 10, a solution of phenolphthalein would exist as a mixture of the two forms and would appear as some shade of pink.

The fact that indicators generally change over one narrow pH range limits the usefulness of individual indicators to determine the actual pH of a given solution. Using phenolphthalein, you could determine that a solution had a pH less than 8, greater than 10, or maybe between 8 and 10. But you could not determine more specifically than that. Litmus is red below pH 4.5 and blue above pH 8.3; between pH 4.5 and 8.3 it is some color in between red and blue. Litmus can thus tell you whether a solution is more acidic than pH 4.5 or more basic than pH 8.3, but it cannot tell you how acidic or basic; nor can it tell you much about the pH range over which the color is changing, that is, between pH 4.5 and 8.3.

A mixture of several indicators, known as a universal indicator, changes color over most of the range of pH values and allows a more definite pH determination. Special paper that has been treated with a universal indicator can do more than simply tell whether a solution is acidic or basic; it can be used to determine the pH of a solution much more specifically. Such indicator paper is known as pH paper. For specific purposes, narrow-range pH paper is sometimes used. In the ranges for which it is available, pH values can be determined to tenths of pH units. For more general purpose work, broad range papers may be used. One type permits the determination of the even-numbered pH values (2-10); another could be used for the odd-numbered values (1-11). A third type permits pH determination to the nearest unit value over the pH range 0-13. In any case, the pH is estimated by comparing the color of the paper with a color chart.

11 Acids, Bases, and Salts

Indicators

The ability of acids and bases to *change the color* of some compounds is another property that is useful to scientists to indicate the acidity or basicity (alkalinity) of a substance. **Indicators** are organic ("carbon-containing") compounds that show a definite color change when they react with acids or bases. One common indicator is *litmus,* obtained from a lichen that grows in the Netherlands, Scandinavia, California,

Fig. 11-9 Litmus paper

In order to obtain very accurate pH values over the entire range, an electronic instrument known as a pH meter may be used. Essentially a voltmeter, the pH meter uses a glass electrode that is sensitive to the hydronium ion concentration in solution. It responds in such a way that the voltage produced is proportional to the pH of the solution. Generally, at least two solutions of known pH are used to "standardize" the meter prior to each use. The pH of the solution in question can then be measured.

The pH of swimming pools is carefully regulated. If the pH drops below 6.8, the pipes in the filters may become clogged with mineral deposits. Generally, the pH should be about 7.5 so that the chlorine compound, hypochlorous acid (HOCl), is present in the correct concentration. If the pH is too high, the chlorine compound decomposes too rapidly in sunlight. If the pH is too low, there will be too much HOCl in the pool; eye irritations and excessive growth of algae will result.

Testing the pH of a urine sample can give doctors important information about their patients. Urine with normal pH is slightly acidic—about 6. Though diet can affect urine's pH, it normally ranges between about 4.5 and 8. If the pH test shows that urine is too acidic or too basic, the patient may have a serious medical problem. When pH is abnormal, crystals can form in the urine. These crystals may lodge in the kidneys to form painful stones which may need to be removed surgically. Sometimes ultrasound waves are used to break up the stones. In some cases, the diet may be modified to prevent the formation of stones.

Manufacturers of hair products also carefully test the pH of their products to make sure they are safe. If the pH of a hair permanent were too high, the permanent would dissolve rather than curl the hair!

and other places. After it is extracted from the lichen and treated, litmus is a bluish chemical that turns red in an acidic solution; the red color will turn back to blue in a basic solution. Both red and blue litmus paper are available for testing whether a solution is acidic or basic. Thus, red litmus paper will change to blue if the solution is basic, and blue litmus paper will change to red if the solution is acidic. A simple way to remember some properties of <u>B</u>ases is to remember the 3 B's: <u>B</u>ase—turns litmus <u>b</u>lue and tastes <u>b</u>itter. Besides litmus, another common indicator in the laboratory is *phenolphthalein* [(FEE nawl THAY leen)]. It is colorless in acidic solutions but turns to a deep pink color in basic solutions.

There are many other indicators that can be used in the laboratory to determine whether the solution of a substance is acidic or basic. In addition, careful choice of a series of different indicators can allow you to determine the relative strength of an acid or base.

Fig. 11-10 Phenolphthalein turns pink in the presence of a base.

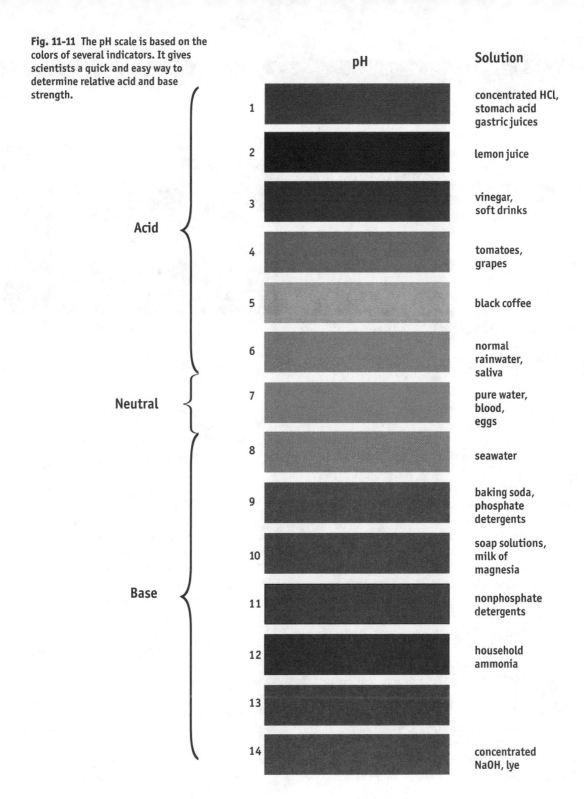

Fig. 11-11 The pH scale is based on the colors of several indicators. It gives scientists a quick and easy way to determine relative acid and base strength.

pH | Solution

Acid

1 — concentrated HCl, stomach acid gastric juices

2 — lemon juice

3 — vinegar, soft drinks

4 — tomatoes, grapes

5 — black coffee

6 — normal rainwater, saliva

Neutral

7 — pure water, blood, eggs

Base

8 — seawater

9 — baking soda, phosphate detergents

10 — soap solutions, milk of magnesia

11 — nonphosphate detergents

12 — household ammonia

13 —

14 — concentrated NaOH, lye

Acid Rain

What is the pH of rain? You might expect pure rainwater to be neutral, but that is not the case. Under normal conditions, rain and snow are slightly acidic because atmospheric carbon dioxide dissolves in them to form the weak acid carbonic acid, which ionizes slightly.

$$CO_2 + H_2O \rightarrow H_2CO_3 \rightarrow H^+ + HCO_3^-$$

Rain and snow usually have a pH of about 6.6. Scientists know that this has been the order of things for thousands of years because they have measured the pH of snow deep within glaciers.

As the burning of fossil fuels (coal and oil) increased during the past century, there was also a decrease in the pH—an increase in the acidity—of snow and rain in certain parts of the industrialized world. Some areas are even affected by acidic pollution that drifts in from industrialized regions that are many miles away. Rain in the northeastern United States, southeastern Canada, and western Europe may have a pH as low as 4; in some cases, it has been as acidic as vinegar or lemon juice, approximately pH 2.5-3! (Remember that each unit decrease in pH represents a tenfold increase in acidity.) Precipitation with a pH lower than the normal 6.6 is termed *acid rain* or *acid precipitation.*

English scientist Robert Angus Smith coined the term *acid rain* in 1872. Smith measured the pH of the precipitation in the industrial region near Manchester, England. He found that as more industry moved into the area and increased its sooty output of air pollutants, the pH of the rainwater fell. His was the first scientific report to draw a relationship between air pollution and acid rain.

What causes acid rain? When sulfur-containing coal is burned for energy (as in power plants), sulfur dioxide is produced. This SO_2 can react further with atmospheric oxygen to form sulfur trioxide, which reacts with water to form the strong acid sulfuric acid.

$$S + O_2 \rightarrow SO_2$$
$$2SO_2 + O_2 \rightarrow 2SO_3$$
$$SO_3 + H_2O \rightarrow H_2SO_4$$

A similar situation occurs when ores containing sulfur are burned during the production of metals such as zinc and copper.

Scientists have also blamed nitrogen oxides for contributing to acid rain. The major source of nitrogen oxides is internal combustion engines, such as are found in automobiles, trucks, and buses. At the high temperatures and pressures inside engines, atmospheric nitrogen and oxygen combine to form nitrogen monoxide, which can then react further with oxygen to form nitrogen dioxide; this NO_2 dissolves in rain to form another strong acid, nitric acid.

$$N_2 + O_2 \rightarrow 2NO$$
$$2NO + O_2 \rightarrow 2NO_2$$
$$3NO_2 + H_2O \rightarrow 2HNO_3 + NO$$

If rain and snow are already naturally acidic from the presence of dissolved carbon dioxide, why is it a problem when other acids, such as sulfuric and nitric acids, are present? Why the difference? Remember that sulfuric and nitric acids are strong acids and, therefore, produce many hydronium ions in solution; carbonic acid, a weak acid, produces relatively few. The additional strong acid in the precipitation lowers its pH considerably.

Lakes, streams, and soils in areas that have a low concentration of alkaline (basic) minerals are more affected by acid rain than are areas that are rich in such minerals. The most common alkaline minerals are limestone, $CaCO_3$, and dolomite, $CaMg(CO_3)_2$; they serve to neutralize excess acid.

Acid rain has many effects on living organisms, some of which are not yet well understood by scientists. There have been cases in which the lakes became so acidic that all the fish were killed. Even at lower acidity than that which will kill fish, other organisms in the aquatic ecosystem are affected adversely. Since many terrestrial animals depend on aquatic organisms for their food, any factor that affects aquatic life eventually also affects them.

When they are inhaled, the gases that result in acid rain can also aggravate human respiratory diseases such as asthma by irritating lung tissue. Acid rain affects plant and animal life by allowing some toxic metals in the soil and lake sediment to dissolve; these can therefore enter the food chain and be concentrated in predatory animals. Aluminum, in the form of aluminum silicates, is more soluble in acidic water; in that form it adversely affects the use of nutrients by plants. Acid rain also makes certain plants more susceptible to disease. Further, acid water dissolves more readily those nutrients that are needed by plants, allowing them to be washed away in the runoff. Clearly, acid rain affects aquatic, plant, animal, and human life.

So what has been done about the problem? Though a relatively few dead fish and trees will not bring an end to the world, any trend that affects an increasing number of lakes and streams is of increasing concern to scientists. A temporary solution to the problem, at least in one extreme situation, was to utilize the fact that acids react with and are neutralized by carbonates.

This information was used in the treatment of several acidic lakes in the state of New York, where there was a lack of naturally alkaline minerals in the soil. Planes, helicopters, and snowmobiles were used to dump carbonates into and around the lakes to neutralize the excess acidity—both that which was already present and that which would come from the melting of acidic snow. Of course, since this was only a temporary solution, something more effective and long-range was needed.

Public awareness of the problem, public pressure, and government legislation have resulted in stricter air pollution standards. As a result, users of high-sulfur coal have either begun using a low-sulfur coal, removed much of the sulfur from the coal prior to burning it, or used scrubbers to remove the sulfur oxides from the exhaust gases. Lime (CaO) in the scrubber reacts with sulfur dioxide or sulfur trioxide to form $CaSO_3$ or $CaSO_4$ respectively, thereby removing the sulfur compounds from the exhaust gases.

Efforts to reduce nitrogen oxide emission from automobile exhaust are more complex. One method uses a catalytic converter to convert the NO back to O_2 and N_2 before it leaves the exhaust system.

Have such efforts been successful in reducing acid rain in the United States? A recent study of the pH of rainwater at thirty-three collection sites across the United States showed a significant reduction in its acidity. The increased pH was accompanied by a decrease in the concentration of

nitrate and sulfate ions. This decrease would be expected if the acidity of acid rain were coming from sulfur and nitrogen oxides whose emissions were being reduced.

What position should a Christian take on environmental issues such as this one? The Bible pictures humans as the stewards of God's physical creation. In the Old Testament, God commissioned Adam to subdue the earth (Gen. 1:28). But we were also instructed to take care of the land God gave us. For example, He instructed the children of Israel to allow the land to rest every seventh year by not planting crops (Lev. 25). In Deuteronomy 22:6-7 God taught His people another important lesson in conservation. When they hunted birds for meat, they were to take either the bird or its young, but never both. In this way the population of the birds would not be destroyed.

Today it is important that we learn how to make wise choices in environmental issues—choices based on scriptural principles and science. We need the products of the industries that discharge sulfur oxides into the air. But we also need to conserve the environment for future generations. We should not selfishly live with only the present in mind by taking what we want and leaving behind a depleted world. Balance is necessary. We must have production, *and* we must work to find creative ways to be better stewards in our technologically advanced society without destroying our environment.

The pH Scale

The hydronium ion concentration in solution can be more specifically designated by a number scale known as the **pH scale,** or simply pH. It ranges in value from 0 to 14, with values less than 7 being acidic and values greater than 7 being basic. A pH equal to 7 is neutral—that is, neither acidic nor basic. Pure water would have a pH of 7.

You should understand that the pH scale is based on exponents; thus, a difference of 1 unit on the pH scale is a factor of 10 difference in hydronium ion concentration. For example, if one solution is pH 4 and another is pH 5, the one that has a pH of 4 is 10 times more acidic—it has a 10 times greater hydronium ion concentration—than the one with a pH of 5.

Though the pH scale is defined on the basis of the hydronium ion concentration, it is important to understand that the total concentration of hydronium and hydroxide ions in any water solution is constant. ***Thus, as one concentration increases, the other must decrease.*** A neutral solution has equal concentrations of hydronium and hydroxide ions. If there is an excess of hydronium ions, the solution is acidic; if there is an excess of hydroxide ions, the solution is basic.

Because of the way in which pH is defined mathematically, the smaller the value of the pH, the larger the concentration of the hydronium ion and the more acidic the solution. On the other hand, the larger the value of the pH, the smaller the concentration of the hydronium ion and the more basic the solution. If the hydroxide and hydronium ions are of equal concentration, the solution is neutral and the pH is 7. This is most easily remembered by associating *lower pH* values with *higher acidity.* You can see how the pH values of a number of common substances compare by examining Figure 11-11.

As you can see from the figure, solutions of soaps (and many detergents) are basic; they are thus able to remove oils and grease quite effectively from skin, clothing, and hair, for example. However, when used too frequently on hair, soaps tend to remove too much of the oil, leaving it dull, brittle, and "lifeless."

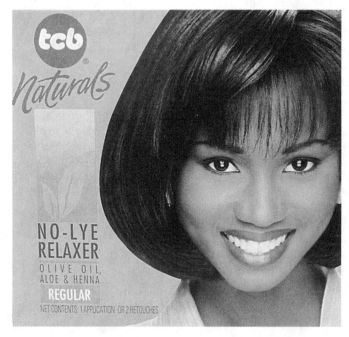

Fig. 11-12 Notice the "No-Lye" label on the box. Although bases are excellent detergents, they are often too harsh to be used for hair care products.

11 Acids, Bases, and Salts

Furthermore, damage to hair can occur if the preparation is too basic (alkaline). Drain cleaners, which have large pH values, actually dissolve hair in drainpipes! Thus, shampoos that are slightly acidic—usually referred to as *nonalkaline*—are better for hair because they allow it to retain some of its natural oils and shine.

SECTION REVIEW QUESTIONS 11B

1. From Table 11-6 you can see that benzoic acid is a weak acid and phosphoric acid is a moderately strong acid. Which acid has a stronger bond to its ionizable hydrogen? Which produces more hydronium ions in water solution?

2. Which color of litmus paper would you use to check the acidity/basicity of a detergent solution? To what color would it change?

3. What indicator turns deep pink in a basic solution?

Salts

Table salt (sodium chloride) is only one of a large class of compounds known as salts. You are probably familiar with several salts in the form of seasonings that you might use in your food. Salts have many different uses, but what relationship exists between acids, bases, and salts?

Salts are ionic compounds that are made up of a negative ion (anion) that comes from an acid, and a positive ion (cation) that comes from a base. Sodium chloride is made up of chloride (Cl^-) anions from hydrochloric acid and sodium (Na^+) cations from sodium hydroxide. Another popular seasoning, monosodium glutamate, has the same cation (Na^+), but its anion, glutamate ($C_5H_8O_4{}^-$), comes from glutamic acid, an amino acid that is common in plant and animal tissue.

Making Salts: Neutralization

By its very definition, you can see that a salt is a product of a **neutralization** reaction: the reaction of an acid and a base to produce a salt (an ionic compound) and water. In the section on acids, you saw that when an acid dissolves in water, it ionizes into positive hydronium ions and negative ions. Using a different strong acid than in the previous example, you can see how HNO_3 splits into a hydronium cation and a nitrate anion.

$$HNO_3 + H_2O \rightarrow H_3O^+ + NO_3^-$$

As you learned in the section on bases, when a strong base dissolves in water, it dissociates into positive metal ions and negative hydroxide ions. For the strong base potassium hydroxide, the ions formed are potassium cations and hydroxide anions.

$$KOH \xrightarrow{H_2O} K^+ (aq) + OH^- (aq)$$

If these acid and base solutions are mixed, all four ions meet in the same solution. The hydroxide ions immediately pull one of the protons from the hydronium ions to form water, thereby neutralizing each other.

$$K^+ (aq) + OH^- (aq) + H_3O^+ (aq) + NO_3^- (aq) \rightarrow K^+ (aq) + NO_3^- (aq) + 2H_2O$$

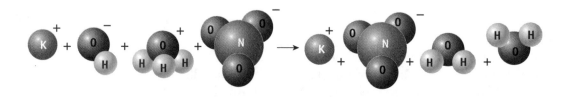

To isolate the salt produced in a neutralization reaction, you would have to evaporate the water from the solution. Once the water is evaporated, these ions *associate* (join together) to form an ionic compound—the salt. In this example, the nitrate anions

TABLE 11-13	Salts from Sample Acid-Base Reactions		
	Bases		
Acids	NaOH sodium hydroxide	KOH potassium hydroxide	Mg(OH)$_2$ magnesium hydroxide
HCl hydrochloric	NaCl sodium chloride	KCl potassium chloride	MgCl$_2$ magnesium chloride
HNO$_3$ nitric	NaNO$_3$ sodium nitrate	KNO$_3$ potassium nitrate	Mg(NO$_3$)$_2$ magnesium nitrate
H$_2$SO$_4$ sulfuric	Na$_2$SO$_4$ sodium sulfate	K$_2$SO$_4$ potassium sulfate	MgSO$_4$ magnesium sulfate

11 Acids, Bases, and Salts

combine with the potassium cations to form solid potassium nitrate (KNO_3) as the water is driven off as a vapor (gas).

$$K^+ \text{ (aq)} + NO_3^- \text{ (aq)} \xrightarrow{\Delta} KNO_3 \text{ (s)} + H_2O \text{ (g)}$$

To sum up, then, in general,
    base cation + acid anion = salt

Types of Salts

Since there are many different acids and many different bases, thousands of different salts can be produced from neutralization reactions. Theoretically, any acid could react with any base to produce a unique salt. The table on page 258 lists three acids and three bases. Notice the nine different salts that can be produced from their reactions with one another.

SECTION REVIEW QUESTIONS 11C

1. Define *neutralization*.
2. How do you typically isolate a salt from a water solution?

SCIENTIFICALLY SPEAKING

acid	hydroxide ion
ionization	base
Brönsted-Lowry	indicators
hydronium ion	pH scale (pH)
Arrhenius	salts
	neutralization

CHAPTER REVIEW QUESTIONS

1. Who was the man who defined acids and bases as electrolytes that produce ions in solution?

2. What model shows acids as proton donors and bases as proton acceptors?

3. Tell what you would observe if you dipped a piece of blue litmus paper in each of the following: (a) tomato juice, (b) a drain cleaning solution, (c) a lemon-lime soft drink.

4. Tartaric acid, citric acid, and malic acid are found naturally in several fruits. Would a solution of one of these acids be more likely to have a pH of 1, 4, or 7?

5. If the pH of normal rainwater is 6.6, how many times more acidic would acid rain be that had a pH of 3.6?

6. Describe the formation of salt. Name three other salts besides sodium chloride.

FACET REVIEW QUESTIONS

1. Most of the sulfuric acid produced in the United States is used for making what?

2. What is the main source of nitrogen oxide pollutants?

3. In what way does a universal indicator help determine pH?

WHAT DID YOU LEARN?

1. Why would you rinse an acid burn with a weak base? Why is it essential that this base be weak?

2. The formula for carbonic acid is H_2CO_3. Even though its formula indicates that it could be a very strong acid like sulfuric acid (H_2SO_4), it is actually very weak and is present in soft drinks. Why is it safe to drink carbonic acid, and why is it included in soft drinks?

3. The hydrochloric acid in the human stomach has a pH of 1. It is strong enough to burn a hole in the carpet, yet we hardly even know it is there. How is the stomach protected from destruction?

Physics in Action

Energy and Momentum

12A **Conservation of Energy**

12B **Forms of Energy**

12C **Momentum**

12

Matter makes up all of the things around you. It is everything that has mass and occupies space. You can examine matter—touch it, taste it, handle it. Matter and energy are two related facets of our physical universe. Matter is the substance of the universe, whereas energy is the mover of matter.

Energy cannot be picked up and examined. In fact, energy is not even a substance. We say that food contains energy or that gasoline is a source of energy, but we cannot isolate energy from either of these. When studying energy, one must take the perspective that energy is an *ability*, not a substance. **Energy** is the ability to do work. For example, food is a source of energy because the body can convert it to another form, such as heat from your skin and movement from your muscles. Understanding how energy is used, the different forms it takes, and how it is conserved is of tremendous interest to scientists because human beings rely heavily on energy resources to maintain their lifestyles. The study of energy is very broad—it transcends all areas of science. Living cells need food to survive; rockets use energy to launch; and power companies must provide electrical energy to millions. Although this "mysterious" ability we call energy may seem a little hard to comprehend, the laws and forms of energy are actually quite simple to understand. We will first examine the two basic categories of energy and use common examples to illustrate.

 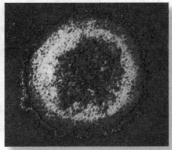 

Conservation of Energy

Any form of energy can be either stored or used up. **Potential energy** is stored energy, or energy at rest. A battery has stored energy that can be used for work later on. The battery is a perfect example of potential energy because it has the ability to perform a tremendous amount of work. Gasoline in a gas tank has enough potential energy to propel the car for several hundred miles. A skier at the top of a hill has the capacity to do work because of his position. He has potential energy. As he skis down the hill, the potential energy is converted into **kinetic energy,** energy in motion. A burning log, a moving vehicle, and falling objects all possess kinetic energy.

We can calculate potential and kinetic energy of certain objects by using formulas.

Potential energy is calculated by multiplying the mass of an object (m) by the acceleration due to gravity (g) and the height of the object (h).

Calculating Potential Energy
PE = mgh
m = mass of object
g = 9.8 m/s²
h = height of object

Fig. 12-1 As a skier skis downhill, he is converting potential energy to kinetic energy. How did he get the potential energy in the first place?

Potential energy

If you lift a 3.00 kg book a distance of 1 m and place it on a shelf, how much potential energy have you given to the book?

FORMULA: PE = mgh

$(3.00 \text{ kg})(9.8 \text{ m/s}^2)(1 \text{ m}) = 29.4 \text{ J}$

Kinetic energy

What would the kinetic energy be of a 5 kg rock thrown through the air with a velocity of 20 m/s?

$$KE = \frac{1}{2}mv^2$$

$$\left(\frac{1}{2}\right)(5 \text{ kg})(20 \text{ m/s})^2 = 1000 \text{ J}$$

Potential energy (PE) is measured in units called joules. A **joule** equals one kilogram-meter squared per second squared and is the most common way of measuring energy.

Kinetic energy is measured in much the same way, with the same units (joules, or J). The kinetic energy of a moving object is calculated by multiplying one-half of the object's mass by its velocity (v) squared. The *velocity* of a moving object refers to its speed (in m/s) and direction.

Because velocity is squared in the kinetic energy equation, doubling the velocity quadruples the kinetic energy. This relationship between velocity and kinetic energy explains why a car traveling at 88 km/hr takes so much longer to stop than a car moving at 44 km/hr.

Calculating Kinetic Energy

$$KE = \frac{1}{2}mv^2$$

KE = kinetic energy
m = mass
v = velocity

Conservation of Energy

God sustains His creation. Hebrews 1:3 tells us that God is "upholding all things by the word of his power." Second Peter 3:7 declares that "the heavens and the earth . . . by the same word are kept in store." Have you ever wondered why so many things occur in cycles? Many natural processes have a recognized conservation principle. Conservation simply means that energy or matter is never destroyed; it is simply converted from one form to another. In Chapter 9 we learned that elements involved in reactions may form compounds that act and look radically different from the original elements, but not one gram of substance is lost. When you think about it, energy is often converted back and forth from potential to kinetic. James Prescott Joule (for whom the SI unit joule is named) pondered conservation principles and wrote about them extensively. A German scientist, Hermann von Helmholtz, expanded on Joule's work. The ideas they propounded were

Fig. 12-2 When people take a trip, the potential energy in the gasoline is converted into various forms of kinetic energy—such as motion and heat.

formed into a concept called the **law of conservation of energy**, which states that *energy can be changed from one form to another but can never be created or destroyed.* We also call this the first law of thermodynamics. No exceptions to the law of conservation of energy have ever been found. When cars use up a tank of gasoline on a long trip, you may wonder what happened to the energy "contained" in the fuel. It didn't just "disappear." The potential energy in gasoline was converted into various forms of kinetic energy such as motion, the heat of the engine, and the heat of the braking action.

Energy and Matter

The bonds that hold atoms together contain tremendous amounts of energy. As we discussed in earlier chapters, these bonds can be very strong or very weak depending on the electronegativity of the elements involved and the number of valence electrons. No one really knows how such forces work in the atom. The best we can do is describe the behavior of these atoms. What is even more intriguing than chemical bonds is the idea that matter and energy are actually interchangeable, one and the same. Scientists have been able to measure radioactive decay reactions that actually show the mass of substances decreasing as it is converted to energy. That means that if we were able to convert the entire mass of a desk into energy, the amount of energy released would be staggering.

SECTION REVIEW QUESTIONS 12A

1. Describe the difference between potential energy and kinetic energy.
2. What is the law of conservation of energy?
3. What do scientists now believe about matter and energy?

Forms of Energy

Physicists theorize that nuclear furnaces in the sun may convert as much as 657 million tons of hydrogen into 653 million tons of helium every second! What happens to the missing 4 million tons of matter? It is converted into energy in the core of the sun and ultimately discharged into space. The sun possesses energy in many different forms: light and heat as evidenced by its solar flame, nuclear energy from its plasma furnace, and electrical and magnetic energy as evidenced by its sunspots. We receive energy from the sun in the form of light and swarms of energetically charged particles called solar wind.

In this chapter we will summarize eight forms of energy: thermal energy, radiant energy, sound energy, chemical energy, electrical energy, magnetic energy, mechanical energy, and nuclear energy. Each form of energy has the capacity to do work. As these forms are converted from one form to another, work is performed (kinetic energy) or stored (potential energy).

Fig. 12-3 If all the earth's fuels were gathered together and burned at the same rate as the sun "burns," they would be consumed in only four days.

Radiant Energy

"Let there be light." When God spoke those words, He instantly energized the universe! Light (or, more generally, radiation) is the ultimate source of all energy in the universe, so it had to be a part of the original six-day Creation. To produce other types of energy, **radiant energy** must be transferred to other forms. Radiation is everywhere! It pervades the universe. It is absorbed and re-emitted by matter. It travels through empty space at 300 million meters per second! It comes in many forms, varying by its wavelengths and energies. This includes radio waves, infrared waves, visible light waves, ultraviolet waves, X rays, and high-energy gamma rays. On the fourth day, God created the sun, the major source of radiant energy in the solar system. For the earth, the sun was made to rule the day and the moon, reflecting the sun's light, to rule the night. Solar radiation not only illuminates the earth but also maintains the entire life and weather systems of the earth by the conversion of radiation into thermal energy. It is interesting that only a small percentage of the available radiant energy that comes from our sun is intercepted by the earth for this purpose.

Mechanical Energy

Mechanical energy is the energy possessed by objects that are in motion or that have the potential to move. Wind possesses mechanical energy. You have probably seen pictures of the terrible destructive power of wind—the 800 km/hr winds of a tornado can lift an entire house and hurl it hundreds of meters through the air. Mechanical energy comes in two forms: kinetic energy caused by motion and potential energy associated with relative position.

Sound Energy

Sound energy is another form of energy that travels in waves. Unlike light waves, which can travel through the vacuum of space, sound energy can travel only through matter: solids, liquids, or gases. It is caused by mechanical vibrations in these media. So it is really another form of mechanical energy. The speed of sound depends on the nature of the matter it travels through. The sound's rate of vibration determines whether or not our ears can detect it. God has designed our ears to respond to rates of vibration between approximately twenty and twenty thousand vibrations per second. But He has equipped many animals to detect vibrations of sound energy in ranges beyond these limits.

Thermal Energy

Thermal energy is related to the motion of molecules in matter. The more vigorous the motion of these particles, the more **thermal energy** a substance possesses. In this way, we see that thermal energy is really a manifestation of mechanical energy on a microscopic scale. Heat is the transfer of thermal energy.

Thermal energy originating with our sun directly or indirectly powers much of nature. For example, the earth's atmosphere is powered by thermal energy. Due to heating effects, the air is circulated throughout our atmosphere in different layers, bands, and zones. The alternating light and dark bands on the gaseous giant planets like Jupiter and Saturn are due to thermal energy originating from the planets themselves and the sun.

The thermal energy from the sun also drives the earth's water cycle. Every day the sun's warmth evaporates over 700 cubic kilometers of water from the earth's oceans, streams, rivers, and lakes. This moisture is carried inland in great billowy clouds and released as rain, mainly over the mountains. The rainwater rushes down slopes to form streams, rivers, and lakes. When we use dams to tap the energy of this moving water, we indirectly tap the thermal energy of the sun.

Chemical Energy

Plants change the energy of the sun into **chemical energy** by a process known as photosynthesis. In **photosynthesis,** plants use light energy to produce the chemicals that "fuel" their growth. The energy of the sun is converted into the chemical energy found in sugar. Humans and animals eat food from plants, thus converting it back into kinetic energy. We also need chemical energy to grow. We fuel our bodies with the chemical energy in food. We also tap the chemical energy of fuels to power our cars and heat our homes.

PHOTOSYNTHESIS

Sun: Thermal energy (kinetic) converted to . . .

Sugar: Chemical energy (potential) converted to . . .

Movement, growth, and heat for our bodies (kinetic)

Electrical Energy

Scientists have developed special photovoltaic cells that can convert the energy of sunlight directly into electrical current. Many of our space probes tap the power of the sun with solar panels. They use the resulting electrical energy to run their instruments.

Electrical energy is associated with the flow of charged particles through a conductor. It is an amazing form of energy. You may not realize it, but all the electrical energy that is used in your home is delivered through a bundle of copper wires as thin as strands of spaghetti.

Magnetic Energy

Magnetic energy arises from magnets and their surrounding magnetic fields. Magnetic energy accomplishes work by producing attractive and repulsive forces that cause certain objects to move. Generators are used to force currents through circuits by varying magnetic fields.

Nuclear Energy

As its name implies, **nuclear energy** comes from the nucleus of the atom. This energy is released by splitting a nucleus or by fusing several small nuclei together. For example, a little bit of mass is lost when hydrogen atoms are fused into a deuterium atom (a hydrogen atom with an extra neutron). This mass (matter) is converted into energy using Einstein's equation $E = mc^2$ (c is the speed of light). A tiny loss of mass results in a large energy release. If

The Changing Forms of Energy

Under the proper conditions energy can be transformed from one type to another. We use energy transformations every day to light our homes, cook our food, and travel to school.

A lamp transforms electrical energy into light energy. An oven transforms electrical energy into thermal energy. A car transforms chemical energy (from gasoline) into mechanical energy (motion). Our bodies transform chemical energy (from food) into thermal energy in our cells, electrical energy in our nerves, and mechanical energy in our muscles.

The items pictured to the right are examples of primary energy transformations that take place in a variety of common devices. Some devices produce more than one form of energy. When an incandescent bulb changes electricity to light, heat is also generated. When an engine converts chemical energy in fuel to mechanical energy, heat and sound are also produced. A device is

efficient if most of the energy that goes into the device comes out in the desired form. Some devices produce the same general form of energy as they take in. A hand-operated eggbeater receives mechanical energy as you turn the crank, and it delivers mechanical energy to the eggs. Is this an energy transformation? No, you are simply altering a single form of energy to make it more useful. The beaters move faster than you could move your hand.

How many types of energy transformation are there? Look at the diagram on page 273; it shows every possible energy transformation. There are twenty-eight lines connecting the different forms of energy. Each of these lines represents *two* directions of change. Therefore, fifty-six energy transformations are possible!

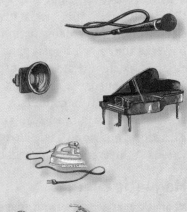

somehow the nuclear energy stored in two one-pound grapefruits could be completely converted into energy, it could supply the U.S. energy needs for an entire year! Two one-pound grapefruits have a mass of 0.9 kg. The energy is $E = 0.9 \text{ kg} \times (3 \times 10^8 \text{ m/s})^2 = 8 \times 10^{16}$ J! The power use in watts, or the rate at which power is expended per second, is this value divided by the number of seconds in a year. Power = Work/time = 8×10^{16} J/$(3.15 \times 10^7 \text{s})$ = 2.54 GW (gigawatts, or billion watts)!

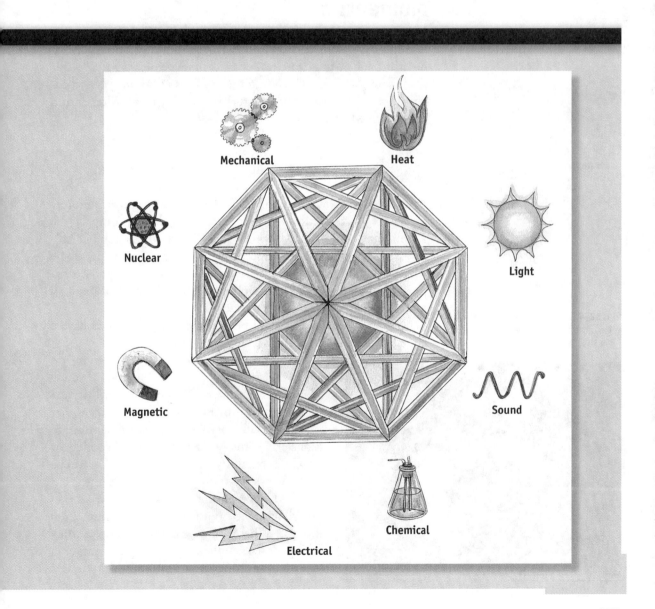

SECTION REVIEW QUESTIONS 12B

1. What process do plants use to convert kinetic energy from the sun into the potential energy of sugar?

2. Why can't sound travel through a vacuum?

3. What does $E = mc^2$ have to do with nuclear energy?

12C

Section

$$1 \text{ J} = \frac{1 \text{ kg} \cdot \text{m}^2}{\text{s}^2}$$

momentum units $= \dfrac{\text{kg} \cdot \text{m}}{\text{s}}$

Momentum

If you were going to describe a particle or object of mass m that was speeding along at velocity v, what quantity would you use to describe it? Newton chose mv, or mass times velocity, as the "quantity of motion" with which to frame his laws of motion. Today scientists call this quantity **momentum** (mo MEN tum). Momentum (p) is defined as mass (m) times velocity (v).

$$p = mv$$

The greater the mass of a moving object, the greater its momentum; and the greater its velocity, the greater its momentum.

Because of the effect of mass on momentum, a slowly moving truck has much more momentum than a slowly moving motorcycle. To illustrate the importance of mass, let us compare the action of a bowling ball knocking down pins to the action of a volleyball traveling at an equal speed and aimed at the same pins. The volleyball will bounce away after knocking down only one or two pins; it is simply too light to produce a strike. Because of its small mass, the volleyball has little momentum.

On the other hand, a small bullet fired from a gun can have a large momentum because of its high velocity.

Fig. 12-4 The faster a bowling ball is rolled, the more momentum it will have to knock the pins down.

Momentum (p) is dependent upon an object's mass and its velocity. If both of these quantities are very small, the object will have a small momentum, and if it collides with another object, it will not have much momentum to "transfer" to the other object. If either mass or velocity is relatively high, the momentum will be high. A massive train moving along a track has very high momentum. A stopped train (v = 0) would have no momentum at all! Just think about it. What would be harder to stop: a truck rolling down a hill at 5 miles per hour or a basketball moving at 15 miles per hour? As you probably guessed, a truck would be harder to stop because of its large momentum due to its large mass. To put it another way, it would take a large force to stop the truck quickly.

As mentioned in the previous paragraph, momentum can be *transferred* from one object to another without a change in total momentum of the entire "system." This is known as the **conservation of momentum.**

As an example, consider the firing of a rifle. The momentum of the bullet firing forward should equal the momentum of the rifle recoiling backward. So the mass of the bullet times its muzzle velocity equals the mass of the rifle times its recoil velocity. This explains why a rifle recoils. It also explains why a powerful gun or bullets produce a greater "kick."

Jets propel themselves forward using the principle of conservation of momentum. The exhaust is fired out at high speeds from the jet engines. The "back" momentum of the exhaust equals the forward momentum that propels the plane's mass forward.

Calculating momentum

What is the momentum of a bullet traveling at 350 m/s if its mass is 0.002 kg?

KNOWN: velocity (v) = 350 m/s

mass (m) = 0.002 kg

UNKNOWN: momentum (p)

FORMULA TO USE: p = mv

SUBSTITUTION: p = 0.002 kg(350 m/s)

SOLUTION: p = 0.7 kg · m/s

Note the units of the answer. There are no special units for momentum as there are for energy. Therefore, we must retain a combination of the units that go into the calculation. Multiplying kilograms by meters per second gives kilogram-meters per second (kg · m/s) for the units of momentum.

Fig. 12-5 This Navy jet illustrates the conservation of momentum.

STOP!

The kinetic energy of a car must "go somewhere" when the car stops. This energy is normally converted to heat in the brakes. If a car comes to a skidding halt, some of the energy is also converted to heat in the tires and on the road.

The U.S. Department of Transportation has conducted extensive tests to determine the distance standard passenger cars need in order to stop on dry, clean, level pavement. The results of these tests are given in the table.

The driver-reaction distance is based on a reaction time of 0.75 seconds. Though the reaction time stays the same at all speeds, the driver-reaction distance increases in direct proportion to the speed. In other words, if you are going faster, more ground will be covered during your 0.75-second reaction time.

The braking distance is the distance needed to stop once the brakes are applied. Researchers found that when the speed is doubled, the braking distance is more than quadrupled. This dramatic increase is caused by the fact that doubling the speed quadruples the kinetic energy, coupled with the fact that automobile brakes work less efficiently at higher speeds.

Adding the driver-reaction distance to the braking distance gives the total stopping distance.

Stopping a car requires more distance than you might think. The figures given here are for ideal conditions. The stopping distance can be much greater when the car is going downhill, when the weather is bad, or when the road is dusty, wet, or gravel-covered.

Speed (mph)	Driver-Reaction Distance (in feet)	Braking-Distance Range (in feet)	Total Stopping-Distance Range (in feet)
20	22	18-22	40-44
25	28	25-31	53-59
30	33	36-45	69-78
35	39	47-58	86-97
40	44	64-80	108-124
45	50	82-103	132-153
50	55	105-131	160-186
55	61	132-165	193-226
60	66	162-202	228-268
65	72	196-245	268-317
70	77	237-295	314-372
75	83	283-353	366-436
80	88	334-418	422-506

Conservation of Energy and Conservation of Momentum

When two objects of unequal mass collide, the lighter object is accelerated after the collision to a much faster speed than the heavier object is. Suppose that a 360-pound defensive football player collides with a 120-pound running back carrying the football in the opposite direction. If they are moving at the same speed before the collision, the lighter man will bounce back at twice his initial speed, while the heavier player is stopped cold.

Another example that illustrates the conservation of both momentum and energy is the collision ball trick. Picture six balls in a row on a metal track. If a single ball is rolled from the left toward the group, the rolled ball hits the first ball of the group and stops dead. At the same instant, the ball at the right-hand end leaves the group at the same speed as the ball that hit the group. The other five balls do not move! They transmit the motion to the ball that rolls away.

If two balls are rolled in from the left, two balls leave from the right.

What happens when seven moving balls hit the six stationary ones?

In this case, one of the seven moving balls keeps moving. This ball, together with the six balls that started in a resting position, makes seven balls in motion after the impact, giving the same momentum as was present before the impact.

Each ball must have the same mass in order for the demonstration to be effective.

Is Perpetual Motion Possible?

For many centuries humans dreamed of building a perpetual-motion machine that, once set in motion, would continue to operate indefinitely without the addition of fuel or energy. The most desirable type of perpetual-motion machine, of course, would be one that could not only keep itself running but also produce additional energy to do useful work. Such a machine would save time and energy. But as soon as the principle of the conservation of energy became established in the mid-1800s, scientists realized that the idea of a machine that would keep itself going was an impossible dream. The moving parts of all machines produce energy-eating friction. Thus, no machine can keep up with its own continuing energy needs, much less develop energy to spare. No one has ever succeeded in building a true perpetual-motion machine.

Even though none of the machines actually worked, some very ingenious ideas were tried. One consisted of a continuous chain running over a series of pulleys. Because the right-hand side of the chain is longer, the inventor of this machine expected the added weight to pull the chain around in a clockwise direction. Though this idea may appear feasible, it turns out that the pulleys on the right take up the additional weight, and the chain fails to move.

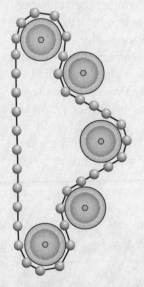

Another attempt at making the perfect machine used eight sledgehammers attached to a large wooden wheel. The handles were able to pivot freely at their attach-

ment point, except for a small spike embedded in the wheel. As one sledgehammer would swing forward, it would suddenly hit the spike and turn the wheel clockwise. The idea was as the wheel turned, the other sledgehammers would continue to fall and hit their spikes, causing a "domino effect." The circular shape of this machine seemed to assure that the machine would continue to rotate forever. The problem with this machine was that there were always more hammers hanging down on the left than on the right. The falling hammers could not produce enough force to overcome the weight of the hammer on the left, and the machine would come to a halt.

Both of these machines were supposed to operate by gravity.

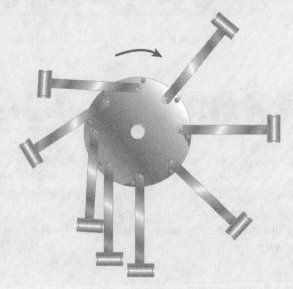

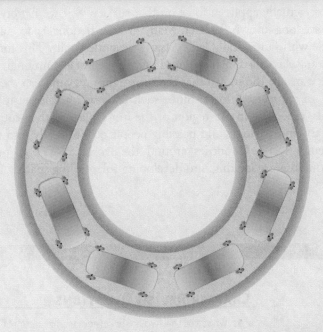

glass enclosed. Inside, brass spheres continually rotate back and forth. No tubing or wires connect the clock to any power source. The clock contains no batteries and never needs to be wound. But it does receive energy from its surroundings. This type of clock operates by responding to changes in atmospheric pressure. It uses this energy to drive a train of gears, which in turn moves the hands of the clock. If its parts never wore out, this device could continue to run indefinitely, but it is not a perpetual-motion machine because it derives its energy from its surroundings.

The law of conservation of energy combined with several centuries of experimental failure has convinced us that perpetual motion in a machine is impossible.

Christian Huygens, the noted seventeenth-century physicist, pointed out that in order for a gravity-operated perpetual-motion machine to work, its overall mass must keep moving to a lower level. But when that mass moves to the lower level, it has no way to return to its original position. When it cannot move any lower, motion stops. Thus, gravity-operated perpetual-motion machines are doomed to failure.

Perpetual-motion buffs also experimented extensively with magnetism. A magnet can produce motion by repelling a second magnet. Suppose we put wheels on a large number of bar magnets and arrange them on a circular track so that each magnet is repelling the one in front of it while also being repelled by the one behind it. Will not the entire circle of magnets now move around the track by mutual repulsion? Again nature fails to cooperate. Since each magnet receives an equal amount of repulsion from in front and behind, there is no unbalanced force on it, hence no motion. What is true for the individual magnets is true for the entire circle of magnets. The circle simply locks itself into place and refuses to move in either direction.

Perhaps you have seen devices that appear to be perpetual-motion machines. One type of clock is especially baffling. This clock is fully

Light Momentum

Light transports energy through a vacuum. This phenomenon is called radiation. But physicists also have found that light striking a surface actually applies a force on that surface. Science fiction writers have long known this fact. Many of their fictional spacecraft are vessels with fantastically large, nearly weightless sails. This form of space travel is called **solar sailing**. The sails present an amazingly large surface area to the sun so that the sun's light rays can push the craft with an appreciable force. Since such craft will accelerate to high speeds, especially in the region of the inner planets, they could be used to send payloads and possibly people economically into interplanetary space. Countries around the world as well as private corporations are looking into developing solar-sailing spacecraft.

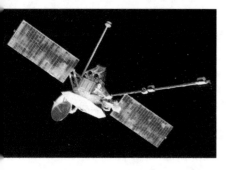

Fig. 12-6 *Mariner 10* was the first spacecraft to use solar-sailing techniques by using the pressure of sunlight reflecting off the solar panels for altitude control.

CHAPTER REVIEW

SCIENTIFICALLY SPEAKING

energy

potential energy

kinetic energy

joule

law of conservation of energy

radiant energy

mechanical energy

sound energy

thermal energy

chemical energy

photosynthesis

electrical energy

magnetic energy

nuclear energy

momentum

conservation of momentum

solar sailing

CHAPTER REVIEW QUESTIONS

1. What are the two basic categories of energy? Give an example of each.

2. Give the formula for calculating potential energy.

3. Name the two scientists that formulated the law of conservation of energy.

4. Give a short description of these eight forms of energy: thermal, radiant, sound, chemical, electrical, magnetic, mechanical, and nuclear.

5. What term describes an object's "quantity of motion"?

6. Suggest an experiment that would demonstrate the conservation of momentum.

7. How does solar sailing relate to momentum?

1. A 5 kg mass has a momentum of 43.2 kg · m/s. What is its speed?
2. Explain how a small mass can have a very large momentum.

$$= \frac{43.2}{5}$$

$$= 8.6\frac{2}{5}$$

$$= \boxed{9}$$

FACET REVIEW QUESTIONS

1. When the speed of a car is doubled, what happens to the braking distance?

2. How does friction affect "perpetual-motion" machines?

WHAT DID YOU LEARN?

1. One early automobile was called the Stanley Steamer. Can you guess what energy transformations took place when one of these automobiles was driven?

2. A carpenter experimented with several hammers of different sizes and finally selected one that was just right for his work. The heaviest hammer he tried had a mass of 1 kg but was very hard to swing. The carpenter found that he was able to swing a 0.5 kg hammer twice as fast as the 1 kg hammer. With which hammer could the carpenter generate more kinetic energy in a given amount of time? Was he smart to select the lighter hammer, which he could swing faster?

3. As a bullet is shot from the muzzle of a gun, the gun kicks backward and momentum is conserved. What actually forces the gun backward—the bullet? the exploding gases? some other force?

4. An engineer designed and built a roller coaster for an amusement park. He made the second hill higher than the first hill. Why was he fired from his job?

Mechanics: Matter in Motion

13A **Kinematics: Velocity and Acceleration**

13B **Dynamics: Newton's Laws**

13C **Gravity**

In "The Boscombe Valley Mystery," Sherlock Holmes rescued a young man who was falsely accused of murdering his father. Young McCarthey was nearby when his father was murdered, and, in the eyes of Scotland Yard's Inspector Lestrade, he had the perfect motive: he would inherit a large fortune! But the inspector had overlooked some very important clues when he made his hasty arrest.

Holmes intervened to show that the real key to the mysterious murder lay in the footprints at the scene of the crime. Yes, the inspector had found the son's footprints near the corpse, but he had missed another set of footprints—very unusual ones! After studying these prints, Holmes concluded that a tall man who limped with his right leg and wore thick-soled hunting boots committed the murder. Lestrade laughed at Holmes's description of the murderer, for it did not fit his prisoner, the young McCarthey, at all. Yet Holmes's careful collection of clues before he jumped to a conclusion had led him to the real murderer. Soon the man Holmes described was captured, and the thankful young heir was set free!

In this story, Holmes taught Lestrade the importance of collecting clues before determining motive, a lesson that Lestrade never seemed to learn. In physics, scientists ignored the same lesson for centuries. Early Greek philosophers tried to explain motion by determining the "motive"—*why* things move—before they had collected all of the clues that would reveal *how* things move. Of course, this led them to many incorrect conclusions. Aristotle believed that arrows flew through the air because the atmosphere closed behind them and pushed them forward! It was not until Galileo Galilei challenged these faulty notions in the seventeenth century that scientists began rethinking the way things move. Galileo proposed that we should study how things move before we conclude why they move. Like Sherlock Holmes, he thought it was best to collect clues rather than jump to an immediate conclusion about motive. His work started a revolution in physics that was completed by the English physicist Isaac Newton. The modern study of motion, called **mechanics,** is based largely on Newton's work regarding his three laws of motion and his gravitational theory. Today we split the study of motion into two parts: **kinematics** (KIN uh MAT iks), the description of *how* things move, and **dynamics** (dye NAM iks), the description of *why* things move. Kinematics is not concerned with mass or force but rather speed, acceleration, and velocity. Dynamics takes into account how mass and force affect motion. Of course, we will begin our study of motion by gathering *clues* from kinematics and then proceed to determine the *motives,* or dynamics.

Fig. 13-1 In this case, Holmes has overlooked the obvious.

Kinematics: Velocity and Acceleration

The American pioneers often crossed stretches of deserts on their westward journey. Sometimes a group of travelers would lose the trail and wander through the desert until they ran out of water and died in the burning sand. A water hole might be just a few miles away, but without landmarks to guide them, people were often misled by the vast desert sand.

Frames of Reference

In science we need landmarks to find the trail. Without them, our studies are as futile as the lost pioneers' wanderings. Scientists call such a landmark a *point of reference.* A group of these landmarks forms a **frame of reference.** Without these the study of physics would be pointless.

In the study of motion, the frame of reference determines what motion will be described. How fast are you moving right now? Suppose that you are in a classroom in New York City. A person in the room with you would claim that you are standing perfectly still, but if someone were observing you from a stationary point above the North Pole, he would observe you moving

Fig. 13-3 If you were in space, your frame of reference would show that the earth is rotating very rapidly, even though it seems to us that our planet is standing still.

approximately 310 meters per second! The person in the room with you does not "see" you move because he is moving at the same speed. The observer stationed over the North Pole sees that you are moving with the earth's rotation. If someone could observe you from outside our solar system, his frame of reference would reveal that you are really moving more than 29,000 meters per second as the earth whirls around the sun! Therefore, no single frame of reference is the *only* one for all motion. Take, for example, a moving train. The motion of the train will be described differently by a person standing by the tracks compared to, say, a plane flying overhead in the same direction of the train or another train on different tracks heading the opposite direction.

Displacement and Average Speed

Once we have identified a frame of reference (for example, a moving train as viewed from a person standing by the tracks), we can determine the change in position of an object, or its **displacement,** over a given time interval. This displacement over a given time interval is called **speed.** The formula for calculating the average speed of a moving object is $v = d/t$ where v is the average speed (see also velocity), d is the distance traveled or displacement, and t is the elapsed time. Since distance is measured in units of length, such as meters or kilometers, and time is often measured in seconds or hours, the units for speed (v) are often m/s or km/hr.

Compare a car that covers 21 m in 1 s and a bicycle that covers 21 m in 3 s. In both cases, the displacement is the same; however, the car is moving 21 m/s, or three times faster than the bicycle moving at 7 m/s (see example below).

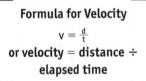

Formula for Velocity

$$v = \frac{d}{t}$$

or velocity = distance ÷ elapsed time

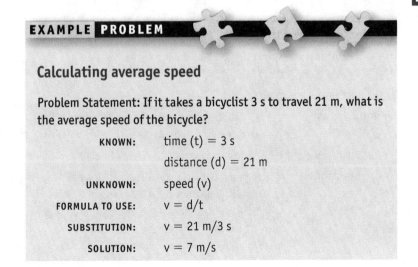

EXAMPLE PROBLEM

Calculating average speed

Problem Statement: If it takes a bicyclist 3 s to travel 21 m, what is the average speed of the bicycle?

KNOWN:	time (t) = 3 s
	distance (d) = 21 m
UNKNOWN:	speed (v)
FORMULA TO USE:	v = d/t
SUBSTITUTION:	v = 21 m/3 s
SOLUTION:	v = 7 m/s

Fig. 13-4 Suppose the route above marks the way to your friend's house. Why would you use the average speed on the trip rather than your fastest speed to calculate the time it takes to make the trip?

Realistically, vehicles speed up and slow down during their motion. For instance, your family makes several rest stops during a typical vacation trip. Therefore, the speed calculated is really an **average speed**.

EXAMPLE PROBLEM

Calculating time when given speed and distance an object has traveled

Suppose that a friend's house is 1.5 km away. How long would it take to cover that distance if you could maintain an average speed of 15 m/s the entire trip?

KNOWN:	speed (v) = 15 m/s
	distance (d) = 1.5 km
UNKNOWN:	time (t)
FORMULA TO USE:	t = d/v (Multiply both sides of the speed equation [v = d/t] by t and then divide both sides by v.)
SUBSTITUTION:	t = 1.5 km ÷ 15 m/s
SOLUTION:	Notice you must first convert m to km, or km to m. If you convert m to km you get t = 1.5 km ÷ 0.015 km/s = 100 s. Or if you convert km to m you get t = 1500 m ÷ 15 m/s = 100 s, or 1 minute and 40 seconds.

Calculating distance when given speed and time an object has traveled

It takes 2 hours for a Japanese bullet train to go from Tokyo to Nagoya. Bullet trains can attain speeds of 225 km per hour. Assume an average speed of 200 km/hr and calculate the distance.

KNOWN:	speed (v) = 200 km/hr
	time (t) = 2 hr
UNKNOWN:	distance (d)
FORMULA TO USE:	$d = t \cdot v$
SUBSTITUTION:	$d = 2 \text{ hr} \cdot 200 \text{ km/hr}$
SOLUTION:	$d = 400 \text{ km}$

Now that we know the formula for finding the speed of an object, we can also adjust the equation to help us find the distance traveled or the time required to make a trip.

Fig. 13-5 Modern bullet trains speed Japanese commuters to their destinations. How long would it take a commuter to travel home if his house were 112.5 km from Tokyo?

Velocity

Displacement involves both distance and direction. For example, a trail map indicates that a waterfall is about 1.5 miles to the north. To get there we must travel on the particular trail that goes in that direction; 1.5 miles in *any* direction will not do. We must go north. Average speed simply tells us how far we went in how long a time but does not tell us the direction. **Velocity** includes both an object's *speed and direction.* Like displacement, velocity includes both **magnitude** (how big) and direction. Quantities of this type are called **vectors.** Quantities that express *magnitude* only, such as speed and distance, are called **scalars.** Is mass a scalar or a vector? Is your height a scalar or a vector? What about force or temperature? How about your age?

In a simple description of motion along a straight line, we can just put a sign, + or -, on the scalar quantity to make it a vector. For instance, if a black BMW is traveling 30 m/s to the east and a green Chrysler is traveling in the opposite direction (west in this case) at 45 m/s, we could specify the velocity of the BMW as +30 m/s and the velocity of the Chrysler as -45 m/s. The -45 m/s tells us that the car is traveling to the west at 45 m/s. Of course, our designation of east as + and west as - is completely arbitrary. We could just as easily reverse them, but they must be opposite: they cannot have the same sign since they are traveling in opposing directions. If the two cars are traveling on the same road, on opposite sides of the yellow line, how fast are they moving away from each other?

Acceleration

When a sprinter hears the starting gun, he changes his speed from rest to a high speed in a short amount of time. We can describe this motion in two ways. We can talk about his average speed, or we can describe how his speed *changed* over time. This latter description is called **acceleration.** Acceleration, *a,* is the rate of the change of velocity in a given interval of time.

The Δ symbol used in this equation stands for the *change in* or *difference.* Since acceleration involves changes in velocity, this symbol makes it easier to write the equation. The change in the velocity is found by subtracting the starting, or initial, velocity (v_i) from the final velocity (v_f) and then dividing by the time interval.

Notice that the units of acceleration can be expressed in units of speed divided by time. The result is 3 m/s/s and is read as 3 meters

> **Formula for Acceleration**
>
> $$a = \frac{\Delta v}{t}$$
>
> **or acceleration = the change in velocity ÷ elapsed time**

Fig. 13-6 When does a runner accelerate (+) and decelerate (−) during a sprint? Is there a point during the race when he is not doing either?

Calculating Acceleration

Problem Statement: A car moving at +5 m/s accelerates to +20 m/s in 5 s. How fast was the car accelerating?

KNOWN:	initial velocity (v_i) = +5 m/s
	final velocity (v_f) = +20 m/s
	total time (t) = 5 s
UNKNOWN:	acceleration (a)
FORMULA TO USE:	$a = (v_f - v_i)/t$
SUBSTITUTION:	$a = (+20 \text{ m/s} - +5 \text{ m/s})/5 \text{ s}$
SOLUTION:	$a = 3$ m/s/s

Kinematics: Velocity and Acceleration

Acceleration

A car comes to a stop from a speed of +30 m/s in 10 s. What is the acceleration of the car? Note: This is sometimes referred to as *deceleration.*

KNOWN:	initial velocity (v_i) = +30 m/s
	final velocity (v_f) = 0 m/s
	total time (t) = 10 s
UNKNOWN:	acceleration (a)
FORMULA TO USE:	$a = (v_f - v_i)/t$
SUBSTITUTION:	$a = (0\ m/s - +30\ m/s)/10\ s$
SOLUTION:	a = -3 m/s/s

per second, per second. Often it is condensed to 3 m/s^2. A sign on the acceleration, +3 m/s^2, emphasizes that the velocity is *increasing* in the same direction as the original motion. Another way to say this is: *the acceleration is acting in the same direction as the initial velocity,* so both have the same sign.

Now suppose that a car moving in the same direction comes to a stop from a speed of +30 m/s in 10 s. The change in the velocity is 0 m/s − 30 m/s = -30 m/s. So the deceleration is -3 m/s^2.

Here the negative indicates that *the acceleration is acting in the opposite direction of the initial motion,* which was positive. Acceleration is a vector also. If it acts in the direction of motion, the velocity will be increasing; and if it acts in the opposite direction of motion, the velocity will be decreasing.

Consider a swinging screen door. If we assign a positive sign to the motion outward, we see that the spring is acting to slow its motion down and to turn it backwards; thus, the acceleration is negative relative to the original motion. The acceleration is acting to turn it around from a positive, forward motion to a negative or backward motion. Indeed, the door slows down, stops and reverses direction and speeds up as it moves in the negative direction. The velocity of the door starts out as positive, decreases, briefly goes to zero, and then becomes negative. A rock thrown upward has much the same motion. Can you describe how its velocity changes with time?

Kinematics gives only an account of the motion. We must enter the domain of *dynamics* in order to find out "why" things move.

1. Displacement is a change of _____.

2. The speedometer currently reads 62 mph, but actually only 54 miles have been covered during the last hour. What is the average speed?

    (a) 62 mph

    (b) 54 mph

    (c) an average of a and b

3. What information does velocity give that speed does not?

13B

Section

Dynamics: Newton's Laws

Medieval scientists believed that all things would slow down and eventually stop if left to themselves. This idea seems logical enough. If your engine quits, the car rolls to a stop. If you stop pedaling your bike, it will slow down and eventually fall over. But as logical as it appears, this assumption was found experimentally to be wrong! The natural tendency of all things is not to slow down and stop. Quite the contrary, when no outside forces work on an object, it will continue in its original state of motion. That is, it will stay at rest if it was at rest; if it was moving, it will keep moving in the same direction and at the same speed.

The Italian physicist Galileo was the first to investigate these ideas. He spent a great deal of time experimenting with falling bodies, inclined planes, projectile motion, and pendulums. On the basis of his experiments, Galileo found that objects would continue moving indefinitely unless they were affected by some outside influence. The English physicist Isaac Newton later extended Galileo's studies to formulate an entire area of science, the field of mechanics, and particularly dynamics—the study of why things move. Isaac Newton was born on Christmas Day in 1642. This was the same year Galileo died. Twenty-three years later, Newton formulated the three laws of motion.

Newton's First Law of Motion

Forces cause change. Forces may slow down an object, as in the case of friction or air drag, or may cause it to speed up or change direction. But what if we took away the forces acting on an object? What we would find is that things like to keep on doing

Fig. 13-7 These bumper cars resist a change in motion.

what they are already doing! In other words, an object in motion will stay in motion, or an object at rest will stay at rest *unless* it is acted on by a force. This statement is known as *Newton's first law of motion.*

Much of this does not seem to make sense in our everyday experience. If you throw a baseball horizontally, it will eventually fall to the ground. It does not sail off in a straight line. If you jump up in the air, you do not continue going up; instead you fall back to earth. So how can Newton's first law be correct? Well, you have not considered all the forces involved, such as gravity, atmospheric drag, and other forces. If there were no other forces acting upon a baseball thrown into space, it would continue on in a straight line until some other force acted upon it. The gravitational pull of the earth is very strong, so we are not able to observe this directly. But astronauts who have gone to the moon and satellites that are speeding through deep space have proved Newton's first law to be correct.

We often describe matter in terms of its physical properties—for example, color, taste, or hardness. As we saw in the last chapter, however, describing matter in terms of energy is more difficult. Energy is more of an "ability" than a physical description. Another ability of matter that is important to understand when discussing motion is called **inertia.** Inertia is a property of matter which causes it to resist a change in the state of motion. If you are riding in a car and the driver slams on the brakes, you jerk forward even though the car has stopped. Your body resisted the change in the state of motion.

Newton's Second Law of Motion

One of the benefits of a small, lightweight car is that moving it takes relatively little force. Such cars have small engines that use very little fuel. Larger, heavier cars need bigger, more powerful engines. The larger cars have more mass, so they have more

Fig. 13-8 Speeding bobsleds have a greater acceleration and inertia when there is extra mass. Olympic rules state that the athletes in the sled cannot have a combined mass greater than 630 kg (1,386 lb.).

inertia. It takes more force to get a big car rolling, and likewise it takes more force to stop it.

These observations show a direct relationship between force, mass, and acceleration for any given object. This relationship is stated in *Newton's second law of motion:* the value of an unbalanced force (F) is equal to its mass (m) multiplied by its acceleration (a).

The unit of force (F) is called the **newton** (N) and is equal to 1 kilogram-meter/second squared. We can use Newton's second law to calculate the force needed to give an object a certain acceleration. An economy car has a mass of approximately 1000 kg. How much force would it take to accelerate such a car 10 m/s^2?

> **Newton's Second Law of Motion**
>
> $F = ma$
> **or force = mass $\times$ acceleration**

$$F = 1000 \text{ kg} \times 10 \text{ m/s}^2$$
$$F = 10{,}000 \text{ kg m/s}^2 \text{ or } 10{,}000 \text{ N}$$

Now let us compare this value to the force needed to give a full-sized car the same acceleration. Let us say that the mass of such a car is 2000 kg.

$$F = 2000 \text{ kg} \times 10 \text{ m/s}^2$$
$$F = 20{,}000 \text{ kg} \cdot \text{m/s}^2 \text{ or } 20{,}000 \text{ N}$$

As you can see, a full-sized car requires twice the force to reach the same acceleration.

Newton's Third Law of Motion

Forces always come in pairs. A force of one object on another results in a force being returned. Have you ever jumped out of a small boat into the water? When you dive into the water, the boat moves backward. Your diving action causes a reaction movement of the boat. Firing a gun does much the same thing. The force of the gun on the bullet results in a force back on the gun called a recoil. These observations demonstrate the **action-reaction principle**, or *Newton's third law of motion.*

Here is another way of writing Newton's third law: *for every action, there is an opposite and equal reaction.* The "action" force is always exerted on a different body than the "reaction" force. In the boat example, the action force was exerted by your feet, and the reaction force was exerted on the boat.

Some action-reaction forces do not involve motion. Notice a book lying on a desk. Can you explain why the book is at rest? What forces are acting on the book? Gravity pulls the book toward the earth. This is its weight. The only other force actually on the book is the force of the table holding the book up. Since the book is at rest, the surface force must balance the weight of the book. So the book stays at rest because the table is strong enough to support it! If we set a 20-ton safe full of gold bars on the table, the table would collapse. Similarly, if you lean on the wall, the force that holds you up is the strength of the wall. If you lean on a cardboard wall in a stage or movie set, it will not hold you up by action-reaction forces.

Of course, some action and reaction forces do involve motion. Without them, rockets could not fly. Rockets do not fly by pushing against the ground. In fact, rockets firing from a 'parking' orbit around the earth work just fine.

13 Mechanics: Matter in Motion

The rocket expels the exhaust gases backward, causing an equal and opposite reaction on the rocket itself, pushing the rocket ahead. The rocket then accelerates. When two objects collide, object 1 pushes on object 2, while object 2 pushes back on object 1. When two masses pull gravitationally on each other, the directions are reversed, but the relation is the same. Object 1 pulls on object 2, while object 2 pulls with an equal and opposite force on object 1.

Let's learn a lesson from Newton's apple—the one that supposedly hit him on the head and made him start thinking about gravity. When an apple is falling, does the apple fall to the earth . . . or does the earth fall to the apple . . . or is it both? According to Newton's third law, both will happen. The force of the earth on the apple is equal to the force of the apple on the earth (about 2 N). Since the earth is 3×10^{25} more massive than the apple, it accelerates at such a slow rate toward the apple that it cannot be detected. So in reality, the earth's inertia is so much greater than the apple's that for all practical purposes the apple falls toward the earth and not vice versa.

SECTION REVIEW QUESTIONS 13B

1. Define *inertia*.

2. State Newton's second law in the form of an equation.

3. If you press on a desk top with a force of 25 N, what force is the table exerting back at you (assuming there is no motion)?

Gravity

Have you ever wondered why people say, "What goes up must come down"? Things fall toward the ground because the earth attracts objects towards itself. This attraction is called the earth's **gravity**. In fact, all the objects in the universe attract each other. We also see that the more massive the object, the greater the attraction. These attractions are called **action-at-a-distance forces** because they act on objects without touching them. How can a force act on an object without touching it? No one really knows, but based on our observations, this principle appears to be universal. Our knowledge about gravitational force has enabled us to put satellites in orbit and men on the moon.

Falling Bodies

Is it true that all bodies fall at the same rate (or acceleration)? Will equal-sized spheres of aluminum and lead fall at the same rate even though lead is heavier? Galileo was very interested in this question. He began his experiments when he was a professor at the University of Pisa in Italy. A popular story says that Galileo dropped various weights from the famous leaning tower to investigate their rate of fall. Although there may be more fiction than fact in the details of the story, we do know that Galileo reached a surprising number of correct conclusions about the way objects fall.

The scientists of Galileo's day held firmly to the two-thousand-year-old ideas of the Greek philosopher Aristotle. Aristotle had proclaimed that a heavier object should fall faster than a lighter object. Galileo challenged this faulty conclusion in two ways—by a "thought experiment" and by an actual physical experiment. Galileo's "thought experiment" showed clear thinking and originality. He imagined two small, equal weights falling side by side. If the weights were released from the same height at the same time, they obviously would strike the ground at the same instant. If the experiment were repeated again with a light but loose chain connecting the weights, the same thing would happen. He imagined that the weights were dropped repeatedly and the chain was shortened each time. Eventually, the two weights would be closely bound together, forming a single weight. This doubled weight would fall in the same amount of time as each of the smaller weights. Aristotle had said that the double weight should hit the ground in half the time the

Fig. 13-9 What did Galileo conclude from his thought experiments in which two chained weights hit the ground at the same time?

13 Mechanics: Matter in Motion

single weights took to fall. Galileo's scientific insight told him that there should be no difference between them.

Galileo later tried dropping many different objects. He found that if the masses of the two objects were great enough compared to their surface areas, then size, shape, and weight made little difference in how fast they fell. You can prove this for yourself. Try dropping a heavy book and a pencil from the same height. They will fall side by side and land at the same time. Remember that the book has more mass than the pencil. Because of this greater mass, the earth attracts the book with a greater force than it attracts the pencil. But the book also has more *inertia* than the pencil, which keeps it from accelerating faster. The force and the inertia exactly offset each other.

Now try dropping a pencil and a piece of paper at the same time. The pencil hits the floor first. In this case, another force enters the picture—air resistance. The air greatly slows down the paper because of the paper's small inertia and large surface area. Now wad the paper into a ball and drop the paper and the pencil again. What happens now that the surface area of the paper is decreased? A smaller surface area will cause a lower air resistance.

What would happen if no air were present when the uncrumpled paper and the pencil were dropped? Galileo predicted that they would fall at exactly the same rate, but to test his theory you would need to drop the paper and pencil in a sealed room with all the air removed by a vacuum pump. Or you could take your experiment to the surface of the moon, where there is practically no atmosphere at all.

Astronaut David Scott did just that. On the *Apollo 15* lunar mission, he took a hammer and a falcon feather (from the Air Force

Fig. 13-10 Apollo astronaut David R. Scott tried an elementary physics experiment on the moon's surface. In this unusual laboratory, he dropped a hammer and a feather from wrist level to find out if both objects would fall at the same rate. Indeed, they did!

mascot) with him in the lunar landing module. Once on the surface of the moon, he dropped the hammer and the feather before the watchful eye of a television camera. In exactly 1.33 seconds the feather and hammer simultaneously hit the surface of the moon.

If we could repeat that same experiment on the earth in a vacuum, we would find that both the feather and hammer would still hit at the same time. However, we would find that is takes less than 1.22 seconds to hit the ground. That is because the earth is larger than the moon and it has a greater "pull" due to gravity. On earth, this "pull," or *acceleration due to gravity, (g),* is 9.8 meters per second per second or 9.8 m/s/s (often written as 9.8 m/s^2). What this means is that a falling object near the surface of the earth will accelerate by 9.8 m/s for every second the object is falling. For example, if you dropped an object from a very tall building, at the end of one second it would be moving 9.8 m/s. After two seconds, it would be moving 19.6 m/s (9.8 + 9.8). After three seconds, the velocity would be 29.4 m/s (9.8 + 9.8 + 9.8). How fast would it be traveling after falling four seconds?

By rolling objects down inclined planes, Galileo discovered that the *distance* that an accelerating object travels is proportional to the square of the time, or

$$d = 1/2 \ at^2$$

For an object falling near the earth, *a* becomes *g* (acceleration due to gravity = 9.8 m/s/s).

EXAMPLE PROBLEM

Distance of fall and acceleration

After dropping a stone from a cliff, you count off 5 s before it hits the ground. How high above the valley floor are you?

KNOWN:	acceleration (g) = 9.8 m/s/s (or 9.8 m/s^2)
	time (t) = 5 s
UNKNOWN:	distance (d)
FORMULA TO USE:	$d = 1/2 \ at^2$
SUBSTITUTION:	$d = 1/2 \ (9.8 \ m/s^2) \ (5 \ s)^2$
SOLUTION:	d = 122.5 m

Suppose you are walking on a hill and you see a valley below. How can you determine how high you are above the floor of the valley?

If you have a stopwatch and good hearing, you could simply throw a smooth rock and time how long it takes it to hit bottom. (You would want to throw it out horizontally or drop it. Why wouldn't you want to throw it down?) Then simply do the calculation.

Drag and Terminal Velocity

When an object falls through the atmosphere, it eventually reaches a **terminal velocity,** the highest velocity at which that object can fall. What limits the velocity of any falling object? As the object falls through the air, the air pushes against it. This push, the air resistance, increases as the object accelerates. Eventually, the push of the air resistance will become as great as the pull of the object's weight. The object stops accelerating. Why? When the force of the air resistance equals the force due to the pull of gravity on the object (its weight), the forces are balanced. Since there is no unbalanced force on the object, there is no force to accelerate the object.

Different objects have different terminal velocities. Objects with very little surface area can reach very high speeds as they fall, but light objects with large surface areas fall at much slower speeds. How does this principle apply to a parachute?

Fig. 13-11 The terminal velocity of a parachute allows parachutists like this one to land safely. What role does the large surface area of the parachute play in determining the terminal velocity?

Weight as a Force

Even though we cannot see or touch the force of gravity, we can measure it. In fact, you probably know the strength of gravity's pull on your body. It is your **weight**. Weight, w, is a measure of the force of gravity. We have already learned that F = ma (see Newton's second law). We have also just learned that the earth "pulls downward" with an acceleration due to gravity equal to 9.8 m/s^2. Therefore, weight can be found by using the same equation (F = ma), substituting "w" in for F and "g" in for a:

$$w = mg$$

In this equation, w is the weight and g is acceleration due to gravity.

It is important to understand the distinction between mass (the amount of matter in an object) and weight (dependent upon the pull of gravity). You can measure mass *directly* by using a balance. Weight is found by using a scale. These two terms are often misused. No matter where you are, your mass never changes—unless you lose or gain mass. Your weight, however, does change depending on your location in relation to other massive objects. For example, if you were to go to Mars your mass would stay about the same. Your weight, however, would change.

EXAMPLE PROBLEM

Calculating weight of an object

If your mass is 50 kg (as measured on a balance), what is your weight?

KNOWN:	acceleration (g) = 9.8 m/s/s (or 9.8 m/s^2)
	mass (m) = 50 kg
UNKNOWN:	weight (w)
FORMULA TO USE:	w = mg
SUBSTITUTION:	w = 50 kg × 9.8 m/s^2
SOLUTION:	w = 490 N

Recall that 1 kg · m/s^2 is equal to 1 newton (N).

Note: 1 kg = 2.2 lb; therefore, if you weigh 120 pounds you can find your weight in newtons by dividing 120 by 2.2.
1 kg/2.2 lb × 120 lb = 55 kg   55 kg × 9.8 m/s^2 = 539 N!

In the example above, the mass was 50 kg. Therefore, the weight in pounds would be 2.2 lb/1 kg × 50 kg = 110 lb.

On Mars, the acceleration due to gravity is only 3.7 m/s². That is because Mars is smaller than Earth. How much would you weigh on Mars?

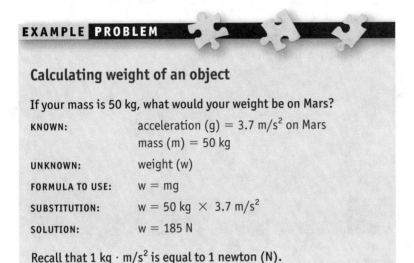

EXAMPLE PROBLEM

Calculating weight of an object

If your mass is 50 kg, what would your weight be on Mars?

KNOWN:	acceleration (g) = 3.7 m/s² on Mars
	mass (m) = 50 kg
UNKNOWN:	weight (w)
FORMULA TO USE:	w = mg
SUBSTITUTION:	w = 50 kg × 3.7 m/s²
SOLUTION:	w = 185 N

Recall that 1 kg · m/s² is equal to 1 newton (N).

Universal Law of Gravitation

In the example above, we found out that the gravity on Mars is less than it is on Earth. Why is this so? Well, we know that *gravitational forces are directly related to the mass of an object.* In fact, only very massive objects such as planets and stars exert enough gravity to be felt. The gravity of the sun is very strong. The gravity of Earth is much less.

We also realize that gravity has a limited range of influence. For example, by the time the spacecraft *Voyager I* and *Voyager II* traveled past Mars, Earth's gravity no longer had any noticeable effect on them. As the distance from an object's *center of gravity* increases, the influence of its gravity becomes weaker. There are slight differences in gravity even on the earth's surface, depending on where you are located! Newton recognized the relationship between gravity as a force, the mass of two objects, and the distance separating the objects. This helped Newton formulate the **Universal Law of Gravitation.**

Newton's law of gravity states that the force of gravity is directly related to the product of the masses of the two bodies. Also, it is inversely related to the relative distance between the objects *squared.* Written as an equation, Newton's Law of Gravity is

$$F = G \frac{m_1 \cdot m_2}{d^2}$$

Pendulum Motion

Pendulums first caught Galileo's attention as he watched a chandelier swing back and forth in a cathedral in Italy. He observed that the period of the pendulum (how long it took to swing back and forth) was very regular. Later, Galileo made experimental pendulums of different weights; these may have been no more than weights hanging on pieces of string. He found that the weight of the pendulum does not affect its period. The only variable that seemed to matter for small angles of swing was the length of the pendulum.

One other factor, however, can change the period of the pendulum. If its location is changed, its acceleration varies because of a change in the strength of gravity. Where the acceleration due to gravity (g) is greater, the pendulum will swing faster. Where g is less, the pendulum will swing more slowly. At the surface of Jupiter, a pendulum would swing considerably faster than it swings on the earth; its period would be much shorter. At the surface of a very small astronomical body that has a low mass, such as the moon, a pendulum would swing very slowly; it would have an extremely long period. If you could put a pendulum on the surface of the sun, it would swing 12.8 times faster there than it would on the surface of the moon!

Acceleration Due to Gravity at Different Places in the Solar System	
Body	g at surface in m/s^2
Sun	274.4
Earth	9.80
Moon	1.67
Mars	3.7
Jupiter	26.46
Saturn	11.76
Neptune	9.80

where m_1 and m_2 are the masses of the two objects and the distance between them is d. G is 6.67×10^{-11} N · m²/kg², a value known as the *universal gravitation constant.* Since the masses are directly related to F, the more massive the objects, the greater the force of gravity between those objects. In fact, if the mass of both objects is doubled, then we increase the force by 2 × 2, or four times.

Since the distance between two objects squared is inversely related to F, the farther apart the objects are, the less the force of gravity between the objects. For example, if the distance is increased by 3 times, then the force is decreased by 9 times! If the distance is decreased to 1/4, the force is increased by 4^2, or 16 times!

Gravity is a very important force in nature. It literally holds the universe together. Yet it is also one of the weakest forces in nature. In I Corinthians 1:27 we read, "But God hath chosen the foolish things of the world to confound the wise; and God hath chosen the weak things of the world to confound the things which are mighty." This reminds us that though we are weak, God can do mighty things with us. Perhaps the greatest power in the universe is manifested when a Christian who loves God with all his or her heart shares burdens with the Lord in prayer. What appears to be weak and foolish has a greater influence than the most powerful physical agents in the universe.

Fig. 13-12 Venus has about the same mass as Earth and is about 2/3 of Earth's distance to the Sun. How does the Sun-Venus force compare to the force between the Sun and Earth? Since the masses are about the same the only difference is d. Inverting 2/3, we get 3/2. Squaring this value, we get 9/4, or about 2 1/4. So the force between Venus and the Sun is about twice that of the Earth-Sun.

Earth Satellites

Satellites are celestial bodies in orbit around another celestial body. Satellites can be natural, like the moon of our earth and the moons of other planets. Or they can be manmade, like the ones that orbit our planet and provide weather, navigation, communications, and intelligence data to receiving stations. The seventeenth-century German astronomer Johannes Kepler was especially interested in the motion of the planets around the sun and the moons around the planets. One might think that because the sun is such a large object, its gravitational pull would be so tremendous that planets would just careen toward it. But Kepler was able to formulate theories that explained how satellites moving at the right speed and position move in elliptical orbits. Since that time, scientists have used Kepler's ideas to put hundreds of satellites in orbit.

A satellite in low earth orbit travels at a speed of 28,000 km/hr. At this speed it circles the globe in about ninety minutes. If a spacecraft attains escape velocity, its speed is 40,000 km/hr. A great many satellites, used mostly for communications, travel in high earth orbits so that their orbital period matches the daily rotation of the earth, twenty-four hours. By using Newton's law of universal gravitation and the size of the earth, one can calculate the altitude of such an orbit—36,000 km. Here the satellite remains apparently fixed in the sky if it has an equatorial orbit. It is really orbiting, but it is circling the earth at the same period as the

JOHANNES KEPLER-German Astronomer (1571-1630)

"**Knowest thou the ordinances** of heaven? canst thou set the dominion thereof in the earth?" (Job 38:33)

Sir Isaac Newton once commented, "If I have seen further, it is by standing on the shoulders of giants." Johannes Kepler was one of those giants. Kepler was the first man to demonstrate that the motions of the planets are precise, predictable, and obedient to definite rules. Kepler's three laws of planetary motion are used extensively today in calculating the orbits of satellites and in mapping routes for space travel. Kepler is also called the Father of modern optics because of his masterful mathematical analysis of lenses and mirrors.

Kepler, a German astronomer and a devout Lutheran, trusted Christ as his Savior at an early age. Although he was persecuted for his Protestant beliefs, he remained true to the Lord through his entire life. Kepler saw himself as God's instrument for revealing the details of His handiwork to men. "Since we astronomers are priests of the highest God in regard to the book of nature," he once wrote, "it befits us to be thoughtful not of the glory of our

minds, but rather, above all else, of the glory of God." Seeking to give his children a thoroughly Christian upbringing, Kepler wrote Bible study guides to aid their understanding. One of these guides, "The Body and Blood of Jesus Christ Our Savior" is still preserved in the University of Tübingen library.

Michael Maestlin, whom Kepler met at the University of Tübingen, inspired Kepler for his life's work. Though he taught his students the old geocentric (earth-centered) theory of the solar system, Maestlin exposed them to the newer ideas of Copernicus in a way that kindled Kepler's imagination. Consuming curiosity compelled Kepler to study the subject on his own. After-class discussions with Maestlin, who was a fellow Christian, sparked new ideas that would lead to the publication of Kepler's first book.

In 1591 Kepler graduated from the Faculty of Arts at Tübingen, receiving the equivalent of today's Master of Arts degree. At that time he felt certain that he was destined for the Lutheran ministry. Accordingly, he enrolled at the Theological Faculty and continued his studies. Before he completed his theological examinations, however, an unexpected opportunity arose. The death of the mathematics and astronomy teacher at the Protestant

surface of the earth below. This is called a **geostationary orbit.** Once pointed, a fixed satellite dish mounted on the earth will always point at the same satellite. This eliminates the need for tracking and reduces costs. Pluto's moon, Charon, orbits as a geostationary satellite.

seminary in Graz, Austria, had created a vacancy. When the senate of the University of Tübingen was asked to recommend a candidate, they chose Kepler. His extraordinary ability had not gone unnoticed.

Kepler's years at Graz were both challenging and rewarding. There he produced his first serious scientific treatise, *The Mystery of the Universe,* an ambitious geometric description of the solar system. The work closed with a magnificent hymn of praise to the Creator. The treatise was well received, and, because he shrewdly placed it in the hands of several leading astronomers (including Galileo and Tycho Brahe [TEE ko brah]), Kepler's name became known in several of the scientific centers of Europe.

As the sixteenth century drew to a close, the political and religious conditions in Graz grew increasingly turbulent. Faced with severe religious persecution, Kepler and his family fled from Graz in 1600. Earlier the same year he had accepted an invitation to visit Prague to see Tycho Brahe, imperial mathematician to Rudolph II, emperor of Bohemia. Recognized as the world's leading astronomer, Tycho had been making remarkably accurate observations of the planets for twenty years. It now remained for someone to "make sense" out of

the massive columns of data he had assembled. Kepler wanted access to these observations, and Tycho was eager to add a theoretician of Kepler's caliber to his staff of assistants. It was indeed Providence who brought together these two giants whose abilities complemented each other so well. Kepler was aware of the unique opportunity that had been afforded him and thankful for the strange turn of events that brought it to pass. He later said, "I see how God let me be bound with Tycho through an unalterable fate and did not let me be separated from him by the most oppressive hardships."

When Kepler arrived in Prague, Tycho assigned him the task of interpreting observations of the planet Mars. These calculations occupied the German astronomer for many years. Kepler explored numerous blind alleys and was often forced to start over again. However, his perseverance bore fruit. He formulated one-by-one the three laws of planetary motion familiar to every student of astronomy:

1. Planets move in ellipses with the sun at one focus.

2. An imaginary line from the sun to a planet sweeps over an equal area in equal time.

3. The square of a planet's orbital period is directly related to the cube

of the mean distance from the sun.

Kepler's third law provided a foundation for Newton's law of gravitation just half a century later. Kepler was well ahead of his time; no one claimed to have anticipated his discoveries. In fact, to other astronomers of his day, the area and ellipse laws were new, unorthodox, and difficult to understand.

Kepler's later life was one of hardships—sickness and death in his family, religious persecution, war, a fire, and a trial in which his mother was falsely accused of witchcraft. But his faith in Christ brought him triumphantly through these tribulations, and he gave God the glory for His sustaining grace.

Kepler's name has been immortalized by his three laws of planetary motion. A prominent crater on the moon has been named in his honor. His native Germany has paid him homage by erecting elaborate monuments to him in Regensburg and Weil der Stadt. His birthplace in Weil der Stadt has been converted into an attractive museum. Any fame he achieved, however, was simply a byproduct of his lifelong endeavor to glorify the name of the heavenly Father. "Let also my name perish," Kepler stated, "if only the name of God the Father . . . is thereby elevated."

1. Summarize Galileo's experiments on falling bodies and how they contradicted Aristotle's teachings.

2. What does g stand for, and what is its value?

3. Distinguish between mass and weight. What is wrong with the following statement: "This bag of potatoes weighs 5 kg"?

CHAPTER REVIEW

SCIENTIFICALLY SPEAKING

mechanics	inertia
kinematics	newton (N)
dynamics	action-reaction principle
frame of reference	gravity (g)
displacement	action-at-a-distance forces
speed	
average speed	terminal velocity
velocity (v)	weight (w)
magnitude	Universal Law of Gravitation
vectors	satellites
scalars	geostationary orbit
acceleration	

CHAPTER REVIEW QUESTIONS

1. What is the difference between kinematics and dynamics?

2. Summarize Newton's three laws of motion.

3. Give an example of how a person's frame of reference can affect his perspective of motion.

4. What is the term we use to denote speed and direction?

5. What is a scalar quantity?

6. What are action-reaction forces? Give an example.

7. An astronaut is comparing her mass and weight on an asteroid many times smaller than the earth to her mass and weight on the earth. In general, what does she find?

8. The sound of thunder travels at the rate of 332 m/s. How long does it take for the sound to travel 1320 m (about 0.8 miles)?

9. Is the natural tendency of all matter to be at rest or in motion? Explain your answer.

10. According to Newton's second law, what is the weight of a 20 kg mass on the earth?

11. Using the law of universal gravitation, does F increase or decrease when the distance (d) decreases?

FACET REVIEW QUESTIONS

1. Name Kepler's three laws of planetary motion.

2. Describe pendulum motion on the planet Jupiter.

WHAT DID YOU LEARN?

1. You realize that you forgot to strap on your parachute seconds after you ejected from your F-16 jet fighter. Your last recorded altitude over Lake Michigan was 3000 m. If you are to have a chance at surviving the fall, what is the best way to position your body? Why?

2. A man is seen in a circus lying on a bed of nails. Describe the action-reaction forces involved. Why don't the nails puncture his skin?

3. Our planet is not a perfect sphere; it is slightly flattened at the poles. Would a native of Alaska experience a slightly stronger or weaker pull from gravity than a person living near the equator? Hint: Gravitational pull varies depending on distance from center of gravity (in this case the center of the earth).

4. What is the importance of a geostationary satellite orbit?

5. Can someone on the earth experience the same effect of weightlessness that astronauts do?

Work and Machines

14A **Making Work Easier**

14B **Other Simple Machines and the Distance Principle**

In 215 B.C. the Roman navy besieged the port city of Syracuse on the southeast coast of Sicily. The attackers thought they had an easy prey, but the tiny nation turned out to be a worthy opponent. It kept the entire Roman navy at bay for over three years. How did the defenders succeed for so long? Mostly by using the ingenious machines of the scientist Archimedes (AHR kih MEE deez).

   As the Romans first entered the harbor, they were greeted by a hailstorm of rocks launched from catapults along the shore. When the ships neared the shoreline, Archimedes' men lowered large hooks from long poles called booms. They embedded the hooks in the wooden hulls, hoisted the ships into the air, and plunged them into the sea. The stubborn Romans sent more ships to conquer the city. This time, as the Roman ships entered the harbor they mysteriously burst into flames. Archimedes had directed the defenders of Syracuse to use their polished shields as mirrors to focus the rays of the hot Mediterranean sun on the sails of the Roman ships. The intense heat ignited the cloth sails, causing the Romans to abandon their ships. The Roman commanders hated and feared Archimedes so much that the instant they took Syracuse they put the scientist to death!

Did Archimedes possess some magic that his enemies did not? No, but what he did possess was knowledge and a great ability to *apply* his knowledge. Scientists before his time had used mathematics in the description of nature, but Archimedes applied his mathematical ideas for the practical control of everyday events. He contributed to the development of levers, pulleys, and other simple devices that we still use today. In this chapter we will explore these simple machines and the ways in which they make work easier for us. Let's begin by looking at what we mean by the word *work.*

Making Work Easier

What is work? The term *work* has many meanings. For example, work is usually associated with effort expended to accomplish a task. That task may be physical, such as mowing a lawn, or intellectual, such as writing a musical composition or teaching a class. In physical science, however, work is being done only if an object moves under the influence of a force. Therefore, the two conditions that define work are a *change in position* (*d* is the symbol for distance or displacement) and an *applied force* (*F* is the symbol for force; F = ma; see Chapter 13). You can push and push on the wall of your classroom until your arms ache and you begin to sweat. Have you done any work on the wall? The answer is no.

Fig. 14-1 This woman accomplishes work only when she moves the weight.

According to our definition, you have not done any work at all since the wall did not move. Scientifically speaking, work involves effort and results. Your effort (F) on the wall has yielded no results; therefore, no work has been done on the wall. No work is done if either the force or distance equals zero.

When a weightlifter pulls a barbell above his head, he does strenuous work, but once the barbell is in position, he is no longer working on the barbell. He is exerting force to hold the barbell in place, but the force is not causing motion. Since there is no change in position, zero work is being done on the barbell.

A weightlifter can change the amount of work he does by adding mass to the barbell. If he adds 10 kg to each side of the barbell, he increases the amount of work he must do to accomplish the lift. Even though he is lifting the barbell the same distance, he is using *more* force to lift the increased mass. Consider the following example. Two weightlifters are lifting the same amount of mass. The first is doing a military press. He pushes 100 kg from his chest to the full extension of his arms. The other is doing a snatch. He must pull the 100 kg from the floor and push it over his head in one continuous motion. Which lifter is doing more work against gravity? Consider both the force and the change in position. Is the force the same? Yes, both are lifting 100 kg. Is the distance the same? No, the lifter doing the snatch must pull the weight from the floor and then push the barbell over his head without stopping, over a greater distance. Therefore, he is doing the greater amount of work.

Fig. 14-2 A puck sliding on ice is not an example of work because no force is being applied.

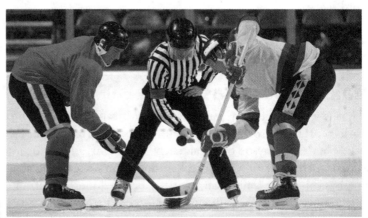

What if an object's position is changed but no force has been applied? Take, for example, a hockey puck gliding on the nearly frictionless ice. As the puck slides with constant speed in a straight line across the ice, is there work being done? The answer is no. The puck is moving, but no force is being applied. So the work being done on the puck at that moment is zero.

Work depends on both force and displacement and is defined as the amount of a particular force applied on an object multiplied by the distance the object is moved. The formula used to calculate work is

$$W = F \cdot d$$

where F = force and is measured in newtons (N), and d = displacement or distance and is measured in meters (m).

Formula for Work
$$W = F \cdot d$$
or work = force × distance

Calculating amount of work done in N · m

Problem Statement: If you push an empty cooler on the surface of a picnic table with a 20 N force for a distance of 2 m, how much work is accomplished?

KNOWN:	force (F) = 20 N
	distance (d) = 2 m
UNKNOWN:	work (W)
FORMULA TO USE:	W = F · d
SUBSTITUTION:	W = 20 N · 2 m
SOLUTION:	W = 40 N · m

If the cooler in the example problem above were full of ice, more force would be necessary. Suppose 40 N were applied to slide the full cooler. The total work done on the cooler would be 40 N · 2 m, or 80 N · m. In the SI system, the newton-meter has been given a special name. It is called a **joule** (JOOL) (**J**). A joule is the work done when a one-newton force moves an object in the direction of the force through a one-meter displacement.

one newton-meter = one joule

1 N · m = 1 J

You learned in Chapter 12 that the joule is also the unit for energy. Through unit analysis, you could prove that energy joules and work joules are the same basic unit ($1 \text{ J} = \frac{\text{kg} \cdot \text{m}^2}{\text{s}^2}$). Now that we have learned the definition of work in a science context, let's see what we can use to make work easier.

Simple Machines

Machines are devices that make work easier. They can be as simple as a pry bar or as complex as a bulldozer. Many simple machines can greatly reduce the amount of effort required to perform a task. Machines with only one or two parts are called **simple machines.**

We will look at six simple machines—the lever, wheel and axle, pulley, inclined plane, wedge, and screw. These simple machines are devices that allow a small force to be as effective as a large force applied without their aid. Many of them date back thousands of years before Archimedes. Machines were first made of stone, later of bronze, and still later of iron and steel. How the Egyptians were able to set huge blocks of stone in place in the pyramids has always been a source of

wonder and amazement, even for our modern world. It is possible that the blocks were pushed along on logs, which served as wheels, then up a sloping road (inclined plane) to the top of the structure.

Machines can make work easier in three ways. First, a machine can increase the amount of force a person exerts. An example of this type of machine would be a wrench. Second, a machine can change the direction of the force exerted. An example of this would be a pulley. Third, a machine can change the speed at which a force acts. A tennis racket is an example of this type of machine.

Machines can increase the force available to do work and speed up the rate at which work gets done. However, a machine can never increase the amount of work done or energy expended. Even in factories where complex machines are driven by large electric motors, the machine can never increase the amount of work done by the motor. There is always a "payoff" or "cost." For example, pliers change a small force and large distance moved at the handles to a large force and small distance moved at the nose.

Fig. 14-3 An ancient Egyptian balance

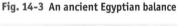

Levers

A simple **lever** is a rigid bar capable of turning about a fixed point called a **fulcrum** (FUL krum). The lever appeared in Old Testament marketplaces in the form of equal-arm balances, or platform balances, which were used to measure silver and gold for trading. A pan was attached to each end of a rigid bar, which was equally divided by a fulcrum. The pans held the precious metals, which were used as the standard for comparison. A person weighed an object by placing it in one pan and the known weights in the other pan. Dishonest traders were known to adjust their balances so that they no longer had "equal arms." In Proverbs 11:1, God's children

are admonished to avoid such practices: "A false balance is abomination to the Lord: but a just weight is his delight."

Although levers were applied throughout the ancient world, Archimedes was the first to mathematically determine the principle by which they work.

The Law of Moments

Imagine a seesaw, a light boy, and a heavy boy. Your job is to balance the boys on the seesaw. You might guess that the heavy boy should sit closer to the fulcrum than the light boy. But how much closer should he sit? The best way to solve this problem is to perform an experiment, gather data, and then analyze the data. First, weigh both boys. Suppose the heavy boy weighs 450 N, twice as much as the lighter boy, who weighs 225 N. Let the boys get on the seesaw, and have them move until they balance it. They can take a number of different positions to balance the lever. For example, when the 450 N boy sits 1/2 m from the fulcrum, the 225 N boy can balance him by sitting 1 m from the fulcrum. When the 450 N boy sits 1 m from the fulcrum, the 225 N boy can balance him by sitting 2 m from the fulcrum. Also, with the heavy boy at 1 1/2 m, the light boy must be 3 m from the fulcrum. This table summarizes the data:

Meters from fulcrum in order to balance	
450 N boy	**225 N boy**
$\frac{1}{2}$	1
1	2
$1\frac{1}{2}$	3

After arranging the data in a table, the physicist usually looks for a pattern that ties the data together. With enough "head scratching," the physicist sees a general principle at work. In this case, the weight of the heavy boy multiplied by his distance from the fulcrum is equal to the weight of the light boy multiplied by his distance from the fulcrum.

$$(450 \text{ N})(1/2 \text{ m}) = (225 \text{ N})(1 \text{ m})$$
$$(450 \text{ N})(1 \text{ m}) = (225 \text{ N})(2 \text{ m})$$
$$(450 \text{ N})(1 \ 1/2 \text{ m}) = (225 \text{ N})(3 \text{ m})$$
$$(\text{weight}_1)(\text{distance}_1) = (\text{weight}_2)(\text{distance}_2)$$

This relationship seems to work, at least for these two boys. Trying this experiment again with different students might yield the following data:

Meters from fulcrum in order to balance	
600 N student	200 N student
$\frac{1}{3}$	1
$\frac{2}{3}$	2
1	3

Again, the products of the weights and the distances are equal in each case:

$$(600 \text{ N})(1/3 \text{ m}) = (200 \text{ N})(1 \text{ m})$$
$$(600 \text{ N})(2/3 \text{ m}) = (200 \text{ N})(2 \text{ m})$$
$$(600 \text{ N})(1 \text{ m}) = (200 \text{ N})(3 \text{ m})$$

Would this principle also hold true for nonliving objects? Substituting sacks of flour or kegs of nails for each of the boys would settle this question. After enough testing, this principle can be confidently applied to all kinds of objects. Only weights of the objects and their distances from the fulcrum are important. This principle can be summarized by this equation:

$$w_1d_1 = w_2d_2$$

The Law of Moments
$$w_1d_1 = w_2d_2$$

In this equation, the first weight (w_1) multiplied by its distance (d_1) from the fulcrum is equal to the second weight (w_2) multiplied by its distance (d_2) from the fulcrum. This principle is called the **law of moments.** It applies to all levers. The distances must be measured from the fulcrum to the exact point at which the weight is applied on the lever arm for the calculations to be correct.

You may use this equation to find unknown values in a lever system. If you know three of the quantities, you can calculate the fourth value.

EXAMPLE PROBLEM

The Law of Moments

Problem Statement: How far from the fulcrum of a seesaw would a 300 N girl sit to balance a 450 N boy who is sitting 1 m from the fulcrum?

KNOWN:	weight$_1$ = 300 N
	weight$_2$ = 450 N
	distance$_2$ = 1 m
UNKNOWN:	distance$_1$
FORMULA TO USE:	$w_1 \cdot d_1 = w_2 \cdot d_2$
SUBSTITUTION:	300 N $\cdot$ d_1 = 450 N $\cdot$ 1 m
SOLUTION:	d_1 = 1.5 m

The law of moments establishes the conditions that must exist if there is to be no rotation of the lever (seesaw)—in other words, if a state of equilibrium is to exist. If the seesaw is not in equilibrium, it will tend to pivot on the fulcrum. This is referred to as **torque** and occurs when the law of moments is not being met.

First-class Levers

Some 1500 years before Christ, early Britons labored to build the astronomical observatory we now call Stonehenge. The gray sandstone slabs that make up the main ring of the observatory were quarried on the Marlborough Downs and hauled 39 km south to the Salisbury Plain. The ancient Britons must have been excellent engineers and craftsmen. Even with modern construction equipment we would find it difficult to do the things they did, but the Britons accomplished them using only simple machines.

The **first-class lever** played an important part in constructing Stonehenge. With first-class levers, a push (**effort**) is applied to one end (the **effort arm**) of the lever in order to move a weight (**resistance**) at the opposite end (the **resistance arm**). The fulcrum is located between the effort and the resistance. Using simple arrangements of timbers and boulders as levers and fulcrums, the ancient builders of Stonehenge maneuvered massive forty-ton stones and arranged them with great precision.

FACETS of the physical world

Mechanical Advantage

Simple machines give the user a mechanical advantage. The term *mechanical advantage* may be misleading. In the problem of moving the stone, you found that you could save effort but that the saving was not "free." You had to pay for it by applying the effort over a greater distance. This hidden cost is an example of the *distance principle:* what is saved in effort is paid for in distance.

One way of expressing how much an effort is magnified by a simple machine is the mechanical advantage (M.A.). It can be calculated in three different ways.

M.A. = (1) resistance/effort = (2) effort arm/resistance arm = (3) distance that the effort is applied/distance that the resistance moves
    = 980 N/245 N   = 160 cm/40 cm   = 40 cm/10 cm

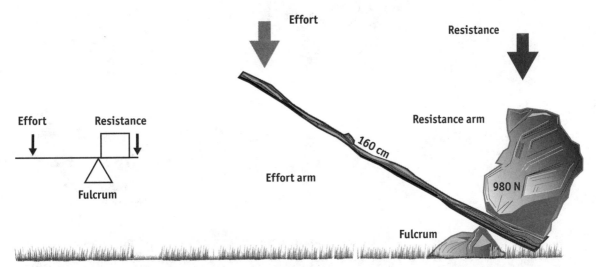

Fig. 14-4 First-class lever

You can use the law of moments to calculate the effort needed to move an object with a first-class lever. Suppose you had to move a stone—much smaller than the stones at Stonehenge! Note the measurements in the drawing above.

$$w_1 \cdot d_1 = w_2 \cdot d_2$$

effort   effort arm   resistance   resistance arm

If we apply them to the law of moments, we can solve for the effort needed to lift the stone.

First, place the known values into the equation.

$$w_1 \cdot 160 \text{ cm} = 980 \text{ N} \cdot 40 \text{ cm}$$

the force to be applied (effort)   the length of the effort arm   the weight of the stone (resistance)   the length of the resistance arm

Next, solve for the effort by dividing both sides by the length of the effort arm.

$$\frac{w_1 \cdot 160 \text{ cm}}{160 \text{ cm}} = \frac{980 \text{ N} \cdot 40 \text{ cm}}{160 \text{ cm}} \quad \text{units cancel}$$

$$w_1 = 245 \text{ N (the units of force)}$$

The effort needed to move the stone was only one-fourth of the weight of the stone! Did you actually do less work? Did you somehow "pay" for the reduced effort? Look at the task again.

You can see that although you applied one-fourth of the effort, the effort arm moved four times as far as the resistance arm.

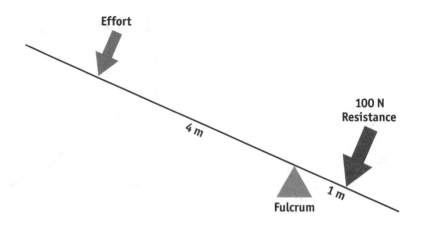

By means of machinery such as levers and pulleys, we can move an object by applying a force much smaller than would be required if we tried to move it directly without the use of a machine. The **mechanical advantage** (**M.A.**) is often described as a measure of the "force-multiplying ability" of a machine. One formal definition is the ratio of the resisting force and the applied force:

$$M.A. = \text{resisting force/applied force}$$

EXAMPLE **PROBLEM**

The Law of Moments and M.A. of a Lever

A force of how many newtons must be exerted 4 meters to the left of the fulcrum of a first-class lever to balance a 100 N weight suspended from the opposite end at a point that is 1 meter to the right of the fulcrum? Calculate the mechanical advantage of the lever.

KNOWN:	force or weight$_2$ = 100 N
	distance$_1$ = 4 m
	distance$_2$ = 1 m
UNKNOWN:	force or weight$_1$
FORMULA TO USE:	$w_1 \cdot d_1 = w_2 \cdot d_2$
SUBSTITUTION:	$w_1 \cdot 4\text{ m} = 100\text{ N} \cdot 1\text{ m}$
SOLUTION:	$w_1 = 25\text{ N}$
	M.A. = resistance (w_2)/effort (w_1)
	M.A. = 100/25
	M.A. = 4

Note: There are *no* units given to M.A.!

Thus, the lever in the example above would have a mechanical advantage of 4 since the resisting force is four times as great as the applied force.

On a seesaw the ratio of the weight suspended (resisting force) to the applied force required to hold it precisely in equilibrium gives us the mechanical advantage of the lever, for the seesaw is a lever. If a weight of 100 N is held suspended by a 10 N force, the lever has a mechanical advantage of 10. If there were no friction involved and if the slightest additional force were added to the 10 N applied force, the 100 N weight would begin to rise.

In other words, moving the effort arm 4 cm will move the resistance arm only 1/4 of this distance or 1 cm! The price you pay to gain M.A. is in the distance over which you must move the effort.

Second- and Third-class Levers

If you arrange the effort, resistance, and fulcrum differently, two other types of levers are possible. In a **second-class lever,** the resistance is located between the fulcrum and the effort. Most doors are second-class levers. The hinges form the fulcrum, the effort is applied at the doorknob, and the weight of the door is the resistance. Another common second-class lever is the wheelbarrow. Where are the effort, resistance, and fulcrum of the wheelbarrow?

When you carry your tray at a cafeteria, you use a **third-class lever**—your arm! The muscle called the biceps exerts an effort on the bones in your forearm. The fulcrum is your elbow, and the resistance is held in your hand. With third-class levers the effort is applied between the fulcrum and the resistance. The resistance arm (the distance from the fulcrum to the point of resistance) is longer than the effort arm (the distance from the fulcrum to the point of effort).

Fig. 14-5 Second-class lever

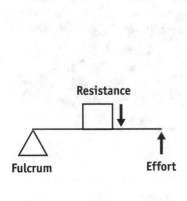

Resistance

Fulcrum   Effort

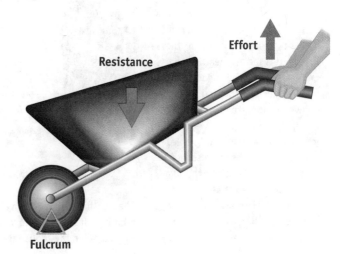

Effort

Resistance

Fulcrum

The mechanical advantage of third-class levers reveals some interesting facts about the body's design. One of the equations for mechanical advantage was

$$\text{M.A.} = \frac{\text{the distance that the effort is applied}}{\text{the distance that the resistance moves}}$$

When the biceps moves the upper forearm 5.0 cm, the hand is moved 35 cm. Therefore, the mechanical advantage is calculated as follows:

$$\text{M.A.} = \frac{5.0 \text{ cm}}{35 \text{ cm}} = \frac{1}{7}$$

FACETS of the physical world

Stonehenge

Hoisting into place a twenty-five-ton pillar of stone would be no small feat. The builders of Stonehenge placed thirty of those stones in a circle thirty meters in diameter. They didn't use cranes or automobiles. The didn't use large flatbed trucks to haul their stone. Why not? Because Stonehenge was built over 3500 years ago!

Stonehenge is thought to be a ritualistic monument built by an ancient civilization known as the Druids. It is located near Salisbury, England, and has become a very famous tourist attraction. Nobody knows why the people built this odd monument. Some say it was purely for ritual, as a tribute or temple. Others think it was some sort of large sundial, predicting the summer and winter solstices.

Archaeologists have developed theories about how the main ring was constructed. According to one

theory, the builders dug a deep pit where each stone was to stand. To erect a pillar, they rolled it on logs until one-third of its length hung over a pit and then lifted the other end and tilted the stone over the

If a mechanical advantage is less than 1, it takes a large effort to overcome a small resistance. Does the action of the forearm seem inefficient?

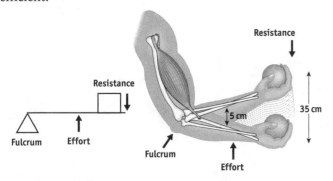

Fig. 14-6 Third-class lever

edge. Next, layer by layer, they built a log structure against the side of the leaning stone so that they could use levers to lift the huge column upright. Workers then hurriedly filled in the pit. But scientists still wonder how these early engineers lifted and placed the four-ton capstones that topped the ring of columns.

Over the thousands of years, Stonehenge has endured not only the notorious weather of England but also vandals. Sometime after the beginning of the first millennium, Roman soldiers apparently knocked some of the stones over. Since then, other stones have fallen over. In the 1950s, five stones were raised to give Stonehenge the approximate look it had in the first century. After 3500 years, seventeen of the original stones stand today. Ten of them are still capped.

First Class

Second Class

Third Class

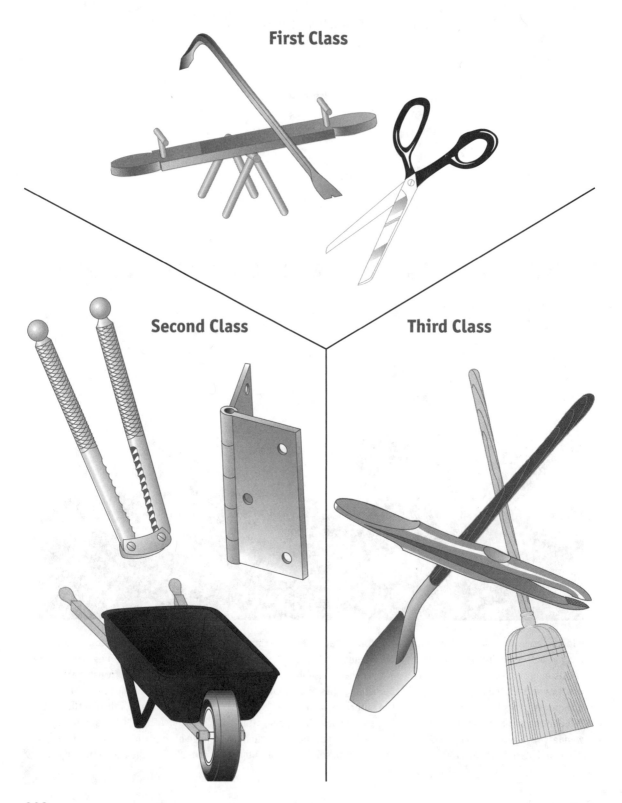

Not if you consider the way this lever functions. Levers that avoid effort "pay" with large movements of the effort arm and only small movements of the resistance arm. However, third-class levers do not avoid effort. Instead, a lot of effort and a small amount of movement on the part of the effort arm result in a large movement of the resistance arm. If God had designed the human body with first- or second-class levers, it would not have the range or speed of motion that we enjoy.

SECTION REVIEW QUESTIONS 14A

1. What are the two conditions that define work?
2. What is meant by mechanical advantage?
3. Give an example of each of the three types of levers.

Other Simple Machines and the Distance Principle

The Wheel and Axle

A simple lever, such as a crowbar, cannot move the resistance very far. To cover distance, the simple lever must be modified. One such modification is called a **wheel and axle.**

A bicycle provides another excellent example of a wheel and axle at work. Your feet provide the effort exerted to the axle by the pedals. This effort is then transferred to the wheels through the sprocket and chain. On a multispeed bike, you may have noticed that when you shift "down" to a lower gear when going up a hill, your feet must move faster (cover more distance). The price you pay to get the bike to pedal more easily is in the distance your feet must move.

Pulleys

A **pulley** is also a modified lever. The effort arm and the resistance arm of a pulley are the same length. Therefore, the mechanical advantage of a *single fixed pulley* is equal to 1. If a single fixed pulley does not save effort or shorten the distance through which the effort is applied, then how are single pulleys useful? This type of pulley changes the direction of an effort. Sometimes this gives a definite physical advantage. Lifting an object with a single pulley attached to the ceiling allows you literally to put your weight into your effort. This is often much easier than bearing the whole effort with your legs, back, and arms.

A *single movable pulley* has a mechanical advantage of 2. The drawing below illustrates why.

As the rope is pulled 1 m, the pulley moves upward only 1/2 m. The motion of the pull is divided in half since two ropes are attached to the resistance. For each meter that the weight rises, the rope must be pulled out 2 meters.

What is the mechanical advantage of this pulley system?

The mechanical advantage is 1. Fixed pulleys change only the direction of the motion. They do not affect the amount of effort needed.

In this pulley system the mechanical advantage is 4. Can you see why? There are four ropes supporting the resistance. Therefore, the effort is only one-fourth of the resistance, but the rope must be pulled four times the distance that the resistance is moved! This gives us a quick way to calculate the mechanical advantage of pulley systems. The number of ropes supporting the resistance will be the same as the value of the mechanical advantage. Such an arrangement of fixed and movable pulleys is called a **block and tackle**.

EXAMPLE PROBLEM

Working with pulleys

Suppose a workman is trying to lift a piano with a six-pulley block and tackle (three fixed and three movable pulleys—see Figure 14-7). If the piano weighs 2400 N, how much effort will be required of the workman? What is the mechanical advantage of the system?

KNOWN:	Since six ropes are attached to the resistance, the M.A. is 6.
	Weight of piano = 2400 N (538 pounds)
UNKNOWN:	Effort required to lift piano
SOLUTION:	Since M.A. is 6, the effort required will be 1/6 the resistance.
	1/6 · 2400 N = 400 N effort (90 pounds)

M.A. = resistance/effort; therefore, effort = resistance/M.A.

In the previous example, how far would the workman have to pull the rope to get the piano to rise 1 m? 2 m? 5 m? Since the M.A. is 6, he would have to pull the rope 6 meters for every meter that the piano moves up or down!

The Distance Principle Applied

The distance principle, sometimes called the work principle, is another way to understand the mechanical advantage of a machine. The **distance principle** states that any *reduction in the effort force* that is required will be "paid" for by an *increased distance* through which that force must act. We saw this principle in action with the lever, wheel and axle, and pulley. It is based on the conservation of energy. The amount of work *in* cannot be greater than the amount of work *out*. If we assume 100% efficiency, they must be equal. Thus, the amount of work done, whether with the original force or the reduced force, will be the

Fig. 14-7 The workman "pays" for reduced effort by pulling a longer distance of the rope.

same. When you climb a mountain, you do the same amount of work against gravity in reaching the top whether you take a path that is short and steep or one that is long and gradual. We already know that work is defined as the product of a force times a distance. In the case of climbing a mountain, the force is the weight of the person, and the distance is the vertical height reached.

Inclined Planes

Historians tell us that the ancient Egyptians did not have pulleys. This fact makes the construction of the pyramids an even more amazing feat of engineering. The simple machine that was used to move the giant limestone blocks into position was the **inclined plane.**

Many earthen ramps were built during the construction process. Lighter stones could be slid up steeper ramps while the heavier stones required long, gradual inclines.

An ancient papyrus dating from 1300 years before Christ gives the approximate measurements of one of these large earthen inclined planes: 384 m long and 32 m high. If the Egyptian engineers had lifted the stone directly into place 32 m above the ground, the work done would have been equal to the force needed to lift the stone multiplied by the distance (32 m). The work needed to lift a 6000 N block would be calculated this way:

$W = F \cdot d$
$W = (6000 \text{ N})(32 \text{ m})$
$W = 192,000 \text{ N} \cdot \text{m}$
$W = 192,000 \text{ J}$

By sliding the stone up the ramp, the same 192,000 J of work was accomplished with much less effort. Of course, the distance principle tells you that the savings in effort must be paid for in increased distance. How could the effort needed to slide the block up the ramp be calculated? You know the total work (192,000 J), and you know the distance over which that work will be accomplished (384 m). Therefore, you can use the work equation to solve for the force (effort) needed to move the stone.

$W = F \cdot d$
$192,000 \text{ N} \cdot \text{m} = F \cdot 384 \text{ m}$
Divide both sides by the 384 m to solve for F.
$192,000 \text{ N} \cdot \text{m}/384 \text{ m} = F (384 \text{ m}/384 \text{ m})$
$192,000 \text{ N}/384 = F$
$500 \text{ N} = F$

Compare the effort needed to push the block up the inclined plane (500 N) with the resistance of the block (6000 N), and you will see why the Egyptians used this simple machine! Can you calculate the mechanical advantage of this machine? One of the ways to calculate M.A. is to divide resistance by effort. The resistance of the block was 6000 N while the effort needed to slide the block was 500 N. The mechanical advantage would be calculated as follows:

$6000 \text{ N}/500 \text{ N} = 12$

Different inclined planes have different mechanical advantages. A short, steep ramp has a lower mechanical advantage than a long ramp with a gradual slope. The distance principle indicates that the mechanical advantage of any inclined plane is the ratio of the length of the incline to its height:

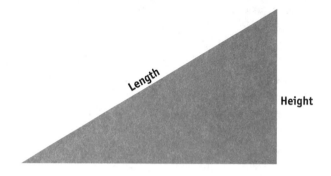

$$\text{M.A.} = \frac{\text{length of incline}}{\text{height}}$$

Of course, friction always opposes motion up an inclined plane. To keep our calculations simple, we have ignored the effects of this force. But in real-life situations you must consider friction's effect.

Today, inclined planes are fairly common. A stairway is a modified inclined plane. It takes a lot of effort to shinny up a pole or to climb a rope, but walking up a stairway is relatively easy. Steep mountains present a challenge to even the most powerful automobile engines. The force an engine can supply is limited. To overcome this problem, engineers design roads to wind back and forth, sloping gently as they go up a mountain. A smaller force applied over the longer distance is able to get the car up the hill. Whether the car goes straight up the hill or winds back and forth, the total work done by the engine is the same.

Wedges

Two inclined planes placed bottom to bottom form a **wedge.** Wedges help split logs more easily. The pyramid builders split the huge rocks they quarried with wedges. Some common examples of wedges are axes, hatchets, chisels, and knife blades.

Screws

An inclined plane wrapped around a cylinder or cone is a **screw.** Cylindrical screws are called bolts. A bolt is threaded so that it will accept and tightly hold a nut. Conical screws are designed to force their way into wood or other compressible materials.

The distance between two adjacent threads on a screw is called its **pitch.** If the pitch is small, the effort must be applied over a great distance. The screw's penetration is small compared to this distance. Therefore, a small pitch indicates a high mechanical advantage. A large pitch would indicate a low mechanical advantage. That is why screws with small pitches are easy to turn.

Applied Inclines

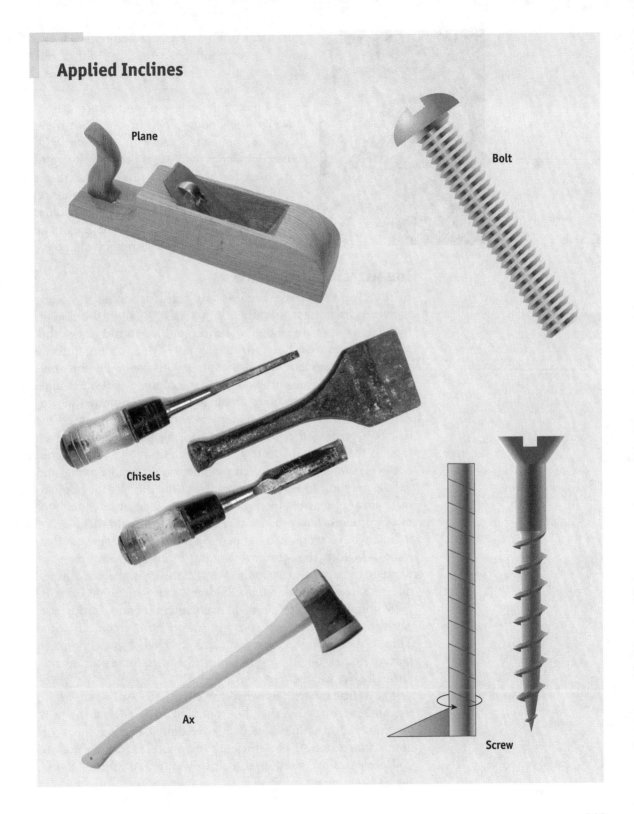

Plane

Bolt

Chisels

Ax

Screw

In order to lift a very heavy object, such as a building, you must use a machine with a very large mechanical advantage, such as a *jackscrew*. The work done on the heavy object is the weight of the object times the vertical distance it rises. However, the amount of effort needed to move that object can be reduced with a jackscrew. Of course the worker will pay a price of having to move the effort through a great distance to get the object to move a very short distance! Therefore, the distance principle applies because the work done in lifting the heavy object will be equal to the work done in pushing the handle.

Fig. 14-8 A jackscrew

Idealization in Science

In this chapter we have been dealing with frictionless machines. However, frictionless machines do not exist! In all of the cases in this chapter, we have ignored the effects of friction and made other assumptions as well. This raises a question: if these assumptions we make are never exactly true, why bother with them? The answer is that they make our problem-solving economical. One simple equation enables us to make predictions for large numbers of similar devices, each of which has its own distinctive features. One equation predicts the force relations for all inclined planes even though the frictional effects will be different in each. If we could not generalize in this way, each problem would require a long and tedious solution to get an exact answer, when in fact the approximate answer predicted by the generalization is accurate enough for most purposes. This practice is called **scientific idealization.**

Since the effort needed to operate a real machine is greater than the ideal effort, the actual work input is always greater than the useful work output. If the only losses occurring in the machine are due to friction, the difference between the work input and the work output is the work done in overcoming friction. In this case: work input = useful work output + work to overcome friction. Thus, it is obvious that in real situations not all of the work put in is recovered as useful work. To describe a machine's actual performance, we use the term *efficiency.*

The **efficiency** tells us what percent of the work put into a machine is returned as useful output. The remainder of the work put into the machine is used in overcoming friction and other nonuseful resistance. The efficiency of an ideal machine would be 100 percent, since work input equals work output; but of course, such a machine is not possible.

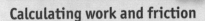

Calculating work and friction

A boy with a mass of 50 kg is pulling a 10 kg sled up a hill covered with snow. Suppose the frictional force is 10 N, and the hill has a height of 30 m, and the distance he walks up the hill is 90 m.

a. How much work does he do against gravity?

b. How much work does he do against friction?

c. What is the total amount of work that he does?

	KNOWN:	boy's mass = 50 kg
		sled's mass = 10 kg
		frictional force = 10 N
		height of hill = 30 m
		distance walked = 90 m

a.   UNKNOWN: Work (W)

FORMULA TO USE: $W = F \cdot d$

To find F, use $F = ma$, where m = the boy's mass plus the mass of the sled (60 kg) and a = 9.8 m/s^2; F = 588 N

SUBSTITUTION: $W = 588 \text{ N} \cdot 30 \text{ m}$

SOLUTION: $W = 17640 \text{ N} \cdot \text{m}$, or 17640 J

b. Remember that friction always works against motion and acts along the entire distance of 90 m.

UNKNOWN: Work (W)

FORMULA TO USE: $W = F \cdot d$

SUBSTITUTION: $W = 10 \text{ N} \cdot 90 \text{ m}$

SOLUTION: $W = 900 \text{ N} \cdot \text{m}$, or 900 J

c. Total work he does is the work he does against gravity (17640 J) plus the work he does against friction (900 J).

SOLUTION: 17640 J + 900 J = 18540 J

Keeping the Body Moving

God designed the human body to use lubricants effectively. Lubricants help reduce the amount of friction between moving surfaces. If your bones met surface-to-surface each time you moved, they would produce tremendous amounts of heat and friction. Your joints would eventually wear out! To avoid this, God covered the ends of the bones with a very smooth material called *cartilage* and filled the joints with a friction-reducing lubricant called *synovial* (sih NO vee ul) *fluid*. Together the cartilage and fluid allow the body to move with very little friction. However, this system can break down. Arthritis, a disease of the joints, attacks cartilage, causing it to become rough and stiff. The increasing friction in the joint makes movements more and more difficult.

God's friction-reducing design also plays an important role in the heart. The heart muscle contracts more than 86,000 times each day. If the friction of this movement were not reduced, the heart would quickly wear out. The heart is surrounded by two layers of tissue that form the *pericardium* (PEHR uh KAR dee um). The outer layer is a tough, resilient film that protects the heart. The thin inner membrane is a delicate layer of tissue that covers the heart itself. Between these two layer is 10 to 15 mL of *pericardial fluid;* this lubricating fluid allows the two pericardial layers to slide effortlessly over each other. This ingenious system allows the heart to function, free from damaging friction.

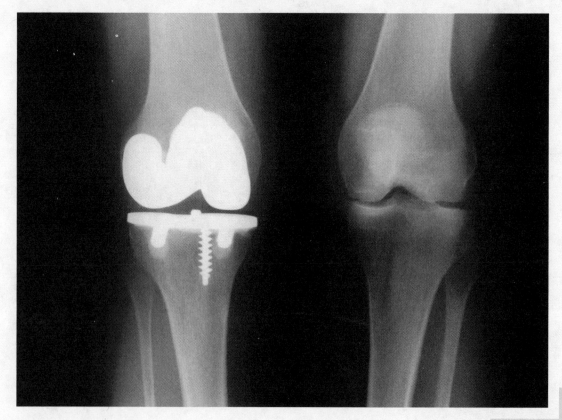

Work and Power

Not only can machines increase the force available to do work, but they can also speed up the rate at which work is done. Let's look at an example. Two construction workers are working on opposite sides of a large warehouse laying a new roof. One worker has a nice electric motor that he is using to quickly pull up buckets of hot tar. The other is slowly pulling up buckets by hand using a rope. To lift a full 90 N (~20 pounds) bucket of tar up to the 4-meter-high roof, it takes (90 N)(4 m), or 360 joules of work. Both the worker using his hands and the one using a machine do the same amount of work to lift one bucket, 360 J. But one does it more quickly. We say that the machine develops more power than the man working with his hands. **Power** (P) is the rate of doing work. Therefore, an equation that can be used to calculate P would be

$$P = Work/time = W/t$$

where work is measured in joules (J) and time is measured in seconds (s). The unit of power in the SI system is the watt (W). One **watt** is the amount of power produced by 1 joule (newton · meter) of work in 1 second.

In the example above, suppose the machine can pull a bucket to the top of the roof in 4 seconds, while the man takes an average of 20 seconds. The power that the machine develops is 360 J/4 s, or 90 W, while the average power that the man can output is 360 J/20 s, or 18 W. The machine has 5 times the power of the man.

$$\left[\begin{array}{c}\textbf{Formula for Power}\\ \textbf{P = W/t}\\ \textbf{or power = work ÷ time}\end{array}\right]$$

SECTION REVIEW QUESTIONS 14B

1. Do simple machines save us work? Explain why or why not.

2. What is the fulcrum of a wheel and axle?

3. What is the distance principle?

4. Compare the power in these two situations:

   A. Lifting 600 N of bricks 10 m high in 30 s.

   B. Lifting 600 N of bricks 10 m high in 120 s.

SCIENTIFICALLY SPEAKING

work	third-class lever
joule (J)	wheel and axle
simple machines	pulley
lever	block and tackle
fulcrum	distance principle
law of moments	inclined plane
torque	wedge
first-class lever	screw
effort	pitch
effort arm	scientific idealization
resistance	efficiency
resistance arm	power (P)
mechanical advantage (M.A.)	watt (W)
second-class lever	

CHAPTER REVIEW QUESTIONS

1. What is work? What two conditions are necessary for work to be accomplished?

2. How does a lever make work easier?

3. How does friction reduce the efficiency of a machine?

4. What machines might have been used in the construction of the pyramids?

5. A 500 N barrel is rolled up a 5 m inclined plane to a platform that is 1 m above the ground. Neglecting friction, what effort is required?

6. What is the mechanical advantage of a jack that is able to lift a 5000 N car with 400 N of effort?

7. Does a fixed pulley multiply force, distance, or neither? Explain. What would a fixed pulley be used for?

8. If 532 J of work can be accomplished in 14 seconds, how much power is generated?

9. What do we call an inclined plane wrapped around a cylinder or cone?

10. If the pitch on a screw is small, does that indicate a high or a low mechanical advantage?

11. What would be the efficiency of an "ideal" machine?

Facet Review Questions

1. What is the friction-reducing fluid that is found in the joints of the body called?

2. How much do the pillars at Stonehenge weigh? What was the simple machine Britons may have used to put them upright?

What Did You Learn?

1. Make a list of household machines that use levers. Identify them as first-, second-, or third-class levers.

2. What are some examples of materials that are used to reduce friction? What machines are they used in?

3. Karen decided to take up isometric exercises. Her first exercise was to press her palms together and push with all of her strength. Although Karen may have been improving her physical fitness, was she accomplishing any work? Explain why not.

Fluid Mechanics

Chapter

15

Why does a plane fly? What causes a boat to float or a curve ball to curve? All of these examples can be explained by the mechanical forces of air and water. As you learned in Chapter 4, both liquids and gases will flow to assume the shape of a container. Collectively, these types of materials are called **fluids. Fluid mechanics** is the study of fluids and their forces.

Characteristics of Fluid Pressure

The particles in a fluid are in constant motion in all directions. As the particles in a fluid move about, they bump into each other and bump into the walls of their container. Moving particles have mass and energy; thus when they bump they exert a force. The force particles exert upon an area is called pressure. Since the particles are moving in all directions, it follows that the force exerted occurs in all directions.

Although pressure is exerted in all directions, it is measured and reported as a force acting on one surface. **Pressure** is defined as the force pushing directly on a given surface. The following formula can be used to describe pressure:

Formula for Pressure
$$P = F/A$$
or pressure = force ÷ unit area

Recall that in SI units, force (F) is measured in newtons (N) while area is usually measured in square meters (m^2). In SI units, the force of 1 N on a 1 m^2 surface causes a pressure of 1 **pascal** (Pa):
$$1 \text{ N/m}^2 = 1 \text{ Pa}$$

Other common units of pressure are the bar and millibar. The bar (b) equals 100,000 Pa, and the millibar is one one-thousandth of a bar. This unit (mb) is commonly used by meteorologists to measure atmospheric pressure. Standard atmospheric air pressure at sea level, for example, is 1013 mb, or about 1×10^5 Pa.

English system units of pressure are also in common use; car tires, for example, are often inflated to 35 pounds per square inch (psi).

It is important at this point to understand the difference between pressure and force. Let's say you have a textbook that has a weight of 10 N. As it sits on your desk, it exerts a *force* of 10 N on the desk. No matter how the book is sitting on the desk, it exerts the same force. It can be lying flat or standing on end.

What pressure does it exert on the desk? Here you do need to be concerned about the orientation of the textbook. Its position will affect the pressure it exerts on a given area of the desk. For example, if it is lying flat it will exert the least amount of pressure on the desk—because the 10 N are spread out over a large area. If, on the other hand, the book is standing on edge, the area has been reduced, so the pressure in the given area increases. Look at the formula for pressure once again:

$$P = F/A$$

Can you see that as the area goes down the pressure must go up? This is an inverse relationship.

As you can see, pressure is dependent upon both the force applied and the area that the force is applied to. Why do you suppose a 110-pound woman wearing high-heeled shoes could do a lot more damage to a wooden floor than a 250-pound man wearing sneakers?

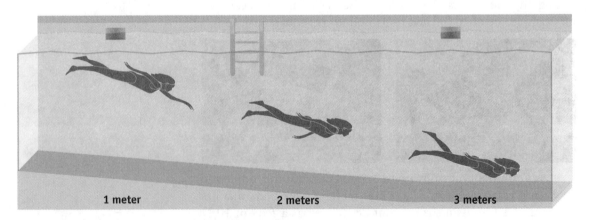

1 meter   2 meters   3 meters

Fig. 15-1 The deeper you go into the water, the greater the pressure.

15 Fluid Mechanics

Pressure and Gravity

When you swim underwater, you feel the pressure of the water against your eardrums. The deeper you swim, the greater the pressure. When your parents take you on a drive up a mountain, or you take off in a jet, you feel your ears pop as the pressure on each side of your eardrums equalizes. Why does pressure change as you move to different locations in the water or atmosphere?

Fluids have weight. Each particle of gas or liquid has mass that is acted upon by gravity (w = mg; see Chapter 13). Greater depths of a fluid have greater pressure. Why is this so?

The swimming pool in Figure 15-1 has been divided into three levels. The water pressure exerted on you is directly proportional to your depth. In other words, the deeper you go into the water, the greater the pressure because the weight or force (F) of the water above you increased. In the formula P = F/A, if force is increased, the pressure must also increase. If you dive a little deeper, say from one meter to two meters below the surface, the water pressure on you is twice as great as it was previously. Likewise, if you swim to three meters below the surface of the water, you will have the weight of three meters of water pressing on you. The pressure change is directly proportional to the depth in the fluid.

The volume or shape of the swimming pool does not affect the pressure. The pressure at a depth of one meter is the same in a backyard pool, an Olympic-sized pool, and in a lake. However, the pressure is slightly different at a one-meter depth in the ocean. Can you guess why? Because equal volumes of fresh water and salt water do not have the same mass, they have different densities (see Chapter 3). Salt water weighs more (is more dense) and thus produces a greater pressure.

The same principle is true for our fluid atmosphere. Contrary to popular belief, air *is* matter and therefore has weight! If you stand by the seashore, you are about as deep as you can get in the atmosphere. It helps to think of a "column" of air above us that extends to the "edge" of our atmosphere. This column pushes down with a certain amount of air pressure. Thus, the atmospheric pressure is nearly its greatest at sea level. If you travel upward in the atmosphere, perhaps by climbing a mountain, you will not be as deep in the atmosphere. As a result, the column of air above is much less, and therefore the pressure is less. Also, since air is highly compressible, on a mountain, the atmospheric pressure is even less than you might expect.

The effects of atmospheric pressure are quite evident. In 1968 the Summer Olympics were held in Mexico City. Because of the elevation above sea level, some of the athletes noticed that they had a hard time getting enough oxygen during the more demanding competitions.

Fig. 15-2 Notice that the greatest "flow" is produced by the hole that is closest to the bottom of the can.

1. What unit is commonly used to measure atmospheric pressure?

2. If the area over which a force is applied is reduced, what happens to the pressure? The force?

3. Would you expect the weight of air pushing down on you from a mountaintop to be greater or less than at sea level?

15B

Section

Fluids in Motion: Hydraulics

Since pressure results from particles exerting force in all directions, pressure *acts* in all directions as well. When you inflate an ordinary balloon, does only one side stretch and expand? Of course not. The pressure pushes equally on all sides of the balloon. What if you increase the pressure in a balloon by pinching one side? The pressure is transmitted throughout the whole balloon equally in all directions as revealed by the stretching of other parts of the balloon in response. Blaise Pascal summed up these observations about fluids in Pascal's principle.

Pascal's principle: Changes in pressure in a confined fluid are distributed equally in all directions throughout the fluid.

Hydraulic Press

The characteristic of fluids revealed in Pascal's principle makes fluid a useful tool for transmitting force from one area to another. It also

allows us to use fluids to increase force. In Chapter 14, we called the tools that increase force *machines.* The machines which use fluids to transmit and/or increase force are called **hydraulic machines.**

You have probably seen hydraulic machines or devices in operation without realizing that fluids provided the key to their operation. The brakes on your family car and an automobile lift at a service station are two common hydraulic machines. How is it that a hydraulic machine can convert a small force to a large force?

Recall that fluids can transmit an applied pressure equally throughout. So if you apply a pressure (P) of one Pascal at one area in a fluid, the fluid can transmit that pressure to a hundred different areas—each with a different force (F), depending on the size of the area (A). Using the equation for pressure (P = F/A), you can solve for F by multiplying both sides of the equation by A.

$$A \cdot P = \frac{F}{A} \cdot A$$

Therefore, $F = P \times A$. If the area goes down, the force must go down, given the fact that the pressure in a fluid is distributed equally throughout. If area goes up, force must also go up.

Examine the car lift shown on page 340. This is an example of a hydraulic press. Remember that the pressure in a fluid is equal throughout. Thus, the pressure on every square centimeter of the small piston is equal to the pressure on every square centimeter of the large piston. Since the large piston has more surface area, more force is applied to it.

For example, suppose the small piston of a hydraulic press has a surface area of 0.01 m^2 and a force of 10 N is applied to it. A pressure of 1000 Pa results and is transmitted through the fluid to the

EXAMPLE PROBLEM

Hydraulics

Problem Statements:

1. What is the maximum force that can be lifted with a press if the input force is 500 N distributed on an area of 1 m^2 while the output force is distributed over 2 m^2?

2. What is the pressure exerted throughout this system?

3. How far would you have to move the input force to get the output force to move 10 cm?

1st) *Since the area on the large cylinder is two times larger than the small cylinder, the force would also be doubled. Therefore, 500 N would convert to a 1000 N force on the large cylinder.*

2nd) *For both the input (500 N/1 m^2) and the output (1000 N/2 m^2), the pressure exerted is 500 Pa.*

3rd) *Since the input force is doubled in this example, the distance this force must move would be two times greater. Therefore, in order to move the output force 10 cm, the input force would have to move 20 cm.*

Mechanical Advantage

Suppose the area of the output piston, A_2, is 15 times larger than the input, A_1.

Therefore, the output force is 15 times larger than the input. One can move a heavy object a small distance by applying a small force through a large distance. The mechanical advantage (see Chapter 14) can be calculated by dividing the output force, F_2, which is called the *resistance,* by the input force, which is called the *effort.* In this example, the mechanical advantage is 15. Moving the input force 15 cm will move the output force only 1 cm!

The Human Circulatory "Hydraulic System"

The human circulatory system is an amazing hydraulic system composed of pumps, valves, and "pipes," which are the blood vessels—arteries and veins.

The heart consists of two pumps, one that pushes the blood through the lungs and another that pushes blood through the rest of the body. Oxygenated blood from the lungs is pumped at high pressure by the left ventricle into a large artery called the aorta, which carries the blood away from the heart. The right ventricle pumps blood at the same rate to the lungs, where it gives up CO_2 and absorbs oxygen. It applies a lower pressure output since there is less resistance to the flow of blood through the lungs than through the rest of the body. Thus, the *rate of flow* is the *constant* in the circu-latory system, rather than the *pressure.* As blood travels to *smaller* vessels, since the vessels decrease in diameter, the *speed must increase;* therefore, the pressure must decrease by Bernoulli's Principle (see page 346).

Blood eventually converges back into the heart through large vessels called veins. Pressure in the circulatory system also varies because of the different heights of the parts of the body. For example, the vessels in the foot have higher pressures than those in the upper part of the leg.

Throughout the system are valves. Valves not only govern the flow of blood in the heart but are also built into the blood vessels to stop the possible back flow of blood.

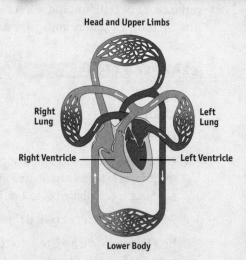

The great human hydraulic system was engineered and created by God. This is one of many complexities we see in the human body and other living creatures that attest to a great designer. It is no wonder the writer of Psalm 139:14 declares, "I will praise thee; for I am fearfully and wonderfully made: marvellous are thy works; and that my soul knoweth right well."

large piston. If the area of the large piston is four times larger than the small one, four times the force results. In this case the resulting force would be 40 N (4 · 10 N). What would be the area of the large piston? $4 \cdot 0.01 \text{ m}^2 = 0.04 \text{ m}^2$. Note that the pressure stays constant throughout the fluid at 1000 Pa. However, just as we learned in Chapter 14 that there is a price to pay for gaining mechanical advantage with simple machines, there is also a price for gaining the increased force applied in the larger piston. The price is once again the distance that the input force must move through. Using the example above, since the input (or applied) force was increased by four times, the distance this force must move will be four times greater than the distance the output force will move. In other words, moving the input force through 12 cm will move the output force only 3 cm (12/4 = 3).

Buoyancy

While playing in the family pool, ten-year-old Beth asked her dad to pick her up and throw her back into the water. Her dad quickly discovered that it was easy to pick her up partway, but as he lifted her out of the water she became heavier and heavier. His vision of flinging her halfway across the pool was quickly reduced to merely tossing her a few feet. At first she was so light—but she apparently gained weight as she rose out of the water. What happened?

Objects (or people) submerged in water (or other fluids) weigh less than they do out of the water. The ancient Greek scholar Archimedes reasoned the explanation for this more than two thousand years ago. He learned that when an object sinks it occupies space where fluid previously was. The fluid that is pushed aside to make room for the object is the displaced fluid. From this information, Archimedes formulated what is now called **Archimedes' principle.** Archimedes' principle states that an immersed object is buoyed up by a force equal to the weight of the fluid displaced.

Since equal volumes of different substances have different densities (and thus have different weights) the displaced fluid and the immersed object will likely have different weights. This means that the buoyant force and the weight of the immersed object will often be different. The relationship between the buoyant force and the weight of the immersed object determines whether the object will float or sink.

Suppose the buoyant force is greater than the weight of the object. What do you think will happen? The object will float. If the buoyant force is less than the weight of the object, the object will sink. Sometimes the two forces are exactly equal. In this case the object can rest at any level in the fluid.

You may have heard the expression "just the tip of the iceberg." The expression implies that a given situation is much more complex or "weighty" than it appears to most people. In other words, most people don't see the whole problem. The expression actually does come from observing icebergs. Since the buoyant force of water is just a little greater than the weight of ice, icebergs float *to* the surface but not *on* the surface. Most of the ice stays submerged beneath the water. This can create hazards for boats since most (up to 90 percent) of an iceberg cannot be seen by ship captains.

Specific Gravity and the King's New Crown

Geologists can easily determine the density of a rock specimen with a piece of string, a spring scale, and a pool of water. They weigh the object in water and out of water and then use Archimedes' principle.

Let's look at an example. Suppose a rock has a mass of 200 grams out of water and 175 grams in water (according to the spring scale). The change in mass (25 g) is equal to the buoyant force. We know this because an object displaces a mass of water equal to its own mass, and, according to Archimedes' principle, an immersed object (the rock in this case) is buoyed up with a force equal to the weight of water it displaces. Since the weight of the displaced fluid equals the buoyant force, the mass of the displaced water is 25 grams. The volume of the displaced fluid is also easily found, since the density of water is 1 g/cm^3. So the volume of the water displaced is 25 cm^3. This is also the volume of the rock, since it displaces its own volume. So the density is 200 grams/25 cm^3 or 8 g/cm^3.

Density determined this way is called *specific gravity*. With this method we are actually determining the density of a substance relative to that of water. We can summarize this method by the following equation:

$$\text{Specific Gravity} = \frac{\text{Weight in air}}{\text{Weight in air} - \text{Weight in water}}$$

Legend has it that Aristotle was charged with the duty of determining if the king's new crown was pure gold or if it had hidden "inferior" metals like silver. Using "bathtub" physics similar to the method above, he found that the density of the crown was *less* than that of gold—the royal metallurgist had cheated the king. We assume that the metallurgist promptly lost his job—or maybe his head!

344

You know that steel is denser than water and will sink in water. Using the terms of Archimedes' principle, we would say that the weight of water which a block of steel displaces is less than the weight of the steel, so the steel sinks. But students often ask, "Ships are made of steel—why do they float?"

The density of a steel ship is not simply the density of the steel used to construct it. Its density is the combined densities of the steel and air volume that it contains. To float, a steel ship is constructed to contain great volumes of air. It is not simply a "block" of steel. The shipbuilder's goal is for the ship to displace a weight of water greater than the weight of the air-steel combination.

Buoyancy is not restricted to liquids. Gases are governed by the principles of buoyancy too. Helium-filled balloons float upward because the helium in them is less dense than the surrounding air. A helium balloon displaces air, and the resulting buoyant force is greater than the weight of the helium. Hot-air balloons operate similarly because hot air is less dense than the cooler surrounding air.

Archimedes' principle allows large undersea creatures, such as whales, to swim with ease and grace. These creatures weigh as much as one hundred tons or more, but their density is only slightly higher than the water's. Since the buoyant force almost equals their weight, their *apparent* weight may be only a few hundred pounds in water!

Moving Fluids

Have you ever enjoyed a frosty milkshake on a hot day? As you slurped the cool, delicious liquid through a straw, you probably were not thinking about science, but scientific principles governing fluids were definitely involved.

When a person sucks on a straw, he does not directly pull the liquid up. What actually happens is that he removes air from inside the straw, decreasing the air pressure on the inside. As a result, the air pressure on the outside pushes the liquid up and into his mouth. In other words, the weight of the atmosphere pushes the liquid up the straw as you "pump" the air out. Drinking through a straw demonstrates a fluid principle. Fluids move from areas of high pressure to areas of low pressure.

Many examples of this principle can be observed every day. When air moves from an area of high pressure to an area of low pressure, we call it *wind*. A vacuum cleaner creates unequal pressure, which causes air and loose dirt to flow from outside to inside the vacuum. When you inhale you expand your chest, which makes the pressure lower inside your lungs, and air flows in.

Fig. 15-3 Bernoulli's principle

Bernoulli's Principle

Try this demonstration. Take two strips of paper and, while holding them with two fingers each, hold them an inch or two apart (see Figure 15-3). Now blow a steady stream of air gently between them. You may have expected the two sheets to separate when you blew between them, but is that what happened? If you did it correctly, the sheets should have pulled closer together.

What you have demonstrated is **Bernoulli's principle,** which says that the pressure of a fluid decreases as its speed increases; in other words, when a fluid moves, it exerts less pressure. The fluid stream of air you blew exerted less pressure between the pieces of paper while the unmoving air on the outer sides remained unchanged. The higher pressure on the outer sides pushed the papers toward each other.

A familiar example of the use of Bernoulli's principle is the design of airplane wings. A cross section of an airplane wing is shown below. Notice that the lower surface is relatively flat and straight while the upper surface is curved. This makes the upper surface larger than the lower surface. As the wing moves forward,

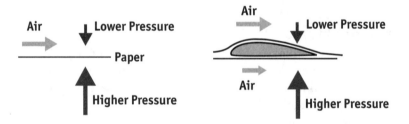

the air above the wing travels a longer distance than does the air below the wing. This means that the air traveling along the upper surface moves faster in relation to the wing than air passing along the lower surface. As a result, according to Bernoulli's principle, the air above the wing exerts less pressure than the air below the wing. This unbalanced pressure on either side of the wings lifts (or pushes) airplanes up.

Another common use of Bernoulli's principle is the baseball pitch known as a curve ball. A curve ball is thrown with a hand motion that causes the ball to spin. Because of the spinning, one side of the ball is traveling through the air faster than the other side. Bernoulli's principle tells us that as fluid speed increases,

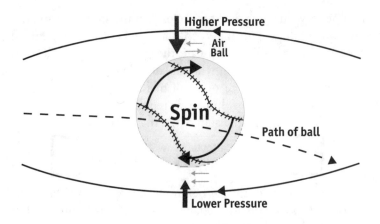

Higher Pressure

Air
Ball

Spin

Path of ball

Lower Pressure

pressure decreases. Thus, less pressure is being exerted on the side of the ball that is traveling faster, and the ball curves in that direction.

SECTION REVIEW QUESTIONS 15B

1. What do we call machines that use fluid to transmit and increase force?
2. Describe the buoyant force of a sinking object.
3. Describe a simple experiment illustrating Bernoulli's principle.

The Gas Laws

As we mentioned earlier, the gas phase of matter can also be considered as we discuss the principles of fluid mechanics. Like liquids, gases take the shape of the container they are placed in. Unlike liquids, they are compressible. We can take a given amount of air and place it within any container. The smaller the container, the greater the pressure the air will exert on the container. Likewise, if the container is enlarged, the pressure will drop because the air molecules have more "room."

For many years, the relationship between pressure and volume of gases has been explained using **Boyle's law.** It states that the volume of a dry gas is inversely proportional to the pressure, assuming that the temperature remains constant. In other words, when the pressure goes up the volume goes down and vice versa. The English chemist Robert Boyle first proposed this law during his experiments with a J-shaped tube, closed at the short end and open at the long end. By pouring various amounts of mercury into the open end, he was able to regulate the pressure of the gas on the short end. Boyle found that when he doubled the pressure on gas, its volume was reduced to one-half of its original size. When he tripled the pressure, the volume was reduced by a third.

This relationship can be stated as a mathematical equation:

Boyle's Law
$$P_1V_1 = P_2V_2$$

P_1 is the pressure of the gas before the change, and V_1 is the volume of the gas before the change. P_2 is the pressure after the change, and V_2 is the volume after the change.

Fig. 15-4 Boyle's J-shaped tube

EXAMPLE PROBLEM

Boyle's Law

Example 1:

Atmospheric pressure is measured by a **barometer** in millimeters of mercury. Normal atmospheric pressure (for which we have used the term *one atmosphere*) is measured as $76\overline{0}$ mm of mercury on a barometer. (The line over the zero indicates that the digit is significant.) If the pressure on 2.00 L of a gas at normal atmospheric pressure ($76\overline{0}$ mm Hg) were increased to 1520 mm Hg, what would be the final volume of the gas?

Solution:

First identify the values of the symbols in the Boyle's law equation:

$P_1 = 76\overline{0}$ mm Hg

$V_1 = 2.00$ L

$P_2 = 1520$ mm Hg

$V_2 = ?$ (The problem directs you to solve for the final volume.)

Now substitute these values into the equation:

$$P_1 \cdot V_1 = P_2 \cdot V_2$$

$76\overline{0}$ mm Hg $\cdot$ 2.00 L$=$ 1520 mm Hg $\cdot V_2$

Divide both sides by P_2 and cancel the units:

$$\frac{76\overline{0} \text{ mm Hg} \cdot 2.00 \text{ L}}{1520 \text{ mm Hg}} = \frac{1520 \text{ mm Hg} \cdot V_2}{1520 \text{ mm Hg}}$$

units cancel   cancels to 1

(continued)

Solve for V_2:

$$\frac{760 \cdot 2.00\,L}{1520} = 1 \cdot V_2$$

$$1.00\,L = V_2$$

Special Note: All of the data given in the problem have at least three significant digits. Therefore, the answer *must* have three significant digits.

Example 2:

A cylinder was expanded from an original volume of 400.0 mL to a final volume of $100\overline{0}$ mL. If the original pressure of the gas inside the cylinder was $304\overline{0}$ mm Hg, what is the final pressure?

Solution:

First identify the values:

$$P_1 = 304\overline{0}\ \text{mm} \qquad P_2 = ?$$
$$V_1 = 400.0\ \text{mL} \qquad V_2 = 100\overline{0}\ \text{mL}$$

Substitute these into the equation:

$$P_1 \cdot V_1 \ = \ P_2 \cdot V_2$$
$$304\overline{0}\ \text{mm} \cdot 400.0\ \text{mL} \ = \ P_2 \cdot 100\overline{0}\ \text{mL}$$

Divide by V_2 and cancel units:

$$\frac{304\overline{0}\ \text{mm Hg} \cdot 400.0\ \cancel{\text{mL}}}{1000\ \cancel{\text{mL}}} = \frac{P_2 \cdot 100\overline{0}\ \cancel{\text{mL}}}{1000\ \cancel{\text{mL}}}$$

Solve for P_2:

$$304\overline{0}\ \text{mm Hg} \cdot 400.0/100\overline{0} = P_2 \cdot 1$$

$$1216\ \text{mm Hg} = P_2$$

Note: This time four significant figures were maintained.

As you can see, pressure or volume changes have a direct effect upon one another. What are some of the practical applications of Boyle's law? Perhaps you have seen air compressors in a garage or workshop. People use compressed air for all types of applications, such as filling tires or balls with air and running powerful air tools.

Those that construct tanks to hold compressed air must be aware that the more air (increased volume) put into a tank the greater the pressure will be on the tank walls. Such calculations involving Boyle's law are crucial—if the tank is not strong enough, it could explode! Maybe you have heard of high altitude weather balloons that are used to measure atmospheric conditions. Meteorologists will only partially fill the balloon with helium gas, because the higher the altitude, the less atmospheric pressure will be exerted on the outside of the balloon. Therefore, the balloon will expand to much greater than its original size.

Why do bicycle tires seem to go flat in the winter? On a cold day, you can pump up a soccer ball indoors until it is firm, but it seems to go soft when you take it outside. What happened? These

EXAMPLE PROBLEM

Charles's Law

At 27° C, an amount of gas has a volume of 2.0 L. What volume will it occupy if it is heated to 87° C? (Assume that the pressure on the gas is constant.)

Solution:

Identify the values:

$V_1 = 2.0$ L

$T_1 = 27°C + 273 = 30\overline{0}$ K

$V_2 = ?$

$T_2 = 87°C + 273 = 36\overline{0}$ K

Substitute the values into the Charles's law equation:

$$\frac{V_1}{T_1} = \frac{V_2}{T_2}$$

$$\frac{2.0 \text{ L}}{30\overline{0} \text{ K}} = \frac{V_2}{36\overline{0} \text{ K}}$$

Cross multiply and cancel:

$$2.0 \text{ L} \cdot 36\overline{0} \text{ K} = 30\overline{0} \text{ K} \cdot V_2$$

$$\frac{2.0 \text{ L} \cdot 36\overline{0} \text{ K}}{30\overline{0} \text{ K}} = \frac{30\overline{0} \text{ K} \cdot V_2}{30\overline{0} \text{ K}}$$

units cancel   cancels to 1

Solve for V_2:

$$\frac{2.0 \text{ L} \cdot 36\overline{0}}{30\overline{0}} = 1 \cdot V_2$$

$$2.4 \text{ L} = V_2$$

examples tell us that there is a relationship between temperature and gas volume. This relationship is called **Charles's law,** named in honor of the French physicist Jacques Charles (1746-1823). This gas law states that if the pressure on a dry gas is kept constant, its volume will be in direct proportion to its Kelvin temperature. In other words, the hotter the gas becomes the greater its volume will be. This relationship can be stated as a mathematical equation:

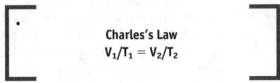

Charles's Law
$$V_1/T_1 = V_2/T_2$$

where V_1 is the original volume, T_1 is the original temperature, V_2 is the final volume, and T_2 is the final temperature.

As with Boyle's law, the final units will always be the same as the original units. The answer that we found "makes sense." The gas was heated 20 percent hotter (on the Kelvin scale), and its volume increased by 20 percent.

In order to explain Charles's law, we have to understand the behavior of gas molecules. When the temperature of a gas is high, the molecules are in a higher energy state. In this "excited" state, the molecules take up more space, and thus the volume of the gas increases. When the temperature is low, the molecules are not as active and will take up less total volume. Notice, however, that the number of molecules never increases or decreases. The volume of gas is simply telling us how much space the gas molecules take up.

SECTION REVIEW QUESTIONS 15C

1. Which law does not deal with changes in temperature?
2. If a gas is heated 20 percent hotter, by what percentage will its volume increase?

CHAPTER REVIEW

SCIENTIFICALLY SPEAKING

fluids	Archimedes' principle
fluid mechanics	Bernoulli's principle
pressure	Boyle's law
Pascal (Pa)	barometer
Pascal's principle	Charles's law
hydraulic machines	

CHAPTER REVIEW QUESTIONS

1. A book may rest in several different orientations on a table, such as lying flat, resting on its long end, or resting on its short end (as on a bookshelf). In what orientation does it apply the greatest pressure? The least amount of pressure?

2. As a hydraulic press exerts an effort of 490 N through a distance of 1 m, it raises a truck 0.25 m. What is the weight of the truck?

3. The water in a large tank weighs about 400 N. How much pressure is applied to the base if the area of the base is 3 m^2?

4. Is an object that floats on the surface of a fluid more dense or less dense than the fluid?

5. As a tractor trailer passes your compact car on the interstate, your car seems to be pulled sideways toward the passing truck. Explain this phenomenon in light of Bernoulli's principle.

6. Will a balloon expand or shrink if placed in a freezer? What law describes this phenomenon?

7. Describe how the "J-shaped tube" experiment helped Boyle formulate the law named for him.

FACET REVIEW QUESTIONS

1. What is the purpose of the right ventricle? Left ventricle?

2. What is the formula for determining specific gravity?

WHAT DID YOU LEARN?

1. Using what you know about fluids, why doesn't the air in a punctured tire just stay there?

2. Would you hypothesize that the base of Hoover Dam is thicker, thinner, or about the same as it is at the top?

3. What property of liquids helps to explain the usefulness of hydraulic machines?

Wave and
Particle Motion

Heat and Temperature

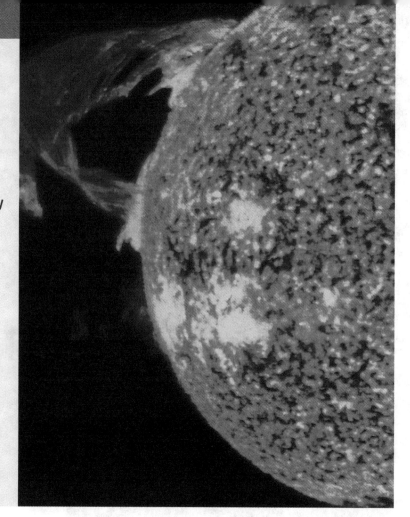

16A **Defining Thermal Energy**

16B **Heat Transfer**

Over the centuries, scientists have proposed, defended, or discarded thousands of theories about the physical properties of matter. Perhaps the greatest debate has centered on heat. Many have sought to explain the presence of heat because it is an easily observable phenomenon. **Heat** is the transfer of kinetic energy present within matter. As we have already discussed, kinetic energy is energy in motion. So the more heat present within an object, the more motion is occurring among the atoms of that particular object. Anyone who has burned himself on an iron or felt the pain of a sunburn knows that God has provided us with a sense of the heat in our environment.

We know that heat can be easily transferred from one object to another, stored, or used to keep us warm in freezing temperatures. We often talk about heat as if it were a substance, but in reality it is just another form of energy. Although we often call heat *thermal energy,* it is better defined as the *flow of thermal energy* from one object to another. Heat is not a substance but rather a description. As we will examine in this chapter, heat is simply the outward expression to our senses of what is happening on the molecular level.

Keeping you warm is not the only function of thermal energy. In the past, thermal energy produced steam that propelled locomotives across continents and ocean liners across the seas. Today steam produced by thermal energy drives huge turbines that generate electricity for cities and industry. In some localities, thermal energy from within the earth (geothermal energy) and thermal energy from the sun (solar energy) help to meet the demands of our energy-hungry society. The benefits of thermal energy—both for now and for the future—make it an important influence in our lives.

Defining Thermal Energy

Many years ago, scientists thought that thermal energy was a weightless, invisible fluid. They named this fluid *caloric* (kuh LOR rik). According to the **caloric theory,** all matter supposedly contained a measurable amount of this fluid; hot objects contained more than cold objects. When a hot object touched a cold object, caloric flowed from the hot object to the cold object until equal quantities of each material contained equal amounts of this mysterious fluid.

The caloric theory remained popular because it seemed to explain many everyday occurrences. Have you ever bought an ice-cream cone on a hot summer day and then raced to eat it before it melted and dripped all over you? The caloric theory would have explained this phenomenon by stating that the caloric in the warm surrounding air flowed into the cold ice cream and made it melt. This description of melting appeared to be correct, but could the caloric theory describe other observations of thermal energy?

The Kinetic Theory of Thermal Energy

In the late 18th century, the observations of an American-born scientist eventually toppled the caloric theory. Benjamin Thompson left America and later arranged to receive a royal title

Fig. 16-1 Count Rumford

in the court of Bavaria. The new count changed his name to Rumford, after his hometown in New Hampshire. He rose quickly in the Bavarian government and was soon appointed minister of war. One of his duties was to supervise the manufacture of weapons. This duty gave Count Rumford an opportunity to observe cannon-boring operations.

The cannon-boring procedure was relatively simple. A solid brass cylinder mounted on a rotating shaft was pushed against a stationary drill bit. As the cylinder was hollowed out, great quantities of thermal energy were released—enough, in fact, to boil the water that was poured into the cylinder to cool the bit. How was this thermal energy produced?

According to the caloric theory, the metal that was drilled from within the barrel released its caloric. As more metal was removed, more caloric should have been set free. Count Rumford devised an experiment to test whether or not the metal itself released the caloric. He pressed a dull drill bit against a rotating cannon barrel for half an hour and found that only a

Fig. 16-2 Rumford compared the amount of thermal energy produced when a cannon was bored with a dull bit to the amount of thermal energy produced when a sharp bit was used. What did he discover?

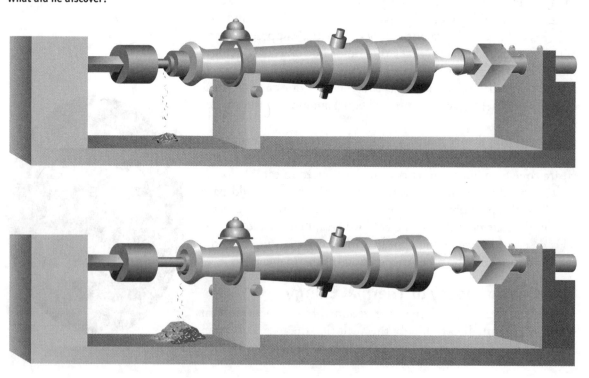

tiny amount of metal, but a large amount of caloric (actually thermal energy) was released. He then compared this amount of caloric to the caloric released when a much larger amount of metal was removed in a much shorter time with a sharp bit. The two amounts of caloric were just about the same. This was astounding! How could two different amounts of the same metal release the same amount of caloric? Count Rumford realized that the caloric theory was incorrect.

If the release of caloric did not account for the thermal energy produced by the cannon-boring, what did? Count Rumford observed that the energy release stopped when the drilling stopped. He reasoned that the motion of the barrel against the bit, and not caloric, produced the thermal energy. Count Rumford did not know how motion produced thermal energy, but his experiments sparked the research that led to the answer—the kinetic theory of thermal energy.

The **kinetic theory of thermal energy** identifies the thermal energy of an object with the motion of its particles (which may be atoms, ions, or molecules). Rub your hands briskly together and see what happens. The faster you rub your hands, the warmer they become. Native Americans found that by rubbing two sticks together they could produce enough thermal energy to start a flame. According to the kinetic theory, rubbing two objects—two sticks, for instance—together causes the molecules in the objects to move faster. As the motion of the molecules increases, the energy in the sticks increases. The more "stirred up" the molecules become, the warmer the sticks become. The total energy of the particles in an object is called the object's thermal energy. When we observe a warm object, we know that the particles that make it up are in a higher energy state, moving at a faster rate than if the object were cold.

Measuring Particle Motion

We describe particle motion with the everyday words *hot* and *cold.* These terms are relative and very subjective. You may feel "too hot" while a friend feels "just right." Unless we can measure the hotness or coldness of objects, these concepts are scientifically useless.

The measurement of an object's hotness or coldness is called its **temperature.** Temperature is expressed in units called *degrees* (°C or F, or kelvins on the absolute scale). As an object becomes hotter, the number of degrees in its temperature increases. Temperature actually indicates the average kinetic energy of an object's particles. As the particles gain kinetic energy, they move faster and the object's temperature rises.

A Short History of Thermometers and Temperature Scales

One of the first thermometers was built in approximately 1600 by Galileo. The "thermoscope," as Galileo called it, consisted of a long, slender glass tube sealed at one end and inverted with its open end in a pan of water. The level of water in the tube rose and fell as the volume of the air trapped inside fluctuated with the temperature. Galileo's thermoscope proved to be fairly accurate; it could clearly indicate the temperature of the hands of the person who held it. Unfortunately, the thermoscope also responded to small changes in atmospheric pressure.

   Later scientists revised Galileo's thermoscope by replacing the air with a combination of water and alcohol and completely sealing it in a tube. Using expandable liquids instead of gases made these thermometers less sensitive to atmospheric pressure changes. Today, many thermometers contain mercury. Mercury's volume changes predictably over a greater range of temperatures than the volume of either water or alcohol.

   In time, scientists added calibrations (kal uh BRAY shunz) to their thermometers so that they could measure specific temperatures. For instance, many scientists marked the level of the liquid in their ther-

mometers as they were measuring the boiling point of water. Then, each time the liquid's level returned to that mark, the scientists knew that the temperature the thermometers were measuring was the same as the temperature at which water boiled.

Gabriel Fahrenheit (FEHR un hite), a German-Polish instrument maker, used three temperatures to calibrate his thermometer: the freezing point of a water, salt, and ice mixture; the freezing point of pure water; and the average temperature of a normal human body. He divided this scale into equal units, or degrees Fahrenheit (°F) between these three key calibrations. The Fahrenheit scale is still used in the United States by most weather forecasters.

In 1742 a Swedish astronomer named Anders Celsius devised a simpler temperature scale. He divided the temperature range between the freezing and boiling points of pure water into one hundred equal temperature intervals. He used intervals of the same size to measure temperatures above and below this temperature range as well. The French commission that designed the metric system later named the freezing point of water 0 degrees Celsius (0°C) and the boiling point 100 degrees Celsius (100°C). The fact that each interval, or degree Celsius, is equal to one-hundredth of the temperature range between these two easily reproducible points makes the Celsius scale easy to calibrate and use. Most countries and almost all scientific laboratories use the Celsius scale to measure temperature.

In 1848 Lord Kelvin developed a temperature scale called the Kelvin scale, which has only positive temperature values. The calibration of the Kelvin scale reflects the fact that negative kinetic energy does not exist. Using the Kelvin scale, we can directly compare the average kinetic energy of the particles in any two objects. For this reason, the temperatures on the Kelvin scale are also known as absolute temperatures. The lowest temperature on the Kelvin scale, 0 K, represents the temperature at which an object possesses an absolute minimum of kinetic energy. This temperature is also known as *absolute zero*.

Once you know the Celsius temperature of an object, its absolute temperature is simple to calculate. The sizes of the temperature intervals, or degrees, in the Celsius and Kelvin scales are the same. Absolute zero (0 K) on the Kelvin scale corresponds to –273°C on the Celsius scale. Therefore, to convert a temperature from the Celsius scale to the Kelvin scale, one simply adds 273 degrees. To convert a Kelvin temperature to the corresponding Celsius temperature, one simply subtracts 273 degrees. The following equations express the relationship between these two scales:

$$C + 273 = K$$
$$K - 273 = C$$

In these equations, C stands for the Celsius temperature and K stands for the Kelvin temperature. Note also that in the modern metric system, temperatures on the Kelvin scale are expressed as Kelvins (K), **not** as degrees Kelvin.

Sample problem 1:

A hummingbird has a body temperature of 43°C. Find the corresponding Kelvin temperature.

Solution:

$$K = C + 273$$
$$K = 43 + 273$$
$$K = 316 \text{ Kelvins}$$

Sample problem 2:

Dry ice sublimates at -78.5°C. What is the corresponding absolute temperature?

Solution:

$$K = C + 273$$
$$K = -78.5 + 273$$
$$K = 194.5 \text{ Kelvins}$$

Sample problem 3:

Liquid nitrogen boils at 77 Kelvins. Convert this temperature to degrees Celsius.

Solution:

$$C = K - 273$$
$$C = 77 - 273$$
$$C = -196°C$$

Fig. 16-3 Glaciers in Alaska

Distinguishing Between Temperature and Thermal Energy

Which is hotter—a ton of molten copper or a glacier in Alaska? Obviously, the molten copper is the hotter of the two. Now for a harder question: Does the copper or the glacier contain more thermal energy? The answer to this question may surprise you. The glacier, though much colder, contains more thermal energy than the molten copper! How can this be?

To understand this seeming contradiction, we need to distinguish between temperature and thermal energy. Temperature measures the *average kinetic energy of an object's particles.* In other words, temperature measures the energy of motion possessed by an average particle in the object. Thermal energy measures *the total energy of all the particles in an object.* Thus, thermal energy includes the energy of motion of all the object's particles.

If two cubes of iron—one large and one small—were heated to the same temperature, their individual atoms would possess the same average kinetic energy. However, the large cube would contain *more* atoms with that average kinetic energy. The total energy of the atoms in the large cube would be greater than the total energy of the atoms in the small cube. Thus, the large cube would possess more thermal energy. If these cubes with identical temperatures were thrown into identical buckets of ice, the large cube would release much more thermal energy and melt much more ice than would the small cube.

By the same principle, the glacier has more thermal energy than a ton of molten copper. The fact that the temperature of the glacier is lower than the temperature of the copper shows that the glacier's particles have less average kinetic energy than the copper particles have. However, the glacier has many more particles than the ton of copper has. Therefore, the total energy of the glacier's particles adds up to more than the total energy of the copper particles. Since thermal energy is a measure of an object's total energy, the glacier has more thermal energy than the molten copper.

Fig. 16-4 Copper melts at 1080 °C. This crucible is pouring molten copper into a smelting furnace, where it will be purified.

Measuring Thermal Energy

Since temperature and thermal energy measure different physical properties, they must be expressed in different units. Temperature, as you know, is measured in degrees or kelvins. Thermal energy is measured in another unit called *calories* (cal).

Historically, a calorie was defined as a certain quantity of caloric fluid. The downfall of the caloric theory made this use of the word obsolete, but the term itself has survived, and today it represents a certain quantity of thermal energy. The **calorie (cal)** is that amount of thermal energy which, when transferred to 1 g of water, causes an increase of 1°C in the water's temperature. If 1 kg of water is heated 1°C, a kilocalorie (kcal) is required. The calorie is a measurement of energy, as is the joule, so sometimes joules are used to measure the amount of thermal energy. At this point you may have

TABLE
16-5 **Approximate Caloric Contents**

Food	Amount	kcal	Food	Amount	kcal
apple	1	66	jam	1 tbsp.	54
bacon	1 slice	49	chocolate ice cream	$\frac{1}{3}$ pint	191
banana	1	87	macaroni	1 cup	168
green beans	$\frac{1}{2}$ cup	16	mayonnaise	1 tbsp.	100
chocolate cake with chocolate icing	2-in. slice	445	milk	8 oz.	151
fudge	1 oz.	112	pancake	4-in. diameter	61
t-bone steak	8 oz.	1078	peanut butter	1 tbsp.	72
hamburger sandwich	1	576	popcorn, plain	1 cup	42
white bread	1 slice	62	potato chips	2 oz.	312
brownie	1	140	French fries	10 2-in. pieces	156
butter	1 tbsp.	100	orange	1	75
Life Saver candy, fruit flavored	1 piece	9	rice	1 cup	187
catsup	1 tbsp.	21	sausage	4 oz.	538
celery	1 stalk	6	soft drink, cola flavored	8 oz.	96
Corn Flakes Cereal	$1\frac{1}{3}$ cups	105	tea	1 cup	1
chocolate-chip cookie	1	51	tomato soup	1 cup	83
egg	1 large	81	spaghetti	1 cup	159
fried chicken	1 drumstick	89	strawberries	$\frac{1}{2}$ cup	28
walnuts, shelled	$\frac{1}{2}$ cup	654			

a hard time understanding the difference between heat and temperature. Temperature is dependent upon the motion of particles in the object and can vary greatly. The measurement of temperature deals more with the *intensity* (hotness or coldness) of thermal energy. Temperature is a quick way of determining the activity level of molecules. Measuring heat in calories does not attempt to explain the intensity, but rather the *amount* of energy present.

The calorie may measure the amount of thermal energy that is transferred from one object to another. It may also measure the amount of thermal energy that a substance could *potentially* release. Calories measure potential thermal energy that a chemical reaction releases or stores, while temperature indicates the average kinetic energy of particles involved in the reaction. One of the most common uses of the calorie is to measure the thermal energy stored in foods. The "Calorie" (capital "C"—Cal), which is found in cooking and diet contexts and which is used to measure the energy stored in foods, is actually the kilocalorie (kcal). In this text, we will use the more accurate term **kilocalorie.**

Starches, sugars, and fats are the main sources of energy for our bodies. One kilogram (about $2\frac{1}{2}$ cups) of sucrose (table sugar) has the potential of releasing over 2000 kcal. The same amount of fat can release three times as many calories. Your body uses the thermal energy of food to provide itself with energy. If your body does not receive enough thermal energy—enough calories—you will become underweight and ill. On the other hand, if you consume more calories than your body needs, you will gain weight.

How much energy do you need? The answer depends on your age, gender, size, and level of physical activity. Nutritionists have

TABLE 16-6	Average Caloric Requirements (kcal)	
Age	Males	Females
1-3	1300	1300
3-6	1600	1600
6-9	2100	2100
9-12	2400	2200
12-15	3000	2500
15-18	3400	2300
18-35	2900	2100
35-55	2600	1900
55-75	2200	1600

determined the average caloric intake needed by individuals of different ages (see Table 16-6). Since different foods contain different amounts of kilocalories, nutritionists have also prepared tables showing the caloric content of most foods. You can determine your intake of kilocalories by measuring the amount of each food you eat and comparing it to the value given for that food in a caloric content chart.

SECTION REVIEW QUESTIONS 16A

1. According to early scientists, what was the weightless and invisible fluid in substances that explained heat?

2. According to the kinetic theory of thermal energy, what accounts for the energy present within matter?

3. Temperature is measured in kelvins, but what is the unit for thermal energy?

Heat Transfer

Remember the last time you opened a car door on a broiling summer afternoon and were met by a blistering blast of hot air? After gingerly seating yourself on the scorching car seat, you quickly became aware of its energy-storing capabilities. The longer you sat there, the more you felt the sun pouring additional energy into you and the car. All these sensations are evidence of heat—the flow of thermal energy from one object to another. Thermal energy can flow by three different processes: conduction, convection, and radiation.

Conduction

When two objects at different temperatures touch each other, heat flows from the hotter object to the cooler object. This process is called **conduction** (kun DUK shun). If you have ever prepared hot chocolate, you already are well experienced in the process of conduction.

The hot chocolate became "hot" because of conduction. A teapot containing water was placed on a hot burner. First, the teapot was heated by contact with the burner. Then the water was heated by contact with the teapot. When you added the water to the chocolate mix, heat was once again transferred. Later, you were warmed by contact with the hot chocolate! Conduction took place as thermal energy flowed from the burner to the teapot, from the teapot to the water, from the water to the chocolate mix, and finally from the hot chocolate to you.

How does conduction transfer thermal energy? When a warm object contacts a relatively cool object, kinetic energy is conducted from the warmer object to the cooler object. This happens as the slower-vibrating particles of the cooler object are agitated by the faster-vibrating particles of the hotter object. Gradually, the hotter particles lose some of their kinetic energy to the cooler particles. When the average kinetic energy of the particles of both objects has become equal, the two objects are at the same temperature and conduction stops. This condition is called **thermal equilibrium.** The hot object transfers energy to the cold object, so the cold object has an increase in energy. But the hot object loses the same amount. The total amount of energy within the system is conserved according to the law of conservation of energy we studied in Chapter 12. No energy is lost or gained.

The process of conduction is obvious when a piece of red-hot iron is plunged into a bucket of cool water. The popping, fizzing, and bubbling of the water testifies that energy from the iron atoms is being transferred to the water molecules. When the popping, fizzing, and bubbling stops, the iron and water have reached equilibrium, and the conduction of thermal energy has ceased.

Conduction is the chief method of heat flow in solids. The atoms of solids are tightly bound to each other. Thus, if one atom vibrates, those around it will vibrate too, so the energy is propagated through the substance. The movement of valence electrons (see Chapter 8) in certain solids is also a way heat is conducted.

Some solids conduct thermal energy better than others. Since metals easily give up their valence electrons, which are free to

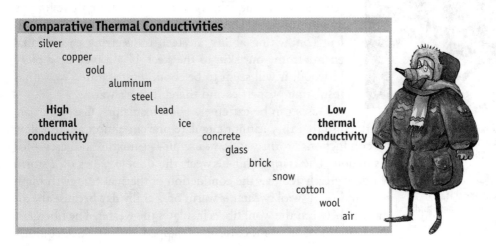

Comparative Thermal Conductivities

silver
copper
gold
aluminum
steel
High thermal conductivity   lead
ice
concrete   **Low thermal conductivity**
glass
brick
snow
cotton
wool
air

conduct energy, metals are generally excellent **conductors** of thermal energy. Silver is the best heat conductor, but it is also very expensive. In most situations, less expensive conductors, such as copper and aluminum, are more practical. Substances that are good conductors of heat are also good conductors of electricity. Conductors have the best practical use in situations that require a large amount of energy to be transferred. In heating and cooling systems, you will often see fins and coils made of metal. The fact that something is a metal and is a good conductor does not mean that it is indestructible. If the temperature of the metal becomes too hot, it could melt.

At the opposite end of the scale are substances such as wool, brick, and glass. These materials resist heat flow and are called

insulators (IN suh lay turz). The ceramic materials used to make the exterior tiles of NASA's space shuttle are excellent insulators. When these tiles are damaged or worn, they can be easily replaced. The tiles protect the space shuttle's occupants from the searing temperatures generated when they reenter the earth's atmosphere. Insulators are "non-conformist"—even though everything else around them may be at high or low temperature, they resist any change in temperature. In fact, *insulator* comes from the Latin word *insula,* meaning "island." An object surrounded by insulating materials forms an "island" of one temperature in the midst of a surrounding "sea" of other temperatures.

Insulators and conductors are an interesting study when it comes to temperature and how the human body senses heat or cold. You may have picked up a piece of "cold" steel with your bare hands. In reality, the steel is the same temperature as the room, if it has been sitting there for any amount of time. The cool sensation comes from the excellent conducting ability of steel, transferring the thermal energy from your skin to the steel. If you pick up a piece of wood, it will seem to be room temperature. Wood has insulating properties and therefore feels warm.

Gases can be extremely good insulators. Gases that are confined so that they cannot circulate prevent almost all heat flow by conduction. Storm windows use air—a mixture of gases—for insulation. The trapped air between the double panes of a storm window greatly reduces the conduction of thermal energy through the window. A wool sweater is warm on a chilly day because the air trapped between the wool fibers insulates the wearer. The fiberglass insulation used in homes also uses trapped air to reduce conduction.

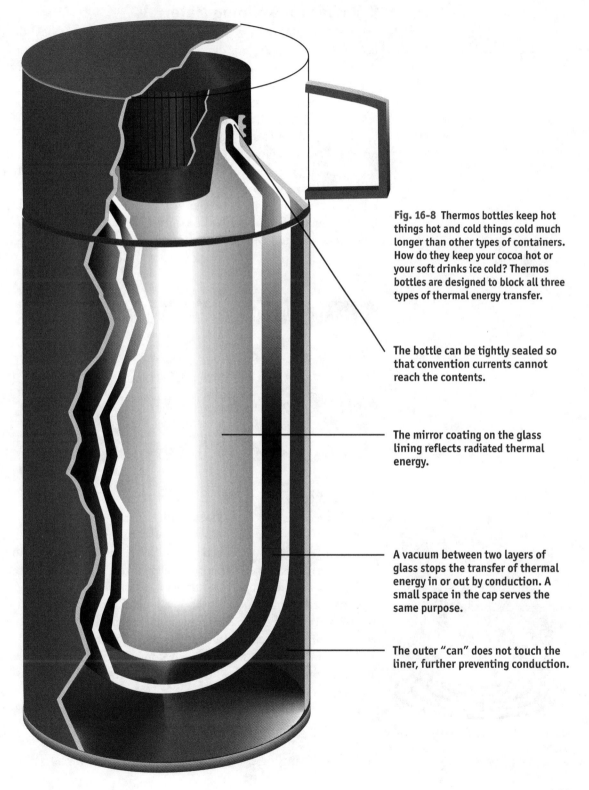

Fig. 16-8 Thermos bottles keep hot things hot and cold things cold much longer than other types of containers. How do they keep your cocoa hot or your soft drinks ice cold? Thermos bottles are designed to block all three types of thermal energy transfer.

The bottle can be tightly sealed so that convention currents cannot reach the contents.

The mirror coating on the glass lining reflects radiated thermal energy.

A vacuum between two layers of glass stops the transfer of thermal energy in or out by conduction. A small space in the cap serves the same purpose.

The outer "can" does not touch the liner, further preventing conduction.

R-Values for Building Materials

Heat conduction through a building material, such as glass, brick, fiberglass, or insulation, is dependent on several factors, including the material's thickness, the contact area, and the difference between the outside and inside air temperatures. There is also a material dependent value. For instance, brick is a much poorer conductor of heat than aluminum siding (only 1/8 as good). By combining the thickness and this material dependent value, we obtain a heat resistance or **R-value.** The larger this value, the better the insulator keeps the cold out. An R-value of 40 would be better than an R-value of 30. Table 16-11 gives the R-values of common materials. A combination of materials increases the total R-value, but it does not add directly. For instance, two 5-mm thick windowpanes with a 5-mm air gap can increase the R-value forty fold over that of a single 5-mm thick windowpane!

TABLE

16-11 R-Values of Common Materials	
Material	R-Value
Dry air	5.5
Fiberglass	3.0
Wood (white pine)	1.3
Window glass (single pane)	0.14
Aluminum	0.00061

Convection

That blast of hot air mentioned earlier that greets you when you open a car door on a warm day illustrates the existence of another method of heat flow—**convection** (kun VEK shun). In convection, moving particles transfer thermal energy from one place (such as the car) to another (such as your face).

Convection and conduction both depend on the movement of matter to transfer thermal energy. What, then, distinguishes convection from conduction? In conduction, the particles are confined and remain relatively stationary. In convection, energy is passed along as vibrating particles flow from high temperature regions to low temperature regions.

In the pot of water shown in Figure 16-9, the hot pan heats the water that is in contact with it. This water expands into a hot "cell" that is lighter than the water around it. Since its density is less, it rises by buoyant forces. As it rises, it cools, decreasing in size and

Fig. 16-9 The convection currents in a pot help to transfer thermal energy throughout the water.

Convection current

Radiator

Fig. 16-10 Convection currents also help to heat this room.

increasing in weight, finally falling back where it is reheated by the pan. This cyclic motion is called a **convection current.** This cycle carries thermal energy upward from the hot pan to the cooler areas of water. These currents also thoroughly mix the water, eventually producing a uniform temperature throughout. Once equilibrium has been reached, the convection process halts.

Convection operates in houses that have radiators or hot-water pipes as heating elements. The air next to these heating elements is heated by conduction of thermal energy from the particles of the pipe or radiator to the particles of air. Once the air is heated, it rises and circulates just as the water in the pot.

Homes with hot-air heating systems are also heated by convection. Warm air enters each room through vents or registers. As the cool air in the room falls and the warm air rises, it creates convection currents that help transfer the thermal energy throughout the room.

Atmospheric convection currents form sea breezes and land breezes, as shown in the diagram on the next page. In the morning sunlight, the land's temperature rises more quickly than the water's temperature. Consequently, the air over the land becomes warmer than the air over the water. Cooler, high-pressure air from over the water flows inland and pushes the warm air aside. This warmer air over the land rises by buoyant forces. This air movement is known

Fig. 16-11 Convection currents over land and sea cause the constant winds that blow on the coast.

as a sea breeze (or lake breeze). At midday, when the temperatures of the land and water are nearly the same, the air moves very little. During the early evening, the land cools more quickly than the water. As a result, the air over the water stays warm longer than the air over the land. The cooler, high-pressure land air flows out onto the water, pushing the warmer air upward and creating a land breeze. Local sea and land breezes moderate the climates of coastal towns.

Radiation

Particles are very thinly distributed in the space between the sun and the earth—so thinly, in fact, that this space is almost a vacuum. Since convection and conduction both depend on matter to transport thermal energy, they cannot explain the heat flow from the sun to the earth. Thermal energy is transferred to the earth by **radiation** (ray dee AY shun)—radiant electromagnetic waves transport energy through space, and that energy is converted to thermal energy at the earth.

Radiant energy does not require the presence of matter to travel from place to place. In fact, radiation travels faster through a vacuum than through transparent materials. Whenever radiation strikes matter, some of the energy is absorbed by the matter and re-radiates as infrared radiation. Although most of the energy arrives at the earth from the sun in the form of visible light, the main source of atmospheric heat is infrared radiation from the ground! Since the greater part of the radiation arriving from the sun strikes the ground, it is absorbed by the rocks, soils, and so on, and is re-radiated back into the atmosphere.

The amount of thermal energy that is absorbed by matter depends on its surface characteristics. For instance, dark-colored materials readily absorb solar radiation; light-colored materials reflect most of it. These properties explain why on a sunny day you may feel warmer wearing a dark-colored shirt than you do wearing a light-colored shirt. They also explain why black automobile seats are much hotter than light-colored seats on a bright summer day.

Applying Thermal Energy

Have you ever burned your mouth on a piping-hot piece of apple pie? When you examined the pie, the crust seemed cool, but when the filling touched your mouth—ouch! Apparently, the pie crust and the pie filling were cooling at different rates. One reason for this difference is that pie fillings are mostly water. It takes a large amount of thermal energy to heat water, but once water is hot, it retains thermal energy better than most substances. The dry crust cools quickly while the watery filling stays hot.

The way a material gains and retains thermal energy is largely due to the composition of the material. Some materials, such as water, gain thermal energy slowly and retain it for a long time. Other materials, such as pie crust, gain and lose thermal energy very quickly. We can tell whether a material has lost or gained thermal energy by measuring changes in its temperature. If you had used a thermometer to check the temperature of the pie filling, you would have seen that it was still too hot to eat.

Fig. 16-12 A radiometer is a sealed glass bulb with freely spinning vanes mounted on its base. Each vane has a black side and a white side. A radiometer can be used to detect radiant heat energy. As the radiant heat energy strikes the vanes, the black side absorbs more heat than the white side. Air molecules move faster on the hot side of the vane and cause the vane to rotate.

Fig. 16-13 The steam rising over hot apple pie gives us an important clue as to why the filling stays hot longer than the crust.

Thermodynamics

Thermal energy, like all forms of energy, has the ability to do work. The English physicist James Joule performed many experiments to establish the relationship between thermal energy and work. He found that 1 cal of thermal energy is capable of performing 4.18 J of work. This relationship (4.18 J/cal) is known as the *mechanical equivalent of heat*. This is a very important finding since it shows that heat is a normal form of energy and that energy is conserved even in thermal processes.

Devices that transform thermal energy into work are called *heat engines*. One common type of heat engine is the steam engine. Hero, a scientist who lived in Alexandria, Egypt, built one of the first steam engines in 120 B.C. He connected two L-shaped pipes to a hollow ball. As heat was applied to water in the ball, steam escaped from the two pipes and caused the globe to twirl. Unfortunately, the engine could not do much more than spin itself. In 1769 James Watt, a Scottish engineer, developed a steam engine that was useful for doing work. Soon steam engines were powering boats, trains, and factories around the world.

While inventors developed increasingly useful heat engines, scientists wondered what principles governed the transformation of energy from one form to another. It was at this time that the branch of physics called thermodynamics was born. **Thermodynamics** (thur mo dye NAM iks; from the Greek words *therme,* meaning "heat," and *dynamikos,* meaning "powerful") deals specifically with the conversion of thermal energy into other energy forms and into work. However, the principles, or laws, of thermodynamics influence many other aspects of modern science.

The *first law of thermodynamics* is the law of energy conservation (see Chapter 12). It states that while energy can be converted from one form to another, it cannot be created or destroyed. It tells us that the total amount of energy in the universe stays the same. This conclusion agrees with Genesis 2:1—"Thus the heavens and the earth were finished, and all the host of them." Since that time God has kept the amount of energy in the universe constant by preserving His creation. God is "upholding all things by the word of his power" (Heb. 1:3).

The *second law of thermodynamics* was formulated by several individuals, one of whom was Lord Kelvin. Lord Kelvin found that the energy in the universe, although it is conserved, becomes less available for performing useful work. One example of the second law is the transformation of energy in a gasoline engine. In a gasoline engine, the chemical energy in the bonds of the gasoline molecules is released as thermal energy and other forms of energy. Some of the thermal energy is used to produce pressure that moves the engine's pistons. However, much of the thermal energy and all other energy is absorbed into the metal of the engine. This energy must be removed from the engine to prevent it from overheating. Some of the thermal energy is removed through a heat

Watt's steam engine

exchanger called a radiator. This thermal energy does not perform useful work. It has not been destroyed, but it can no longer be used.

The second law of thermodynamics can be written in several equivalent forms; one modern way to put it is as follows:

Energy naturally becomes unusable. The amount of decay and disorder never decreases with time.

In other words, the amount of randomness or disorder in a system always increases over time but can never decrease on its own. The scientific measurement of the amount of unusable energy in a system is called that system's **entropy** (EN truh pee). Entropy measures the randomness, or disorder, in a system. (As energy becomes less orderly, it has less ability to do work.) According to the second law of thermodynamics, the entropy of the universe is always increasing. In other words, everything in the universe runs down! This is exactly what is meant in Isaiah 51:6—"Lift up your eyes to the heavens, and look to the earth beneath: for the heavens shall vanish away like smoke, and the earth shall wax old like a garment . . . but my salvation shall be forever, and my righteousness shall not be abolished."

Think of all the processes that show an increase of entropy.

For example, a book put back up on a shelf has a higher gravitational potential than it had on the floor. The book naturally stays on the shelf (entropy staying the same) or falls down to the ground (entropy

Hero's steam engine

increasing). In fact, the book will tend to fall to the lowest available state, the ground. Once the book is on the ground, can it ever naturally rise off the ground and go back to the shelf? The second law says no. It cannot decrease its entropy! It does not matter how long we wait. It will never do this. We can input useful work and lift it back into place if we wish, but it will not lift itself naturally. Energy naturally flows from a high potential to low potential, never the other way around.

Hot water in a bathtub cools off as time passes. The temperature will eventually go to that of its surroundings. We would be quite surprised if the heat available in the air collected back into the tub's water and made it hot again!

Watches, batteries, and even people run down. Can their used-up energy be recovered? You may rewind a watch, recharge a battery, and rest and eat to "recharge" yourself, but none of these processes recover the original energy. If we consider all the natural processes that we can observe in the universe, we can see that all of nature is running down.

The second law of thermodynamics is a biblical principle. Both Hebrews 1:11 and Psalm 102:26 describe the earth and the heavens as waxing old like a garment. In the same way that clothing gradually wears out, the universe is gradually using up its supply of available energy. The second law also supports the biblical account of Creation. The fact that the universe is running down implies that it must have been "wound up" sometime in the past.

No one has ever found a single exception to the first and second laws of thermodynamics. Both laws fully agree with Scripture and with every scientific observation that has been recorded.

Both the first and second laws of thermodynamics present serious problems for the theory of evolution. For example, the second law refutes the evolutionary idea that matter organized itself from disorder and chaos into order and complexity.

Specific Heat

How do scientists measure the amount of thermal energy needed to change the temperature of specific materials? Scientists use calories to measure thermal energy. One kcal of thermal energy raises the temperature of 1 kg of water 1°C. But does this amount of thermal energy raise the temperature of all substances 1°C? No, each substance reacts differently to thermal energy. Scientists call the amount of energy needed to raise the temperature of 1 kg of a substance 1°C the **specific heat** of that substance. Some substances have small specific heats. It takes only 0.22 kcal to raise the temperature of 1 kg of aluminum 1°C. Lead requires still less energy— a mere 0.031 kcal—to raise the temperature of each kg 1°C. Other substances, such as hydrogen and helium, have high specific heats. They must absorb large quantities of thermal energy before their temperatures change. Every substance has its own specific heat. Tables of specific heats can be used to help us identify materials and use them more efficiently. Specific heat is expressed as kcal per kg per degree Celsius, kcal/kg°C—the number of kcal needed to raise the temperature of 1 kg of a material 1°C. Look at the specific heats shown in Table 16-14.

Compared to other substances, water has a very high specific heat. This property makes water useful for absorbing excess thermal energy. Because a small amount of water can absorb a large

TABLE 16-14	Specific Heats
Substance	Specific Heat (cal/g°C or kcal/kg°C)
Alcohol (ethyl)	0.46
Aluminum	0.21
Copper	0.09
Glass	0.20
Gold	0.03
Iron	0.11
Lead	0.03
Salt (sodium chloride)	0.02
Silver	0.05
Water	1.00

amount of thermal energy from a hot engine, water is used as an engine coolant. Water's high specific heat also enables the Gulf Stream, the Japan Current, and similar currents to carry large amounts of thermal energy over great distances. England has a moderate climate because of the warming of the Gulf Stream.

Thermal Energy Transfers

Have you ever put ice into a cup of hot chocolate to keep it from burning your tongue? How does the ice cool the hot chocolate? When the ice is placed in the hot chocolate, thermal energy flows from the hot drink into the cold ice and causes it to melt. The water produced as the ice melts continues to absorb thermal energy and becomes warmer until the chocolate and the water have the same temperature. The end result: the hot chocolate is no longer as hot (it has lost thermal energy), and the ice is no longer cold (it has gained thermal energy). Now the hot chocolate is less likely to burn your tongue.

Not all the thermal energy transferred from the hot chocolate was used to raise the temperature of the ice and then of the water as the ice melted. Some of that energy was used to change the ice from a solid to a liquid. At 0°C water can exist as either a solid or a liquid. It takes 80 cal more per gram of water to change the solid structure of ice into a liquid. This extra energy does not change the temperature of the ice; it simply helps the water molecules over-come the attractive forces that hold them in the solid state. Scientists call this extra energy the **heat of fusion.** Since water needs 80 cal to change each gram of solid to the liquid phase, its heat of fusion would be 80 kcal/kg.

Changing a substance from the liquid state to the gaseous state also requires some extra energy. The extra energy for a substance's liquid-to-gas phase change is called the **heat of vaporization** (vay pur ih ZAY shun). Water needs 540 cal to change each gram of liquid to steam at 100°C. Therefore, water's heat of vaporization is 540 kcal/kg. There is no temperature change during the water-to-steam transition. All 540 cal used to evaporate a gram of water go toward separating the water molecules from one another to form steam. After water has become steam, its temperature remains 100°C until additional energy is added to it. To calculate the energy needed to change 10 g of water at 100°C into steam at 100°C, you would multiply the number of grams that are evaporating by the calories per gram needed to cause the evaporation.

$$(10 \text{ g}) \times \left(\frac{540 \text{ cal}}{\text{g}}\right) = 5400 \text{ cal}$$

Every substance possesses its own heat of fusion and heat of vaporization. Table 16-15 shows the heats of fusion and vaporization for several common substances.

TABLE
16-15 **Thermal Characteristics of Materials**

Heats of Fusion and Vaporization

Substance	Melting point	Heat of fusion	Boiling point	Heat of vaporization
Alcohol (ethyl)	-116°C	24.9 kcal/kg	79.0°C	204 kcal/kg
Aluminum	660°C	94.0 kcal/kg	1800°C	2520 kcal/kg
Copper	1080°C	49.0 kcal/kg	2300°C	1150 kcal/kg
Gold	1060°C	15.9 kcal/kg	2600°C	
Iron	1540°C	7.89 kcal/kg	3000°C	1600 kcal/kg
Lead	327°C	5.47 kcal/kg	1620°C	207 kcal/kg
Silver	960°C	26.0 kcal/kg	1950°C	565 kcal/kg
Salt (sodium chloride)	801°C	124 kcal/kg	1450°C	
Tin	232°C	13.8 kcal/kg	2260°C	
Water	0°C	80.0 kcal/kg	100°C	540 kcal/kg

Thermal Expansion

The concrete and steel of the Verrazano-Narrows Bridge in New York City span 1298 m from Brooklyn to Staten Island. That is, on a cold winter day they do. On a hot summer day, the concrete

and steel stretch to 1299 m! An increase in thermal energy causes most materials to expand—a process known as **thermal expansion.** Bridge designers must leave gaps, called finger joints, between the sections of the roadbed so that the bridge can expand without buckling. Roads and sidewalks are also built with compressible strips between the concrete slabs to allow the concrete to expand and contract as the temperature changes. The picture above compares power lines in the summer and winter. Can you guess what happened?

As particles are heated, they become more energetic and vibrate more vigorously; therefore, they take up more room. This increased volume of the particles increases the length, width, and height of a heated material. Solids, liquids, and gases all exhibit thermal expansion—some more than others. For instance, during the same temperature increase, brass expands almost seven times as much as porcelain.

Some thermostats use the different expansion rates of different metals to control the temperatures of ovens and houses. Brass, for example, expands more than steel. If strips of these two metals are placed back to back and bonded together, they form a bimetallic (by muh TAL ik) strip. When a bimetallic strip is heated, one side expands more than the other, causing the strip to bend. In many thermostats, a bimetallic strip is coiled like a watch spring. As the temperature drops, the bimetallic strip uncoils a tiny bit, pressing a movable arm against an electrical contact. This allows electricity to flow through the movable arm to the heating element. As the temperature rises to the proper level, the coiled bimetallic strip contracts and coils more tightly, pulling away from the movable

arm. When the movable arm is no longer pressed against the electrical contact, electricity can no longer flow to the heating element. Thermometers can also be made using bimetallic strips.

Pyrex glassware (test tubes, flasks, and other utensils) is used in many laboratories because it can withstand sudden changes in temperature. This useful characteristic results from Pyrex's low expansion rate. Ordinary glass, because of its larger expansion rate, shatters or cracks if it is subjected to a quick change in temperature. When one part of an ordinary glass utensil is rapidly heated, it expands. Since glass conducts heat poorly, the rest of the utensil remains cool and does not expand. The stress produced by the size difference within the same piece of glass cracks or shatters the utensil.

Inexpensive thermometers use the expansion and contraction of mercury or alcohol to measure changes in the surrounding temperature. As the temperature rises, the liquid expands and pushes up through a narrow, cylindrical hollow in the glass tube of the thermometer. When the temperature drops, the liquid contracts, and its level in the glass tube drops. Other properties of matter, including *electrical resistance,* are also temperature dependent. An electronic thermometer is based on this principle.

Water behaves uniquely as its temperature changes. Most substances contract steadily as their temperatures drop. Water also contracts as it is cooled—at least, until its temperature drops to 4°C. As its temperature falls below 4°C, water begins to expand. At 0°C water turns to ice, and still it expands. In fact, as it freezes, water expands about 11 percent!

Because density = mass/volume, an increase in volume decreases the density. A given volume of water is smallest at 4°C because the density is greatest at this temperature. Water at 4°C tends to sink to the bottom of the lake. Colder temperature water (0°C) rises and freezes on the surface.

This expansion makes ice less dense than water and allows ice to float. If God had not designed water to expand as it freezes, rivers and lakes could freeze from the bottom to the top, killing all the life in them. However, since ice expands and is less dense than liquid water, it forms an insulating layer that helps to shield the underlying water (and the plants and animals in it) against freezing. God made water with this unusual property to preserve the life He created.

Fig. 16-18 Why does water on the surface of a lake, stream, or river freeze first?

TABLE 16-19	Thermal Expansion Rates
Substance	Thermal expansion from 30 °C to 40 °C
Aluminum	0.238 mm
Brass	0.169 mm
Concrete	up to 0.127 mm
Lead	0.292 mm
Nickel	0.131 mm
Ordinary glass	up to 0.128 mm
Pyrex glass	up to 0.035 mm
Silver	0.94 mm
Stainless steel	0.164 mm
Wood (across grain)	up to 0.730 mm
Wood (along grain)	up to 0.110 mm

CHAPTER REVIEW

SCIENTIFICALLY SPEAKING

heat

caloric theory

kinetic theory of
    thermal energy

temperature

calorie (cal)

kilocalorie (kcal)

conduction

thermal equilibrium

conductors

insulators

R-value

convection

convection current

radiation

thermodynamics

entropy

specific heat

heat of fusion

heat of vaporization

thermal expansion

CHAPTER REVIEW QUESTIONS

1. Define the term *calorie* and explain how it came into use.

2. As the temperature of an object increases, what happens to the motion of the particles? What do we call this theory?

3. Name three substances that are insulators and three that are conductors.

4. Explain why a double-paned window is such a good insulator.

5. What do we call the gradual, cyclical process in which warm particles mix with cold particles so that a uniform temperature is eventually reached?

6. According to your knowledge of specific heat, would water or alcohol cool an engine faster?

7. What common household item must undergo thermal expansion in order to work properly?

8. Why are expansion joints placed in large bridges and in concrete sidewalks?

SECTION REVIEW QUESTIONS 16B

1. What is the difference between conduction and convection? Which requires the "circulation" of matter?
2. What is the difference between a conductor and an insulator?
3. When a substance is heated, what happens to the volume?

FACET REVIEW QUESTIONS

1. Why do scientists prefer using the Celsius scale instead of the Fahrenheit?
2. What is happening to the entropy of the universe?

WHAT DID YOU LEARN?

1. What advantages would there be to having some aluminum parts in an engine instead of iron parts? What would the disadvantages be?
2. In winter, a wooden floor will feel warmer to your bare feet than a tile floor will, even though they are actually the same temperature. Why does the wood feel warmer?
3. On a hot summer day, your parents fill the car's gas tank completely. You notice later that the gasoline is spilling from under the gas cap. Why?
4. A scientist reports in his research findings that certain substances are "hot" and "cold" but does not report temperatures. Why is this a poor method of recording data?

Electricity

17A Static Electricity
17B Electric Current

17

Try this experiment: take a piece of paper and drop it. Why does it fall to the floor? That's an easy one—gravity pulls it down.

Now try this experiment: tear off a few small bits of paper and put them on the table. Run a comb through your hair and then hold it over the bits of paper. You can get them to jump up and stick to the comb. Why do they do that? The answer is **static electricity**. This type of electricity deals with charges that exist between stationary objects, or objects at rest.

Static Electricity

People have observed static electricity throughout history. Moses mentioned lightning (one of the most spectacular results of static electricity) over three thousand years ago (Exodus 19:16). Over two thousand years ago, the Greeks observed that a piece of amber they had stroked with wool or fur could "magically" attract certain lightweight objects.

Notice that the force of static electricity can be stronger than the force of gravity. As the bits of paper sit on the table, gravity is pulling them down. The force of static electricity from the comb is able to overcome gravity and pick them up.

Fig. 17-1 A comb with an electric charge can pick up bits of paper.

Fig. 17-2 A large buildup of electric charge can have dramatic effects.

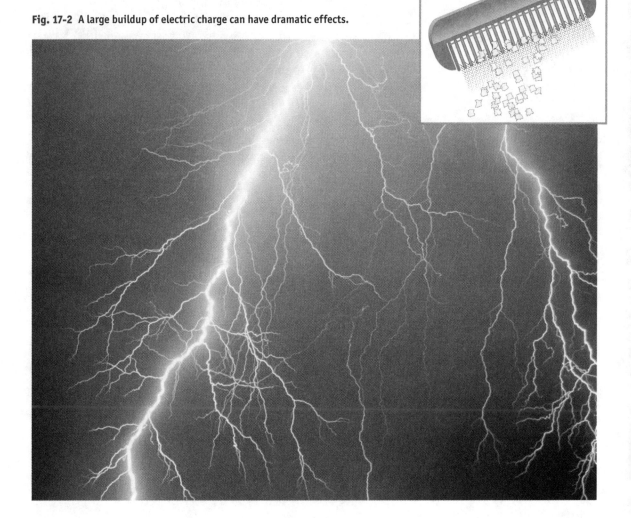

Electric Charge

Recall from Chapter 6 that atoms are made up of three fundamental particles: electrons, protons, and neutrons.

Protons and neutrons are tightly stuck together in the center, or nucleus, of the atom. It is difficult to change the nucleus of an atom. Electrons, on the other hand, are found around the nucleus on the outside of the atom. Valence electrons are much easier to add or remove than the protons and neutrons. As you learned in Chapter 8, these changes in electrons are the basis of chemical reactions.

Each of these particles (proton, electron, neutron) has several properties. In Chapter 6, you learned that they have mass. One effect of mass we can observe is gravity, the attraction that all masses have for each other (Chapter 13). The paper's mass causes it to be attracted to the earth's mass, pulling it to the floor.

These particles also have a property called *charge.* Unlike mass, which has only attractive effects, charged particles can either attract or repel. These two kinds of effects suggest that there must be two kinds of charge—positive and negative. We know there are two kinds of charge because we can observe objects either attracting each other (like the comb and the paper) or repelling each other.

Consider the following experiment, which you can do yourself. Hang a plastic ruler by a string. Rub one end vigorously with a cloth, preferably a wool cloth, or a piece of fur. This will give the ruler a negative charge.

Hold another ruler in your hand and rub it with the same cloth. It will have the same charge. Bring this ruler near the tip of the hanging one, but do not let them touch. You should be able to see your ruler repel, or push away, the hanging ruler.

Now hold a glass rod in your hand and rub it with a silk cloth. The rod will have a positive charge. Bring the glass rod near the hanging plastic ruler. It should attract, or pull, the plastic ruler.

Now hang a glass rod by the string. Rub it with silk to charge it, and repeat the experiments. The results should be as listed in the table below:

Charge of first object	Charge of second object	Result
+	–	Attract
+	+	Repel
–	+	Attract
–	–	Repel

The **law of charges** summarizes this table: like charges repel; unlike charges attract. Additionally, an object can have equal amounts of positive and negative charge. Such an object would act as if it were not charged at all.

Most atoms are made up of more than one proton and neutron. They normally have equal numbers of positive charges (protons) and negative charges (electrons). The effects cancel, and the atom generally acts as if it were not charged at all. We say the atom is *neutral.* Everyday objects are made up of neutral atoms and are therefore neutral themselves.

Valence electrons, however, are easily removed from atoms. Simple rubbing can do it. This is what happens when you walk across a carpet floor and then feel a shock when you touch a doorknob. Your shoes and the carpet have exchanged some electrons.

When we rub two objects together, one will lose electrons and the other will gain electrons. The object that loses electrons is left with an excess of protons. It has a net positive charge. The other object gained electrons and has an excess of them. It has a net negative charge.

Wool has a weak *affinity* for electrons. Rubbing most materials with a wool cloth will remove electrons from the wool. The cloth becomes positively charged, and the object becomes negatively charged.

The exception would be a material that has an electron affinity even weaker than wool. For example, Lucite, a hard transparent plastic material, has an even weaker affinity for electrons than wool does. A wool cloth will rub electrons off a Lucite rod, resulting in a negatively charged cloth and a positively charged rod.

When an object has an excess of electrons, we say that it is storing a negative charge. When an object has a shortage of electrons, we say it is storing a positive charge. Scientists use this principle to build charge-storing electronic components called **capacitors.** In a capacitor, positive and negative charges are stored in objects separated so that the charges cannot move between them.

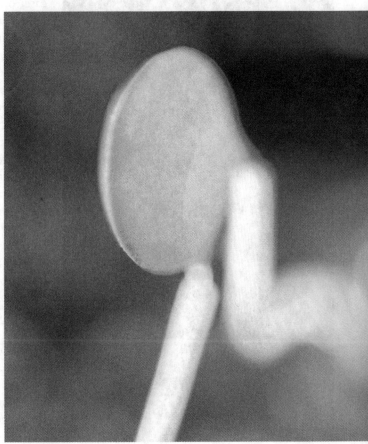

Fig. 17-3 Capacitors store electric charges on conductors separated by an insulator.

Electrical Induction

Recall the comb and paper experiment at the beginning of this chapter. The comb attracted the bits of paper. Why? The comb, run through your hair, became charged. What about the bits of paper? Were they charged? The law of charges says that oppositely charged objects attract. Is this what happened?

No, the paper was probably not charged. There is another way that objects can attract each other. **Induction** is the charging of an object by shifting the paths of its electrons. The charged object, when brought near, will produce a temporary charge within the paper.

Remember that the paper, although it is neutral, contains both protons and electrons. When the comb is brought near, the electrons are repelled, pushed toward the back side of the paper. The protons are left nearer, toward the front side of the paper. The comb attracts these nearby protons, as if the paper itself had a net positive charge.

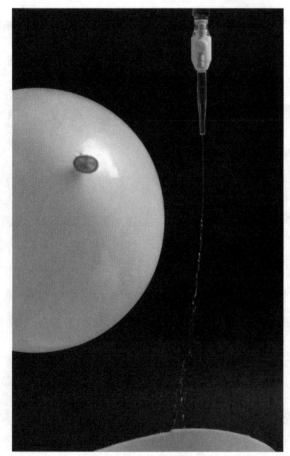

Fig. 17-4 The polar molecules of water are easily attracted by an electric charge.

When two objects attract each other, it could be for one of two reasons. In one case, the objects have opposite charges. In the other case, only one object has a charge. The charged object *induces* a charge in the other.

Water molecules are particularly easy to attract this way, because the H_2O molecule itself is naturally polarized. This means that the positive and negative charges within the molecule are naturally separated.

You can demonstrate the attraction for a polarized water molecule using a balloon and a water faucet. Charge the balloon by rubbing it with a cloth, preferably wool. Turn on the faucet so that a narrow, smooth stream of water flows out. Bring the balloon near without touching the water. The charged balloon will attract the water molecules and cause the stream to bend.

Water molecules play an important role in how objects lose their charge as well. In the comb experiment at the start of the chapter, the comb's charge will dissipate slowly even if you don't touch it. The extra electrons can "leak off" onto water molecules in the air. For this reason, all of the demonstrations in this chapter work best in dry weather. Induced charges also play an important role in modern electronics. A capacitor, described in the previous section, can store charge on its conductive plates. In addition, when the conductors are charged, they can induce a charge in the insulator in between. This induced charge enhances the charge-storing capability of a capacitor.

Detecting Charges

How can you tell whether an object has a positive charge, a negative charge, or no charge at all? Scientists have designed an instrument called an **electroscope** that uses the law of charges to detect charge. The simple electroscope shown in Figure 17-6 consists of a flask with a one-holed rubber stopper, a metal rod, a few leaf-shaped pieces of aluminum foil, and a metal sphere.

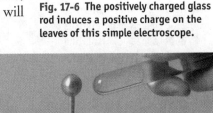

Fig. 17-5 A Braun electroscope uses a stem and needle rather than leaves.

The metal rod in the electroscope not only serves as a support for the metal leaves and metal sphere but also carries charge from the sphere down to the leaves. If we place a negative charge (extra electrons) on the sphere, some of the extra electrons travel down the rod to the metal leaves, making both leaves negatively charged. In accordance with the law of charges, the leaves will repel each other and swing apart. On the other hand, if the sphere is positively charged, the metal rod will conduct electrons away from the leaves, making them both positively charged. Once again, the leaves will swing apart because of their like charges.

Fig. 17-6 The positively charged glass rod induces a positive charge on the leaves of this simple electroscope.

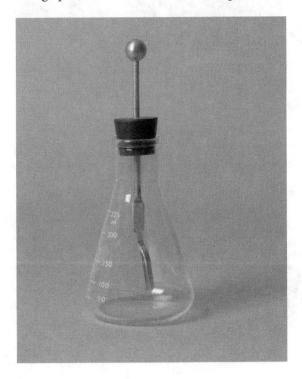

These mechanical electroscopes can detect only relatively large charges. This shortcoming is caused by the fact that tiny electrical charges produce only tiny electrical forces of repulsion, which cannot move the relatively large mass of a metal leaf or pointer. Today, most laboratories use electronic electroscopes. Instead of relying on mechanical movement, these electroscopes measure the charge on an object by applying the charge to a capacitor and then measuring how long it takes the capacitor to lose the charge.

Sparks Are Flying—
The Van de Graaff Generator

In 1931 Robert Van de Graaff (VAN deh graf), a Princeton physicist, invented one of the first devices that produced large amounts of charge. In the *Van de Graaff generator,* a motor-driven belt passes over two pulleys made of insulating materials. At one point, the belt receives negative charges from an electron source called a *comb* ("ground comb"). The moving belt carries the negative charges to a metal "collector comb." Since the charge on the belt is more negative than the charge on the comb, electrons flow from the belt onto the collector comb. From the collector comb the electrons flow onto a large metal sphere. The longer the Van de Graaff generator operates, the more negative charge collects on the large metal sphere. The charge cannot flow off the metal sphere because the support for the sphere is made of an insulating material, which does not conduct charge well.

Of course, there is a limit to the amount of charge that can be

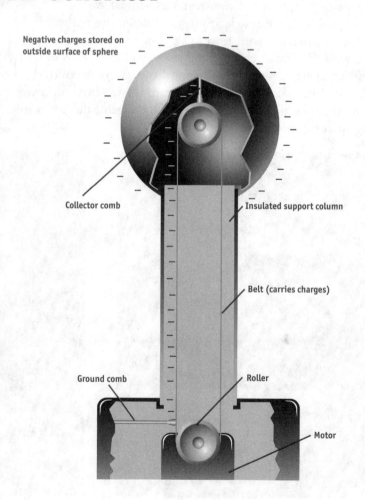

Negative charges stored on outside surface of sphere

Collector comb

Insulated support column

Belt (carries charges)

Ground comb

Roller

Motor

Using Charges

Several biological systems use static electricity. The human body's muscles and nervous system use electrical charges to function. As a heart muscle cell begins to contract, for example, the electrical charge on the cell changes. This change can be picked up with a sensitive electronic instrument called an electrocardiograph. The resulting pattern of changes can tell a doctor much about the condition of the heart.

As the negative charges flow from the generator, they collect on the individual fibers of hair. As "like repels like," so the negatively charged hair strands try to "escape" from one another.

collected on the metal sphere. As soon as the concentration of negative charge on the sphere and collector comb has reached the same level as the concentration of negative charge being delivered by the moving belt, no more negative charge will flow from the belt to the sphere.

The charge that accumulates on the metal sphere of a large Van de Graaff generator can produce a tremendous electrical force. Sparks up to 4 m long can be produced between a large Van de Graaff generator and a grounded object. (A *spark* is a visible transfer of charge from one object to another.)

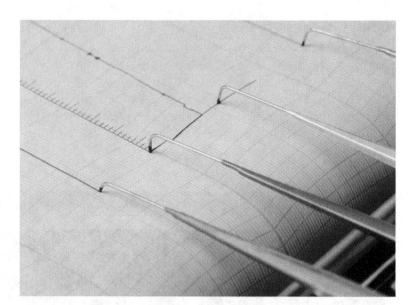

Fig. 17-7 An EKG records the changing electric charges in a human heart as it beats.

Fig. 17-8 Electrostatic precipitator

Electrostatic principles also operate in the pollution-control systems of some factories. As smoke travels from machinery to the smokestacks, it passes charged electrodes that give the smoke particles a static charge. Just before the smoke enters the smokestacks, the charged particles are collected on oppositely charged metal

plates. Much of the remaining "smoke" that is released through the smokestack is harmless steam. Frequently, the particles attracted to the electrodes contain valuable chemical substances that can be reclaimed. This type of antipollution device, called an electrostatic precipitator, substantially reduces air pollution.

Moving Charges

As you may recall from Chapter 16, some materials allow electrons to move through them easily with little resistance. We call these materials *conductors.* Metals such as copper and aluminum are good conductors. Electrical wires are made out of these materials. Other materials do not allow electrons to move easily. We call these materials *insulators.* Glass, wood, and rubber are all insulators. The plastic coating on the outside of an electrical wire is an insulator.

TABLE 17-9	Relative Conductivity of Various Substances	
Poor conductors—good insulators	rubber, glass, wood
Semiconductors	silicon, germanium
Good conductors—poor insulators	iron, aluminum, copper, silver

Most materials are either excellent conductors or excellent insulators. Only a few materials fall in between. We call such materials **semiconductors.** These materials allow limited electron flow. Common examples include carbon and silicon. Transistors and other computer chips are made out of semiconductor materials.

When objects with different charges are brought together, some of the electrons may move from one to the other. This is what happens when you walk across the carpet on a dry day and then touch a doorknob. The spark you feel is caused by electrons jumping from you to the doorknob.

The loss of static electricity as electrons move to another object is called electric discharge. Lightning is a common and dramatic form of electric discharge. Lightning is produced when a cloud discharges its excess electrons.

SECTION REVIEW QUESTIONS 17A

1. What is the law of charges?
2. Explain induction as it relates to the paper and comb experiment.
3. What do we call materials that allow limited electron flow and are used in electronics?

Lightning

Lightning strikes somewhere on the earth about one hundred times every second. The United States is a frequent target—about one hundred people are killed every year in the United States by lightning, and hundreds of others are injured or have property damaged by this powerful, natural discharge of electrical current. In a normal year, more people are killed by lightning than by tornadoes and hurricanes combined.

Lightning usually strikes within parts of the same cloud. In less than a second, a single lightning bolt may jump up to three kilometers and heat the air along its channel up to 10,000°C. The tremendous increase in pressure generated by the sudden expansion of this heated air produces a clap of thunder often audible over twenty kilometers away. One lightning stroke is usually followed by another stroke along a slightly different path. Scientists have detected up to forty strokes in less than a second.

In 1752 Benjamin Franklin demonstrated by his famous kite experiment that lightning is a form of electricity. During a thunderstorm, Franklin flew a kite from a long length of wet twine. Stationing himself under a dry shed, Franklin held a dry silk string attached to a key connected to the twine that held the kite. He observed that sparks flew from the key whenever he brought it near objects physically attached to the ground. He wondered if these sparks were identical to the electrical charges he could store in his Leyden jars. He tested his hypothesis by touching the key to a grounded Leyden jar. As Franklin suspected, charge flowed from the key to the jar just as it did from other sources of static electricity. His conclusion: lightning is static electricity.

What causes lightning? Most lightning occurs during a thunderstorm as rain falls over an area of warm, rising air. Although it is not fully understood, a charge separation occurs in large clouds. The base of the cloud acquires an overall negative charge, and the top portion of the cloud accumulates an overall positive charge. These opposite charges continue to accumulate in the cloud. At the same time, the negatively charged base of the cloud induces a positive charge on the earth. At about ten thousand volts per centimeter, the difference in potential becomes too great. This force eventually breaks down the insulating capacity of the air and a lightning bolt "discharges" the excess electrons.

The bolt of lightning produced as charge jumps from the earth to the cloud may release more power than the combined peak capacity of all the electrical power plants in the United States. However, because the bolt lasts less than a second, the energy it releases is worth less than twenty dollars!

Recent research shows us that forked lighting is not the only type. Rarer forms, such as sheet lightning and ball lightning, have been observed by scientists, but their causes remain a mystery. *Red sprites* are great fountains of reddish lightning that have been seen only in the stratosphere, over twelve miles above the surface of the earth. These red sprites may shoot up to fifty miles in height and are found in only the biggest, most severe thunderstorm systems. Types of lightning called *blue jets* behave in a similar fashion.

Benjamin Franklin also invented one of the best protections against lightning—the lightning rod. A lightning rod is a pointed, upright metal rod fastened to the roof of a building and connected to the ground by a wire leading from the base of the rod. The lightning rod serves to conduct charge to the ground. If lightning does occur near the rod, it will be attracted to the highest object in the area (the lightning rod) and will be conducted harmlessly to the earth through the wire.

Occasionally, Scripture uses lightning to symbolize judgment. For example, in Psalm 18:14 David exclaims, "Yea, he sent out his arrows, and scattered them; and he shot out lightnings, and discomfited them." Lightning is a fitting symbol for judgment because it possesses not only great destructive power but also great speed. But we sometimes forget that lightning serves a useful purpose. You may wince at the statistic that lightning starts 75,000 forest fires each year. In most cases, however, forest fires actually help forests because they clear out decaying vegetation, providing much-needed nutrients to the new seedlings. Lightning also combines atmospheric nitrogen with oxygen to form nitrates. Nitrates are then carried down to the soil by precipitation and are used to fertilize plants and help them produce needed proteins.

Here are some important safety rules that will help you protect yourself from lightning during a thunderstorm.

1. The safest shelter during a thunderstorm is a building protected by lightning rods or a shielded metal enclosure such as a car. Stay in a protected place if you can.

2. Stay away from isolated trees, high points of land, and bodies of water because lightning is most likely to strike these locations.

3. If you are caught in an open area, lie down flat.

4. Indoors, keep away from windows and outside doors. Close all windows; lightning has been known to enter buildings through open windows. Avoid using electrical appliances and touching plumbing. Lightning can strike and kill or seriously injure you as you touch a faucet or telephone.

Electric Current

Electric discharges are short-lived. An object has only a limited number of excess electrons to lose. When they are gone, the discharge ceases. In order to use electricity to perform useful work, we need a continuous flow of charge.

Modern civilizations could not exist without a continuous flow of electricity. Cars, elevators, freezers, hair dryers, fluorescent lights, and hundreds of other convenient and time-saving devices require electricity to operate. In almost all these devices, moving charges provide the energy for the work that is accomplished. Electricity that involves continuously moving charges is called **electric current.**

Identifying Current

As discussed earlier, electrons are far easier to move than protons. Nearly all electric current involves the flow of electrons, which are negatively charged.

Recall that electrons cannot be created out of nothing. A steady flow of electricity requires a steady supply of electrons. To better understand this, let's look at the way decorative fountains are designed.

A steady supply of water is needed for the fountain. It is wasteful and expensive to constantly spray new water into the air and then allow it to drain away. Nearly all fountains collect the water, return it to the pump, and recirculate it again and again.

Fig. 17-10 Modern society is totally dependent upon the reliable flow of electric current.

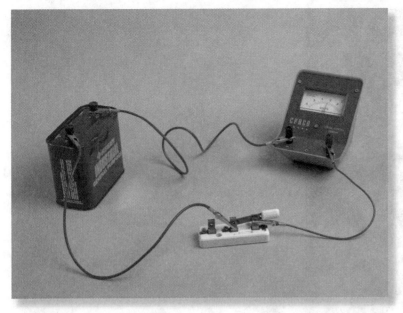

Fig. 17-11 A simple electrical circuit is a circular path for electricity.

Electrical systems use a similar approach. A path is provided for electrons to return to the source to be used again. Such a closed path is called an electric **circuit**.

Sources of electrical energy, such as flashlight batteries, do not create electrons. They are simply electron "pumps" that push electrons through the circuit.

Fig. 17-12 A light bulb has two contacts: one for current to enter and another for current to exit.

This is the reason a flashlight battery has two connections, a positive end and a negative end. The battery pumps the electrons to the negative end where they exit. They flow through the circuit and return to the positive end. Look carefully at the base of a light bulb (Figure 17-12). It also makes two connections, one for the electrons to enter and another for the electrons to exit.

Any break in the conductor keeps electrons from flowing around a circuit. A circuit can be broken intentionally with a switch. A simple **switch** is a conductor that can be moved so that it either bridges or does not bridge the gap between two wire conductors. When the conductors do not make contact, electrons cannot flow across the break, and

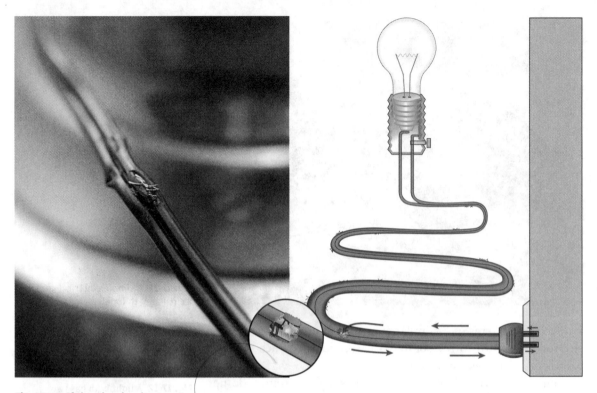

Fig. 17-13 If the wires in a lamp cord touch, the electrons will follow the "easiest" path. We call this a short circuit.

both the circuit and the switch are said to be *open*. When the conductors do make contact, electrons can flow through the connected conductors, and the circuit and switch are said to be *closed*. A switch acts like a drawbridge. When the switch is open, the drawbridge is up and the electrons cannot jump the wide gap. When the switch is closed, the drawbridge is down and electrons can travel across. The spark that often occurs when a switch opens is really a stream of electrons jumping across the tiny gap.

Electrons will take the path of least resistance. This tendency is frequently to blame when electrical appliances break down. For example, picture a lamp cord that has frayed so badly that the wires inside it touch each other. If the electrons flowing into the cord flowed all the way through the lamp, it would convert some of their energy into light. Rather than traveling the entire circuit, however, the electrons take a shortcut through the point where the wires touch. We call this shorter path for the electrons a **short circuit**.

Causes of Current

Electrons move through a circuit only if an electrical force pushes them. What is an electrical force? Where does it come from? What part does it play in electrical circuits? We can compare electric current to a water-pump system. A pump creates pressure. It can push

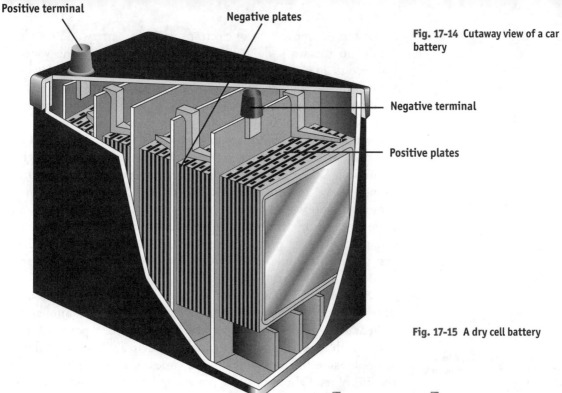

Positive terminal

Negative plates

Negative terminal

Positive plates

Fig. 17-14 Cutaway view of a car battery

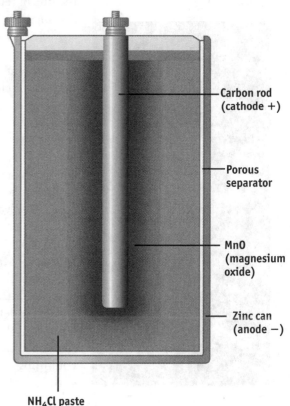

Fig. 17-15 A dry cell battery

Carbon rod (cathode +)

Porous separator

MnO (magnesium oxide)

Zinc can (anode −)

NH₄Cl paste

water through pipes from a low elevation to a higher elevation. The higher the pump pushes the water, the more work the pump does. As the water is raised, it gains potential energy. As it flows back to its original level, it can be used to do work.

A battery is like an electrical pump. Instead of pumping water, a battery pumps electrons. Inside a battery, a chemical reaction pushes electrons from one place to another. As this process continues, the place losing electrons becomes positively charged, and the place gaining electrons becomes negatively charged. The positive terminal has a shortage of electrons. The negative terminal has an excess of electrons. These electrons are ready to travel through a circuit. The chemical reaction provides the pressure to make them move.

Chemical reactions are only one way to move electrons. For example, in Chapter 18 you will learn about generators that produce electricity using magnetism.

How is the movement of electrons within a battery and circuit similar to the work done in a water-pump system? The water pumped to an elevation will do work if it is allowed to flow downward. Similarly, the electrons that a battery pushes onto its negative terminal will do work if they are allowed to flow through a circuit.

If you wanted to build a water-pump system that would give the water a large amount of potential energy, you would find a location where the water could be pumped up a very high mountain. When the water was released, it would be capable of doing a large amount of work. But to pump the water up the mountain you would need a strong water pump. If you want a large amount of electrical energy to flow through a circuit, you also need a strong "pump." Some batteries are stronger than others: the stronger the battery is, the more electrons it can push onto its negative terminal.

Water naturally flows from high elevations to lower elevations, or from places of high pressure to places of low pressure. Similarly, current always flows from places with higher electrical potentials to places with lower electrical potentials. These places may be different objects or different points in the same object. In Figure 17-16 the line of red light in the tube is given off by a stream of electrons flowing between two electrodes at different potentials.

We measure the difference between electrical potentials in units called **volts (V).** Because moving a single electron involves such a tiny amount of energy, volts are defined in terms of moving a large number of electrons. A special unit has been defined to specify a standard number of electrons. This unit is the **coulomb (C)** (KOO lom). A coulomb is the charge carried by 6,250,000,000,000,000,000 (6.25×10^{18}) electrons! A voltage of 1 V is a potential that can move 1 coulomb of charge (6.25×10^{18} electrons) using 1 joule of energy.

The greater the number of electrons that flow through a circuit in a given amount of time, the greater the amount of current that flows through the circuit. We measure current in units called **amperes** (AM pirz; abbreviated A), sometimes shortened to *amps.* Measuring electrical current in amperes is like measuring water flow by counting the number of liters of water that pass a point in a pipe every second (liters per second). Electrical current is defined by the movement of a charge. A circuit with a current of 1 ampere has 1 C of charge (6.25×10^{18} electrons) moving past a point in the circuit every second. How many coulombs of charge flow in one second past a point in a circuit with 2 A of current?

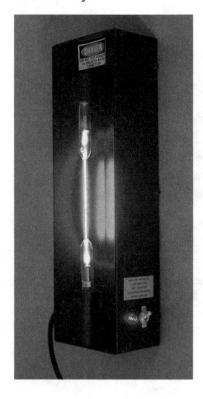

17-16 Electron movement can be quite dramatic. This is current flowing in a tube of mercury.

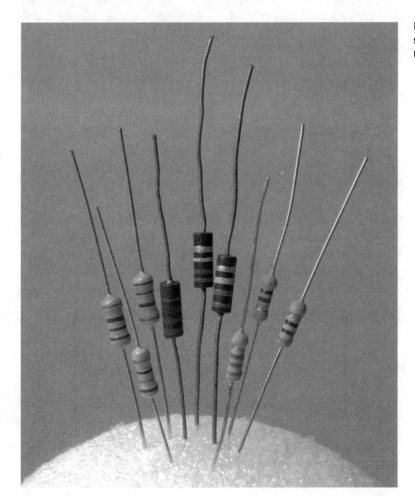

Fig. 17-17 Resistors are color-coded to show the relative amounts of resistance they provide.

Controlling Current

How do the moving charges of electrical current do work in electrical devices? Again, compare electricity and water. Moving water can do work. For instance, the water flowing down a mountain can turn a water wheel. The water uses some of its energy to push the paddles as it flows by. The water wheel can then use the energy it gains from the water to do work by turning a turbine.

The electrical parallel to a water wheel is a resistor. A **resistor** is any object or substance that hinders the flow of electrons. Resistors in your home include the heating element on a stove, the filament in a light bulb, and the speaker on your radio. Just as water uses energy to flow past a water wheel, electrons use energy to flow through resistors. As you might expect, insulators have large resistances, semiconductors have medium resistances, and conductors have very small resistances.

A German schoolteacher named Georg Simon Ohm explored the relationship between voltage, current, and the resistance of various devices. He observed two important facts. You can experiment with resistors and observe these facts for yourself.

First, choose a resistor and observe the current that flows when various voltages are connected. You will discover that the *current is directly proportional to the voltage.* If you double the voltage applied to a resistor, the current also will double. Since voltage is the "pressure'" that forces electrons through the resistor, this fact is no surprise.

Second, choose a fixed voltage supply and attach various sizes of resistors. You will discover that the *current is inversely proportional to the resistance.* If you double the resistance, the current will decrease by one half. This is also expected, because resistors limit the flow of current.

Putting these two facts into a single equation leads to **Ohm's law.**

$$\text{Formula for Ohm's Law}$$
$$I = \frac{V}{R}$$
This equation is commonly rearranged and written as
V = IR or Voltage = current times resistance

Today we measure resistance in units called **ohms** (Ω). It takes 1 V of potential difference to push 1 A of current through a resistor with a resistance of 1 Ω. It takes 2 V to push 2 A of current

Fig. 17-18 Georg Simon Ohm

EXAMPLE PROBLEM

Calculating resistance

A car headlight experiences a current of 4 A when connected to the car's 12-V battery. What is the resistance of the headlight?

KNOWN:	Current (I)	= 4 A
	Voltage (V)	= 12 V
UNKNOWN:	Resistance (R)	
FORMULA TO USE:		R = V/I
SUBSTITUTION:		R = 12 V/4 A
SOLUTION:		R = 3 V/A or
		R = 3 Ω (since 1 V/A = 1 Ω)

Fig. 17-19 The heating element in an electric stove has a low resistance, allowing a large amount of current to flow and producing large amounts of heat.

through a 1-Ω resistor. How many volts would it take to push 10 A through a 2-Ω resistor?

All electrical devices have some resistance. Therefore electrons always lose energy as they pass through electrical devices. As explained in Chapter 12, energy is never actually lost but is converted into other forms of energy. For example, if you are making a coffeecake, you may use an electric mixer to convert electrical energy into the mechanical energy necessary to spin the beaters. An electric oven converts electrical energy into the heat energy that bakes the cake.

The resistive devices in an electrical device are called **loads.** A circuit may contain more than one load and may be arranged in many different ways. Two common arrangements have specific names. In a **series circuit** there is only one path for the electrons to follow. All the electrons from the source flow through all the loads in sequence and then return to the source. In a **parallel circuit,** the electrons have several paths to follow. Only some of the electrons pass through any one load. The rest of the electrons flow through the other loads.

For example, if two or more light bulbs are connected in series (Figure 17-20), the electrons that pass through the first bulb must also pass through the second and third bulbs. Therefore, the same amount of current flows through all the light bulbs. If any one bulb burns out (the thin, current-carrying filament breaks), the circuit is broken and the current stops flowing through all the bulbs.

If two or more bulbs are connected in a parallel circuit (Figure 17-22), each bulb represents a separate path for electrons. The current from the power supply divides, and only a portion goes through each bulb.

If one of the light bulbs in the parallel circuit is turned off or burns out, electrons will continue to flow through the other branches, and the other bulbs will continue to burn. Houses are nearly always wired in parallel for this reason.

Because wires made of good conductive material have very little resistance, they are used to carry current between electrical energy

FACETS of the physical world

Michael Faraday (1791-1867)

What do silver-plated spoons, electric generators, polarized sunglasses, and liquid ammonia have in common? The answer is Michael Faraday (FAIR uh day). His work made these and many similar innovations possible. Science historians rate this man as one of history's greatest experimental physicists.

Faraday was born in England and grew up there. His early life was filled with books. He spent much time as an apprentice to a bookbinder, browsing through scientific writings. When he was only twenty-one years old, he became fascinated with the teachings of Sir Humphrey Davy, a well-respected chemist. Davy mentored young Michael, who soon followed his lead in studying chemistry.

Faraday's pioneering work in electrochemistry showed that compounds can be broken down into elements by an electrical current. Faraday called this decomposition reaction *electrolysis*. Today many

industries use electrolysis in processes that include plating spoons with silver, powering batteries, and extracting aluminum from its ore. Perhaps Faraday's greatest contribution to chemistry was his discovery of the ringed, six-carbon structure known as benzene. The benzene molecule would revolutionize the study of organic chemistry.

As he grew older, Faraday became more and more interested in electricity and magnetism. While experimenting with magnets, Faraday discovered that rotating magnets can induce a current and produce electricity. This discovery was the basis for electric generators, transformers, and electric motors. Faraday also contributed to the study of polarized light and the liquefaction of gases. Perhaps most noteworthy of all is Faraday's discovery of the "field" of force that surrounds a magnet. This concept became one of the major developments in the history of physics.

What made Michael Faraday the successful scientist that he was? He had the right attitude toward science, himself, and God. A devout Christian, Faraday based his attitudes on the firm foundation of Scripture. He viewed science as a constant search to see order and consistency in God's creation. Faraday wanted to discover and understand as much as he could about God's universe. To do this, he disciplined himself to become a model researcher. Faraday believed that the ideal scientist should be enthusiastic but always careful; he must constantly test his theories against the facts. If fact and theory do not match, theory must be discarded. These were high standards, but Faraday drove himself to meet them.

Faraday's Christianity motivated him not only to excellence but also to humility. Despite his notable achievements, Faraday never forgot that he could make mistakes, and as

sources and loads. However, each type of wire can carry only a limited amount of current without overheating and possibly starting a fire. **Fuses** are used to prevent electrical fires by interrupting the current before the wires become too hot. Fuses are made of metals with low melting points and are rated according to how much current they can carry without melting and breaking the circuit. For example, if more than 10 A of current pass through a fuse with a current rating of 10 A, the wire in the fuse will melt and break the flow of current in the circuit. Automobiles have fuses to control their electrical systems, but most houses no longer have fuses.

a result, he carefully scrutinized his work for errors. In the words of one of his biographers, Faraday led a "life-long strife to seek and say that which he thought was true, and to do that which he thought was kind." Faraday's humility made him both an exemplary scientist and a shining testimony for Christ.

Faraday's contributions to science were firmly rooted in his faith. As an earnest student of the Bible, Faraday made nearly three thousand notes in the margin of his Bible. To his knowledge of the Bible, he added enthusiasm and intense love for God. Even his heavy research schedule could not distract him from the all-day Sunday services and midweek prayer meeting of the small church he attended in London. Another great scientist, John Tyndall, noted that "a good deal of Faraday's weekday strength might be attributed to his Sunday exercises. He drinks from a fount on Sunday which refreshes his soul for the week."

Faraday knew that God's Word is sure. While he carefully searched out and analyzed scientific knowledge, he realized that knowledge of God comes from the Bible by simple faith. A reporter once asked Faraday about his speculations on the hereafter. "Speculations?" replied the astonished physicist. "I have none; I am resting on certainties. 'I know whom I have believed, and am persuaded that he is able to keep that which I have committed unto him against that day'" (II Timothy 1:12). Although some of Faraday's scientist friends smiled scornfully at his beliefs, they could not say that they were the product of a weak mind or that they failed to produce a godly life.

Michael Faraday commanded respect and admiration across the globe. For many years he served as director of the Royal Institute's laboratory in London. His election as a Fellow of the Royal Society was only

one of about ninety-five honors he received for his outstanding achievements. Psalm 1:2-3 promises that those who delight in the law of the Lord will prosper. Certainly this promise was fulfilled in the life of Michael Faraday. He stands both as a scientific hero and as an inspiring example of a Christian who applied his faith to everyday life.

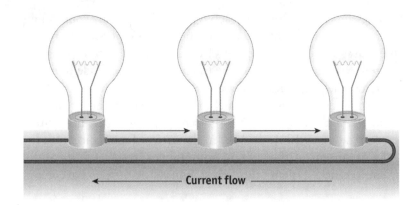

Fig. 17-20 In a series circuit, all the bulbs carry the same current.

Current flow

Fig. 17-21 Fuses interrupt the flow of electricity when overload occurs.

Since replacing burned-out fuses can become tedious and expensive, a device known as a **circuit breaker** has been designed. Circuit breakers are automatic switches that turn themselves off when the current is excessive. They are not damaged like fuses and can simply be turned back on to restore power.

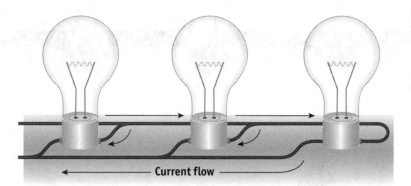

Current flow

Power and Current

Power measures how fast work is done. Power can be calculated by dividing the total amount of work done (in joules) by the time it took to do the work (Chapter 14). The unit of power is the **watt (W).** A machine that does 1 J of work in 1 s uses 1 W of power. The more quickly a circuit uses energy, the larger the power. For example, a 100-W light bulb uses twice as much energy per unit of time as a 50-W light bulb. The extra energy is used to produce more light in the 100-W light bulb. Machines in many factories use thousands of watts of power. The power ratings of these machines are expressed in **kilowatts (kW),** or units of 1000 W.

We often refer to companies that sell electrical energy as "power companies." However, the electric company usually charges you only according to how much energy you use, not according to the power you draw. The "power meter" behind your house displays

Fig. 17-23 Electric companies charge customers by the kilowatt-hour.

Bright Ideas

Many of the appliances we use daily—toasters, irons, electric stoves and ovens, fluorescent and incandescent lights, to name a few—produce heat or light from electrical energy. How does electrical current produce light and heat?

We know that electrons lose energy as they pass through a resistor. Where does this energy go? Most of the energy of the electrons is converted into thermal energy in the resistor. The more current is pushed through any given resistor, the more thermal energy (heat) is produced.

In toasters, irons, stoves, and similar appliances, electrical current passes through materials such as nichrome (an alloy of nickel, iron, and chromium) or carbon. When enough current flows through a heating element made of one of these substances, the element glows red-hot.

Forcing current through an electrical device can also produce light. The first electrical lights were arc lights. The British chemist Sir Humphrey Davy found that a bright spark would flash continually between two carbon rods if they were connected to the terminals of a high-voltage battery. Lights based on this principle produced a very bright and glaring light. Consequently, arc lights were not often used in homes. Today, carbon arc lights provide extremely bright light for large motion-picture projectors,

searchlights, and spotlights.

Current flowing through wires can also produce light. The word *incandescent* means "glowing with great heat," so lights made from wires that glow when current passes through them are called *incandescent lights*. As nineteenth-century scientists learned more about electricity, they realized that incandescent light was a promising way to produce light efficiently. Unfortunately, their tests quickly revealed an obstacle: each wire that produced a fairly bright light also burned out quickly. During the last half of the nineteenth century, Thomas Alva Edison tested thousands of different substances as the conductors in incandescent light bulbs. Platinum, human hair, cotton, and bamboo were just a few of the materials he tried. Finally, in October 1879 he succeeded: a carbonized thread formed a long-lasting incandescent filament. Edison found that if he enclosed the carbonized filament in a glass bulb and removed the air from within the glass, the filament lasted even longer. The lack of oxygen in the bulb kept the thread from oxidizing and burning out quickly. In the wake of Edison's discovery, light bulbs rapidly became the major source of light in American homes.

Today carbon filaments have been replaced by more sturdy and efficient materials, primarily tungsten wire. Tungsten wire has a higher resistance than most other metals, allowing for relatively short filaments. In addition, tungsten's very high melting point (about 3410°C) allows tungsten filaments to burn hotter and brighter without melting.

Fluorescent light bulbs produce light from current much differently from the way incandescent light bulbs do. In *fluorescent lights,* sodium or mercury vapor fills a long tube that has electrodes at each end. When enough voltage is supplied to the electrodes, the molecules are ionized; that is, valence electrons in the atoms are removed from their paths. Current then flows through the tube, carried by the free electrons and the ions in the tube. Periodically, free electrons rejoin the ions and produce invisible ultraviolet light. When the ultraviolet light strikes the inner coating of the tube, a bright, uniform light is given off.

Units of Measurement—Electricity

1 joule = 1 newton meter

1 watt = 1 joule/second

1 coulomb = 6.25×10^{18} electrons

1 ampere = 1 coulomb/second

1 volt = 1 joule/coulomb

1 ohm = 1 volt/amp

Formulas:

Ohm's law: V = IR (voltage = current × resistance)

P = IV (power = current × voltage)

both electrical power (the rate of use) and electrical energy (the amount used). The spinning dial shows the power. The faster it spins, the greater the power. The numbers show the total energy used. The more times it spins, the greater the energy used. Ten slow spins or ten fast spins both add up to the same amount of energy. Therefore, it costs just as much to operate a 100-W light bulb for ten hours as it does to run a 1000-W blow dryer for one hour. The light bulb uses 100 J per second; the blow dryer uses 1000 J per second. The light bulb has to run ten times longer than the blow dryer to use an equal amount of energy (the same number of joules).

CHAPTER REVIEW

SCIENTIFICALLY SPEAKING

static electricity	amperes (A)
law of charges	resistor
capacitors	Ohm's law
induction	ohms (Ω)
electroscope	loads
semiconductors	series circuit
electric current	parallel circuit
circuit	fuses
switch	circuit breaker
short circuit	watt (W)
volts (V)	kilowatts (kW)
coulomb (C)	

CHAPTER REVIEW QUESTIONS

1. Describe what will happen if you repeatedly run a comb through your hair and then bring it near some scraps of paper. What does this experiment illustrate?

2. Would you classify most objects on the earth as positive, negative, or electrically neutral?

3. Describe a capacitor and what it does with electrons.

4. What is electric current?

5. Which is a stronger electron "pump," a 6-V flashlight battery or a 12-V car battery?

6. If a 120-V source is pushing 1 A of current through a light bulb, what is its resistance?

7. What current flows through a 40-W light bulb connected to a 120-V source?

8. What is a coulomb?

9. Explain the difference between power and energy. What are the units for each?

10. If you double the resistance in a circuit, what will happen to the current?

We know that power can also be calculated using the equation power = current × voltage. If at least two of these values are known, we can solve many different types of problems involving electricity. As you can see, the various units of electricity—watts, volts, amps, ohms, coulombs—are all interrelated. Studying these relationships is the key to understanding electricity.

SECTION REVIEW QUESTIONS 17B

1. If a string of Christmas lights goes out when one bulb is removed, are the bulbs wired in series or in parallel?

2. What is the most common device used to protect today's homes from electrical overload?

3. State Ohm's law in the form of an equation.

FACET REVIEW QUESTIONS

1. What did Faraday discover about rotating magnets?

2. Who devised the first truly useful incandescent light bulb?

3. How does a thundercloud induce a charge on the earth?

4. Where are negative charges stored on a Van de Graaff generator?

WHAT DID YOU LEARN?

1. Inside the beautifully carpeted store, you rush to finish your Christmas shopping. At last you have found your final gift. As you hand the cashier your money, a spark jumps from your finger to the cashier's finger, startling both of you. Explain exactly what happened when the spark jumped and why.

2. To refuel a jetliner at a large airport, the fuel operator connects cables from the fuel truck to the airplane before refueling begins. Why do you suppose he does this?

3. Susan decided that to do her part to save electrical power, she would use her electric hair dryer on the medium setting of 800 W instead of the high setting of 1200 W. However, instead of five minutes it now takes ten. Has she reduced her power? Has she used less energy? Which setting will result in a lower electric bill?

4. If you have spent any time traveling, perhaps you have seen huge, seemingly endless stretches of high electric transmission lines. What kind of voltage—high or low—would you expect in these lines and why?

Magnetism

18A **Magnetic Forces**

18B **Electricity and Magnetism**

18C **Using Magnetism**

18

The properties (both real and imagined) of magnets are woven throughout the lore of antiquity. Ancient Greeks first described magnetism in their early writings. The Greeks found "lodestones" in Magnesia in Asia Minor. These mysterious stones could attract and hold iron shavings.

To people long ago, these magnetic properties seemed magical. Some proposed that magnets were evil objects possessed by invisible spirits. Others claimed that magnets could heal sickness and cure headaches. In the Middle Ages the superstitions associated with magnetism made owning a magnet hazardous to your health!

Possessing a lodestone might brand you as a wizard or a witch and earn you a fiery reception from an angry crowd. Yet it was during this time that practical uses for magnets were first discovered.

Until then, sailors had navigated the oceans solely by visual observations of the sun and the stars. A sudden storm or an overcast sky was sometimes fatal for these early travelers. Without their celestial guideposts, sailors had no way to keep their ships from drifting many miles off their appointed courses.

Sometime during the Middle Ages, an inventive person noticed that if a lodestone were placed on a piece of wood and floated on water, it would always orient itself in a north-south direction. Using this property of lodestones, men designed crude compasses that gave sailors and other travelers accurate directions, regardless of the atmospheric conditions.

In 1269 Petrus Peregrinus de Maricourt of France observed that iron shavings sprinkled near a lodestone were attracted primarily to two separate spots on the lodestone. From this observation, Maricourt determined that the magnetic force of the lodestone was concentrated at these two locations. Today we call the two areas of concentrated magnetic force on a magnet **magnetic poles.**

In 1600 Maricourt's discovery was followed by another important step toward understanding magnetism. William Gilbert, an English physician, was fascinated by magnets. He conducted many experiments and compiled a book that listed all of the then-known properties of magnets. He explained how the behavior of a compass was due to the earth's being a magnet itself. Some of the "facts" in Gilbert's book, such as the medicinal properties of magnets, were hardly scientific. Yet Gilbert had brought the study of magnetism to the attention of the scientific world.

Magnetic Forces

Could magnetism be a product of "magnetic charges" just as electricity is a product of positive and negative charges? This possibility directed the efforts of many early investigators.

Objects can be positively charged on one end and negatively charged on the other. However, an object can also be positively charged all over. Is the same true of magnets? Can a magnet be a north pole all over? Early investigators thought this might be true. These scientists believed that large concentrations of "boreal (BOR ee ul) charge" formed north magnetic poles and that large

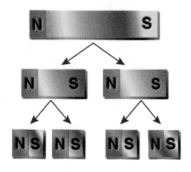

concentrations of "austral (AWS trul) charge" formed south magnetic poles. They supposed that these "magnetic charges" could be separated onto different objects, giving an object only one type of magnetic pole.

No one has ever observed such an object. Objects that have a north magnetic pole always have a south magnetic pole. If you cut a magnet in half, you will end up with two smaller magnets—each with a north and a south magnetic pole. Scientists have found that even when magnets are divided as many times as is physically possible, each of the microscopic fragments has both a north and a south magnetic pole. Scientists continue to look, but so far no one has demonstrated the existence of "magnetic charges" (monopoles).

Fig. 18-1 When a magnet is cut in two, two new magnets are formed with north and south poles on each.

Electric and Magnetic Fields

The effects of magnetism are very similar to the effects of static electrical charges. They both produce forces that we can observe. They both can attract or repel. The area around an object where these forces act is called a *field.* Scientists use diagrams of fields to help picture how these forces act.

Consider an electrode (a charged conductor) with a negative charge. Suppose we bring a positively charged object nearby (Figure 18-2). According to the law of charges, it will be attracted to the negative electrode no matter where we put it. The closer it gets to the electrode, the stronger the attraction. The strengths and directions of the electrical force at every point around the electrode are collectively called the **electric field.**

To draw the field, draw arrows all over the paper pointing in the direction of the force (Figure 18-3). Connect into lines the arrows that are pointing in the same direction. These lines are called **lines of force.** Arrows on each line of force show in which direction the electrical force will move a positive charge.

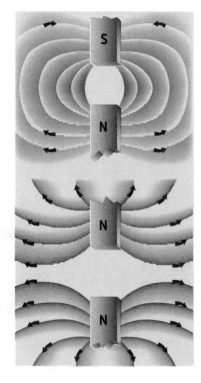

Fig. 18-2 The lines of electrical force surrounding a negative electrode

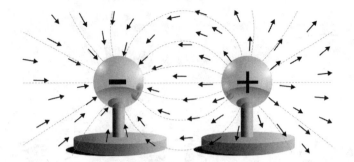

Fig. 18-3 The lines of force surrounding positive and negative electrodes

By convention, the arrows on electric field lines are always drawn to show what would happen to a positively charged object placed in the field. A negatively charged object would be pushed in the opposite direction.

Electric fields are always directed away from a positive charge and toward a negative charge. A single line of force does not show how strong the force is. However, in an area where the force is strong, the lines of force always bunch close together. The closer the lines, the stronger the force. Where is the electric field strongest in Figure 18-3?

The paths of these lines of force are different for different electric fields. Notice the direction of the lines of force in the field around the two electrodes in the figure below. The arrows on lines of force show the direction in which the electrical force will move. Which electrode in this figure has a positive charge? Which one has a negative charge? Actually, *both* electrodes have a positive charge, as you can see from the direction of the lines of force.

Fig. 18-4 The electric field around two adjacent, positively charged electrodes; notice that the lines of force point away from both of them.

Scientists also use **magnetic fields** to show the strength and direction of magnetic forces (Figure 18-5). In magnetic fields, the lines of force point in the direction in which the magnetic forces act on a north magnetic pole. *Since opposite magnetic poles attract each other, magnetic lines of force always point toward south magnetic poles and away from north magnetic poles.*

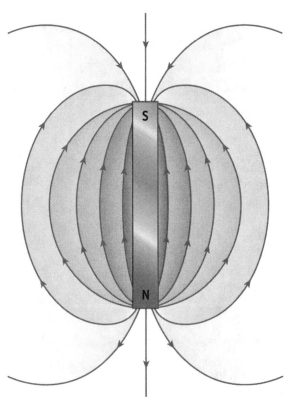

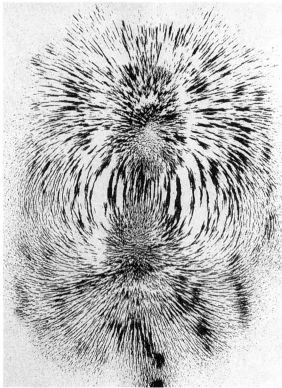

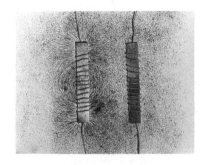

Magnetic Materials

Magnets attract only a small group of materials. We say that these materials are **ferromagnetic.** These magnetic materials include iron, nickel, cobalt, and a few others. Steel (an alloy of carbon and iron) and alnico (an alloy of aluminum, nickel, cobalt, and iron) are commonly used to form the powerful magnets used in motors, speakers, and other applications. Materials that are attracted slightly to magnets are said to be **paramagnetic,** such as aluminum or certain transition metals and rare-earth elements. The strength of the attraction in paramagnetic materials often varies according to the temperature.

The photograph to the left contrasts the effect of both strongly and weakly magnetic materials on magnetic fields. Each magnetic field is created by a coil of current-carrying wire. When aluminum (weakly magnetic) is placed in the center of a coil, the magnetic field becomes only slightly stronger. When iron is placed in the coil, the magnetic field grows much stronger. The iron filings around each of the bars indicate the relative strengths of the fields.

There are many theories to suggest why certain materials are ferromagnetic. We know that we can *induce* magnetism in iron by running an electric current through it. We have also observed that by stroking an iron nail against a strong magnet, we can temporarily give the nail magnetic properties. Scientists believe that ferromagnetic materials possess **domains.** Domains are tiny regions present within the metal that normally are arranged in random directions. These domains are said to possess a *magnetic moment* so that each domain itself acts as a tiny magnet. The magnetic moments cancel each other out until a strong magnet comes along and realigns the moments so that there is a net magnetic field. This is how a magnet can temporarily induce magnetism in any ferromagnetic material.

Natural magnets, such as lodestone, would seem to be the easiest to explain. However, we have only recently been able to explain why such materials are magnetic. We call materials like lodestone **ferrimagnetic.** It seems that lodestone is made up of two different types of iron ions. Because each iron ion is present in different amounts within a piece of lodestone and each ion has a different magnetic moment, the lodestone always seems to display magnetic properties. There is a net magnetic moment, producing a magnetic field.

It should not be surprising that large amounts of thermal energy can disrupt these domains. Although it varies for different substances, the **Curie temperature** is the point at which the substance can no longer exhibit magnetism. The Curie temperature for iron is about 770 degrees Celsius.

Some materials are not at all attracted to magnets. Table salt and mercury are actually repelled from the magnetic field of a strong magnet. If you placed salt crystals in a magnetic field, the salt would weaken the magnetic field noticeably. Many scientists believe that the domains in the salt actually line up against the lines of force in the magnetic field.

Fig. 18-6 A strong magnet can induce magnetism in a nail.

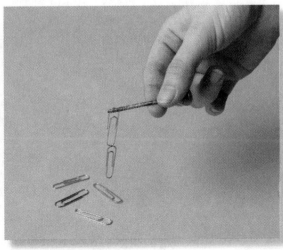

Earth's Magnetic Field

What makes a compass point toward the magnetic north pole? William Gilbert believed that the earth itself was a gigantic bar magnet. Its magnetic field is aligned in a generally north-south direction. A compass contains a very light bar magnet positioned so that it can turn easily on a pivot. This bar magnet aligns itself along the north-south direction of the earth's magnetic field. Then, when the "N" marking on the compass dial is lined up with the north pole of the compass magnet, all the directions on the compass dial can be read.

Did you know that the earth has two north poles? The **geographic north pole** is at the "top of the earth," right on the axis of the earth's spin. The **magnetic north pole,** where the earth's magnetic field is concentrated, is approximately 1500 km away. It is located near Ellef Ringnes Island, a Canadian island in the Arctic Ocean. Compasses are attracted to the magnetic north pole, not the geographic north pole. In some parts of the world, the difference is important. If you lived in Barrow, Alaska, your compass would point 30° east of true geographic north!

Is the magnetic north pole of the earth really a north magnetic pole? Remember that it attracts the north poles of magnets. Are the north poles of magnets attracted to other north magnetic poles? No! They are attracted to south magnetic poles. The "north pole" of the earth must be a south pole magnet.

Does it bother you that this is backwards? Remember that opposite poles attract. If the "north" pole of the earth and the "north" end of a compass needle are to attract each other, one or the other has to be a south magnetic pole! They can't both be north. So the names were chosen to match the compass needle. The north end of the needle is a true magnetic north pole.

Fig. 18-7 The earth's magnetic field has its magnetic pole near what we call the "north pole" of the earth (the geographic north pole).

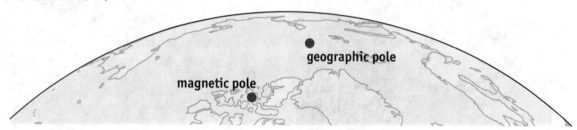

geographic pole

magnetic pole

Auroras

As the sun burns it gives off light. It also gives off a stream of charged particles consisting mainly of electrons and protons. We call this stream of particles the *solar wind*.

The solar wind can be damaging to living things. It is one of many things that make space flight dangerous. Fortunately, most of the solar wind reaching the earth is "caught-up" in the earth's magnetic field.

As you will learn in this chapter, electricity and magnetism are related. Magnetic fields can create and alter electric currents. But electric currents are just moving electrons. Whether they are moving through a wire or through outer space, they are still influenced by magnetic fields.

When the solar wind reaches the earth, some of the particles are deflected away into space. Others circle the earth, trapped by the earth's magnetic field. Few of them make it to the surface. The earth's magnetic field is a blanket created by God to protect us from the solar wind.

Research has shown that the earth's magnetic field is decreasing. This magnetic field is known as the *magnetosphere*. When the magnetic field is gone, so is our protection from the solar wind. Nobody knows exactly when this magnetic field will disappear, if ever, but many think it will not be for at least another three thousand years.

Some of the protons and electrons that circle the earth collide with atoms in the atmosphere. They cause the air to glow with bright shimmering bands of colorful light. We call these glowing lights in the sky *auroras*. These lights are most often seen around the magnetic poles of the earth. The auroras seen in the Northern Hemisphere are known as the *northern lights,* or *aurora borealis*. They are often seen in Alaska and Canada, and sometimes in the northern states of the continental United States.

The ones in the southern areas of the earth are called *aurora australis,* or *southern lights*. Scientists can predict auroras and time them with the appearance of sunspots approximately every eleven years. Sunspots signify the release of high-energy atomic particles from the sun and coincide with the appearance of the more spectacular auroras. Although sunspots and auroras seem like just an interesting display of natural galactic "fireworks," they have also been known to seriously disrupt satellite, radio, and telephone communication. However, the effects of solar wind would be far more damaging if the magnetosphere were not here to protect us.

1. Where is the magnetic force of a magnet primarily concentrated?
2. What English physician wrote a book describing the properties of magnets?
3. What material did ancient Greeks find to be magnetic?

18B

Section

Electricity and Magnetism

In the late 1700s and early 1800s it was believed that electricity and magnetism were related, but no one could demonstrate the connection. It had been observed on ships struck by lightning that their compasses would often be affected. Several scientists tried to duplicate this effect in the laboratory without success.

In 1820 the Danish physicist Hans Christian Oersted was attempting to create an electrical discharge in a classroom demonstration. When he sent a current through the wire, he noted that a compass on the table nearby deflected. The current carrying wire had produced a magnetic field.

Fig. 18-8 Oersted discovered that current flowing through a wire creates a magnetic field strong enough to alter the direction of a compass.

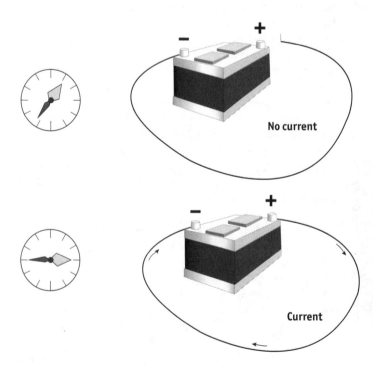

Oersted immediately began experimenting with the wire and the compass and found that the compass pointed in different directions depending on its position around the wire. From his observations Oersted determined that magnetic lines of force form circular loops about a current-carrying wire.

Figure 18-9 shows a current-carrying wire. The arrow along the wire shows the direction of conventional current (opposite to electron flow). The direction of the magnetic field (the direction in which a north magnetic pole will be attracted) can be found by the *right-hand rule*. If you point your right thumb in the direction of the flow of the current, the magnetic lines of force will point in the direction in which the rest of your curled fingers point.

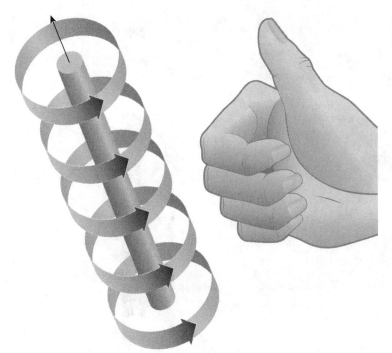

Magnetism from Electricity

Only a week after Oersted's discovery was announced in France, André Marie Ampère (ahm PEHR), a French physicist, announced that he had discovered a magnetic attraction between two parallel wires carrying current in the same direction. Ampère found that when he replaced one of the wires with a magnetic pole, the remaining current-carrying wire was deflected away from or attracted to the magnet. The wire's movement depended on the direction of the current in the wire.

Ampère also discovered that increasing the current in the wire increased the strength of the surrounding magnetic field. Later, scientists discovered that coiling a current-carrying wire increases the force of the magnetic field still further. Each loop of a coiled current-carrying wire produces an equal magnetic force. When the magnetic fields of each of these closely packed "magnets" are added together, the result is a fairly strong magnetic field. Coiled wires that are used as magnets are called **solenoids** (SO luh NOYDZ), or electromagnets.

Special electrical switches called **relays** use solenoids to turn electrical circuits on and off. When electrical current is passed through a solenoid relay, the magnetic force produced by the solenoid pulls a switch closed, turning the circuit on.

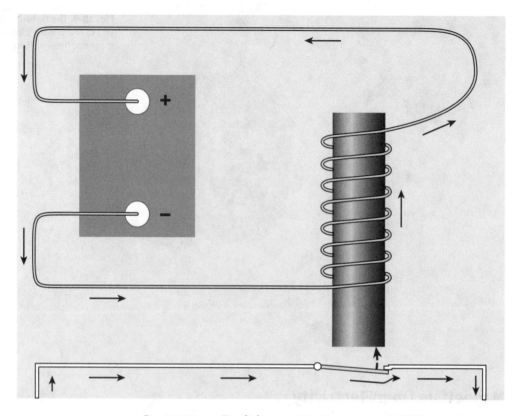

Fig. 18-10 In a solenoid relay, current flowing through the wire creates a magnet. The solenoid attracts the metal switch and closes the circuit.

In 1823 an English experimenter named William Sturgeon observed that placing a magnetic material inside a solenoid increased its magnetic field. In fact, a solenoid with an iron core produced enough magnetic force to lift a piece of iron twenty times as heavy as the iron core! These strong electromagnets play a crucial role in many of the appliances you use daily.

Electricity from Magnetism

Electric current produces a magnetic field. Does it work the other way as well? Can a magnetic field produce an electric current? The answer is yes. If a magnet is moved through a coil of wire (Figure 18-11), a current is produced in a wire. Interestingly enough, the current flows only when the magnet is *moving*. When the magnet stops moving, the current stops. Moving the coil has the same effect as moving the magnet.

How does a magnetic field produce an electric current? The magnetic forces in a magnetic field affect the motion of electrically charged particles. When magnetic forces near a conductor increase or decrease, they set the charged electrons in the conductor in motion. The more quickly the magnetic force increases or decreases, the faster the electrons move.

Generators

Devices called **generators** use magnets to convert mechanical energy into electrical energy. In a generator, some type of engine rotates large numbers of wire coils through strong magnetic fields. As the coils experience changing magnetic forces, large amounts of current are produced in the coils. Most of the electricity we use each day is supplied by electrical generators.

Fig. 18-11 Moving the magnet or the wire up and down produces current. We call this magnetic induction.

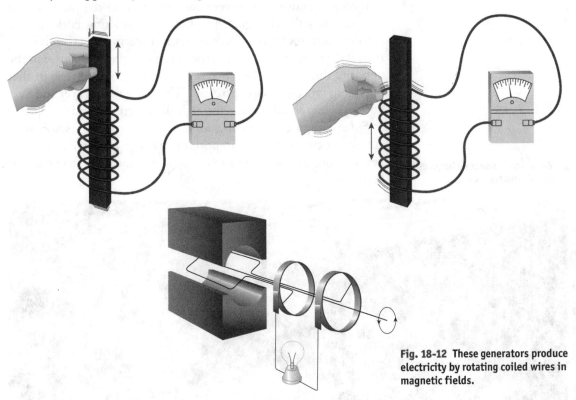

Fig. 18-12 These generators produce electricity by rotating coiled wires in magnetic fields.

The mechanical energy necessary to turn the generator shaft usually comes from one of three sources:

1. Fossil fuels are sometimes burned to produce thermal energy, which is then used to turn water into steam. This steam is forced through turbines, causing the turbines to rotate. The turbines then turn the shafts that rotate coils of wire inside the generators.

2. Hydroelectric plants use the falling water of dams or natural water-falls to provide the energy to turn turbines. Niagara Falls and Hoover Dam are two well-known sites of hydroelectric plants.

3. Atomic energy derived from fissioning uranium-235 can also be used to turn water into steam. This steam is then used to turn turbines like those used in fossil-fuel power plants.

What kind of current does a generator produce? Since the wire coil in a generator rotates through a magnetic field, its position in the magnetic field is constantly being reversed. Consequently, the wire coil in a generator produces a current that moves first in one direction and then in the opposite direction in a repeating cycle. We call an electric current that regularly changes directions an **alternating current (AC).** The electricity that comes into our homes is alternating current. The oscilloscope screen in the photo below demonstrates the changing direction of alternating current. The current increases in one direction until it reaches a maximum and then it decreases to zero. Then the current begins to increase in the opposite direction. When it reaches a maximum current in that direction, it decreases to zero again. This cycle occurs over and over as the generator coil rotates through the magnetic field.

Since computers and some home appliances are very sensitive to current fluctuations, it is important that the *frequency,* or cycles per second, be constant. In the U.S., we measure frequency in **hertz (Hz).**

Fig. 18-13 An oscilloscope helps us to visualize alternating current.

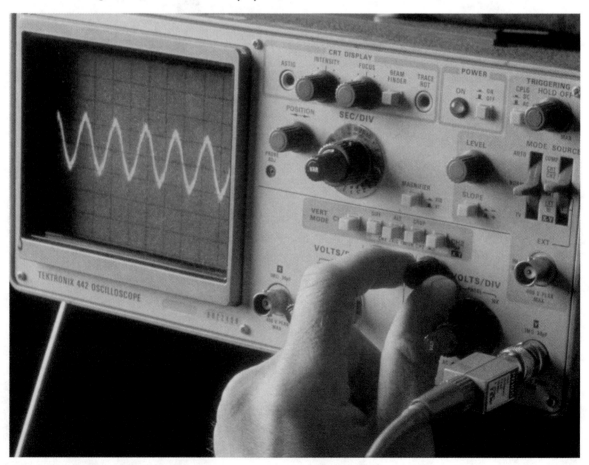

In the United States, electric companies provide 60 Hz service to homes and businesses. That means that when you look at a light turned on in your house, it really is turned "on" and "off" sixty times a second. This happens so fast that your eye cannot detect it. In some other countries, the frequency is less and electric appliances must be adapted in order to work on that lower frequency. Frequency measurements apply not only to AC electricity but to other cyclical measurements as well. We will study these in later chapters.

The current produced by a battery does not change directions and is called **direct current**, or **DC.** Direct current maintains a constant rate of flow in one direction. There is no cycle, or changing of current. Direct current is valuable because it is portable. Everyone knows how inconvenient cords hooked up to AC current can be, and we enjoy the freedom batteries give us to use camcorders, flashlights, and power tools wherever we want to. The problem with direct current is that it quickly drains down, whereas alternating current always seems to be there and there is always plenty of "juice."

SECTION REVIEW QUESTIONS 18B

1. How do electromagnets work?
2. Does a magnet sitting still in a coil of wire generate electricity?
3. Generators convert what form of energy into electrical energy?

18C

Section

Using Magnetism

Magnetism plays a vital role in modern life. Hundreds of appliances, including electric drills, mixers, and washing machines, depend on magnetically driven motors. These electric motors convert electrical energy into mechanical energy—the opposite of generators. Telephones, radios, and televisions all operate through the use of magnetic and electrical fields. Let's examine some more uses for magnetism as it relates to electricity.

Transformers

Flowing through a wire, a DC current produces a constant magnetic field. This constant field is unable to produce any electricity in nearby wires. An AC current, on the other hand, is constantly changing. It produces a magnetic field that is constantly changing. The changing magnetic field of an AC conductor can be used to generate current in other conductors.

Suppose two coils are placed close together. An AC current is supplied to the first coil. The resulting magnetic field produces an alternating current in the other wire. Two coils of wire used in this way to transfer electric current from one coil to another are called a *transformer*. Just as a magnetic material placed inside a solenoid improves its performance, so a magnetic material will improve a transformer. Most transformers consist of coils of wire wrapped around a metal core.

In a good transformer, the voltage produced in the second coil depends on the ratio of the number of turns (or loops) in the first coil to the number of turns in the second coil.

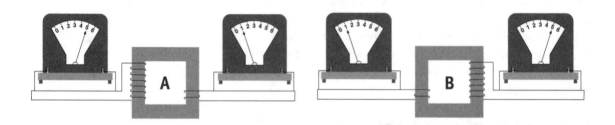

Fig. 18-14 A step-down transformer (A) and a step-up transformer (B)

In the figure above (A), the first coil has more turns than the second coil. The alternating current in the first coil produces a very strong magnetic field. This field sets in motion many electrons in the second coil, but these moving electrons do not possess a large amount of energy. Therefore, the voltage in the second coil is lower than the voltage in the first coil. Because this arrangement of conducting coils produces a smaller voltage in the second coil, it is known as a **step-down transformer.**

In the figure above (B), the second coil has more turns than does the first coil. The magnetic field produced by the alternating current in the first coil sets in motion only a small number of the electrons in the large second coil. Each of the moving electrons in the second coil gains a large amount of kinetic energy. Therefore, the voltage in the second coil is greater than the voltage in the first coil. This arrangement of AC conducting coils is known as a **step-up transformer.**

The relationship between the number of turns and the voltage in a transformer can be expressed by the following equation:

$N_1/N_2 = V_2/V_1$

N_1 and N_2 are the number of turns in the input coil and the output coil. V_1 and V_2 are the corresponding voltages.

For example, suppose a wall transformer needs to convert 120 V into 12 V. In this example, $V_1 = 120$ V, and $V_2 = 10$ V.

Suppose the input coil has 1000 turns ($N_1 = 1000$). How many turns should the output coil have?

$$1000 / N_2 = 120 / 12$$

Solving this equation yields $N_2 = 100$

The second coil should have 100 turns.

Power companies use step-up and step-down transformers to conserve energy. The wires used to carry electricity have low resistance but may be miles long. Energy is wasted in running current through these long wires. If large voltages are used, the currents can be lower and less power is wasted in the lines.

However, large voltages are dangerous. So the power company uses high voltages for its transmission lines and then uses a transformer to reduce the voltage at your house.

At a power plant, the alternating current produced by the generators is converted by step-up transformers into high-voltage, low-current electricity. The high-voltage power lines that crisscross the countryside carry voltages of up to 765 kilovolts (kV) to the areas in which power is needed. In each of these areas, huge step-down transformers convert this electricity into high-current, medium-voltage (about 11 kV) electricity. The locations of these step-down transformers are commonly called power substations. Near individual homes smaller transformers reduce the electricity's voltage to 110 V or 220 V, the voltage required by most household appliances. You may have seen these cylinders mounted on power poles near your house.

Fig. 18-15 A power substation

Fig. 18-16 A transformer near your home steps the voltage down to 220 V.

SAMUEL F. B. MORSE—
AMERICAN INVENTOR (1791-1872)

You may be familiar with the quotation "What hath God wrought!" These were the first words ever sent by intercity telegraph. But can you name the source of the quotation— Numbers 23:23 —or tell the story of how it was selected? This fascinating story begins with the labors of the great Christian inventor Samuel F. B. Morse. In his mind was born the first means of communication that could transmit messages instantly from city to city.

Samuel Morse was born in Charlestown, Massachusetts, in 1791. As the son of the town pastor, he was reared in a Christian home, but he did not accept Christ as his Savior until early adulthood. He received his education at Philips Exeter Academy in Andover and at Yale College (known now as Yale University). Science did not seem to be his strongest subject, although it did interest him. In fact, his primary work early in life was not as a scientist but as a painter and sculptor.

The year following his graduation from Yale, he traveled to England to study with Benjamin West, the most respected artist of that time. The training Morse received during his four years abroad catapulted him into the ranks of America's foremost artists. He later painted such notables as President Monroe, Noah Webster,

and General Lafayette. Also during this period, Morse came under the influence of William Wilberforce and his group of evangelical Christians known as the Clapham Sect. Morse was thoroughly impressed with Wilberforce and stated afterward, "What I saw of

him in private gave me the most exalted opinion of him as a Christian." The godly witness of the Clapham Sect soon brought Morse to trust Christ as his own Savior. Upon returning to America he lost no time in making a public profession of his faith at his own church.

On his second trip to Europe, the idea of the telegraph began to take shape in Morse's mind. In Paris he saw the French *semaphore* system of communication. Signals were relayed from mountaintop to mountaintop by means of flags and symbols. How much better this was, he thought, than the mail system back home. During the return voyage, Morse determined a specific plan of attack. When he disembarked in New York Harbor, his notebook contained sketches of the first crude electric telegraph. It was based on a simple idea—that an electric circuit could transmit a coded message by opening and closing the current to that circuit. The transmission of these electric pulses would produce a series of pulses, and the receiver could interpret the length of the pulses as words and numbers.

Providentially, Morse received an appointment as professor of sculpture and painting at the University of the City of New York. This position provided him with a place in which to experiment and with a means of attracting assistants. After many months of labor, he was ready to demonstrate his collection of voltaic cells, coils, and wires for his colleagues at the university. He even developed a special code of dots and dashes to represent each letter of the alphabet, now known as Morse Code. Several showed interest in the invention, and he soon enlisted the help of a small group of friends. But only one, a fellow Christian named Alfred Vail, was to stick with him to the project's completion.

One of the earliest public demonstrations of Morse's telegraph took place in Vail's hometown, Morristown, New Jersey. The sender and receiver were both at the same location, but the signals traveled through some two miles of coiled wire between the two units. The spectators were enthusiastic, and the Morristown *Jerseyman* extravagantly praised Professor Morse and his invention. In 1838 Morse and Vail gave a demonstration at the Franklin Institute in Philadelphia. Again the equipment functioned successfully and a favorable report was issued—the first acclaim from representatives of the scientific community.

The next demonstration took place in Washington. Among those witnessing the demonstration were President Van Buren and several members of the cabinet. Morse and Vail hoped to secure funds for a trial line between two major cities some distance apart. Unfortunately, the country was suffering a severe depression, and as one congressman informed Morse, "The treasury and the government are both bankrupt."

Morse, however, kept praying and persevering. Late in 1842 he set up a demonstration line between the rooms of the House Committee on Commerce and the Senate Committee on Naval Affairs. He remained faithfully on duty by his equipment, sending sample messages for the legislators and answering their questions. By the end of the year, the Committee on Commerce had submitted a favorable report on Morse's telegraph. Representative Ferris, the chairman of the committee, recommended that $30,000 be appropriated to set up a trial intercity telegraph system.

The committee's resolution passed fairly easily in the House. However, when the bill reached the Senate on the last day of the session, Morse prepared for the worst. In fact, by the end of the day, Morse believed the situation to be utterly hopeless. He returned to his hotel room, had his devotions, and retired for the night.

The next morning at breakfast, a waiter informed Morse that he had a visitor in the hotel parlor. Much to his surprise, Annie Ellsworth, the daughter of the Commissioner of Patent, had come to bring the good news—his bill had passed around midnight and had been quickly signed by President Tyler. In appreciation for her message, Morse made Miss Ellsworth a promise—when the lines were finally completed from Washington to Baltimore, she would be allowed to choose the text for the first message. Thus, on May 24, 1844, the famous four words from the book of Numbers were transmitted from Baltimore to Washington and back again. Morse was delighted that these words of Scripture had been chosen for the first intercity telegraph demonstration. In a letter to his brother he wrote, "It is in my thoughts day and night, 'What hath God wrought!' It is His work, and He alone could have carried me thus far through all my trials and enabled me to triumph over the obstacles, physical and moral, which opposed me."

Fig. 18-17 A giant electromagnet can lift a car when the current is flowing.

Electromagnets

Since 1823, when Sturgeon developed the first practical electromagnet, electromagnets have been built and utilized in many different ways. Electromagnets have proved especially useful for lifting sections of iron and steel. If you visit an iron reclamation plant (a junkyard), you will probably see a crane lifting cars and trucks by means of a large, flat disk. This disk is an electromagnet. When electric current is allowed to flow through it, the disk produces a magnetic force that can pick up extremely heavy pieces of metal. When the metal has been moved to the proper position, it can be released by turning off the current in the electromagnetic disk.

Electromagnets are also useful for sorting metals, particularly aluminum and iron. If a mixture of iron and aluminum materials is carried on a moving belt through a weak magnetic field, the iron pieces will be strongly deflected to one side, while the aluminum materials will pass on without being affected. Aluminum refineries use such electromagnetic sorters to keep iron products from contaminating the aluminum they reclaim from recycled aluminum cans.

Particle accelerators, large machines used in nuclear research, use electromagnets to bend the paths of moving electrons into a circle. As the current in the electromagnet is increased, the magnetic field becomes stronger and the path of the charged particles is bent into a smaller circle. The electromagnets in the particle accelerators act as shepherds, herding the electrons back into the path where they can be accelerated by the electrical field of the accelerator. Some of the particle accelerators constructed in recent years contain special electromagnets called **superconducting magnets.** Superconducting magnets have cores of tin, niobium, and certain other materials that have been cooled to temperatures of about 4 K. At such temperatures, these substances allow large currents to flow with no resistance. They greatly increase the magnet's strength and therefore its ability to direct the paths of electrons.

You use an electromagnet every time you ring a mechanical doorbell. A doorbell is basically a switch (the doorbell button) connected in series with an electromagnet. When you push the doorbell button, the switch closes and electricity flows through the wire coil of the electromagnet. The resulting magnetic field around the electromagnet pulls a small metal clapper, causing it to strike a bell. However, the metal clapper itself is also part of the circuit. When the clapper moves to strike the bell, it breaks the circuit. Since current stops flowing through the electromagnet, the magnetic field begins to die away, and the clapper returns to its original position. This movement, in turn, closes the circuit, starting the entire cycle over again.

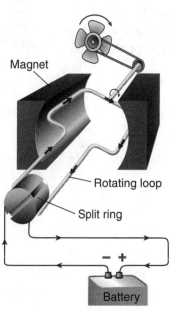

Fig. 18-18 A doorbell circuit

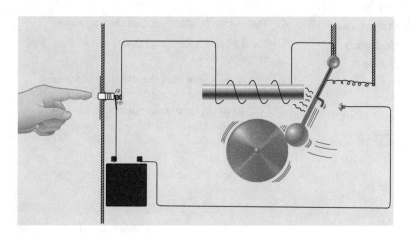

Electric Motors

Electric motors use the magnetic force between an electromagnet and a permanent magnet (or in some cases a stationary electromagnet) to cause the electromagnet to rotate a shaft. The rotating electromagnet in an electric motor is called an **armature** and consists of a current-carrying wire coil around a magnetic material. Some electric motors operate from direct current, some from alternating current, and others from both types of current.

Fig. 18-19 A DC motor

1. What kind of transformer results from wrapping more coils around the first core than the second?
2. What kind of magnet is a doorbell?
3. Why doesn't DC current work in transformers?

CHAPTER REVIEW

SCIENTIFICALLY SPEAKING

magnetic poles	solenoids
electric field	relays
lines of force	generators
magnetic fields	alternating current (AC)
ferromagnetic	hertz (Hz)
paramagnetic	direct current (DC)
domains	step-down transformer
ferrimagnetic	step-up transformer
Curie temperature	superconducting magnets
geographic north pole	armature
magnetic north pole	

CHAPTER REVIEW QUESTIONS

1. Describe the magnetic pole arrangement if one magnet is cut into two pieces.
2. In what direction are the "lines of force" aligned in an electrical field? In a magnetic field?
3. Describe the difference between the two north "poles."
4. What is significant about Curie temperature?
5. Would a battery-operated device use an AC or a DC motor?
6. If you view a wire from the end from which conventional current is entering, does the magnetic field go clockwise or counterclockwise?

7. What is the difference between paramagnetic and ferromagnetic materials?

8. Why do power companies use high-voltage transmission lines? How do they lower the voltage for household use?

9. What does the term *frequency* mean, and how is it measured?

10. What materials have a resistance of zero?

FACET REVIEW QUESTIONS

1. What did Morse see in Europe that inspired him to invent the telegraph?

2. What do we call the magnetic field that surrounds the earth?

WHAT DID YOU LEARN?

1. Why would a moving magnet very near your computer cause severe problems?

2. What do you think would happen to a magnet if it were dropped and hammered repeatedly?

3. An EEG measures the amount of brain activity of humans using small electrodes attached to the head. The electrodes are placed on the skin and never touch the skull or brain, yet the test seems to allow doctors to predict and measure seizures and even thought patterns. Based on what you have learned, how is this possible?

Sound Waves

Chapter

19

The human ear is a delicate and sensitive organ. From birth, we use our ears to establish contact with other human beings. Our entire culture seems to be built on verbal communication, from the radio to the classroom. We learn to talk by listening to others talk. Without hearing, one finds that life becomes more difficult. Perhaps you know people who are deaf or have difficulty hearing. You may be amazed that they seem to get along very well, despite their disability. Many use sign language, read lips, or even learn how to speak without hearing their own voice. You may be surprised to see them answer a telephone or even react to some noises. Could it be that sound can often be detected *without* the ears? Have you ever "felt" a sound? Maybe it was a low-flying jet over your home that caused the pictures to rattle on the wall. Or perhaps you have stroked a cat and felt the low purr as it welcomed your attention. In this chapter we will examine the fascinating properties of sound—how it is produced, transmitted, and interpreted.

Sound Waves

Sound is the form of energy detected by our ears. This energy is carried through the air by means of **waves.** Sound waves are difficult to picture because they are longitudinal. How do you create a sound wave? To make a sound, something must "push on" the air. For example, you can talk because your vocal cords vibrate and push on the air. A piano makes sound because the strings vibrate and push on the air. A whistle makes sound because you blow through it, pushing the air.

A tuning fork is one of the simplest ways to make sound. When it is tapped, the tines vibrate back and forth, making a very pure sound. If you look closely, you may be able to see the vibrations. These vibrations push on the air, creating waves. To see the waves, dip the tips of the tuning fork in a dish of water. The tuning fork will make waves in the water just like it makes waves in the air.

Figure 19-1 illustrates what happens to the air when the tuning fork is vibrating. First the tuning fork moves out, pushing the air and compressing it. Then it vibrates back, pulling away from the

Fig. 19-1 Compressions and rarefactions from a tuning fork

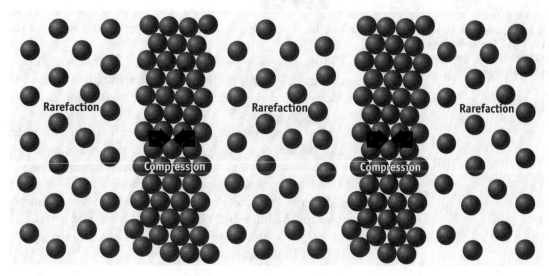

Rarefaction

Rarefaction

Rarefaction

Compression

Compression

Fig. 19-2 Earthquakes are vibrations of the earth's crust. The waves traveling through the earth sometimes yield catastrophic damage.

air and leaving the air spread out. The compressed (higher density) areas are called **compressions.** The stretched out (lower density) areas are called **rarefactions** (rehr uh FAK shunz). As the tuning fork vibrates back and forth, a sequence of compressions and rarefactions is created. We often use the word *sound* to refer to vibrations of matter we can detect with our ear. Often we can detect sound through our sense of touch since sound is vibrating matter. Perhaps you have been able to "feel" the telephone as it rings in your hand. On a much larger scale, earthquakes are vibrations of the earth's crust. During an earthquake, sometimes one can hear deep, rumbling sounds. But as you well know, the destructiveness of earthquakes does not come from the "sound" that they produce—it comes from the vibrations.

What Carries Sound Waves?

Robert Boyle conducted an experiment that clarified the true nature of sound. In 1660 Boyle suspended "a watch with a good alarm" from a thread in a glass jar and pumped all the air out of the jar. With his assistants, he "silently expected the time when the alarm should begin to ring," but the time passed and the experimenters did not hear the alarm.

To confirm his experiment, Boyle opened a valve and allowed air to enter the jar. As the air rushed in, the alarm grew louder and louder. Boyle had demonstrated that sound needs a medium—in this case, air.

Will sound vibrate through mediums other than air? Swimmers know that sound travels clearly through water. If you put your ear against an oak table, you can hear sound travel through wood. Sound travels exceptionally well through metals. Train robbers in the Old West put their ears to the iron rails to learn whether or not a train was approaching. Indians are said to have used a variation of this trick; Indian hunters would listen with an ear to the ground to locate the thundering herds of buffalo.

The Speed of Sound Waves

How fast does sound travel through air? In 1708 William Derham of England calculated the speed of sound through air. Stationing an observer some distance away, Derham fired a cannon into the air. Using the length of time between the observance of the cannon flash and the sound of its boom, Derham calculated the speed of sound. He averaged the results of several trials and came up with a value that was surprisingly accurate. Since Derham's time, scientists have measured the speed of sound through air with precise instruments. Today, the accepted value is 332 m/s at 0°C and 338 m/s under standard atmospheric conditions. As you can see, the speed at which sound travels through a medium is affected somewhat by the temperature of that medium. The molecules in a cold medium move slowly, reducing the speed at which the vibration of sound can be transmitted.

The speed at which sound travels through a medium also depends on the density of the medium. The denser the medium, the faster the sound travels. Thus, sound travels faster in liquids than in gases and (generally) faster in solids than in liquids.

Fig. 19-3 Boyle's silent alarm experiment provided crucial evidence to support the theory that sound did not travel through a vacuum.

The Speed of Sound in Various Mediums	
Medium	Representative Speed
Air at 0°C	332 m/s
Water	1500 m/s
Wood (oak)	3830 m/s
Iron	5955 m/s

The Characteristics of Sound Waves

Sound is not the only form of energy transmitted by waves. As we will learn in Chapter 20, light is also transmitted in waves. The key difference is that sound needs matter in order to be transmitted, but light does not. As we saw with Boyle's experiment, when the matter is removed, sound is not transmitted.

No doubt you have seen several different types of musical instruments. Each one produces a distinct sound. The shape of the instrument, the materials it is made of, and the shape of the room in which it is played all can affect the type of sound that reaches your ear. It seems that all sounds are different, and there are many different ways to measure sound. Consider several values we could measure in sound waves.

- Pitch (high or low?)
- Intensity (loudness)
- Quality (violin or piano?)

In addition, we can measure the actual speed of the sound waves, even the size of the sound waves. All of these factors play a role in every single sound you hear.

Frequency and Pitch

Pitch is how high or how low a tone sounds to our ears. Pitch is directly related to **frequency**, or cycles per second of the sound waves. The higher a sound's frequency, the higher its pitch. The

---

Nature's Loudest Sound

What would you guess is the loudest sound ever produced in nature? The roar of a mighty waterfall? The rumbling of a devastating avalanche? The clap of an 80,000 ampere stroke of lightning? These events are indeed loud, but the world's record for sheer sound intensity in nature is held by volcanoes. Volcanoes are the earth's safety valves. Pressure generated by geologic activity inside the earth occasionally builds up to a level where "something has to give." Sometimes this pressure escapes gradually in a series of small volcanic eruptions. At other times it is suddenly unleashed in a single violent upheaval.

One of the most violent volcanic eruptions ever recorded took place in 1883 on the island of Krakatoa (krah kuh TO uh) between Java and Sumatra. Two-thirds of the island was instantly demolished. The column of dust, ashes, and pumice that blasted into the upper atmosphere took more than two years to settle

to the ground. The force of the blast blew out windows up to 160 km away! The monumental explosion was heard clearly in the Philippines 2240 km away, in Ceylon (today's Sri Lanka) 3200 km away, and on Rodrigues Island 4800 km across the Indian Ocean. Pressure changes recorded on barometers indicated that the sound waves actually traveled around the world—not once, but four times!

keys at the left end of the piano keyboard produce notes that are low in pitch. The other end of the keyboard produces high notes.

Recall from Chapter 18 that frequency is measured in hertz (Hz); a frequency of one vibration per second is designated as 1 Hz. The bottom note on the piano has a frequency of about 27 Hz. The highest note has a frequency of about 4200 Hz. Young children can hear pitches ranging from about 20 to 20,000 Hz. As a person grows older, his eardrums become less elastic, and the upper limit of the frequencies he can hear is reduced.

Archaeologists and volcanologists working together have deduced that an even more destructive eruption occurred in ancient times on the island of Thira (formerly Santorini) in the Aegean Sea. Thira's crater is several times as large as Krakatoa's, meaning that four or five times as much material was ejected. What was originally a sizeable, round island is now a thin crescent of land with a 300-m cliff facing the center of the submerged crater. The bottom of the crater lies another 300 m beneath the surface of the water! Monstrous sea waves and heavy falls of volcanic ash from the eruption are now known to have inflicted heavy damage on the nearby island of Crete. Interestingly, the inhabitants of Thira itself, warned of the danger by severe earthquakes, successfully fled the island in ships.

Volcanoes are awe-inspiring spectacles. They speak to us of God's power and wrath. "Which removeth the mountains, and they know not: which overturneth them in his anger. Which shaketh the earth out of her place, and the pillars thereof tremble." (Job 9:5, 6)

On May 18, 1980, Mount St. Helens, a beautiful volcanic peak in Washington's Cascade Mountains, erupted with the force of a 10-megaton bomb. It spewed out 400 million tons of debris at temperatures over 600°C. The explosion left a crater 2 km wide and 3.8 km long, and streams of gas, ash, and mud desolated 520 sq km of forest. (By comparison, the blast of Krakatoa's eruption was almost twenty times as powerful.)

The Mount St. Helens eruption produced some dramatic geological features, including a large canyon with layered walls similar in appearance to a miniature Grand Canyon. That such features could be produced in a single rapid catastrophe surprised many geologists.

Sounds of any pitch travel at the same speed. This is a good thing! What would it sound like if the bass (low frequency) notes from the choir traveled faster than the soprano (high frequency) notes? You would hear them at different times—the choir would not sound "together." This does not happen, so we conclude that all pitches must travel at the same speed.

Think about the shape of a grand piano. The low strings are long because they need to produce large waves. These large waves have a low frequency. The high strings are much shorter because they produce short waves. The same is true for band instruments. What instrument produces low notes? A tuba, for example, which is a large instrument. What instrument produces high notes? A piccolo, perhaps, which is a tiny instrument. Low notes are long waves; high notes are short waves.

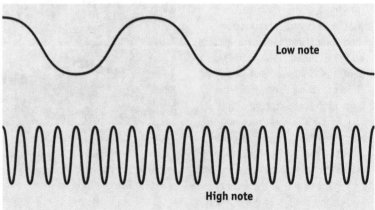

Low note

High note

There are some sound waves that our ears do not respond to. **Infrasonic** (IN fra SAHN ik) **waves** are too low in frequency for the ear to hear, and **ultrasonic** (UL truh SAHN ik) **waves** are too high in frequency for the ear to hear. Dog whistles produce ultrasonic sounds. A dog's ears detect these sounds, but human ears do not. Ultrasound is also used for medical imaging and treatment.

Loud and clear: Sound quality and volume

Loudness is the response of your ear to the intensity of a sound wave. Loudness is related to the power of sound energy hitting a surface. It is commonly expressed in units called **decibels (db),** named for Alexander Graham Bell. A one-decibel increase is a barely noticeable change in volume. A ten-decibel increase sounds twice as loud.

The very softest sound level that can be heard is called the **threshold of hearing.** The threshold of hearing is chosen to be a volume of 0 db. The level of a whisper is about 20 db; normal conversation is about 60 db; and the noise of a vacuum cleaner is about 80 db. At 120 db, called the *threshold of pain,* sound becomes painfully loud. The decibel scale is *logarithmic* as opposed to being *linear.* If the db scale were linear, twice the decibel level would be twice as loud. But this is not the case. Obviously twice the volume of a normal conversation (60 db × 2 = 120 db) is not painfully loud.

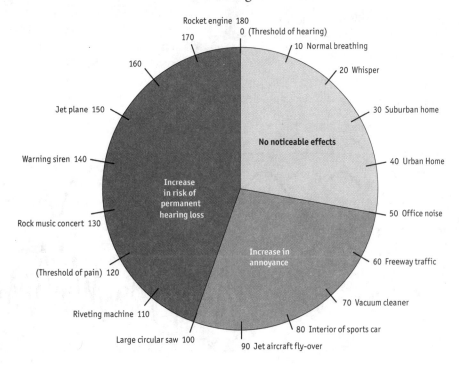

Fig. 19-4 The blue wave, green wave, and red wave are all the same pitch because they have the same frequency. But the blue has a greater amplitude, thus a greater volume. The red wave has a lesser amplitude and thus a lower volume.

Therefore, a 120 db sound is much more than twice the volume of a normal conversation. In fact, 120 db is almost a *trillion times* as loud as the threshold of hearing!

The loudness of a sound is directly related to the **amplitude,** or height of the wave. The greater the amplitude, the higher the volume. The amplitude of the wave directly corresponds to the number and kinetic energy of molecules going through the compressions and rarefactions of wave motion. Our ear perceives a sound as loud because of the sheer size of the waves hitting our eardrum.

Rocket engine 180
170
160
Jet plane 150
Warning siren 140
Rock music concert 130
(Threshold of pain) 120
Riveting machine 110
Large circular saw 100

0 (Threshold of hearing)
10 Normal breathing
20 Whisper
30 Suburban home
40 Urban Home
50 Office noise
60 Freeway traffic
70 Vacuum cleaner
80 Interior of sports car
90 Jet aircraft fly-over

No noticeable effects

Increase in risk of permanent hearing loss

Increase in annoyance

Because it is difficult to measure amplitude of sound waves, the decibel is the preferred way of measuring sound intensity.

Tuning forks produce sound with essentially a single pure tone or frequency. When a musical instrument plays the same note, why does it sound different from the tuning fork? Because musical instruments play *mixtures* of notes. When a trumpet, for example, plays a middle C, it plays at the same time a mixture of other, quieter notes. This mixture of notes gives the trumpet its unique sound. We call the unique sound of an instrument its quality. It is often the characteristic of quality that helps us distinguish between music, or pleasant sound (such as a resounding cymbal—see Psalm 150), and noise (such as a clanging cymbal—see I Corinthians 13:1)!

Vibrating strings illustrate the way instruments produce mixtures of notes. If you pluck a guitar string, for example, it easily and naturally begins vibrating in one big wave from end to end (Figure 19-5). The string produces this same tone each time it is plucked. This tone is called the *fundamental* tone. The string also vibrates in other patterns, with more than one crest along the string. These shorter, faster vibrations produce new tones called *overtones*. When you pluck the string, it typically does several of these vibrations all at the same time, producing a mixture of tones. The fundamental is the loudest and determines the note people hear, but the quieter overtones give the guitar its unique quality.

Fig. 19-5 This diagram shows a fundamental tone and two overtones. All of these vibrations take place at the same time. The diagram below shows the overtones of selected instruments.

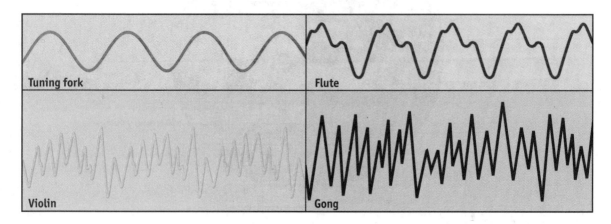

SECTION REVIEW QUESTIONS 19A

1. What do sound waves need in order to travel?
2. Can you hear a 25,000 Hz sound?
3. Why do a clarinet and a trumpet that are both playing a perfect middle C have different sounds?

19B

Section

Sound Phenomena

The statuary hall of the United States Capitol building is sometimes called the Whispering Gallery. The architect of the Capitol building unintentionally designed the elliptical room so that its hard plaster walls reflect sound from one end of the room to the other. Although no one in the center of the room would notice, a person at one end of the hall could easily hear the hushed conversation of persons at the other end. This is one of the many interesting sound phenomena that we will discuss in this section.

Acoustics

When we speak of a building's **acoustics** (uh KOO stiks), we mean the building's effect on sounds. Any type of enclosure will reflect sounds. How well it reflects sounds is another matter. The science of acoustics is the study of controlling the sounds that reach our ears. Using this science, architects can build auditoriums with good acoustics. In a poorly designed auditorium, listeners in the front seats may be able to hear well, while those in other seats cannot. Sounds may be uncomfortably loud in one section and muffled in an adjacent section. Reverberations—multiple echoes of sounds—may distract listeners seated behind the platform.

Years ago, before public-address systems became available, hard, concave surfaces were

placed behind speakers' podiums to reflect the sound of speaker's voices. Today, the walls of many auditoriums and stages are designed to put the principles of sound reflection to good use.

Often the sides of a stage are equipped with slanted surfaces (called "splays") that reflect sound outward to the audience. Other auditoriums utilize convex (curved outward) wall surfaces along the seating area to reflect sound to various points in order to achieve a more even distribution of sound. It is also important to

FACETS of the physical world

The Ear

The human ear is an amazing organ. Man has never duplicated its complex anatomy and physiology by a working model. The ear is clear evidence of an intelligent designer.

Sound enters the ear through the external ear and the external auditory canal. The external ear helps us determine the direction of a sound source by blocking sounds coming from behind. The external auditory canal serves as a resonating chamber, amplifying many different frequencies throughout the middle range of the audible spectrum.

The inner end of the auditory canal is formed by the tympanic (tim PAN ik) membrane, or eardrum, which separates the outer ear from the middle ear. This thin, flexible membrane vibrates in response to extremely tiny movements of air in the auditory canal. A normal eardrum responds to pressure changes that move it as little as a billionth of a centimeter. Ordinary sounds move the eardrum about a millionth of a centimeter.

Before sound impulses in the ear can be converted into nerve impulses and sent to the brain, they must enter the liquid that contacts the nerve endings in the inner ear. Transmitting sound from air to a liquid presents a challenging problem. Have you ever sat in a boat and tried to talk to someone swimming underwater? Since most of the sound energy would simply bounce back from the water's surface, you may not be heard underwater at all. This problem is solved very neatly by the mechanism of the middle ear.

The middle ear consists of the eardrum and three bones called the hammer, the anvil, and the stirrup. Suspended by ligaments, these bones function as little levers. The hammer transmits vibrations from the eardrum to the anvil. The anvil in turn passes the vibrations along to the stirrup. The footplate of the stirrup covers the oval window, the entrance to the fluid-filled inner ear. The fulcrums of the three bones are positioned in such a way that

the force of their vibrations increases about 1.5 times from the eardrum to the oval window. A much greater gain in force comes about by pressure amplification. Because the area of the eardrum is approximately twenty-two times the area of the oval window, the pressure of a vibration is increased twenty-two times as it is transmitted to the oval window. Together, the lever action and pressure amplification in the middle ear increase the force of vibrations about thirty-seven times!

Several structures in the middle ear protect it from injury. Two tiny muscles, controlled by the brain, restrict the vibration of the eardrum and the stirrup as a safeguard against uncomfortably loud sounds. The Eustachian (yoo STAY shun) tube connects the middle ear cavity with the throat and helps to equalize the air pressure on both sides of the eardrum. If your ears "pop" as you ascend or descend rapidly in an elevator or airplane, you know that your Eustachian tubes are doing

remember that sound is a form of energy—the greater the force, the longer the sound waves will travel. Sound cannot travel on forever, because like all energy, it is changed to other forms. When designing auditoriums, the designers must realize that although acoustics are good, nothing can compare to sheer volume and power. Even the most acoustically advanced auditorium has some type of amplification system to increase the amplitude of the sound waves.

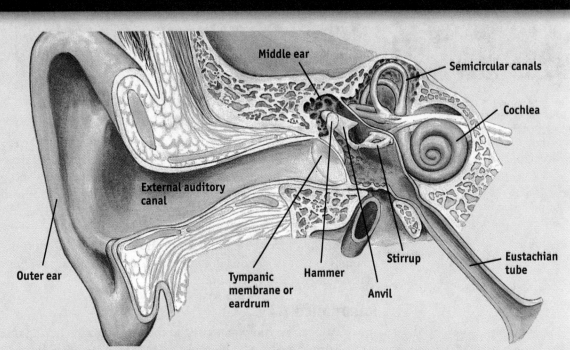

Middle ear

Semicircular canals

Cochlea

External auditory canal

Outer ear

Tympanic membrane or eardrum

Hammer

Anvil

Stirrup

Eustachian tube

their job. The sound is caused when you yawn or swallow, opening your Eustachian tubes, and the eardrum, which has been pushed outward by the unequal pressure, snaps back into place.

The inner ear is the most intricate and least understood part of the ear. It contains two fluid-filled organs: the semicircular canals (the organs of balance) and the cochlea (KAHK lee uh), the snail-shaped

tube in which sound is converted into nerve impulses.

Imagine that the cochlea can be unrolled. Running almost the entire length of the cochlea is a delicate partition that divides it into two fluid-filled parts. At the oval window, the stirrup transfers sound vibrations to the fluid of the cochlea. The vibrations travel through the fluid to the organ of Corti, which runs the length of the

partition and contains thousands of sensory cells and nerve endings. Differences in structure allow only certain sensory cells in the organ of Corti to be moved by a certain frequency of vibration. The sensory cells relay to the auditory nerve thousands of separate signals that indicate the pitch, loudness, and quality of a sound. The auditory nerve conducts these signals to the brain, which interprets them as sound.

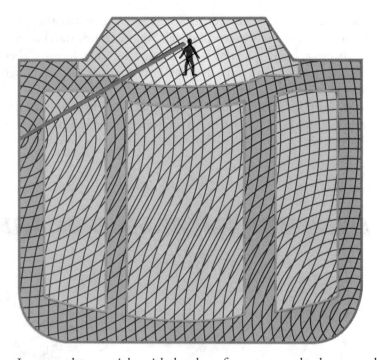

Fig. 19-6 Walls and ceilings that are composed of hard surfaces cause repeated echoes. Sound-absorbing acoustical tiles (above) help reduce reverberations.

In general, materials with hard surfaces are used where good sound reflection is desired. However, if sound is reflected back too strongly, reverberations may occur. These repeated echoes can be prevented by covering walls and ceilings with materials that absorb some of the sound energy from each sound wave that strikes them. Soft, porous materials make good sound absorbers. A large number of small holes or openings greatly improve the sound-muffling qualities of almost any material. Acoustical tiles are designed with many such holes to trap sound energy.

Resonance

If two strings of a violin are tuned to the same pitch, plucking one of the strings will cause the other to vibrate. This phenomenon, called **resonance** (REZ uh nunce), will not occur when the strings are tuned to different pitches.

All objects have frequencies at which they prefer to vibrate. If a sound matching a *natural frequency* is played near an object, the object itself begins to vibrate. You may have noticed a car that rattles only at certain speeds or a radio that buzzes only when it is playing certain sounds. These are examples of resonance.

Resonance plays a number of important roles in our daily lives. Resonance in your sinuses (the hollow spaces in the bones of your skull) amplifies the sounds of your voice. The resonant air column housed in the auditory canal of your ear amplifies incoming sounds in the middle range of the audible spectrum. The sound boxes (large wooden bodies) of stringed instruments also function as resonant chambers.

Have you ever blown across the opening of a bottle to produce a hooting noise? The air rushing over the opening at the proper angle creates vibrations that resonate in the bottle. Can wind cause larger objects to resonate?

On November 7, 1940, the Tacoma Narrows Bridge in Washington was destroyed when a strong wind caused it to vibrate. As the winds continued, the vibrations resonated throughout the center span, getting larger and larger. The internal stresses became so great that the huge suspension bridge literally fell apart. Engineers have since learned how to design bridges to avoid this problem.

Beats

When waves pass through each other, they cause an interesting effect. Scientists call this phenomenon *interference.* If two sound waves have slightly different frequencies and about the same amplitude, they interfere with each other in such a way that the intensity of the sound rises and falls regularly. Although both individual sound waves may have constant volume, the volume of the combined sound pulsates in a regular pattern. These regular changes in intensity are called **beats** (not to be confused with the units of musical rhythm or the percussive strokes used to punctuate music).

Exactly how do beats develop? When two waves that differ only slightly in frequency interfere, they produce a high amplitude

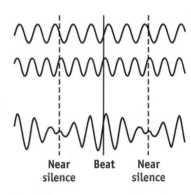

Near silence   Beat   Near silence

Fig. 19-8 Two sound waves of similar frequency will produce a beat when their waves are synchronized. Areas in which the waves are not "in phase" result in destructive interference—near silence.

(a loud sound) at some times and a low amplitude (a quiet sound) at other times. Thus, the sound builds up and dies down periodically. The loud sound is the beat, and it occurs when the sound waves are "in phase" and match up perfectly. The quiet between beats means that the waves are not matched up and are just interfering with one another, in effect canceling each other out.

Beats are sometimes used to tune musical instruments. As the frequencies of two sounds are brought closer and closer (for example, the sounds of a piano string and a tuning fork), the time between beats decreases until the beats disappear. The two sounds then have exactly the same pitch.

The Doppler Effect

The pitch of a sound reaching your ear will vary if either you or the source of the sound is moving. If you are standing at the side of a road and a car approaches with its horn blowing, you hear a certain pitch. As the car passes and leaves you, the pitch of the sound decreases. This phenomenon, called the **Doppler** (DAH plur) **effect,** is named in honor of the Austrian physicist Christian Doppler, who offered a correct mathematical description for it in 1842.

The Doppler effect is the result of relative motion between a sound source and a listener; either the source or the listener or both may be in motion. If the two are coming closer together, extra waves arrive at the ear of the listener each second, and the pitch seems higher. If the motion is such that the two are moving farther apart, fewer waves than normal arrive at the ear of the listener each second, and the pitch seems lower.

Fig. 19-9 The Doppler effect

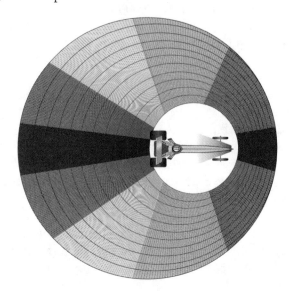

1. What type of floor surface or covering would be best for reducing reverberations?

2. What sound phenomenon would a piano tuner listen for in tuning the piano strings?

3. When a train is moving towards you, does its whistle sound higher or lower in pitch than it does when the train is standing still? What is this phenomenon called?

19C

Section

Applications of Sound

The most important application of sound is the one that you are most familiar with—the human voice, one of the most complex of all musical instruments. It seems that no two humans share the exact pitch, tone, and quality of voice. The larynx (LEHR ingks), or voice box, located inside your windpipe, produces the musical (and sometimes unmusical) sounds of your voice by means of two flexible vocal cords. When you direct air across these cords, they vibrate and produce sound. You tighten your vocal cords to produce high tones and relax them to produce low tones. More complicated sounds are produced by varying the shape and position of your lips, tongue, and teeth.

As mentioned before, the sinuses add resonance because their shape serves to amplify the voice. Without the sinuses, the voice sounds "nasal" (try talking while holding your nose or while you have a bad cold)!

The flexibility of the human voice is amazing. The Russian bass Ivan Ribroff had the ability to sing tones over a four-octave range. Some singers have even been able to shatter wine glasses by matching their voice pitch with the natural frequency of the glass. Such a feat would require tremendous force and voice control!

Though nature provides us with vocal cords, man has devised musical instruments to create musical harmonies that stir the spirit and emotions. As we examine the science behind such instruments, keep in mind that God has given man the knowledge and ability to create such instruments—and we should seek to honor God even through our music. As we mention throughout this book, music is just another tool God has given us to enjoy our physical world. Whether it is playing the flute or guitar, piano or violin, we must do all things for the glory of God (I Cor. 10:31).

Stringed Instruments

There are hundreds of different stringed instruments in various parts of the world. All these instruments produce sound through vibrations of tightly stretched strings. The bridge, one of the supports for the strings, conducts vibrations from the strings to the front plate of the instrument. This plate amplifies the sound through resonance.

For acoustic instruments (those not needing electrical amplification), the lower the instrument's range, the larger its sound box must be.

The pitch of a vibrating string depends on three factors—the string's length, tension, and mass per unit length. The player adjusts the length of the strings by adjusting the placement of his or her fingers on the "neck" of the instrument. The tension of each string is regulated by tuning pegs. The tighter the string, the higher the pitch. The mass per unit length of each string depends on the material and the thickness of the material. On any given instrument the lower-pitched strings are noticeably thicker and heavier than the higher-pitched strings.

Using rubber bands of various thicknesses and lengths, you can experiment with these same three factors. The farther you stretch the rubber band, the higher the pitch (tension). The thicker or wider the rubber band, the lower the pitch (mass per unit length). The longer the rubber band, the lower the pitch (length).

Brass Instruments

Brass instruments (or horns) produce sound by means of a vibrating air column. These air columns have one thing in common with the strings of stringed instruments: the greater their length, the lower their pitch. You can easily see how the length of the air column in a trombone is varied. When the slide is extended, the air column is lengthened and the pitch is lowered. Most other brass instruments have valves or keys by which players can change the length of the air columns.

The air column in a brass instrument is set in motion by the vibration of the player's lips against the mouthpiece. By controlling lip tension, the player can regulate the rate of vibration and thus produce several different pitches at each length of the air column. Because there is no way to change the length of the air column in a bugle, bugle players must produce all the different pitches by changing the tension in their lips.

Because of their strong overtones, the brass instruments were historically the loudest instruments in bands and orchestras. Their easily audible tones made them popular among military leaders for signaling instructions to troops.

Woodwind Instruments

The woodwinds are instruments whose pitch is varied by opening or closing various holes in the side of a vibrating air column. In most woodwinds, such as the clarinet, saxophone, oboe, and flute, flaps controlled by keys cover or uncover the holes. In other woodwinds, such as the bagpipe and the recorder, the player's fingers open and close the instrument's holes.

Percussion Instruments

Percussion instruments generate tones when they are struck. Included in the percussion family are drums, cymbals, tambourines, triangles, bells, chimes, xylophones, castanets, and wood blocks—to name a few. The piano is classified as a percussion instrument because its strings vibrate and produce sound when they are struck with hammers.

As in other instruments, physical size is important in determining the pitch of percussion instruments. The small snare drum has a much higher pitch than the large bass drum. Changing the tension of the drumhead can also change the pitch on a particular drum. The bars of a xylophone are longest at the low-pitched end of the scale and shortest at the high-pitched end.

The Bible refers to some percussive instruments in Psalm 150, but it first mentions musical instruments in Genesis 4:21—"Jubal . . . was the father of all such as handle the harp and organ." The ancient harp had only a few strings, each tuned to a different fixed pitch. Other early instruments similar to the harp included the lyre, the sackbut, and the psaltery. Early organs, and even pipe organs today, use a series of pipes in which air is made to vibrate. The length and diameter of the pipes determine the pitch.

Sound Technology

Whenever we think of sound, we usually try to explain it in terms of the human voice, common sounds, and music. However, there are several other important aspects of sound wave technology that must be mentioned. Among these are sonar, sound amplification, and synthesizers.

The use of **sonar** became widespread during WWI and WWII because of its usefulness in detecting enemy submarines. The word

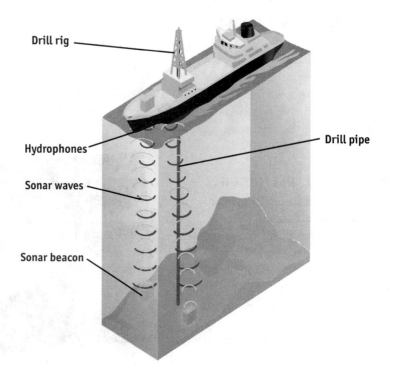

Fig. 19-10 Offshore oil rigs use an extremely advanced sonar system to stay fixed on a precise location.

Drill rig

Hydrophones

Sonar waves

Sonar beacon

Drill pipe

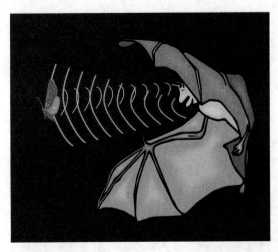

Fig. 19-11 Echolocation enables bats to locate insects in midflight with pinpoint accuracy.

sonar is actually an acronym that stands for *SO*und *N*avigation *A*nd *R*anging. Sonar technology uses sound waves traveling through water to locate underwater vessels, wrecks, or even geologic formations. Sound waves are reflected if they hit a solid, reflecting surface. A typical sonar system consists of a submerged device used for producing sounds waves and a *hydrophone* to pick up the reflected waves. Sonar devices are so sensitive that they can actually produce an image of the underwater object. Scientists discovered the wreck of the *Titanic* using sonar, and they have also used it to examine parts of the doomed ship buried under several feet of sediment. Although underwater cameras give us the best views of the *Titanic,* the cameras are useless at finding wreckage in sediment. Sound waves can penetrate sediment, allowing researchers to "see" buried objects. Sonar is also used by huge offshore oil rigs to stay on location while drilling. By placing sonar beacons on the ocean floor and hydrophones underneath the rig, a computer on board will "pilot" the massive vessel and make adjustments as the ocean currents shift and the wind attempts to blow the rig off course.

When we think of living things, we normally do not think of them possessing sonar—unless they are bats. Some types of bats use **echolocation** to find insects at night and to find their way around pitch black caves. The bat emits a high-pitched frequency beyond the range of human hearing. These ultrasonic waves are reflected off of insects, and the bat can interpret the "data" provided by the sound—distance, speed, even the size and type of insect! As you may imagine, biologists continue to be baffled by the bats' ability to "see" using sound. God's design in nature can be seen in thousands of ways, but perhaps none is as fascinating as the sonar given to the peculiar flying mammal we call the bat.

Ultrasound

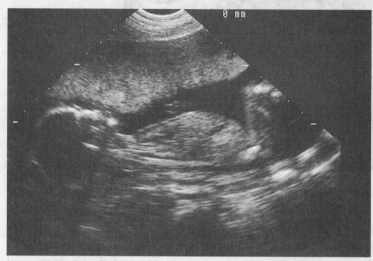

Ultrasonic waves, those sound waves that are at frequencies too high for humans to hear, have some important uses. Ultrasonic cleaners are used by jewelers to clean fine jewelry. The rapidly vibrating waves in the water help to dislodge dirt in the cracks and corners of the jewelry.

Doctors sometimes use ultrasound for treatment of unwanted tissue or objects in the body (such as cancer cells or kidney stones). Very high intensity ultrasonic waves are focused on the target area, destroying the tumor or stone.

Doctors also use ultrasound as a diagnostic tool. A pulse-echo technique is used, similar to a submarine's sonar. A low intensity pulse of ultrasound is directed into the body. Echoes from various parts of the body are detected. Scanning the body produces multiple echoes,

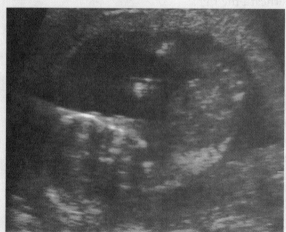

which are used to draw an image, or *sonogram,* of the various organs.

Unlike X rays, which are known to be harmful and must be used in limited amounts with great care, ultrasound has no known harmful effects. For this reason, ultrasound is a major diagnostic tool for pregnancy. The picture below shows an ultrasound image of a 14-week-old human fetus. This tiny baby already has a beating heart. The ultrasound technician takes a small hand-held device called a *transducer* and places it over the mother's abdomen. The transducer emits the ultrasonic waves and interprets them as they are reflected from the tissues of the unborn child. The ultrasound image is unique and very fascinating. As the pregnancy progresses one can often see the bones quite well because the sound waves are reflected strongly from these hard structures. Soft tissue, although not as distinct, can be seen as well, along with most major organs. The image above shows a fetus at 20 weeks.

An *echocardiogram* is a special ultrasound image of the heart. It can give an image of the heart from the inside out, showing heart murmurs, tissue damage, and coronary artery blockage. Since heart disease is still the number one cause of death in the United States, scientists are working every day to make ultrasound technology more detailed and accurate, allowing physicians a window to the previously hidden world of internal workings of the human body.

Sound Amplification

The megaphone is one of the simplest ways to *amplify* or increase the loudness of sound. It consists of a funnel-shaped tube, the small end being where the sound waves enter. The reflecting sound waves inside the funnel increase the *amplitude* of the sound waves, causing a louder sound. Interestingly enough, if you point the large end at the source of sound and listen at the smaller end, the same effect will be produced. Perhaps that is why people sometimes "cup" their ears when they are unable to hear someone speak from a distance.

In the performing arts, sound amplification and production have become an absolute necessity. A microphone and loudspeaker can amplify sound using electronic signals. The loudspeaker has a solenoid with a magnetic field that varies continuously as the sound waves enter the microphone. There is also a permanent magnet located inside of the loudspeaker near a cylindrical paper cone. The interaction between these magnets in the loudspeaker causes the paper cone to vibrate, amplifying the original sound. *Synthesizers* are able to electronically reproduce almost any musical instrument. Using digital instructions, the synthesizer will then convert these electrical signals into sound waves.

SECTION REVIEW QUESTIONS 19C

1. What is the name of the organ that produces sound in humans?
2. What determines the pitch of a pipe in a pipe organ?

CHAPTER REVIEW

SCIENTIFICALLY SPEAKING

sound	decibels (db)
waves	threshold of hearing
compressions	amplitude
rarefactions	acoustics
pitch	resonance
frequency	beats
infrasonic waves	Doppler effect
ultrasonic waves	sonar
loudness	echolocation

CHAPTER REVIEW QUESTIONS

1. What unit do we use to measure the loudness of sound?

2. Give some simple measures one can use to improve the acoustics in a large auditorium.

3. Define natural frequency and give an example of how it can affect matter.

4. If there is a beat occurring, what does that say about the frequency of the two sounds?

5. Name the four major categories of instruments described in the chapter.

6. Does sound travel through water, and if so, is it faster or slower through water than through the air?

7. Can a trumpet and a harp play the same pitch? The same quality? The same loudness?

8. Who sings higher frequencies, sopranos or basses?

9. What animal uses sonar to locate prey and fly in darkness? What is the specific term given to this ability?

10. How can sonar sometimes be more useful than underwater cameras when examining wreckage on the ocean floor?

FACET REVIEW QUESTIONS

1. Give two ways that physicians use ultrasound.

2. What is another name for the eardrum?

3. What other natural phenomenon often accompanies volcanoes and why?

WHAT DID YOU LEARN?

1. In science fiction films and television shows, "battles" between ships in outer space show screeching lasers and loud explosions. Why is such a portrayal totally inaccurate?

2. Are there certain objects that sonar cannot detect underwater? Describe the composition of such objects and how they would be able to escape detection.

3. Describe the quality of sound inside your school's gymnasium and explain the reasons that those acoustics exist.

4. What are the similarities between sound waves and the "ripple" effect when one tosses a stone into a pond?

The Electro-magnetic Spectrum

Imagine that you are floating peacefully in a canoe out on a lake. A motorboat zooms past at high speed. The large waves behind the boat tip your canoe, and under you go. This is another obvious energy transfer. But look more closely. Did the water move from the boat to you? No! If you watch a stick floating in the water between you and the boat, it simply bobs up and down as the wave passes. The water has somehow transferred energy from the boat to you just by bobbing up and down. These types of energy transfers are called *waves*. Waves are rhythmic disturbances that transfer energy from one place to another. When you hear the cheers at a ball game, you are experiencing the effects of sound waves. Sound waves, like water waves, involve the motion of matter. For sound waves, the air is usually what is "waving." Sound waves and water waves are examples of **mechanical waves.** We have already discussed sound waves in Chapter 19, but there are other types of waves. These other types of waves have the same function as sound—to transfer energy. And just as we measure sound, we can also measure the amplitude and frequency of these waves. But there are some dramatic differences. These waves are silent and can travel through the bleakness of vacuum. Some of the high-frequency waves can go right through a strong concrete wall! Although you cannot hear these waves, you may be able to see some. Others you can feel or even use to cook food in minutes instead of hours. Some are even powerful enough to kill living things!

Electromagnetic Waves vs. Sound Waves

Think of the energy we receive from the sun. How does it get here? By light waves, you might say—but there is no water or air or anything between us and the sun to carry the wave to us. Light waves are one of a whole family of waves we call **electromagnetic waves** in what is referred to as the electromagnetic spectrum. This type of energy transfer requires no matter at all. Light waves are a type of electromagnetic wave, but are they the only kind? The answer might surprise you. Radio waves, microwaves, X rays, and infrared and ultraviolet light are all electromagnetic waves. Just as there are sounds that we cannot hear (for example, ultrasonic, like a dog whistle), most waves on the electromagnetic spectrum are not visible to the human eye.

Wave Measurement

All waves, whether mechanical or electromagnetic, have characteristics in common. Figure 20-1 shows a cross section of a typical wave. The highest points on a wave are called **crests.** The lowest points are called **troughs.** The distance that a wave rises or falls from its normal rest position is called the **amplitude** of the wave. One wave is made up of a crest and a trough. Since the vibrations of a wave travel up and down in a repeating pattern, scientists call one wave a cycle.

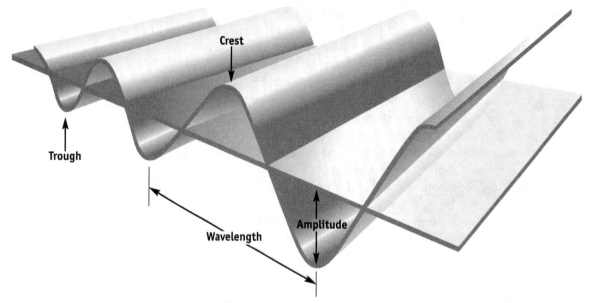

Crest

Trough

Wavelength

Amplitude

Fig. 20-1 The structure of a wave

The length of a wave can be measured in several different ways, but the most convenient way is to calculate the distance from one crest to the next crest or from one trough to the next trough. This measurement is called a **wavelength** and is symbolized by the Greek letter lambda (λ).

The number of wavelengths that pass a given point in one second is called the **frequency** of a wave. Scientists measure frequency in units called **hertz** (Hz), which stand for one cycle per second. Two multiples of this unit are commonly used for waves that vibrate many times per second. One kilohertz (kHz) equals 1000 cycles per second, and 1 megahertz (MHz) equals 1,000,000 cycles per second!

The Velocity of Waves

Although waves travel from place to place, the individual particles of the material through which they move are displaced very little or not at all after the waves "move" by. How can this be? Picture a string that is stretched tight. When you wiggle the string, the vibrations clearly travel down the string, but other than the up-and-down motion of the vibration, the string remains in place.

How fast are these vibrations traveling? Waves travel at a variety of speeds. Water waves on the shoreline of a large body of water travel only a few meters per second. Sound waves in air move much faster. Under typical conditions, a sound wave can travel about 332 m/s. Light waves in outer space zip along at an incredible 300,000,000 m/s—fast enough to go from the earth to the moon in 1.3 seconds!

Fig. 20-2 When a string is wiggled, the vibrations travel down the string, but the particles in the string do not.

The **velocity** of a wave is mathematically related to two of its other characteristics: frequency and wavelength. The following equation ties these three quantities together:

$$v = f\lambda$$

where f stands for the frequency measured in hertz (Hz), and λ stands for wavelength measured in meters (m). Recall from Chapter 13 that the unit for velocity (v) is meters per second.

EXAMPLE PROBLEM

Calculating the speed of a wave

Problem Statement: Suppose that waves on a beach are arriving 1 every 5 s and that the spacing between them is 20 m. What is the velocity (or speed) of these waves?

KNOWN: Frequency (f) = 1 wave/5 s = 1/5 Hz

Wavelength (λ) = 20 m

UNKNOWN: Speed (v)

FORMULA TO USE: $v = f\lambda$

SUBSTITUTION: $v = 1/5 \text{ Hz} \times 20 \text{ m}$

SOLUTION: $v = 4 \text{ m/s}$

Calculating distance of lightning strike

Problem Statement: Suppose you see a lightning bolt and 7 s later you hear the thunder. How far away is it?

KNOWN: When lightning strikes, the light from the bolt travels so fast, it reaches your eyes almost immediately. Sound, however, travels relatively slowly—at about 332 m/s. In 5 s, the sound will have traveled a little over 1600 m or 1 mile. Therefore, simply by counting the seconds that elapse between the time you see the lightning and the time you hear the thunder, you can determine approximately how many miles away a lightning strike is. Five seconds is approximately 1 mile.

SOLUTION: Since 7 s elapsed, the lightning must have occurred about 1.4 miles distant.

Types of Waves

Most waves are classified into two major groups, depending on the direction of their vibration. If the vibration is at right angles to the direction of travel, the wave is said to be a **transverse wave.** Light waves and vibrations on a string are examples of transverse waves.

Fig. 20-3 The vibrations of a transverse wave are at right angles to the direction of travel.

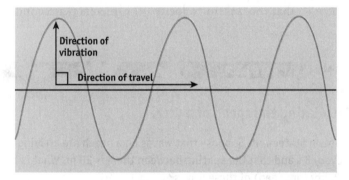

If the vibration occurs in the same direction that the wave is traveling, the wave is a **longitudinal** (LON ji TOOD un ul) **wave.** Sound waves are the most familiar example.

Water waves do not fit clearly into either category. On the surface they look transverse—the water is clearly bobbing up and down. However, the individual particles in a water wave also move back and forth somewhat. The result is that they move in circles.

Fig. 20-4 In this longitudinal sound wave, the molecules of air vibrate in the same direction as the sound wave itself.

Therefore, they have both transverse and longitudinal motion. They are constantly changing the direction of their motion.

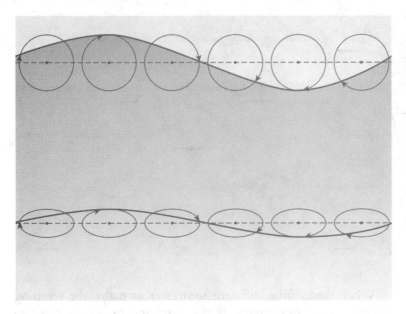

Fig. 20-5 The movement of particles in a water wave. As the wave vibrates up and down, the particles move in a circular motion. They actually return to approximately where they began! Their forward motion is matched by the same amount of backward motion.

Picture a long rope stretched between two boys. At the same instant, each boy flicks his end of the rope upward, sending pulses toward the other. What happens when the pulses meet at the center of the rope? Since both pulses are upward displacements of the rope, they add together for a brief instant as they pass through each other. At that instant there is a single pulse as high as both the pulses together. They will pass through each other and continue. The ability of two pulses to encounter, survive, and move on as before comes as a surprise to many people.

Let us repeat the experiment, but this time have one of the boys flick the rope downward as the other flicks it upward. Two pulses now approach each other, the one an upward displacement of the rope, the other a downward displacement. What would you expect to happen as the pulses pass through each other this time? If they are of equal height but oppositely directed, as in this case (one up, the other down), there will be a brief moment during which they cancel each other. They will pass by each other and move on unchanged. During the moment of cancellation the rope will be approximately straight. However, since the waves are still traveling along the rope, all the energy of both waves is still present. Cancellation is the "subtraction" of the two pulses. It can also be thought of as the addition of a positive quantity and a negative quantity.

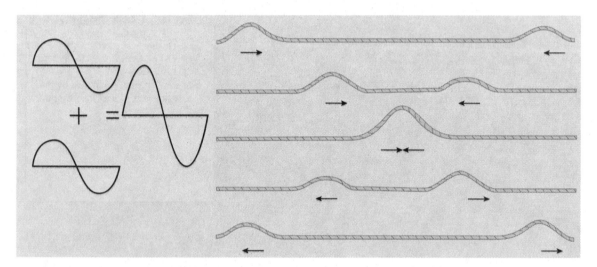

Fig. 20-6 Constructive interference

When waves from different sources cross paths, the resulting effect is called *interference.* If the crests and troughs of the two waves exactly coincide with each other, the waves are said to be *in-phase;* they will add together. This reaction is called **constructive interference.** Waves that are in-phase reinforce each other, producing higher crests and deeper troughs.

If the crests of one wave coincide with the troughs of another, they will cancel each other. These waves are said to be out of phase. *Out-of-phase* waves create **destructive interference.** Often when waves interfere, both constructive and destructive interference can occur.

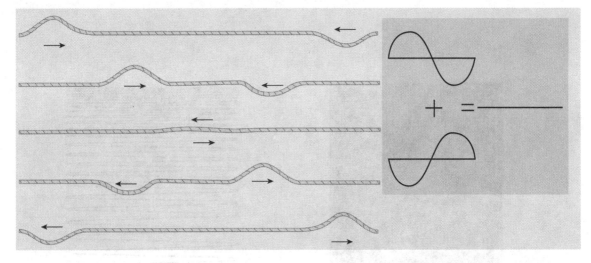

Fig. 20-7 Destructive interference

The Electromagnetic Spectrum

As the name implies, electromagnetic waves have both an electrical and a magnetic nature. These two parts (an electrical component and a magnetic component) vibrate at right angles to each other. As the waves become shorter in wavelength and higher in frequency, they become more energetic. Thus, radio waves (which have long wavelengths) are the least energetic, and gamma rays (which have very small wavelengths) are the most energetic members of the electromagnetic family.

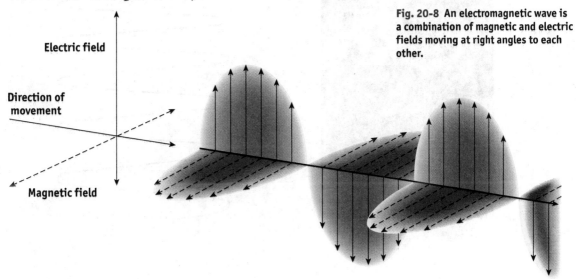

Fig. 20-8 An electromagnetic wave is a combination of magnetic and electric fields moving at right angles to each other.

Electric field

Direction of movement

Magnetic field

The Electromagnetic Spectrum

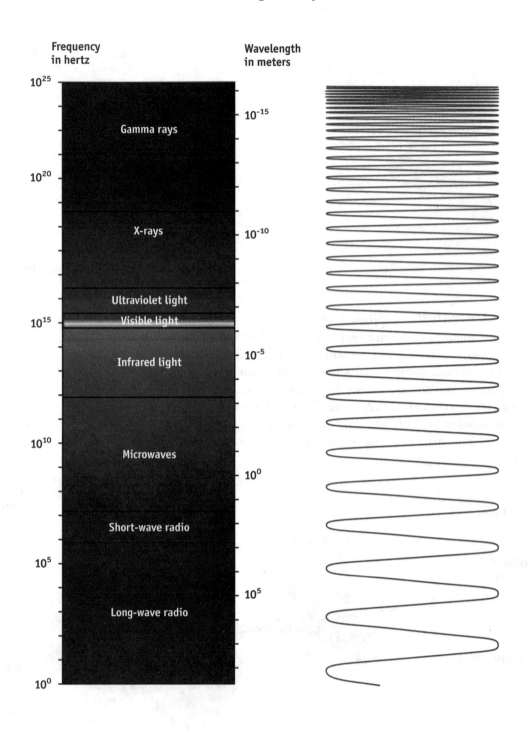

Frequency
in hertz

Wavelength
in meters

10^{25}

10^{-15}

Gamma rays

10^{20}

X-rays

10^{-10}

Ultraviolet light

Visible light

10^{15}

Infrared light

10^{-5}

10^{10}

Microwaves

10^{0}

Short-wave radio

10^{5}

10^{5}

Long-wave radio

10^{0}

Light waves, gamma rays, and radio waves are members of the large family of *electromagnetic waves*. All of these travel at the speed of light (3.0×10^8 m/s) and are capable of traveling through a vacuum. Together, these different electromagnetic waves form a continuum referred to as the electromagnetic spectrum (Figure 20-10). The rest of this chapter describes some of the many forms of electromagnetic radiation.

Radio Waves

The portion of the spectrum called **radio waves** includes both radio and television signals. How many different radio and television stations could you receive in the room where you are studying? Probably several. All those signals are streaming through the room right now. Imagine what it would be like if we could see all those waves! We are flooded with them constantly. The idea that they are traveling right through your body might disturb you, but they are completely harmless. Even the strongest radio and television waves are too weak to do any harm. It is also important to remember that radio waves are not sound waves. We use a radio to interpret the signals from stations. The radio converts the electromagnetic radiation into sound waves that allow us to hear a broadcast coming from miles away—a brilliant, convenient transfer of energy.

The frequencies of radio waves are specified in kilohertz or megahertz. A 1-MHz (1000 kHz) wave in the center of the AM radio band has a wavelength of 300 m. Below the AM band (lower in frequency) is the long-wave region of the radio spectrum. These waves are long indeed. A 0.1-MHz (100 kHz) wave has a wavelength of 3000 m! Long waves are used for shore-to-submarine communications systems and for guiding planes into airports. Using the formula $v = f\lambda$, let's illustrate how wavelength calculations are performed. Keep in mind that radio waves, like all forms of electromagnetic waves, travel at a certain velocity known as the speed of light. The value of the speed of light is 3.0×10^8 m/s in a vacuum.

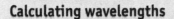

Calculating wavelengths

Problem Statement: Suppose an AM radio station is assigned a frequency of 1260 kHz. What is the wavelength of this wave?

Known:	Frequency (f) = 1260 kHz or 1,260,000 Hz
	Speed (v) = 3×10^8 m/s
Unknown:	wavelength (λ)
Formula to use:	$v = f\lambda$
Substitution:	$(3.0 \times 10^8 \text{ m/s}) = (1,260,000 \text{ Hz})\lambda$
Solution:	$\lambda = 238$ m

Above the AM band (higher frequency) is the short-wave region of the radio spectrum. A wave with a typical short-wave frequency, 10 MHz, has a wavelength of only 30 m. These shorter waves are reflected to the earth from the ionosphere (an ionized layer of the earth's atmosphere extending from roughly 100 km upward), allowing them to travel great distances. Short waves are used for a variety of services—international broadcasts, amateur radio, time signals, military communications, ship-to-shore radio systems, and citizens band (CB) radio. FM radio stations, TV stations, police and fire departments, and mobile telephone services utilize still higher short-wave frequencies. A 100-MHz wave, in the middle of the FM band, has a wavelength of only 3 m.

Radio waves are also used in astronomy. Radio telescopes receive these waves from space! These are not messages from space beings but rather radiation generated in space. By studying the frequencies and relative strengths of the radiation, astronomers are able to gather data about materials in interstellar clouds and other objects in space. Astronomers also transmit radio waves, which bounce off the moon or a planet, giving important clues about the object's characteristics.

Imagine how much time and effort Paul Revere could have saved using a radio station to broadcast his famous warning of the British invasion. Instead he literally yelled at the top of his lungs to get someone to hear him and had to ride an exhausting two hours to Lexington. Since then, radio has allowed people to communicate instantly, whether on the battlefield or in the car on their way home from school. Although the radio seems quaint when compared to computers and cell phones, it was one of the first means of mass communication and remains one of the most important.

Microwaves

The frequencies used for radio astronomy merge into the next region of the electromagnetic spectrum, **microwaves.** The frequencies for microwaves range from about 1000 MHz to 100,000 MHz (10^9 Hz to 10^{11} Hz). Wavelengths range from approximately 0.3 cm to 30 cm. Microwaves can be generated electronically, in much the same way radio waves are generated.

Microwave ovens use these same waves to cook food. Microwaves set up within the oven a changing electric field, which affects water molecules in the food. Water has polar molecules with positive and negative ends. The changing electric field causes the water molecules to turn first one way, then the other. As the molecules turn, they collide with other molecules, giving off energy in the form of heat. Thus, the inside of the food is heated almost as quickly as the surface. Cooking time is greatly reduced because it is not necessary to wait for the heat to move from the surface to the interior of the food as in a standard oven.

Fig. 20-9 How radar works

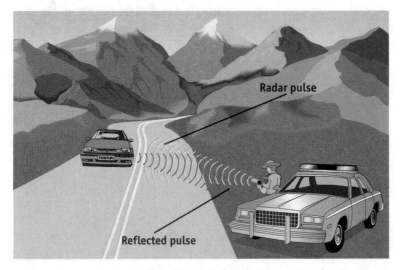

Radar pulse

Reflected pulse

Microwaves are also used in **radar** (*RA*dio *D*etection *A*nd *R*anging). They can be reflected by relatively small objects such as automobiles, airplanes, and ships, and large objects such as storm systems and landmasses. Transmitters beam powerful microwave pulses at the object being studied. The reflected radiation is received by an antenna, and the time interval between transmission and reception is measured. This time interval reveals the distance from the transmitter to the object. Traffic police use radar pulses to determine a car's speed.

Infrared Waves

Moving up the spectrum to still higher frequencies and higher energies, we come to **infrared** (IN fruh RED) **waves.** The prefix "infra" means below. The frequency of this type of energy is just below red visible light. You may recall from Chapter 16 that we defined heat as the kinetic energy present within matter. Heat increases as the motion of the particles increases. When an object is hot, it is radiating infrared rays into the surrounding areas.

Sir William Herschel (1738-1822), an English astronomer, discovered infrared radiation. He refracted rays from the sun through a triangular block of glass called a **prism** to separate the different colors. Herschel placed a thermometer in the various colors of the spectrum and recorded their temperatures. To his surprise, the thermometer was hottest in the region just beyond the red end of the spectrum. The temperature he recorded in this infrared region was greater than in any other part of the spectrum. He called the energy he uncovered "rays of heat."

An **incandescent** (IN kun DES unt) object (one heated to glowing) is a good source of both infrared and visible light energy. You have probably noticed that incandescent lights give off a lot of heat as well as light. A large part of the energy the bulb uses is released as infrared radiation rather than visible light. Fluorescent lights produce a larger percentage of visible light and much less infrared. Because fluorescent lights waste less energy as heat, they are more economical to operate. Another example of an incandescent object is the burner of an electric stove. A hot burner emits an orange glow. It radiates both visible and infrared energy. Can you predict what will happen when the burner is turned off? The color will disappear, but for a time the burner will still emit infrared energy. You can readily detect this energy by holding your hand near the burner. Human skin contains sensitive infrared receptors (detectors) that are plentiful in certain locations, such as on the face and back of the hand. Devices used to detect infrared energy include thermometers, thermostats, and infrared-sensitive film.

Visible Light

Visible light extends in frequency from 4.3×10^{14} Hz (red light) to 7.5×10^{14} Hz (violet light). Its waves are exceedingly short, having lengths ranging from 4×10^{-5} cm (violet) to 7×10^{-5} cm (red). Such small lengths are often written in units of nanometers

High-Tech Heat Wave

Infrared technology is invading areas of industry and business. From the air force to your local police, infrared waves are getting the attention of lots of different people. Why all the fuss? When a scientist develops devices to sense infrared radiation, the effect is equivalent to adding a sixth sense, a new pair of "eyes" that opens up a previously unknown world. The difference is that we do not need light, only the invisible infrared energy that is all around us.

On a dark night, an escaping convict's best chance to get away is to hide out in the woods. Under the cover of darkness, he could remain hidden at least until daylight. A police helicopter searchlight might detect him, but an alert criminal will just evade it when he hears the chopper approach. But now the good guys have a new, silent weapon. Using special infrared video cameras, police officers can "see" the body heat of the fugitive and track him at will. This special "night vision" allows officers to catch fleeing suspects and search for missing persons under the cover of darkness. Night vision is just one of the ways we can use infrared radiation for our own benefit.

The military has a full arsenal of heat-seeking missiles that search out enemy jets by detecting infrared radiation from their engines. Satellites can use infrared photography from space to show much more detail of rivers, mountains, and city locations. Physicians are now using thermography to detect tumors and examine blood flow within patients. Humans are not the only ones interested in heat waves. Rattlesnakes have heat-sensitive pits on their heads, so they can actually detect heat from the small rodents they eat for food. Not only does this allow them to sense their prey in dark conditions, but it also helps them to know if the animal is dead or alive.

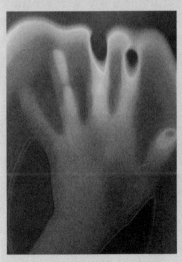

(10^{-9} m). Using these units, the wavelength of visible light ranges from 400 nm to 700 nm. Visible light is thought to be generated by the outer electrons of atoms when they are given extra energy. The additional energy vibrates them and raises them to higher orbitals. When they fall back to their normal levels, they give off light. Depending on the source of the visible light, there can be higher frequency waves present. Sunlight is a combination of visible, ultraviolet, and infrared radiation. Not only can you feel the heat from the sun on your skin (infrared radiation), but you can also see the light.

Ultraviolet Light

The prefix *ultra-* means "beyond." **Ultraviolet light** is just beyond violet light in frequency. Its vibrations are too fast for the human eye to detect. The frequency range for ultraviolet light is about 10^{15} to 10^{17} Hz. Because it cannot be seen, it is sometimes referred to as "black light." It is also referred to as UV light, UV rays, or UV radiation.

Ultraviolet light can be harmful to humans. It can damage your eyes and your skin. The chromosomes in your cells are highly organized into a chemical code known as DNA. This code determines important cell functions such as growth and reproduction. Remember, like all waves, UV light transfers energy. Energy is the ability to do work, and when work is accomplished, molecules get moved around and electron levels are disrupted. Because DNA is a code, it is definitely not wise to interfere with the code. That would be like giving someone your telephone number all scrambled. They would never be able to reach you. As a result, skin cells of those who spend large amounts of time in the sun sometimes experience a change in their DNA, also known as a *mutation*. Skin cancer is one of the most common cancers, and scientists have linked an increased risk of skin cancer to those who do not protect themselves from UV rays.

X rays

W. K. Roentgen (RENT gun) (1845-1923), the first winner of the Nobel prize, discovered **X rays** in 1895 while studying cathode rays (streams of electrons). X rays have frequencies ranging from about 10^{17} to 10^{21} Hz. They are generated when high-energy electrons are rapidly decelerated (slowed down) by striking the electron shells of atoms.

The best-known property of X rays is their ability to penetrate deeply into most types of matter. This has made them useful in medical work for viewing internal structures of the body. X rays are used

in industry to inspect metal objects for internal defects. X rays have also been used to determine whether or not a painting is genuine.

X-ray astronomy (observing astronomical objects using X rays instead of visible light) is a recently developed area of science. X-ray telescopes have been placed in satellites to gather information concerning X-ray emissions from the sun and other astronomical bodies. X rays are produced by gases at very high temperatures, such as those that exist in the atmosphere of stars. Thousands of X-ray sources have now been identified in deep space.

As you are beginning to see, the higher we go in frequency, the more deeply these electromagnetic rays are able to penetrate matter. Although X rays can easily go through skin, they penetrate bone to a lesser extent and reflect off of the hard bone surface. The reflected waves are recorded on special film; thus, we are able to see the bones. Once again, X rays do have their drawbacks. They can damage cells to a greater extent than UV light. X-ray technicians are highly trained and try not to expose radiation to body parts unnecessarily. Pregnant women are often forbidden to receive X rays because of potential harm to the developing cells of the baby.

Gamma Rays

Gamma rays are very similar to X rays but originate from the nuclei of atoms rather than from electrons. Their frequencies overlap with those of X rays but extend even higher, ranging from 10^{-20} Hz upward. Gamma rays are the most energetic form of electromagnetic radiation known to man. Their wavelengths are the shortest known, ranging from 10^{-9} cm downward. This is a mind-boggling billionth of a centimeter, and most gamma rays have wavelengths even shorter than this.

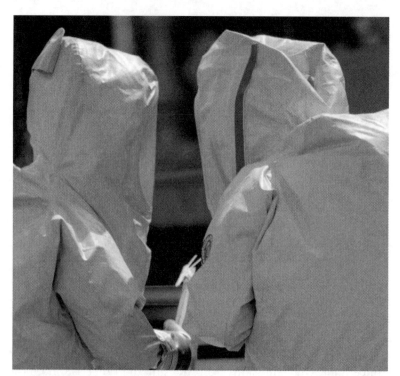

Fig. 20-10 Employees who work around gamma radiation must take elaborate precautions to protect themselves from harm.

In medicine, gamma radiation is used to treat cancer. Almost instantly, gamma rays can destroy cells, a very useful procedure when combating tumors, especially in the brain. Gamma rays represent the most destructive form of electromagnetic radiation because they have the highest energy per ray (photon). They can travel right through humans, steel, and concrete walls and can cause great damage to matter, including destroying chemical bonds and even changing atoms from one element to another. Several *radioactive elements* release gamma radiation as they go through alpha and beta decay (Chapter 6). Although gamma rays are usually released in small amounts, anyone working around uranium or plutonium is well aware of the risks of exposure to these deadly rays.

Astronomers have detected gamma rays streaming from the center of many galaxies, including our own. Smaller bursts of gamma rays occur randomly across the sky, coming from unknown sources.

SECTION REVIEW QUESTIONS 20A

1. What are the high and low points of a wave called?
2. What are the two types of interference?
3. List the seven types of electromagnetic waves discussed in the chapter, in order from lowest to highest frequency.

The Properties of Light

Both light and sound travel in the form of waves. Both have characteristic ranges of frequencies and wavelengths. Yet, despite their many similarities, the two are different in several important ways. For instance, light is an electromagnetic wave, but sound is a mechanical wave. Light can travel through a vacuum; sound cannot.

All you need to do to confirm this last difference is to look at the sky on a clear day. The brightly glowing sun dominates your view. It is clearly visible even though over 150 million kilometers of space separate it from the earth. But what about sound? If you have ever heard a roaring fire, you can imagine the tremendous sound that the astronomical furnace we call the sun could produce. But who has ever heard the sun? The light easily makes the 150-million-kilometer trip to the earth, but no sound does.

The sun is the primary source of radiant energy in our solar system. Other more down-to-earth sources include flames, heater coils, and incandescent lamps. Each of these sources releases a broad range of radiant energy. We call the portion of radiant energy that we can see **visible light.** Together, both visible and invisible radiant energy make up the broad range of frequencies and wavelengths known as the electromagnetic spectrum.

Fig. 20-11 The colors of the visible spectrum, in order, are red, orange, yellow, green, blue, indigo, and violet. They are easy to remember if you use this simple device: the first letters of the names sound like a man's name - Roy G. Biv.

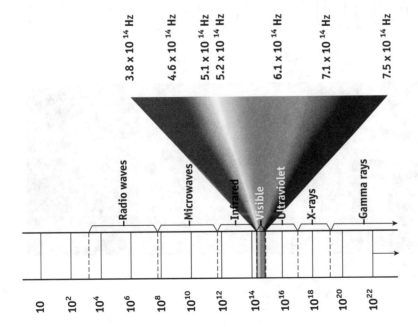

The Visible Spectrum

Visible light consists of waves of electromagnetic radiation of various wavelengths. These wavelengths make up only a narrow slice of the complete spectrum of electromagnetic radiation. This slice is called the visible spectrum.

We see light as colors. Even sunlight, which appears to have no color, is really a mixture of all the colors. Sunlight reveals its secret in the majesty of a rainbow. The colors of the rainbow blend into each other in a continuous spectrum. Each of the colors—red, orange, yellow, green, blue, indigo (purple), and violet, have a range of frequency at which they are present. We can identify colors by a specific frequency and wavelength. For example, waves with lengths of 700 nm and 690 nm are two slightly different shades of red.

A *luminous* (LOO muh nuss) object emits light waves. Some luminous objects produce white light. White light contains almost all the colors of the spectrum. Our sun produces white light.

Some luminous objects, such as a laser, produce a single color of light. These luminous objects are *monochromatic* (from the Greek *monos*, meaning "single," and *chroma*, meaning "color"). All the

Fig. 20-12 The colors of the rainbow are caused by different wavelengths of light.

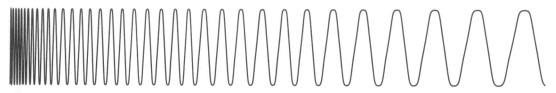

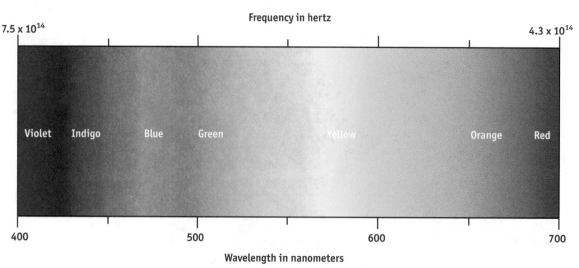

waves emitted by a monochromatic source have the same frequency and the same wavelength. A fluorescent light contains many monochromatic sources, giving what is called a **line spectrum.** The many lines of this spectrum represent the different colors produced by the different glowing gases in a fluorescent tube. The individual colors from a fluorescent tube combine to give the overall effect of white light.

An *illuminated* object reflects light waves. While the sun is a luminous object, the moon is an illuminated object. It reflects the light of the sun. Many illuminated objects appear to have different colors. For example, three cars in the same sunlight may appear to be three different colors. Why is this true? Why, for instance, does a red car look red? The paint on a red car absorbs all light except light with the wavelength we see as red. Red light waves are reflected from the paint and then sensed by your eyes. What colors does blue paint absorb? What color does it reflect?

Fig. 20-13 A line spectrum shows the various monochromatic waves that combine to form the light emitted from some particular sources of light.

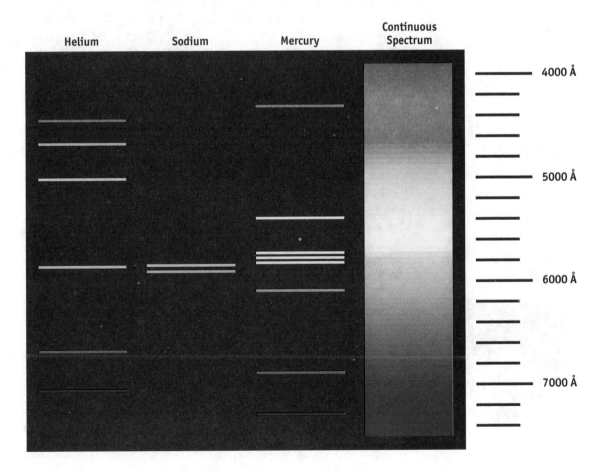

The colors of illuminated objects help to shape our moods and alter our tastes. Would you eat a sandwich made with green ham on blue rye with bright purple cheese? Psychologists who study our responses to color have uncovered information that helps us design not only soothingly colored work places but also better warning systems. We psychologically associate red with danger or warning—fire extinguishers, stop signs, and fire trucks are just a few examples. Notice how most police cruisers in your neighborhood are easily distinguishable from other cars because of their bold, two-tone color scheme and flashing blue lights.

Color Perception

There are many colors, such as brown, that are not in the rainbow. What is "brown light"? There is no wavelength of light corresponding to brown, or peach, or the myriad of other colors we see. These colors are *mixtures* of rainbow colors. When a mixture of colors shines into our eyes, our eyes and brain translate this mixture into a new color. The most familiar example is white light. White light is a mixture of the entire visible spectrum. When we look at a white object, a whole rainbow of color is striking our eyes. However, we see not a rainbow but the color white. A prism is necessary to separate the colors so that we can see them individually.

When only parts of the visible spectrum are mixed, we see colors other than white. For example, mixing red and green light causes our eyes to see yellow (Table 20-14). Every color in the world can be simulated with various mixtures of only three rainbow colors: red, green, and blue. These are the three **additive primary colors.** When we mix these colors in equal proportions, two at a time, we end up with yellow (red/green), magenta (red/blue) and cyan (blue/green). Mix all three, and we get white. Mix them in different proportions, and thousands of shades of these colors will result.

TABLE 20-14 Additive Primary Colors

Color Mixing	
Primary Colors	Result
Red/green	yellow
Red/blue	magenta
Blue/green	cyan
Red/blue/green	white

Color televisions take advantage of this property of our eyes. A color television screen contains dots of only these three colors.

When other colors need to be displayed, mixtures of these three colors are used instead. A close look at a yellow object on a television screen will reveal only red and green dots. There is no yellow light there at all! Our eyes interpret the color as yellow.

Yellow, cyan, and magenta are the **subtractive primary colors.** They are called subtractive because when they are mixed, the only color present is that which is reflected. All of the others are absorbed. Think of mixing yellow and magenta. We know that yellow is made up of green and red, and magenta is red and blue. When we mix magenta and yellow, only the color orange is reflected from the object. When we mix all three subtractive primary colors (cyan, yellow, and magenta), all of the colors of the spectrum will be absorbed and the object will be black. Many types of printers use color cartridges to produce near photo-quality images. As you might have guessed, these cartridges contain only three types of ink—blue-green (cyan), reddish-blue (magenta), and yellow. The computer and the printer determine the exact proportions needed to produce thousands of different shades of color.

TABLE 20-15	Subtractive Primary Colors
Color Mixing	
Yellow/magenta	orange
Cyan/magenta	purple
Cyan/yellow	green
Cyan/yellow/magenta	black

The Speed of Light

An American scientist named Albert Michelson made the first accurate measurement of the speed of light in the 1920s. Michelson measured the time it took for a beam of light to pass between Mount Wilson and Mount San Antonio in California. He obtained a value of approximately 300,000,000 m/s (3×10^8 m/s). Scientists code this value with a small letter *c.*

The Speed of Light in Various Mediums	
Medium	**Approximate speed**
air	300,000,000 m/s
water	223,000,000 m/s
glass	200,000,000 m/s

The speed of light depends on what it is traveling through. Light travels fastest in a vacuum. The chart on page 479 reveals that light moves more slowly in denser mediums. Can you think of a reason for this decrease in speed of light?

At 3.0×10^8 m/s, light should travel about 18 million km per minute. Since the sun is 150 million km away, its light takes approximately 8.3 minutes to get to the earth. We could say that the sun is about 8.3 *light-minutes* away, defining the light-minute as the distance light travels in a minute. Sunlight takes over five hours to reach the planet Pluto. We could, therefore, say that Pluto is more than *five light-hours* from the sun.

In discussing distances to stars, astronomers use a larger unit, the *light-year* (ly). The light-year is defined as the distance light travels in a year (approximately 10 trillion km). The nearest stars, Alpha Centauri and its two neighbors, are about 4.3 light-years away. Essentially, when you "see" an object in space, you are looking back in time to when the light left that object. For example, since Alpha Centauri is 4.3 light-years away, the light we now see left 4.3 years ago! The Orion Nebula is about 1600 light-years away.

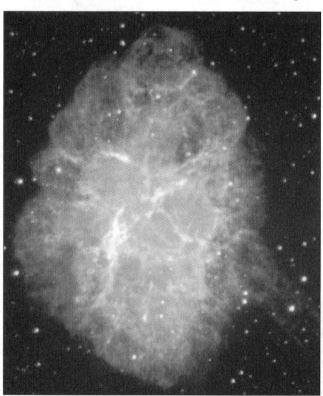

Fig. 20-16 The Crab Nebula is about 615 light years away.

The Intensity of Light

Intensity is a measure of how bright the light from a light source is. To tell exactly how bright a light is, we must be able to compare it to a known standard. Years ago, scientists used a specific type of candle as a standard of intensity. Candles, however, could not be made with exact uniformity, and even a single candle does not burn with a perfectly steady light. Therefore, scientists developed a more accurate unit of intensity called the **candela** (**cd**) (kan DEL uh). This unit is based on the intensity of light from a standard incandescent source operating at a specific temperature. Since the candela is an exact standard, it can be reproduced in laboratories around the world. Interestingly, ordinary incandescent light bulbs produce about one candela of light energy for each watt of electrical power they use. Fluorescent tubes are considerably more efficient than incandescent bulbs; fluorescent lights produce about 4 cd per watt.

When you read a book indoors, the amount of light, or illumination, you receive on the printed page depends on two factors—the intensity of the light source and the distance of the light source from the page.

The illumination of an object is directly proportional to the intensity, or brightness, of the light source. In other words, a lamp that produces 100 cd will illuminate the page twice as much as a 50-cd lamp the same distance away. A 200-cd lamp will provide twice as much light as the 100-cd lamp, and so on.

On the other hand, illumination is *inversely* proportional to the *square* of the distance from the light source. Moving twice as far from a lamp reduces the illumination from the lamp to one-fourth

Fig. 20-17 High intensity lighting is used to illuminate a large stage. Altering the color and intensity of the light can create visual moods that influence the way the audience perceives the performance.

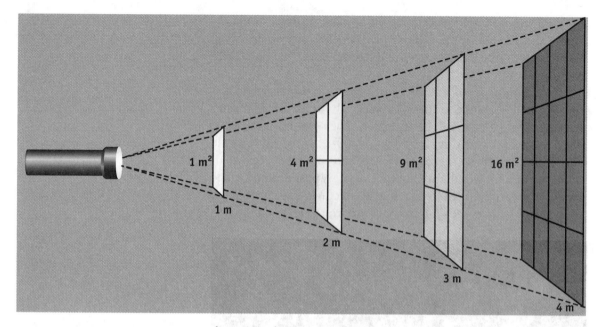

Fig. 20-18 The inverse square law states that illumination is inversely proportional to the square of the distance from the light source. This diagram illustrates why. The same cone of light must spread out to illuminate larger and larger areas.

the original amount. Moving three times as far from the lamp cuts the illumination to a mere one-ninth the original amount. Distance from the light source, therefore, is a far more critical factor in illumination than you might think. This type of relationship is called an *inverse square law,* a situation frequently encountered in the world of physics.

Photographers use *light meters* to measure the exact amount of illumination on their subjects. Inside a light meter is a photoelectric cell that changes light energy into an electric current. The brighter the illumination, the more electric current is produced by the photoelectric cell. This current is used to deflect a needle across a scale that is calibrated in units of illumination. Using the reading from this scale, the photographer adjusts the lens opening and shutter speed of his or her camera to fit the illumination on the subject.

The human eye can detect an amazing range of intensities. Although it can function in bright sunlight, it can also adjust to operate in nearly total darkness—light only one-billionth the intensity of sunlight!

Fig. 20-19 A photographer's light meter

SECTION REVIEW QUESTIONS 20B

1. How do you distinguish an illuminated object from a luminous object?

2. What are the colors of the visible spectrum, from highest to lowest frequency?

3. What is the SI unit for light intensity?

Reflection and Refraction

Have you ever watched dust particles dance through a sunbeam? Have you ever sliced through darkness with a beam of light from a flashlight? Have you ever noticed the beam of light from a slide projector? All these observations tell us that light travels in straight lines.

A **beam** of light consists of a very large number of individual light waves traveling together in a straight line. Scientists use the fact that light waves travel in straight lines to help describe the behavior of light. They represent the directions of light waves by straight lines called **rays.** The study of the movement of light in straight lines is called *ray optics.*

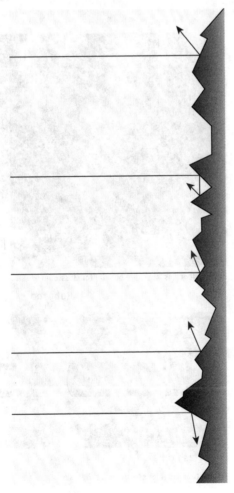

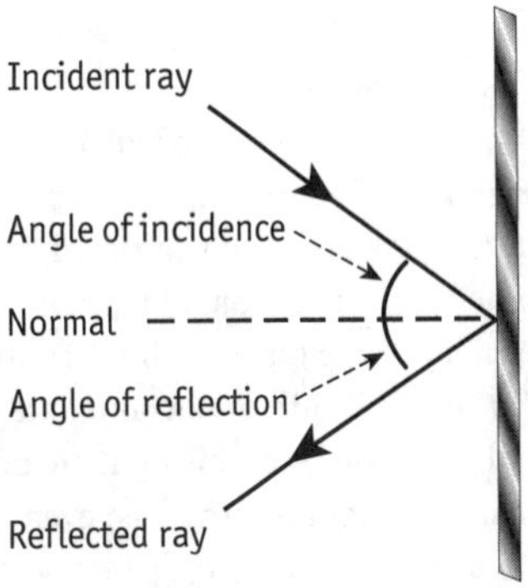

Fig. 20-21 **Reflection in a plane mirror**

Incident ray

Angle of incidence

Normal

Angle of reflection

Reflected ray

Fig. 20-20 **Light is diffused from a rough surface because the beams of light are reflected in many directions.**

Reflection

Pitch-black darkness surrounds you. The windows of your room have been sealed so that no light can enter. The lights have been turned off. Can you see anything? You are probably thinking that this is a silly question, but it provides us with an observation that will help us answer the question "How do we see things?" You cannot see in the dark because you see objects by sensing the light that is reflected by or emitted from them.

FACETS of the physical world

Lasers: The Best and The Brightest

Laser stands for Light Amplification by the Stimulated Emission of Radiation. A laser produces a coherent, concentrated, monochromatic beam of light. An ordinary lamp produces incoherent (in ko HEAR unt), or uncoordinated, light. The waves of this light are of many different lengths, and even those of the same length are not in step with one another. Incoherent light spreads out as it travels: the light beam becomes wider and less intense with distance.

In a beam of coherent light, every wave is the same length and is synchronized in lock-step formation with every other wave. Coherent light does not spread out and become diffuse. This unique behavior of coherent light is the key to the usefulness of lasers.

The "straightness" of laser beams has made them useful tools for measuring distances. If a scientist knows the time it takes for a laser beam to cover a distance, he can use the speed of light to calculate the

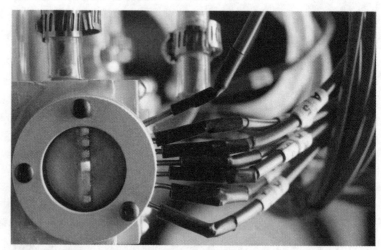

Helium Neon gas lasers are popular for classroom use.

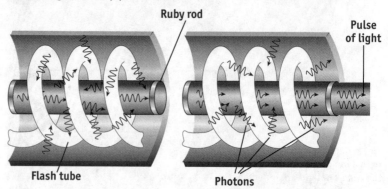

A flash tube provides energy for a ruby laser.

Different objects reflect light differently, depending on the shape of their surface and the angle at which light strikes them. When a beam of light is reflected from a polished flat surface, a simple relationship holds true: the angle at which incoming rays strike the reflecting surface is equal to the angle at which the reflected rays leave the same surface. Scientists normally measure angles of incoming and reflected rays from a line drawn perpendicular to the reflecting surface at the point where the ray strikes

distance. For instance, after *Apollo 11* astronauts placed a laser reflector on the moon, NASA scientists directed a laser beam toward it. By timing the transmission of the laser, NASA scientists were able to measure very accurately the distance between the earth and the moon. Surveyors use lasers to measure distances on the earth, and geologists use lasers to measure the movement of the earth's crust along fault lines.

Pulsing laser beams are used to carry large amounts of information, such as audio (sound), video (television images), and computer data across long distances. Certain types of laser beams generate a tremendous amount of heat at whatever point they strike. These lasers are used in industry to weld sheet metal and to fuse sections of glass or plastic. Using lasers, opthalmologists have begun a quiet revolution in the treatment of common eye disorders such as nearsightedness and farsightedness. *Photorefractive keratectomy* (PRK) uses a laser to remove small parts of the cornea, literally reshaping the eyes in the process. When success-

Diode lasers are small, rugged, and relatively inexpensive. They have found a wide variety of uses from laser pointers to CD players.

ful, this procedure gives patients nearly 20/20 vision.

The first lasers utilized solid ruby rods surrounded by a flash tube to stimulate emission. Ruby is a crystal of aluminum oxide that also contains chromium atoms. These chromium atoms absorb green light and blue light, giving ruby its famous brilliant red color. Liquid and gas lasers are also possible. The development of small, inexpensive semiconductor lasers has made possible a host of applications, from CD players to fiber optic communications.

it. This line is called the **normal.** An incoming ray is called an **incident ray.** An outgoing ray is called a **reflected ray.** The angle between an incident ray and the normal is called the **angle of incidence.** The angle between a reflected ray and the normal is the **angle of reflection.** The **law of reflection** states that the angle of incidence is equal to the angle of reflection.

The image formed by a **plane mirror** (flat mirror) is the result of many separate light rays, each obeying the law of reflection. This reflected image appears to be exactly the same distance behind the mirror as the actual object is in front of the mirror. Thus, if you stand one meter from a plane mirror, your image will appear to stand one meter behind the mirror—two meters away from you. If you stand five meters from the mirror, your image will appear to stand ten meters from you. The farther you are from your image, the smaller it appears. Plane mirror images are also reversed left to right. When you see yourself in a mirror, you do not see yourself as others see you; instead, you see your "mirror" image.

Are there really images behind mirrors? No, rays of light only *appear* to be originating behind mirrors. Your eyes are tricked into thinking the light is coming from there. Scientists call the images

Fig. 20-22 Concave mirrors reflect all parallel light rays through a definite point—the principal focus.

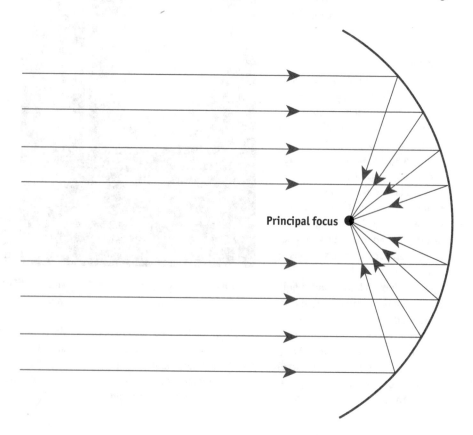

Principal focus

20 The Electromagnetic Spectrum

we see in plane mirrors **virtual images** because the rays of light that form the image are not actually behind the mirror where the image appears to be.

Concave mirrors (mirrors that "cave in") also obey the law of reflection. Figure 20-22 shows parallel rays approaching a concave mirror. When a separate normal is drawn at the point where each ray strikes the surface of the mirror, the angle of reflection equals the angle of incidence for each ray. Notice that the incident rays are also parallel to the line that is perpendicular to the center of the mirror. This line is called the *principal axis.* If a concave mirror is well designed, the reflected rays all pass through a definite point on the principal axis called the **principal focus.**

Have you ever looked into a spoon? Your reflection is upside-down. The light that strikes this concave mirror is not all parallel to the principal axis. Figure 20-23 shows a dog and its image reflected from a concave mirror. Light rays from each point on the dog are reflected from the mirror to a single point. Together, all these points make up a complete focused image of the dog. Because the light rays actually pass through this image, scientists call it a **real image.** A real image could be projected onto a screen. Could a virtual image be projected onto a screen?

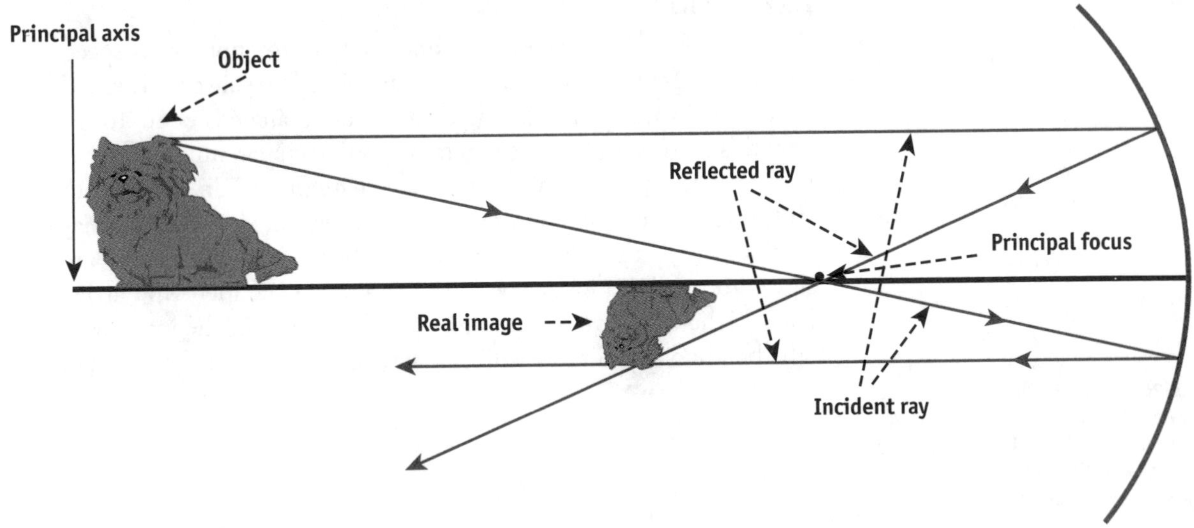

Notice that each ray of light reflected from a concave mirror is reflected onto the opposite side of the principal axis from its starting point. Thus, the image formed by a concave mirror beyond the principal focus is upside-down, or inverted. In Figure 20-23 the image of the dog is smaller than the actual dog, and inverted.

Fig. 20-23 A concave mirror produces an inverted image smaller than the original.

Concave mirrors are used in *reflecting telescopes* to bring parallel rays of light from a star to a focus at the principal focus of the telescope. From this point the light can be reflected to an eyepiece lens by means of a small plane mirror. Concave mirrors may also be used in the reverse direction. When a light is placed at the focal point, it sends light rays fanning out in many directions. When these rays reach the concave mirror, they are reflected as parallel rays. This arrangement is used to produce concentrated beams of light in flashlights, spotlights, searchlights, and automobile headlights.

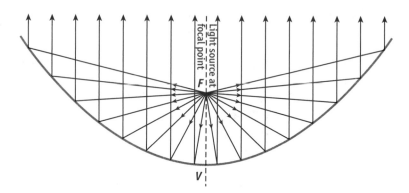

Fig. 20-24 Reflection of light rays in an automobile headlight

Refraction

When a ray of light passes from one medium to another, its speed changes as the going gets easier or harder. As a result of this speed change, light that enters a new medium at an angle is bent. To see why this is true, look at the diagram of soldiers marching in formation (Figure 20-25). The soldiers are marching at an angle from land into a swamp containing waist-deep water. The entire formation is bent because the men who arrive at the water earlier are slowed down for a longer period of time than the men who arrive later. Light waves can be thought of as behaving in the same way. The bending of light as it enters a new medium is called **refraction**.

Fig. 20-25 As the soldiers enter the swamp, the first arrivals slow down, and the whole formation bends. In a similar way, light rays bend as they enter a new medium.

In Figure 20-26, a beam of light passing through the air strikes a block of glass at an angle. The normal is perpendicular to the surface of the block. Notice that the beam of light bends toward the normal as it enters the glass, a denser medium. Inside the new medium, the ray again follows a straight line. Examine the beam as it leaves the glass. Since the ray is now entering a less dense medium (air), it bends away from the normal.

The refraction of light as it enters water causes many illusions. Have you ever tried to net a fish in an aquarium? When you lowered the net into the water, did you find that you had "overshot" the fish? Refraction of light fools you by making the fish seem closer than it really is.

Another interesting effect of refraction is the bending of the sun's rays, which is evident when the sun is just below the horizon. The refraction that takes place as the sunlight enters the atmosphere from space causes us to see sunrises a little earlier than we otherwise would and sunsets a little later than we otherwise would. Thus, refraction slightly lengthens the period of daylight each day. On the equinoxes (approximately March 21 and September 23), when you would expect days and nights of exactly equal length, refraction actually causes the days to be a bit longer than the nights.

On hot days, the refraction of light causes illusions called *mirages*. If a layer of hot, less dense air is located next to the

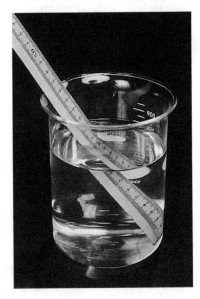

Fig. 20-26 Light refraction through a block of glass

ground beneath a layer of cooler, denser air, the density difference between the two layers will cause light rays to bend gradually upward. This refraction of light often fools people in the scorching heat of a desert into thinking that they see pools of water ahead. Similarly, as you drive along in a car on a hot day, the highway may appear wet in the distance. These mirages are due to refraction.

Lenses use the properties of refracted light to magnify or reduce images. When parallel rays enter a lens, each ray is bent the right amount so that all the rays meet at a single point. This point, like the focus

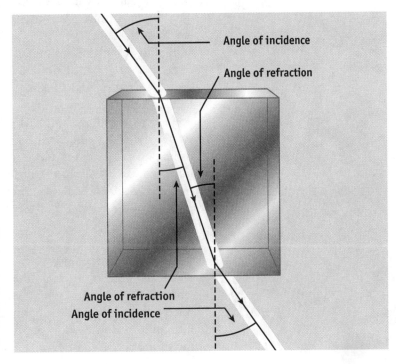

Angle of incidence

Angle of refraction

Angle of refraction
Angle of incidence

"NICE DIVE! TRY USING REAL WATER NEXT TIME!"

point produced by a concave mirror, is called the principal focus. The distance from a lens to its principal focus is called the **focal length** of the lens.

Besides eyeglasses, some of the most useful applications of refraction are made possible by putting two or more lenses together. In a refractor telescope, a large lens, called an *objective,* focuses light from distant objects, while a smaller lens, called the eyepiece, magnifies the focused image. In a compound microscope, multiple lenses make magnifications of more than 1000 times possible. For example, if the lower lens (objective) has a magnification of 100X and the upper lens (eyepiece) has a magnification of 15X, the overall magnification of the microscope will be the product of the two, or 1500X!

Dispersion

The electromagnetic waves that make up the various colors contained in sunlight all have different wavelengths but travel at the same speed in empty space. Entering a medium such as glass or water affects these wavelengths differently. If white light passes through a prism, the longer wavelengths are bent the least while the shorter wavelengths are bent the most. This causes the various

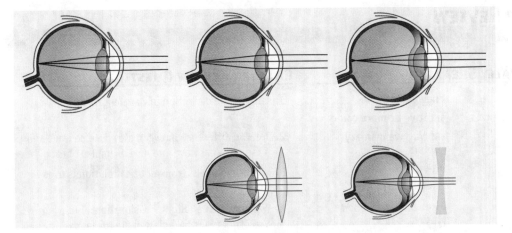

colors to separate from each other. The separation of white light into its differently colored light waves is called **dispersion**.

A rainbow is the result of dispersion. As sunlight shines through rain, each raindrop acts both as a prism and as a concave mirror. Therefore, the sunlight is both divided into its colors and reflected back to observers on the ground.

Fig. 20-27 With normal vision, the image is projected onto the retina (a) Farsightedness—the eyeball is too short and the image is projected behind the eye. A convex lens is used to correct the problem. (b) Nearsightedness—the eyeball is too long and the image is projected in front of the retina. A concave lens is used to correct the problem.

SECTION REVIEW QUESTIONS 20C

1. State the law of reflection.
2. What is unique about the image formed by a concave mirror?
3. Does light passing through a lens illustrate reflection or refraction?

Fig. 20-28 A rainbow is caused by the dispersion of light through water droplets in the atmosphere.

CHAPTER REVIEW

SCIENTIFICALLY SPEAKING

mechanical waves	line spectrum
electromagnetic waves	additive primary colors
crests	subtractive primary colors
troughs	intensity
amplitude	candela (cd)
wavelength	beam
frequency	rays
hertz (Hz)	normal
velocity (v)	incident ray
transverse wave	reflected ray
longitudinal wave	angle of incidence
constructive interference	angle of reflection
destructive interference	law of reflection
radio waves	plane mirror
microwaves	virtual images
radar	concave mirrors
infrared waves	principal focus
prism	real image
incandescent	refraction
ultraviolet light	lenses
X rays	focal length
gamma rays	dispersion
visible light	

CHAPTER REVIEW QUESTIONS

1. What is the definition of wavelength, and what is its symbol?

2. Tell the difference between a transverse wave and a longitudinal wave and give examples of each.

3. What type of electromagnetic radiation is used in radar?

4. We know that sunlight is visible light, but what two other types of radiation are present within the rays of the sun?

5. Predict the results of an experiment exposing plant seeds to gamma or X-ray radiation for several seconds and then planting them. Propose a hypothesis for your results.

6. Give a brief description of the additive and subtractive primary colors and how they are used to produce various other colors.

7. Respond to the following questions about the speed of light: (a) What is the speed of light, and what is the letter used to represent it? (b) How long does it take for light to travel from the sun to the earth? (c) What is the approximate distance of a light year? (d) Does light travel faster through air or through water?

8. How does distance affect light intensity?

9. Contrast virtual images with real images.

10. Explain dispersion in the context of a rainbow.

FACET REVIEW QUESTIONS

1. What is the difference between coherent and incoherent light?

2. Give some advantages for using infrared waves for night vision.

WHAT DID YOU LEARN?

1. When a rock is dropped into a pool of still water, waves begin to spread out around the rock. What happens to the amplitude, wavelength, and frequency as time passes?

2. Why does the technician usually place a lead "blanket" over the patient's abdomen during a chest X ray?

3. Suppose you decide that instead of going out in the hot sun, you are going to sit in front of a window to get a suntan. Several hours later, you discover that you are not any more tanned than when you started. Can you give an explanation for this result?

4. In Genesis 9:11-16, God made a promise never again to destroy the earth with a flood and placed the rainbow in the sky as a reminder to us. Using your knowledge of rainbows, what does this event apparently say about the world before the Flood? Use a Scripture verse to support your answer.

Appendix A

Units of Measure: Common Conversions

For Units of	When You Know the Number of		Multiply by	To Find the Number of
Length	millimeters	x	0.039	= inches
	meters	x	3.281	= feet
	meters	x	1.094	= yards
	kilometers	x	0.621	= miles
Area	square meters	x	1.196	= square yards
	hectares	x	2.471	= acres
Volume	liters	x	1.057	= quarts
	cubic meters	x	1.308	= cubic yards
Mass	grams	x	0.035	= ounces
	kilograms	x	2.205	= pounds
Temperature*	degrees Celsius	x	9/5 (then add 32)	= degrees Fahrenheit

For Units of	When You Know the Number of		Multiply by	To Find the Number of
Length	inches	x	25.4	= millimeters
	feet	x	0.305	= meters
	yards	x	0.914	= meters
	miles	x	1.609	= kilometers
Area	square yards	x	0.836	= square meters
	acres	x	0.405	= hectares
Volume	quarts	x	0.946	= liters
	cubic yards	x	0.765	= cubic meters
Mass	ounces	x	28.35	= grams
	pounds	x	0.454	= kilograms
Temperature*	degrees Fahrenheit	x	5/9 (after subtacting 32)	= degrees Celsius

*Formula for converting degrees Celsius to kelvins: $K - °C + 273$

Appendix B

Elements and Their Symbols

Actinium Ac
Aluminum Al
Americium Am
Antimony Sb
Argon Ar
Arsenic As
Astatine At
Barium Ba
Berkelium Bk
Beryllium Be
Bismuth Bi
Bohrium Bh
Boron B
Bromine Br
Cadmium Cd
Calcium Ca
Californium Cf
Carbon C
Cerium Ce
Cesium Cs
Chlorine Cl
Chromium Cr
Cobalt Co
Copper Cu
Curium Cm
Dubnium Db
Dysprosium Dy
Einsteinium Es
Erbium Er
Europium Eu
Fermium Fm
Fluorine F
Francium Fr
Gadolinium Gd
Gallium Ga
Germanium Ge
Gold Au

Hafnium Hf
Hassium Hs
Helium He
Holmium Ho
Hydrogen H
Indium In
Iodine I
Iridium Ir
Iron Fe
Krypton Kr
Lanthanum La
Lawrencium Lr
Lead Pb
Lithium Li
Lutetium Lu
Magnesium Mg
Manganese Mn
Meitnerium Mt
Mendelevium Md
Mercury Hg
Molybdenum Mo
Neodymium Nd
Neon Ne
Neptunium Np
Nickel Ni
Niobium Nb
Nitrogen N
Nobelium No
Osmium Os
Oxygen O
Palladium Pd
Phosphorus P
Platinum Pt
Plutonium Pu
Polonium Po
Potassium K
Praseodymium Pr

Protactinium Pa
Promethium Pm
Radium Ra
Radon Rn
Rhenium Re
Rhodium Rh
Rubidium Rb
Ruthenium Ru
Rutherfordium Rf
Samarium Sm
Scandium Sc
Seaborgium Sg
Selenium Se
Silicon Si
Silver Ag
Sodium Na
Strontium Sr
Sulfur S
Tantalum Ta
Technetium Tc
Tellurium Te
Terbium Tb
Thallium Tl
Thorium Th
Thulium Tm
Tin Sn
Titanium Ti
Tungsten W
Ununbium Uub
Ununnilium Uun
Unununium Uuu
Uranium U
Vanadium V
Xenon Xe
Ytterbium Yb
Yttrium Y
Zinc Zn
Zirconium Zr

Appendix C

Scientific Notation: A Shorthand Way to Write Numbers

Scientific notation is a great time saver because it simplifies writing very large or very small numbers. For example, the mass of the sun is 2.0×10^{30} kg. To write this out would require thirty zeros. The mass of an electron is 9.1×10^{28} g, which would require twenty-seven zeros if written as an ordinary number.

Numbers that are multiples of 10 are represented this way:

$$1,000,000 = 10^6$$
$$100,000 = 10^5$$
$$10,000 = 10^4$$
$$1,000 = 10^3$$
$$100 = 10^2$$
$$10 = 10^1$$
$$1 = 10^0$$
$$0.1 = 10^{-1}$$
$$0.01 = 10^{-2}$$
$$0.001 = 10^{-3}$$
$$0.0001 = 10^{-4}$$
$$0.00001 = 10^{-5}$$
$$0.000001 = 10^{-6}$$

Numbers that are not multiples of 10 are represented as a product of two numbers: one number (before the times sign) that falls between 1 and 10, and one number that is a power of 10. For example, the number 186,000 would be written as 1.86×10^5, which is equivalent to 1.86 times 100,000. The number 93,000,000 would be written 9.3×10^7.

Appendix D

Understanding Words in Science

Scientists are sometimes accused of speaking a language all their own. They may use words that you have never heard before. But if you break down these complex words into simple parts, and you know the meaning of each part, you will find that you understand many of them after all. When you encounter a difficult scientific word, find the parts on this table and try to determine the meaning of the word. Here is an example:

magnetohydrodynamics
> *Magneto* means magnetic force;
> *hydro* means fluids;
> *dynamic* means power.

Therefore magnetohydrodynamics is power from magnetic fluids.

Numbers

mono	one
di, bi	two
tri	three
tetra, quadra	four
penta, quinta	five
hexa, sexta	six
hepta	seven
octa	eight
nona	nine
deka	ten
cent	hundred

Conditions

a, an	without
ab	departing from
alter	change
anti	opposed to
aud	hear
auto	self-generated
co, con	together
de	loss, removal
en	inside
equa	same
exo	outside
extra	beyond
hemi	half
hetero	different
homo	same, more
hyper	excess
hypo	less than, below
inter	between
intra	within
iso	equal
mal	bad
mega	great, large
micro	small
ortho	straight, regular
oxy	oxygen
pan	all
poly	many
post	after
pre	before
sub	underneath
super	above

Scientific roots

bio	life
chrom	color
dyna	power
geo	earth
graph	record
gyro	turn
helio	sun
hydra	water
hydro	fluid
kine	moving
logy	study of
luna	moon
magneto	magnetic force
meter	measurer
phon	sound
photo	light
scope	see (instrument used for seeing)
son	sound
stella	star
tele	far
therm	heat

Appendix E

SI Units: Derived Units and Formulas

The units used to make quantitative measurements in science are based on SI base units

SI Base Units

Length	meter	m
Mass	kilogram	kg
Time	second	s
Temperature	kelvin	K
Amount of substance	mole	mol
Electric current	ampere	A
Luminous intensity	candela	cd

In order to measure other physical quantities, other units have been devised that are based on the SI units. Here is a summary of the derived units most commonly used in physical science. They are presented in a logical sequence since the units are often defined by using other units. This helps to show the relationships between all formulas and will aid you as you learn them.

Newton (N)

The newton is the unit for **force** and **weight.** The formula for force is:

$$F = ma$$

where F is the force in newtons (N), m is the mass in kilograms (kg), and a is the acceleration in meters per second per second (m/s^2).

The formula for weight is the same, except we substitute g for a. The constant g represents the acceleration due to gravity on earth and the value is 9.8 meters/second/second (9.8 m/s^2). Sometimes the formula is expressed as:

$$w = mg$$

where w is the force in newtons (N), m is the mass in kilograms (kg) and g is the acceleration due to gravity (9.8 m/s^2).

$$1 \text{ newton} = 1 \frac{\text{kilogram} \cdot \text{meter}}{\text{second}^2} \text{ or } N = kg \cdot m/s^2$$

Joule (J)

The joule is the unit of **work** and **energy.** One joule is equal to one newton-meter (N · m).

The formula for work is expressed as:

$$W = f \cdot d$$

where W is the work in joules, f is the force in newtons (N), and d is the distance in meters (m).

The joule is also the unit for potential energy. The formula for potential energy is:

$$PE = m \cdot g \cdot h$$

where *PE* is the potential energy in joules (J), *m* is the mass of the object in kilograms (kg), and *h* is the height of the object in meters (m).

The formula for kinetic energy is:

$$KE = \tfrac{1}{2} mv^2$$

Where *KE* is the potential energy in joules (J), *m* is the mass of the object in kilograms (kg), and *v* is the velocity of the object in meters per second (m/s).

$$1 J = N \cdot m \quad \text{or} \quad 1 J = 1 \text{ kg} \cdot \text{m/s}$$

Kilogram-Meters per Second (kg · m/s)

Newton described momentum as the "quantity of motion." Momentum is expressed in kg · m/s. The formula for momentum is:

$$p = mv$$

where *p* is the momentum, *m* is the mass in kilograms (kg), and *v* is the velocity in meters per second (m/s).

Watt (W)

Joules per second (J/s) is equivalent to a watt (W) and is the unit for **power.** The formula for power is:

$$P = w/t$$

where *P* is the power in watts (W), *w* is the work in joules (J), and *t* is the time in seconds (s).

$$1 W = 1 J/s \quad \text{or} \quad 1 W = 1 N \cdot \text{m/s}$$

Another convenient formula when solving for power: P = IV (power = current × voltage).

Coulomb (C)

The coulomb is equal to 6.25×10^{18}

electrons and is the unit of **electrical charge.**

Ampere (A) *SI unit*

The ampere, or amp, is the measurement of **current** (or electron flow) in a circuit. One amp (A) is equal to one coulomb (C) of charge moving past any given point in 1 second.

$$1 A = 1 C/s$$

Volt (V)

The volt is the measurement of **potential difference** in an electrical circuit. One volt is equal to one joule per coulomb.

$$1 V = 1 J/C$$

Ohm (Ω)

The ohm (represented by the Greek letter omega, Ω) is the unit of **electrical resistance.** One ohm is equal to 1 volt per amp.

$$1\Omega = 1 V/A$$

The relationship between current, voltage, and resistance is called *Ohm's Law* and has the formula:

$$V = IR$$

where *V* is the voltage in volts (V), *I* is the current in amps (A), and *R* is the resistance in ohms (Ω).

Pascals (Pa)

The pascal (Pa) is the unit of **pressure.** One pascal is equal to one newton per square meter (N/m^2).

The formula for pressure is:

$$P = F/A$$

where P is the pressure in pascals (Pa), F is the force in newtons (N), and A is the area in square meters (m^2).

$1 \text{ Pa} = 1\text{kg}/(\text{m} \cdot \text{s}^2)$

Square meters (m^2)
The square meter is a unit of **area.** The formula for area is:

$A = l \cdot w$

where A is the area in square meters (sm^2), l is the length in meters (m), and w is the width in meters (m). Other common units for area are often used for simplicity (cm^2, km^2).

Cubic meters (m^3)
The cubic meter is the unit of **volume.** The formula for volume is:

$V = l \cdot w \cdot h$

where V is the volume in cubic meters (m^3), l is the length in meters (m), w is the width in meters (m), and h is the height in meters (m).

The unit for **density** is kg/m^3 and is the mass per unit volume of a substance. The formula for density is:

$D = m/v$

where D is the density (kg/m^3), m is the mass in kilograms (kg), and v is the volume in m^3. Density is often expressed in grams per milliliter (g/mL).

The liter is 1000 cm^3, or 1000 mL. One m^3 is equal to 1000 liters.

Meters per second (m/s)
Meters per second is a measurement of an object's **velocity** (the rate at which an object changes position). The formula for speed, or velocity, is:

$v = d/t$

where v is the velocity in meters per second (m/s), d is the distance in meters, and t is the elapsed time in seconds (s).

Speed is also measured in m/s, but no direction is specified.

Meters per second squared (m/s^2)
The rate of increase in velocity over time is known as **acceleration.** *Deceleration* is the rate of decrease in velocity. The formula for acceleration and deceleration is

$a = \Delta v/t$

where a is the acceleration in meters per second squared (m/s^2), Δv is the change in velocity in meters per second (m/s), and t is the elapsed time in seconds (s).

Hertz (Hz)
Hertz, the measurement of cycles per second, are used to measure wave motion. One hertz (Hz) is equal to one wave per second. The velocity of a wave is mathematically related to its frequency and wavelength. The formula expressing this relationship is:

$v = f\lambda$

Where v is the velocity in meters/second (m/s), f is the frequency in hertz (Hz), and λ (the Greek letter *lambda*) is the wavelength in meters (m).

Appendix F

Physical Science Laws and Theories

Archimedes Principle (Ch. 15)
An immersed object is buoyed up by a force equal to the weight of the fluid displaced.

Bernoulli's Principle (Ch. 15)
The pressure of a fluid decreases as its speed increases.

Boyle's Law (Ch. 15)
The volume of a dry gas is inversely proportional to the pressure, assuming that the temperature remains constant. When the pressure goes up, the volume goes down.

$$V_1P_1 = V_2P_2$$

V_1 is the initial volume, P_1 is the initial pressure, V_2 is the volume after change, and P_2 is the pressure after change.

Charles's Law (Ch. 15)
If the pressure on a dry gas is kept constant, its volume will be in direct proportion to its Kelvin temperature. The hotter the gas becomes, the greater its volume will be.

$$\frac{V_1}{T_1} = \frac{V_2}{T_2}$$

V_1 is the initial volume, T_1 is the initial temperature, V_2 is the volume after the change, and T_2 is the temperature after the change.

Coulomb's Law (Ch. 2)
The force of attraction or repulsion between two charged bodies is directly proportional to the product of the two charges and inversely proportional to the square of the distance between them. Written as an equation, the relationship is:

$$F = k\,\frac{q_1q_2}{r^2}$$

where F is the force, q_1 is the magnitude of the first charge, q_2 is the magnitude of the second charge, r is the distance from the charges, and k is the proportionality constant (9×10^9 n $\cdot$ m^2/C^2).

This law is the mathematical description of the *law of charges.* It is also very similar to Newton's Law of Universal Gravitation.

Einstein's Theory of General Relativity (Ch. 6)
Mass and energy are equivalent. As energy is lost, mass is also lost. A particle's mass changes with its speed. The greater the speed, the greater the mass. This relationship is represented by the equation

$$E = mc^2$$

where E equals the energy in joules, m equals the mass, and c is the speed of light (3.00×10^8 m/s).

Hooke's Law (Ch. 13)
The more force there is on a spring, the more the spring will expand. The force on the spring is directly proportional to the stretch of the spring.

Law of Conservation of Energy (First Law of Thermodynamics) (Ch. 12)
Energy can be changed from one form to another, but it can never be created or destroyed.

Law of Conservation of Momentum (Ch. 12)
Momentum can be *transferred* from one object to another without a change in total momentum of the entire "system."

Law of Definite Composition (Ch. 5)
Every compound has its own unique molecule with its own unique combination of elements.

Law of Definite Proportions (Ch. 6)
A chemical compound is always made up of the same elements in the same proportions.

Law of Electrical Charges (Ch. 17)
Like charges repel; unlike charges attract. Positive charges are attracted to negative charges.

Law of Magnetic Poles (Ch. 18)
Like magnetic poles repel; unlike poles attract. North magnetic poles are attracted to south magnetic poles.

Law of Mass Conservation (Ch. 3)
In all chemical and physical changes, matter is neither created nor destroyed.

Law of Moments (Ch. 14)
This law applies to levers.

$$w_1 d_1 = w_2 d_2$$

In this equation, the first weight (w_1) multiplied by its distance from the fulcrum (d_1) is equal to the second weight (w_2) multiplied by its distance from the fulcrum (d_2).

For other simple machines, the *distance principle* is often applied using the same formula. It says that any reduction in the effort force that is required will be "paid for" by an increased distance through which that force must act.

Law of Reflection (Ch. 20)
For a ray of visible light, the angle of incidence is equal to the angle of reflection.

Newton's Law of Universal Gravitation (Ch. 13)
The force of gravity is directly related to the product of the masses of the two bodies. Also, it is inversely related to the relative distance between the objects *squared*. Written as an equation, the relationship is:

$$F = G \, \frac{m_1 m_2}{r^2}$$

where F is the force, m_1 is the mass of one body, m_2 is the mass of the second body, r is the distance between the center of the two masses, and G is the universal gravitational constant (6.67×10^{-11} N $\cdot$ m^2/kg^2).

Newton's First Law of Motion (Ch. 13)
Objects at rest tend to remain at rest, and objects in motion tend to stay in motion until acted upon by some outside force. The property of matter that resists a change in the state of motion is called *inertia*.

Newton's Second Law of Motion (Ch. 13)
The value of an unbalanced force is equal to its mass multiplied by its acceleration. This relationship is expressed in the equation

$$F = ma$$

Newton's Third Law of Motion (Ch. 13)
For every action, there is an equal (in strength) and opposite (in direction) reaction. This is often called the *action-reaction principle.* When a mass exerts force upon another mass, the second mass exerts an equal and opposite force upon the first mass.

Pascal's Principle (Ch. 15)
Pressure changes in a confined fluid are distributed equally in all directions throughout the fluid.

Second Law of Thermodynamics (Ch. 4, 16)
Although the total energy in the universe is conserved, it is becoming less and less available for work. The randomness and disorder (entropy) of the universe is increasing.

Glossary

A

absolute zero The temperature on the Kelvin scale at which an object would possess an absolute minimum of kinetic energy.

acceleration The rate at which velocity increases in a given amount of time.

accuracy How close a measurement is to the true value.

acid Any substance that is capable of donating protons.

acoustics The effect of materials and their shapes on sound.

action-at-a-distance forces Forces that act on an object without touching it.

action-reaction principle See **Newton's third law of motion.**

additive primary colors Red, green, blue; form various colors when mixed in different proportions. When all three are mixed, they reflect white. See **subtractive primary colors.**

alkali metals Group 1 (IA) elements that each have one valence electron.

alkaline-earth metals Group 2 (IIA) elements that each have two valence electrons.

alloy A homogeneous mixture of metals.

alpha decay A nuclear reaction in which an alpha particle is emitted.

alpha particle A particle made up of 2 protons and 2 neutrons; a helium nucleus.

alternating current (AC) An electric current that regularly changes the direction of its flow.

amalgam A solution with a liquid solute and a solid solvent.

ammeter A device that measures the current flowing through a circuit.

amorphous solid A solid in which the particles are held in random placement.

Ampere (A or amp) The unit used to measure the amount of current that flows past a point in one second.

amplification The process of increasing the magnitude of a quantity such as voltage or current.

amplitude The distance that a wave rises or falls from its normal rest position.

amplitude modulation (AM) Varying the amplitude of a transmitted electromagnetic wave in accordance with the sounds impressed upon it.

analysis Breaking down materials into simpler substances for study.

analyze Looking for relationships among data.

angle of incidence The angle between the incident ray and the normal.

angle of reflection The angle between the reflected ray and the normal.

angstrom 10^{-10} meter; a hundred-millionth of a centimeter.

anion An ion with a negative charge.

applied science Scientific activities directed toward solving specific problems.

Archimedes' principle The buoyant force exerted on a body in a fluid is equal to the weight of the fluid displaced.

armature The rotating electromagnet in an electric motor.

Arrhenius acid or base Defines acid as a substance that increases the concentration of H^+ when dissolved in water and a base as a substance that increases the concentration of OH^- when dissolved in water.

atmosphere A unit of gas pressure equivalent to 760 mm of mercury on a barometer.

atom The fundamental particle of an element.

atomic mass The total of the masses of the particles in an atom.

atomic mass unit (amu) A unit used to measure the mass an atom; 1/12 of the mass of a carbon-12 atom.

atomic number The number of protons in the nucleus of an atom.

B

balance An instrument for measuring mass.

barometer A device used to measure atmospheric pressure.

base Any substance that is capable of accepting a proton.

basic salt A salt that contains a hydroxide ion.

battery A device that chemically pumps electrons through a circuit.

beam A very large number of individual light waves.

beat The destructive interference of two sound waves with slightly different frequencies and similar amplitudes.

Bernoulli's principle States that the pressure of a fluid decreases as its speed increases.

beta decay A nuclear reaction in which a beta particle is emitted.

beta particle A free electron emitted from a nucleus in nuclear decay.

bias A mental leaning or inclination.

binary compound A compound that is composed of two different elements.

block and tackle An arrangement of fixed and movable pulleys connected by ropes; has a high mechanical advantage.

boiling The rapid phase change from liquid to gas.

boiling point The temperature at which a material changes rapidly from liquid to gas.

boiling point elevation The effect whereby a solute raises the boiling point of the solvent in which it is dissolved.

Boyle's law The volume of a dry gas is inversely proportional to the pressure it exerts, if the temperature remains constant.

Bronsted-Lowery theory of acids The theory that defines an acid as a proton donor; developed by J. N. Bronsted and T. M. Lowery.

Brownian movement The constant random motion of particles in a liquid or a gas.

buoyant force An upward push on matter exerted by a fluid.

C

caloric theory A theory that defined thermal energy as a substance that flowed from hot bodies into cold bodies.

calorie (cal) The amount of thermal energy required to increase the temperature of 1 g of water 1 degree C.

Calorie (Cal) 1000 calories.

candela The metric unit of light intensity.

capacitor An object or device that stores an electric charge.

cation An ion with a positive charge.

Celsius scale A temperature scale based on the properties of water. The Celsius scale has 100 degrees between the freezing point and the boiling point of pure water.

chain reaction A nuclear change that occurs when one unstable nucleus emits neutrons, which cause other nuclei to split and release neutrons, which hit other nuclei and continue the reaction, releasing a tremendous amount of energy.

Charles's law The volume of a gas at constant pressure is directly proportional to its Kelvin temperature.

chart A table of information arranged for convenient analysis.

chemical bond The attraction that holds atoms together.

chemical change A change in a material that alters its identity.

chemical composition The elemental makeup of a material.

chemical energy Energy that is stored in the position of electrons in an atom.

chemical formula A shorthand method of expressing the makeup of a compound (pure substance).

chemical property A property that describes how matter will react and change in the presence of other kinds of matter.

circuit A circular conducting path.

circuit breaker A safety device that switches to break a circuit if current becomes too high.

circuit load The resistance of an electrical device.

classify To put into groups.

coefficient A number placed before a formula to balance an equation.

coherent light Light in which all waves have the same length and oscillate together.

colloids Heterogeneous mixtures in which particles of one substance are partially dispersed in another substance.

color Our perceptions of the different frequencies of visible light as red, orange, yellow, green, blue, indigo, and violet.

communication Sharing data and conclusions with others.

commutator A split metal ring that rotates with the wire coil in a DC electric motor to change the direction of the magnetic field.

compound A substance formed when two or more atoms of different elements chemically join together.

compressibility How much more the atoms of an object/substance can be packed together.

compression A region where air molecules are pushed closer together than normal by the energy of a sound wave.

concave mirror A mirror that curves like the inner surface of a sphere.

conclusion An answer that seems to best fit the data analysis.

condensation The phase change from gas to liquid.

condensation point The temperature at which a material changes from gas to liquid.

conduction The flow of thermal energy from an object to another object through contact.

conductor Any substance that will allow the flow of thermal energy; in electricity, a substance that holds its valence electrons loosely, allowing the flow of electricity.

conservation principles The principles that govern the way matter and energy are interchanged; that matter and energy cannot be created or destroyed.

constructive interference The inphase reinforcement of waves as they pass through each other.

control group In an experiment, the group that experiences no change in the variable.

convection The flow of thermal energy from one place to another by the movement of particles.

convection current A mass of moving particles that carries thermal energy.

coulomb (C) The unit of electrical charge.

covalent bond A chemical bond formed by atoms sharing electrons.

Creationism The view that the universe was spoken into existence by the miraculous acts described in Genesis 1 and 2.

Creationist One who believes the biblical account of the Creation.

crest The highest point on a wave.

crystal lattice A solid structure formed by a regular alternating pattern of positive and negative ions.

crystalline solid A solid in which the particles are held in a fixed repeating pattern.

Curie temperature The temperature at which a permanent magnet loses its magnetic field.

current The flow of charges.

current electricity The effects produced by moving charges.

cycle One complete wave motion.

D

data (singular, **datum**) Scientific information.

deceleration The rate at which velocity decreases in a given period of time.

decibel (db) The smallest difference in intensity between two sounds that the human ear is capable of detecting.

declination The correction of values between true north and magnetic north for any given location.

degree A unit of temperature.

density The mass in a unit of volume.

desalination A technological process that removes salt from seawater so that it is fit for human consumption.

destructive interference The out-of-phase cancellation of waves as they pass through each other.

diatomic molecule A molecule formed of two identical atoms bonded together.

diffusion The process of mixing by particle motion.

dipole A molecule that has both negatively and positively charged poles caused by the unequal distribution of electrons.

direct current (DC) An electric current that flows in only one direction.

direct proportion A relationship in which one value increases as the other value increases.

dispersion The separation of white light into different-colored light waves.

displacement A change in position of an object.

dissociation The process whereby a solvent breaks up an ionic solid.

distance principle States that any reduction in the effort force will be paid for by an increased distance through which that force must act.

domains Microscopic regions of materials that may be lined up to produce a magnetic field of force.

Doppler effect The effect of motion on sound; named in honor of the Austrian physicist Christian Doppler.

double bonds Occur when two pairs of electrons are shared in a covalent bond.

ductile Capable of being drawn into wire.

dynamics The branch of mechanics that describes why things move.

E

echocardiogram Ultrasound image of the heart. See **sonagram.**

efficiency The percent of work input returned as useful output.

effort The force that must be applied to a simple machine to make it produce work.

effort arm The distance from the fulcrum to the effort.

electrical energy Energy that is associated with the flow of charged particles through a conductor.

electrical potential A measure of the electrical charge on an object.

electric field of force The sum of the strengths and directions of the electric forces at all the points around an electrical source.

electricity The attraction of unlike charges and repulsion of similar charges based on the relative amounts of positively charged protons and negatively charged electrons. See also **static electricity** and **current electricity.**

electric motor A device that uses the force between magnets to produce mechanical energy from electrical energy.

electrolysis A decomposition reaction that decomposes the reactants by an electric current in solution.

electrolyte A solute that ionizes in solution and conducts electricity.

electromagnet A solenoid with a core of magnetic material.

electromagnetic waves Energy in wave form that is capable of traveling through a vacuum: radio waves, microwaves, etc.

electron A negatively charged particle with an extremely small mass.

electron configuration The number and position of electrons in the energy levels of an atom.

electron dot notation A method of representing atoms and ions that uses an element's symbol for the nucleus and inner electrons and a series of dots for the valence electrons.

electronegativity The measure of how strongly an atom holds its electrons.

electron orbital The probable location of a specific electron in an energy level.

electroscope A device that detects charges.

element Any substance that cannot be broken down into simpler substances by ordinary chemical means.

endothermic reaction A reaction that requires thermal energy.

energy The ability to do work.

energy level A region in an atom that contains electrons of a certain energy.

entropy The amount of disorder and randomness in a system; unusable energy.

equilibrium In the context of heat flow, the state at which thermal energy is no longer being transferred.

evaporation The phase change from liquid to gas.

evolution The belief that the physical universe somehow structured itself out of self-existing matter, and that its parts continue to organize themselves into more complex structures as time progresses.

evolutionist One who attempts to explain the origin of things by theories of gradual development.

exothermic reaction A reaction that gives off thermal energy.

experiment A carefully designed arrangement for testing a specific hypothesis.

experimental group In an experiment, the group where the variable is altered.

F

family A vertical column on the periodic table; also called a group.

ferromagnetic Strongly attracted to magnets.

filling order The order in which electrons are added to the energy levels of an atom.

first-class lever A lever in which the fulcrum is located between the effort and the resistance.

first law of thermodynamics Energy may be converted from one form to another but cannot be created or destroyed.

fission The splitting of a nucleus.

fluids Liquid or gas phases of matter.

fluid mechanics The study of fluid movement and forces.

focal length The distance from a lens to its principal focus.

force A push or a pull that acts on an object.

formula equation An equation that uses symbols to represent a reaction.

formula unit The basic repeating unit of an ionic solid.

frame of reference A system of reference points from which the position and motion of an object can be determined.

free electron theory A description of metallic bonding that uses randomly shared electrons to explain the properties of metals.

freezing The phase change from liquid to solid.

freezing point depression The effect whereby a solute lowers the freezing point of the solvent in which it is dissolved.

frequency The number of waves that pass a given point in one second.

frequency modulation (FM) Varying the frequency of a transmitted electromagnetic wave in accordance with the sounds impressed upon it.

friction A force that opposes the motion of an object.

fulcrum The fixed point about which a lever turns.

fundamental The lowest tone that a vibrating object produces.

fuse A safety device that melts to break a circuit if current becomes too high.

fusion The joining together of smaller nuclei into a larger one.

G

galvanization A process by which a metal is coated with a thin layer of zinc.

galvanometer A device that measures very slight changes in electric current.

gamma rays A form of radiation consisting of high-energy electromagnetic waves; electromagnetic waves that originate in the nucleus of an atom; the type of electromagnetic waves with the highest frequencies.

gas The state of matter in which the disruptive forces completely overcome the attractive forces, allowing particles unlimited movement.

gas pressure Force exerted on a unit of area by gas particles colliding with a surface.

generator A device that uses magnetic fields to convert mechanical energy into electrical energy.

geographic north pole Point at the "top of the world" where the axis of the Earth spins. See **magnetic north pole.**

graph A visual way to show relationships among data.

gravity The attraction that any object in the universe has toward other objects in the universe.

group Another name for a family on the periodic table.

H

halogens Reactive elements in Group 17 (VIIA) that have seven valence electrons.

heat The kinetic energy present within the particles of matter; the transfer of thermal energy.

heat of fusion The amount of thermal energy needed to change a substance from its solid phase to its liquid phase.

heat of vaporization The amount of thermal energy needed to change a substance from its liquid phase to its gaseous phase.

Henry's law The greater the pressure on a liquid, the greater the amount of gas that will remain dissolved in that liquid at any given temperature.

hertz (Hz) The unit of frequency; one cycle per second.

heterogeneous mixture A mixture with different appearances in different parts.

homogeneous mixture A mixture that appears the same throughout.

Hooke's law The stretch of a spring is directly proportional to the force on the spring.

humanism The philosophy that considers man the center of all things and the ultimate authority in the universe.

hydration The process of surrounding solute particles with solvent molecules.

hydraulic machines Machines which use fluid to transmit or increase force.

hydronium ion The ion formed by the donation of a hydrogen ion to a water molecule; H_3O^+.

hydroponics A type of gardening in which plants are grown in special liquid solutions.

hydroxide ion A polyatomic ion with a negative charge, consisting of an oxygen atom and a hydrogen ion; OH^-.

hypothesis (plural, **hypotheses**) An educated guess at the solution of a problem.

I

incandescent Heated to glowing.

incident ray An incoming ray (toward the reflecting surface).

inclined plane A slanted surface used to raise objects.

indicator An organic compound that shows a definite color change when it reacts with an acid or a base.

induction Charging an object by shifting the paths of its electrons.

inertia The property of matter that causes objects to resist change in the state of motion.

infrared waves Electromagnetic waves with frequencies lower than visible light but greater than radio waves.

infrasonic Sound waves that are too low in frequency for the human ear to hear. See **ultrasonic.**

insulator A substance that does not conduct electricity or heat very well.

intensity The measure of how bright the light from a light source is or the loudness of sound.

interference The interaction of waves as they pass through each other.

inverse proportion A relationship in which one value increases as the other value decreases.

inverse square law Illumination is inversely proportional to the square of the distance from the light source.

ion A charged atom or group of atoms formed by the loss or gain of electrons.

ionic bond A chemical bond in which electrons are transferred from one atom to another.

ionization The process of splitting a molecule into charged particles.

isotopes Different forms of the same element that have different numbers of neutrons.

J

joule (J) The SI unit of energy; equal to 1 Newton-meter of work.

K

kelvin (K) The basic unit of temperature in the metric system.

Kelvin scale A temperature scale that begins at absolute zero.

kilogram (kg) The mass of a liter of water; 1000 grams.

kilowatt (kW) 1000 watts.

kinematics The branch of mechanics that describes how things move.

kinetic energy The energy of motion.

kinetic theory The theory of matter that describes the states of matter in terms of attractive forces and kinetic energy.

kinetic theory of thermal energy Identifies the thermal energy of an object with the motion of its particles.

L

laser A device that produces a narrow beam of coherent, monochromatic light; light amplification by the stimulated emission of radiation.

law A statement of a consistent pattern of phenomena in nature; a theory that has been verified through numerous experiments and observations.

law of charges Like charges repel; unlike charges attract.

law of conservation of energy Energy can be changed from one form to another but can neither be created nor destroyed.

law of definite composition Every compound has its own unique molecule with its own unique combination of elements.

law of definite proportions A chemical compound is always made up of the same elements in the same proportions.

law of magnetic poles Unlike magnetic poles attract and like magnetic poles repel.

law of mass conservation In all chemical and physical changes, matter is neither created nor destroyed.

law of moments The method for computing the amount of force exerted by levers with unequal arms; $w_1d_1 = w_2d_2$

law of reflection The angle of incidence must be equal to the angle of reflection.

law of the conservation of momentum Without outside influence, the total momentum of objects before a change must equal the total momentum of the objects after a change.

lens A transparent object that uses the property of refraction to magnify or reduce images.

lever A rigid bar capable of turning about a fulcrum. See **first class lever, second class lever,** and **third class lever.**

Lewis dot structures See **electron dot notation.**

light Electromagnetic radiation of any wavelength, but usually used in relation to visible light or ultraviolet light.

light energy The energy produced by various wavelengths of the electromagnetic spectrum.

light-year The distance light travels in a year.

lines of force Show the direction the electrical force will move a positive charge.

line spectrum A display of the various frequencies of light emitted by a source.

liquid The state of matter in which the attractive forces and the disruptive forces are balanced, allowing particles limited movement.

liter (L) The volume of a cubic decimeter.

load The resistive devices in an electrical circuit.

lodestone Naturally magnetic mineral.

longitudinal wave A wave whose vibration is in the same direction that it is traveling.

loudness Related to intensity; how strong or weak a sound is to an observer.

lubricant A substance used to reduce the friction between surfaces.

M

magnet An object that is surrounded by a magnetic field and is attracted to ferromagnetic material such as iron and steel.

magnetic energy Energy that is stored in a magnet and its surrounding field.

magnetic field of force The sum of the strengths and directions of the magnetic forces at all the points around a magnetic source.

magnetic north pole Point in Canada where the earth's magnetic field is concentrated. See **geographic north pole.**

magnetosphere Another name for the earth's magnetic field.

malleable Capable of being hammered or rolled.

mass The quantity of matter in an object.

mass number The sum of the protons and neutrons in the nucleus of an atom; also known as atomic mass.

matter Anything that has mass and volume.

mechanical advantage (M.A.) The amount by which a machine magnifies effort (force).

mechanical energy The energy that an object possesses because of its motion or its potential to move.

mechanical waves Rhythmic disturbances of a medium: sound waves, water waves, etc.

mechanics The study of motion.

melting The phase change from solid to liquid.

melting point The temperature at which a material changes from solid to liquid.

meniscus Curve seen at a liquid's surface, especially in a graduated cylinder.

metal An element that tends to give up electrons in a chemical reaction.

metallic bond A chemical bond in which metal atoms are thought to randomly share their valence electrons.

metallic luster The shiny appearance of freshly cut or polished metal.

metalloid A substance that has properties of both metals and nonmetals.

meter (m) The basic unit of length of the metric system; 39.37 inches.

metric system A decimal system of measurements based on the meter; SI.

microwaves Electromagnetic waves with wavelengths from 0.3 cm to 30 cm, and with frequencies that range from 10^9 Hz to 10^{11} Hz.

miscibility The property that allows two liquids to be soluble in each other.

mixture A physical combination of two or more pure substances.

modulation The impressing of sound or patterns of light on a transmitted wave.

molecule A particle made up of two or more atoms chemically joined together; a particle formed by a limited number of atoms bonded covalently; the basic unit of a covalent compound.

momentum Mass multiplied by velocity; a quantity of motion.

monochromatic Luminous objects (such as a laser) that reflect only one wavelength and frequency of light. See **visible light, laser,** and **line spectrum.**

moral judgment A decision made on the basis of right and wrong.

mutation-selection theory The belief that living things evolved from more primitive life forms by random changes in the DNA.

N

nanometer 10^{-9} meters.

natural frequency The frequency at which objects prefer to vibrate.

neutralization The reaction between an acid and a base that produces a salt and water.

neutron A neutral particle in the nucleus of an atom, with approximately the same mass as a proton.

newton (N) The metric unit of weight.

Newton's first law of motion Objects at rest tend to remain at rest, and objects in motion tend to remain in motion (in the same direction and at the same speed) until acted on by some outside, unbalanced force.

Newton's second law of motion The value of an unbalanced force (F) is equal to its mass (m) multiplied by its acceleration (a).

Newton's third law of motion For every action there is an equal and opposite reaction.

noble gases Stable elements found in Group 18 (VIIIA) that have eight valence electrons.

nonelectrolyte A solute that does not ionize in solution and will not conduct electricity.

nonmetal An element that tends to gain electrons in a chemical reaction; poor conductor of heat and electricity.

nonpolar molecule A molecule that does not have electrical poles.

normal An imaginary line drawn perpendicular to the surface of a mirror.

normal salt A salt that is chemically neutral.

nuclear bombardment reaction Occurs when the nucleus is struck with atomic particles or other nuclei.

nuclear change A change that occurs in the makeup and energy of the nucleus of an atom.

nuclear chemistry The study of reactions involving atomic nuclei.

nuclear energy The energy that is stored in the nucleus of an atom.

nucleus The center of an atom, which contains protons and neutrons.

nuclide symbol A special notation for isotopes that shows both the atomic number and the mass number.

O

observation The collection of data through the use of the senses.

ohm (Ω) The unit used to measure resistance.

ohmmeter A device that measures resistance.

Ohm's law Voltage equals the current multiplied by the resistance.

orbitals Regions of most probable location of electrons. See **quantum model.**

oscillation A regular back-and-forth motion of electrons in a circuit.

overtone A multiple of a fundamental tone.

oxidation numbers Symbols that indicate the number of electrons that an element gains or loses as it bonds.

P

parallel circuit A circuit with two or more paths for the electrons in it to follow.

paramagnetic Slightly attracted to magnets.

particle model A model of matter in which all matter is made up of tiny particles in constant motion.

pascal (Pa) Unit of pressure equal to one newton of force over a square meter (N/m^2).

percentage by mass A method of expressing the concentration of a solute as a percentage of the total mass of the solution.

period A horizontal row in the periodic table, also called a series.

periodic law The chemical properties of the elements are periodic functions of their atomic numbers.

periodic table A table of the elements arranged by atomic number into vertical columns called families or groups, and horizontal rows called periods.

phase change A physical change in the state of a material caused by a change in temperature.

phenomenon (plural, **phenomena**) Any fact, circumstance, or experience that is apparent to the senses.

Photorefractive keratectomy (PRK) Using laser beams to reshape the eye and improve vision.

photosynthesis Process that plants use to convert light energy into chemical energy.

pH scale A scale that is used to indicate the relative concentrations of hydronium ions in a solution.

physical change A change in a material that does not alter its identity.

physical property A property that can be observed and measured without changing the kind of matter being studied.

physical universe The totality of matter and energy created by God.

picture tube A large vacuum tube that changes electrical impulses to light patterns in a television set.

piston A solid cylinder that slides within another cylinder.

pitch The distance between two adjacent threads on a screw; how high or low a tone sounds to an observer (related to frequency).

plane mirror A flat mirror.

plasma The state of matter in which particles travel at such tremendous speeds that they become electrically charged.

polar molecule A molecule that has partially charged electrical poles.

polyatomic ion A group of several atoms that act as a single charged particle.

potential difference The difference of the electrical potential between two places.

potential drop See **potential difference.**

potential energy The energy of position; stored energy.

power The amount of work done in a given period of time; $P = W/t$.

precipitate A solid formed during a reaction; insoluble in water.

precision The degree of agreement between replicate measurements of the same quantity.

prejudice Discarding evidence because of a strongly held bias.

pressure The force pushing directly on a given surface.

principal focus A point through which the rays reflected or refracted from a surface will pass.

prism A triangular block of glass that is used to separate visible light into various colors.

product A substance (on the right hand side of the equation) that is produced by a chemical change.

proton A positively charged particle in the nucleus of an atom; 1836 times heavier than an electron.

pulley A modified lever consisting of a rope that moves around a grooved wheel; can be movable or fixed.

pure science Scientific activities motivated by interest or curiosity and performed to gain knowledge for its own sake.

pure substance A substance that is made up of only one kind of particle and is the same throughout.

Q

qualitative data Descriptive information not involving numbers.

quality A subjective value dependent on the mixture of tones and overtones in a particular sound.

quantitative data Measurable or numerical information.

quantum model Represents the location of electrons as general and indefinite, with electrons being present in cloud-like orbitals.

R

radar Radio detection and ranging devices that detect objects through the transmission and reflection of microwaves off of surfaces.

radiation The transportation of thermal energy without the use of matter.

radioactivity The emission of rays and particles from an unstable nucleus.

radio astronomy The study of radio waves emitted by astronomical objects.

radiocarbon dating A method for finding the approximate age of once-living material by measuring its carbon-14 content.

radio waves Electromagnetic waves with wavelengths between 1 and 10 m long and with frequencies below those of visible light waves.

rarefaction A region where the air molecules are spread apart by the energy of a sound wave.

rays Representations of the directions of light waves.

reactant A substance (on the left-hand side of an equation) that undergoes a chemical change.

reaction mechanism A theoretical explanation of how individual atoms behave during a chemical reaction.

real image An image that is produced in front of the plane of a mirror.

rectification Changing alternating current to direct current.

reflected ray An outgoing ray (away from the reflecting surface).

reflection The return of waves after striking a surface.

refraction The bending of waves as they pass from one medium into another.

relay A switch used to turn solenoids on or off.

resistance The force against which a simple machine works; opposition to the flow of electrons.

resistance arm The distance from the fulcrum to the resistance.

resistor Any object that resists the flow of electricity.

resonance The transfer of energy from one object to another object with the same natural frequency.

reverberations Multiple echoes of sound.

R-value A measurement of the insulating ability of a substance. See **insulator.**

S

salt A substance that is formed from the negative ion of an acid and the positive ion of a base.

saturated Containing the maximum amount of a solute that can be dissolved in a given amount of solvent under normal conditions.

scalar Quantities that express magnitude only.

science The systematic use of observations to describe the physical universe.

scientific idealization Approximating an answer when an extremely accurate one is not needed.

scientific method A systematic way of solving a problem by making observations.

scientific notation Using the power of 10 to express very large or very small numbers.

screw An inclined plane wound around a cylinder or cone.

second (s) The basic unit of time; 9,192,631,770 vibrations of a cesium atom.

second-class lever A lever in which the resistance is located between the fulcrum and the effort.

second law of thermodynamics Although the total energy in the universe is conserved, it is becoming less and less available for work.

semiconductor A substance that holds its electrons in a way that allows a partial flow of electricity.

series Another name for a period in the periodic table.

series circuit A circuit with a single path for all the electrons in it to follow.

short circuit A situation in which an electrical current passes through a path shorter than the entire circuit.

SI The abbreviation for the expanded metric system called *Systéme International* (French for International System).

significant digits (figures) All of the certain digits plus one doubtful digit in a measurement.

simple machine One- or two-part devices that make work easier: lever, wheel and axle, pulley, inclined plane, wedge, screw.

solar sailing Using the force of light waves to propel objects through space.

solenoid Coiled wires used to form a magnet.

solid The state of matter in which the attractive forces limit the particles to vibrating in place.

solubility The maximum amount of a solute that can dissolve in a given amount of solvent under normal conditions.

soluble Dissolvable.

solute The substance that is dissolved in a solution.

solution A homogeneous mixture of two or more substances.

solvent The substance that does the dissolving in a solution.

sonagram An image produced by ultrasonic waves reflecting off organs within the human body. See **echocardiogram** and **ultrasonic.**

sonar A type of listening device that uses sound waves to locate objects; sound navigation and ranging. See **ultrasonic.**

sound Mechanical waves that can often be detected by our ears.

sound energy Energy that is produced by vibrating matter and transmitted through a medium.

specific gravity A method of determining the concentration of a solution by comparing the density of the solution to the density of water.

specific heat The amount of thermal energy needed to raise the temperature of 1 g of a substance 10 C.

spectator ion An ion that is present in a solution where a reaction is taking place but which does not participate in the reaction.

speed The rate at which an object changes position.

speed of light (c) 300,000,000 m/s.

spring scale An instrument for measuring weight.

static electricity The effects produced by stationary charges.

stationary electric charges Electric charges that are at rest.

step-down transformer A series of coils that uses induction to produce a lower voltage.

step-up transformer A series of coils that uses induction to produce a higher voltage.

subgroup One of the families of transition elements.

sublimation The phase change directly from solid to gas or from gas to solid.

subscript A small number placed beside the symbol of an element in a formula to indicate the number of atoms of that element contained in the compound represented by that formula.

subtractive primary colors Yellow, cyan, and magenta; when they are mixed in various proportions, they absorb all other colors except the one that is reflected. When all three are mixed together, they absorb every color, showing black. See **additive primary colors.**

superconducting magnet A magnet made from special materials and kept at extremely low temperatures.

supersaturated Having dissolved more than the normal amount of solute in a given amount of solvent.

survey The process of gathering data about an existing situation or object.

suspension A heterogeneous mixture consisting of small particles spread throughout a liquid or gaseous medium, from which they will eventually settle out.

switch A device that can be used to break (open or close) a circuit.

symbol A scientific abbreviation for the name of an element; consists of one or two letters with the first letter always capitalized.

synthesizer A device that converts electrical signals into sound waves; able to reproduce sounds from many musical instruments.

T

technology The practical application of scientific knowledge.

teleology The study of design or purpose in nature.

temperature The measure of the average kinetic energy in a material.

terminal velocity The limit of the velocity at which an object can fall through a gas or a liquid.

ternary compound A compound that is composed of three or more different elements.

theistic evolution The attempted harmonization of evolution with belief in a god.

theory A partially verified idea that relates a number of different observations.

theory of relativity $E=mc^2$; an equation that establishes the relationship between loss of mass and loss of energy; that mass and energy are equivalent.

thermal energy The total energy of the particles in an object related to the motion of the molecules or ions in matter.

thermal expansion An increase in the volume of a substance caused by the addition of thermal energy.

thermodynamics The branch of physics that deals with thermal energy.

thermography Using infrared radiation to diagnose and detect human disease.

third-class lever A lever in which the effort is applied between the fulcrum and the resistance.

threshold of hearing The very softest sound level that can be detected by an observer.

transition elements Strong metals in Groups 3-12 (IB through VIIIB).

transuranium element An element with an atomic number higher than that of uranium.

transverse wave A wave whose vibration is at right angles to the direction in which it is traveling.

triple bond A bond in which three pairs of electrons are shared by the elements.

trough The lowest point on a wave.

Tyndall effect When light passes through a liquid, the light will not be dispersed; an observation showing the presence of a true solution.

U

ultrasonic Sound waves that are too high in frequency for the human ear to hear. See **infrasonic, sonagram** and **sonar.**

ultraviolet light Electromagnetic waves that are just beyond visible light in frequency.

unbalanced forces The unequal forces on an object that cause the object to move.

unit analysis A mathematical tool for converting units.

universal statement An absolute statement using "all" or "none."

unsaturated Capable of dissolving more of a solute.

V

valence electrons The electrons in the outermost energy level of an atom.

value judgment A decision regarding the rightness, beauty, worth, or some other immeasurable characteristic of an object or action.

Van de Graaff generator A metal sphere with a pulley driven device capable of generating a tremendous amount of static electrical charge.

vector Quantities that express magnitude and direction.

velocity The rate at which an object changes position in a specified direction. See **terminal velocity.**

verification The process of testing the correctness of a solution.

virtual image The images that appear to exist beyond a mirror.

viscosity The thickness of a fluid.

visible light Electromagnetic waves with wavelengths ranging from 4×10^{-1} cm to 7×10^{-5} cm, and with frequencies ranging from 4.5×10^{14} Hz to 7.5×10^{14} Hz; the portion of radiant energy that can be sensed by our eyes. See also **light.**

voltage The amount of push needed to cause electrons to move between two points.

voltmeter A device that measures the potential difference between two points in a circuit.

volume Any space defined by length, width, and height.

W

water displacement method Measuring the volume of an irregularly shaped object by submerging it in water contained in a graduated cylinder and taking before-and-after measurements.

watt (W) The SI unit of power; 1 joule of energy per second.

wavelength (λ) The distance between adjacent troughs or peaks.

waves Rhythmic disturbances that transfer energy through space or matter.

weak electrolyte A solute that can ionize only partially and conducts electricity weakly.

wedge Two inclined planes placed "back-to-back."

weight The measure of the force of gravity on an object.

wheel and axle Modified lever in which the effort arm and the resistance arm revolve around a central fulcrum.

word equation An equation that uses words to represent a reaction.

work The product of the force applied on an object multiplied by the distance the object moved; $w = F \times d$.

X

X-ray astronomy The study of astronomical objects using X rays instead of visible light.

X rays Electromagnetic waves with frequencies higher than ultraviolet light; strong enough to penetrate body tissues.

Index

opal, 59
Oppenheimer, Robert, 130
organ of Corti, 445
origins See Creationism, evolution
osmium, 58
osmosis, 224-25
osteoporosis, 60
overtone, 442
oxalic acid, 241
oxidation numbers, 186-88
    definition, 186
    electronegativity, 187
    multiple, 187
    of common elements, 187
    polyatomic ions, 193
oxygen, 79, 95
    diatomic, 93
    dissolved in water, 231
    in air, 143, 146
    oxidation number, 187-88
    rocket fuel, 75
    symbol, 92
oxygen family, 146
ozone, 13

P

paper, 58
parallel circuit, 403
paramagnetic, 416
particle accelerator, 430
particle model, 71
Pascal (Pa), 337
Pascal's principle, 340
pendulum, 41
percentage by mass, 215, 233
pericardial fluid, 332
pericardium, 332
period, 151
periodic law, 137
periodic table
    conductivity of elements, 155, 157
    development, 134-38
    families (groups), 142-43, 149-50
    periods (series), 151-53
    subgroups, 146

    transition elements, 146
    transuranium elements, 149
Permasep filter, 224
perpetual motion, 278-79
phase change See matter, solid, liquid, gas
pH scale, 247, 253, 256-57
phenomenon (plural, phenomena), 7
philosophy, 7, 8
phosphate ion, 193
phosphoric acid, 238, 247
phosphorus, 146
Photorefractive keratectomy (PRK), 485
photosynthesis, 271
piezoelectric effect, 60
plane mirror, 486
planets, 73
plasma
    characteristics, 80
    in nuclear fusion, 128
    neon lights, 80
platinum
    density, 59
plutonium, 149
polar molecule, 222
pollution
    in acid rain, 254-55
    remedies, 255
polyatomic ion, 193
potassium, 143
potassium hydroxide, 249
potassium permanganate, 72
potential difference See also volt, voltage
    measurement of, 400
potential energy
    calculation, 265
    definition, 265
power
    and electrical energy, 407
    definition, 333
    measurement, 333
precipitate, 209, 227
precision, 64
prejudice, 12

pressure
    fluid, 337
    formula, 337
    gas, 350-51
    measurement, 337
principal focus, 487
prism, 470
problem, 21
product, 198
protein, 100
proton, 112
pulley, 324
    block and tackle, 325
    fixed, 324
    movable, 324
    mechanical advantage, 324
pure science, 5
pure substance, 98

Q

qualitative data, 23
quality, 437
quantitative data, 23
quantum model, 113
quartz, 60, 69

R

radar, 469
radiation See also waves; electromagnetic spectrum
    nuclear, 119
    thermal, 372-73
radio
    AM/FM, 467
    transmitter, 468
radioactive dating
    carbon-14, 125
    limitations, 125
    types of, 124-25
radioactivity
    definition, 119
    discovery, 119
radio astronomy, 468
radio telescope, 468
radio waves, 467
radium, 143
    in minerals, 146
    properties, 146

melting point, 378
superconductor, 431
Titanic, 453
Townes, Charles, 6
transition elements, 146
transuranium element, 149
transverse wave, 462
Trinity test site, 130
triple bond, 174
tritium, 128
trough, 459
Truman, Harry S., 131
truth, 34
tungsten, 409
turbine, 70, 423
tympanic membrane, 445
Tyndall effect, 101

U

ultrasonic, 440
ultraviolet light, 472
unit analysis, 48
universal statement, 33
University of California (Berkeley), 149
uranium
beta decay, 149
in atomic weapons, 130
nuclear energy, 127
radioactive dating, 125

V

vacuum, 459
valence electrons, 141
value judgment, 8
Van Allen belts, 80
Van de Graaff generator, 390-91
Van de Graaff, Robert, 390
vector, 288
velocity, 288
acceleration, 288
deceleration, 289-90
terminal, 299
verification, 26
vestigial organ, 13
vinegar, 244, 253

virtual image, 487
viscosity, 77
visible light, 470, 475-76
vitamin, 238, 241
voice, 449
volcano, 438-39
voltage, 400
volume, 54-57
volumetric flask, 57
vulcanization, 27

W

water
boiling point, 83
composition, 92
currents, 371
cycle, 51
density, 59
desalination, 224-25
formula, 97
freezing, 377
heat of fusion, 377
heat of vaporization, 378
melting point, 378
molecular structure, 97
phases, 75
polar molelcule, 222, 388
specific heat, 376
sublimation, 84
waves, 458
water displacement method, 57
watt (W), 333, 407
Watt, James, 374
wavelength (λ), 460
waves
characteristics, 459-60
electromagnetic, 459
longitudinal, 435
mechanical, 459
reflection, 484
refraction, 488
sound, 435
transverse, 462
velocity, 461
weak electrolyte, 170
weather balloon, 78
wedge, 328
weight, 52-53
wheel and axle, 323
Winkler, Clemens, 136

wood
electrical conductivity, 393
thermal expansion, 382
Wood's metal, 219
word equation, 197
work
definition, 309
measurement, 311

X

xenon, 32
X-ray astronomy, 473
X rays
discovery, 472
uses, 473

Photograph Credits

The following agencies and individuals have furnished materials to meet the photographic needs of this textbook. We wish to express our gratitude to them for their important contribution.

AIP Niels Bohr Library
AJC Staff Photo
Almaden Research Center
Aluminum Company of America (ALCOA)
American Iron and Steel Institute
Andersen Windows, Inc.
Arizona State University
Association of Universities for Research in Astronomy, Inc. (AURA)
Dr. Jerry Bouquot
Cal Tech
Bureau International des Poids & Measures
Bureau of Reclamation
George R. Collins
Corbis
Corel Corporation
Jan Curtis
Terry M. Davenport
Digital Stock
James Donovan
Duke Power
Earthquake Engineering Research Center
Eastman Chemicals Division
Edgar Fahs Smith Collection
Don F. Figer
Films for Christ
Dave Fisher
A. Fruchter
General Electric Co.
Geophysical Institute
Godden Collection
Goodyear Tire and Rubber Co.
Jeff Hester
Hubble Heritage Team
IBM Corporation

The ITER Project
John Jenkins
Jet Propulsion Lab (JPL)
Ellyson and Manda Kalagayan
William Keller
Lawrence Berkeley National Laboratory
The Maxillofacial Center, Morgantown, WV
National Aeronautics and Space Administration (NASA)
National Archives
National Institute of Standards and Technology (NIST)
National Space Science Data Center (NSSDC)
Ohaus Corporation
PPC Industries Electrostatic Precipitators, Inc.
PhotoDisc, Inc.
Sgt. Russ Pollanen
STS-68 Crew
Paul Scowen
Jean Shifrin
Six Flags over Georgia
Smithsonian
Soil Conservation Service
Space Telescope Science Institute (STScI)
John William Strutt
United States Air Force Photo
United States Department of Agriculture (USDA)
United States Department of Defense and Technology
University of Alaska
University of California, Berkeley
University of California, Los Angeles (UCLA)
University of Pennsylvania Library
Unusual Films
www.arttoday.com
Washington State Historical Society, Tacoma
Dawn L. Watkins
Yellowstone National Park

Cover/Title Page
PhotoDisc, Inc.

Contents Pages
Courtesy of NASA/JPL/Cal Tech v(top left); Corbis v(bottom left); PhotoDisc, Inc. v(right), vi(top left, right); Digital Stock vi(bottom left)

Introduction Pages
PhotoDisc, Inc. vii(both), viii, ix; NASA, A. Fruchter and the ERO Team (STScI) x

Unit 1 Opener
Courtesy of NASA/JPL/Cal Tech

Chapter 1
PhotoDisc, Inc. 2, 5, 7, 9(bottom left, bottom middle); Terry M. Davenport 3(top three); Eastman Chemicals Division 3(bottom left); Hubble Heritage Team (AURA/STSCI/NASA) and NSSDC 3(bottom right), 15(bottom); Corbis 4, 9(bottom right); Dawn L. Watkins 6, 12; Dave Fisher 8(top); Bureau of Reclamation 8(bottom); Films for Christ 11; www.arttoday.com 15(top)

Chapter 2
Dawn L. Watkins 20, 31; Unusual Films 24, 25, 28(facet), 33; Goodyear Tire and Rubber Co. 27; PhotoDisc, Inc. 28(top), 34(both); www.arttoday.com 32

Unit 2 Opener
Corbis

Chapter 3
Ohaus Corporation 40, 51(both); Bureau International des Poids & Measures 43; Unusual Films 45(all), 47(top), 55, 61(both), 63; NIST 47(bottom), 60; NASA 50; PhotoDisc, Inc. 54

Chapter 4
PhotoDisc, Inc. 68, 69, 76(left, middle), 80(left, middle), 85; Dawn L. Watkins 70, 77(all), 83(both); IBM Corporation, Research Division, Almaden Research Center 72; Unusual Films 74(all), 76(right), 78(bottom all), 82, 84; William Keller, Yellowstone National Park 75; Corel Corporation 78(top); Eastman Chemicals Division 80(right); John William Strutt, Third Baron Rayleigh. New York: Longmans, Green & Co., 1924. Courtesy AIP Niels Bohr Library 87

Chapter 5
PhotoDisc, Inc. 90, 93(bottom), 95(left); Unusual Films 91(all), 94, 95(right), 98, 101; IBM Corporation, Research Division, Almaden Research Center 92; Lawrence Berkeley National Laboratory 93(top); Dawn L. Watkins 100

Unit 3 Opener
PhotoDisc, Inc.

Chapter 6
PhotoDisc, Inc. 106, 113(top), 115, 129, 131; www.arttoday.com 108, 110, 112; Edgar Fahs Smith Collection, University of Pennsylvania Library 113(bottom); National Archives 117(both); Digital Stock 124; The ITER Project 129(Fig. 6-27); U.S. Air Force Photo 130

Chapter 7
PhotoDisc, Inc. 134, 147(top right), 148, 150, 156(both); Edgar Fahs Smith Collection, University of Pennsylvania Library 135; Unusual Films 142, 147(right margin); 153(left), 154; NASA 146; Dawn L. Watkins 147(top left); American Iron and Steel Institute 147(top middle); Dr. Jerry Bouquot, The Maxillofacial Center, Morgantown, WV 152; National Archives 153(right)

Chapter 8
PhotoDisc, Inc. 160, 161(top), 174, 175, 178(top right); Digital Stock 161(bottom); Unusual Films 164, 170(all), 178(bottom right); Dawn L. Watkins 165; USDA 176; ALCOA 178(left)

Unit 4 Opener
PhotoDisc, Inc.

Chapter 9
AJC Staff Photo/Jean Shifrin 184; George R. Collins 188; PhotoDisc, Inc. 189, 204(bottom), 207, 210; Dawn L. Watkins 193, 204(top); Unusual Films 203, 205(both), 208, 209, 211; ALCOA 206(all)

Chapter 10
PhotoDisc, Inc. 214, 216, 217, 220, 226, 231(top); Soil Conservation Service 221; Unusual Films 227; Dawn L. Watkins 228, 229, 231(bottom), 235

Chapter 11
Dawn L. Watkins 238, 256; PhotoDisc, Inc. 239, 242, 254; Unusual Films 243, 244, 251(both), 252

Unit 5 Opener
Digital Stock

Chapter 12
Corel Corporation 264; PhotoDisc, Inc. 265(all), 266, 268, 269(both), 270(middle, bottom), 271(all), 272, 276, 279; Corbis 270(top), 274, 275; NASA 280

Chapter 13
PhotoDisc, Inc. 282, 287, 289(both), 294; Corel Corporation 284, 293; Courtesy of Six Flags over Georgia 292; www.arttoday.com 299, 304; Smithsonian 302; NASA 303

Chapter 14
Dawn L. Watkins 309, 330; PhotoDisc, Inc. 310, 312, 321, 323(left), 332; Corel Corporation 323(right), 329(plane, ax); www.arttoday.com 329(chisels)

Chapter 15
Dawn L. Watkins 337(both), 338(all), 339, 346; Unusual Films 340, 348; PhotoDisc, Inc. 344

Unit 6 Opener
PhotoDisc, Inc.

Chapter 16
Corbis 356; www.arttoday.com 357; PhotoDisc, Inc. 362, 363, 373(top), 381; Dawn L. Watkins 364, 373(bottom), 380; photo courtesy of Andersen Windows, Inc. 368; Godden Collection, Earthquake Engineering Research Center, University of California, Berkeley 378

Chapter 17
PhotoDisc, Inc. 384, 385, 387, 392(top), 396, 406; Unusual Films 388, 389(all), 397(both), 400, 401, 407; Duke Power 391; PPC Industries Electrostatic Precipitators, Inc. 392(bottom); NASA and Geophysical Institute, University of Alaska 395; Dawn L. Watkins 398, 403; www.arttoday.com 402, 405; General Electric Co. 408; General Electric Co., Nela Park 409

Chapter 18
PhotoDisc, Inc. 412, 427(bottom); Unusual Films 416(both), 417(both), 427(top); NASA and STS-68 crew 419(top); courtesy of Jan Curtis 419(bottom); Corbis 424; www.arttoday.com 428; John Jenkins 430

Chapter 19
Corbis 434, 443; Unusual Films 435; PhotoDisc, Inc. 436, 438(both), 439(both), 450(both), 451(both); Dawn L. Watkins 446; Washington State Historical Society, Tacoma 447(both); courtesy of James Donovan 454(top); courtesy of Ellyson and Manda Kalagayan 454(bottom)

Chapter 20
Don F. Figer (UCLA), NASA, and STScI 458; PhotoDisc, Inc. 467, 471(bottom left, bottom right), 474, 484, 485, 491; U.S. Department of Defense and Technology, Sgt. Russ Pollanen, U.S. Air Force 471(top); NASA 471(bottom middle); Corbis 473; Jeff Hester and Paul Scowen (Arizona State Univ.), NASA, and NSSDC 480; Unusual Films 481, 482, 489; NASA Ames Homepage 488